9/12

RELIGION AND ATHEISM
IN THE U.S.S.R. AND EASTERN EUROPE

The Carleton Series in
Soviet and East European Studies

*The Communist States at the Crossroads: Between Moscow
and Peking*
Ed. Adam Bromke. Intro. Philip E. Mosely (New York:
Frederick A. Praeger, Publishers, 1965; London: Pall Mall Press,
1965)
(Japanese translation, Jiji Press, Tokyo, 1967; Marathi translation,
Janapad Prakashan, Bombay, 1969.)

East-West Trade
Ed. Philip E. Uren. Intro. Hon. Mitchell W. Sharp (Toronto : The
Canadian Institute of International Affairs, 1966).

The Communist States and the West
Ed. Adam Bromke and Philip E. Uren (New York, Frederick A.
Praeger, Publishers, 1967;
London : Pall Mall Press, 1967).

*The Soviet Union under Brezhnev and Kosygin: The Transition
Years 1965–1968*
Ed. John W. Strong (New York: Van Nostrand Reinhold, 1971).

The Communist States in Disarray, 1965–1971
Ed. Adam Bromke and Teresa Rakowska-Harmstone (Minneapolis :
University of Minnesota Press, 1972).

Religion and Atheism in the U.S.S.R. and Eastern Europe

Edited by
BOHDAN R. BOCIURKIW
and
JOHN W. STRONG

Assisted by
JEAN K. LAUX

Macmillan

First published 1975 by
THE MACMILLAN PRESS LTD
London and Basingstoke
Associated companies in New York
Dublin, Melbourne, Johannesburg and Madras

SBN 333 15060 0

Printed in Great Britain by
Cox & Wyman Ltd,
London, Fakenham and Reading

Contents

Preface

The idea of this volume was conceived at an international symposium on religion and atheism in Communist societies which was organised at Carleton University in April 1971 by the Institute of Soviet and East European Studies. Many of the contributors to this volume were participants in this symposium. Other contributions were commissioned in order to broaden the analytical framework of the survey and to make its coverage more comprehensive.

This survey is an international effort, with contributions from Canada, the United States, Great Britain, France, Germany, Switzerland and Yugoslavia. An attempt has also been made to approach the problems involved from the viewpoints of several disciplines – as historians, political scientists, sociologists, philosophers and legal scholars.

The book examines various aspects of religion and atheism in the Soviet Union and all other East European Communist states since World War II. The points of emphasis include philosophical confrontation between religion and Communism in these countries; Church–State relations; the impact of political and socio-economic changes on popular religiosity and the socio-political orientation of institutional religion. While all Communist states of Eastern Europe are covered in this volume, different aspects of the problem are being examined in the individual Communist countries; two contributions represent comparative, cross-national surveys of the major 'international' religions of the area – Catholicism and Judaism, respectively.

Four sections may be discerned in the volume. The first one, containing two articles on religion and Communism, counterposes a Western Christian and a Yugoslav Marxist approach to the problem. The second part comprises seven articles exploring various aspects of religion and atheism in the U.S.S.R., including the largest and, relatively, most favoured Church and several 'minority' religions, ethno-cultural and sociological ramifications and functions of religion, secularisation. The third section contains two 'across-the-area' surveys of Catholicism and Judaism, respectively, adding an important (and yet most difficult to attain) comparative perspective to the problem. The remainder of the volume consists of nine 'country-surveys' covering Poland, German Democratic Republic, Czechoslovakia, Hungary, Romania, Bulgaria, Yugoslavia and Albania.

The most striking conclusion of the symposium appears to be that except for the doctrinal commitment of the ruling Communist parties to the eventual establishment of a fully atheistic society, and their insistence on wielding effective controls over the activities of religious organisations, there are indeed very few common features in the official treatment, legal status and political influence of institutional religion in the individual Communist countries. This finding underlines the limited impact of the 'Soviet model' of church–state relations on other Communist systems and dramatises the extent to which history, culture and nationalism have modified the effect of Marxism–Leninism on religion in the individual Communist states.

The editors wish to acknowledge with thanks the help they received in the preparing of this volume: to Professor Jean K. Laux for her invaluable contribution as assistant editor; to the individual contributors for their patience and understanding as the editors editorialised their prose; to the administration of Carleton University for their assistance and encouragement; to Miss Stefania Hawrylak and Mrs Penny Larue for their valuable clerical work in preparing the manuscript; and lastly but not least to the Canada Council for its generous support of the 1971 International Symposium which generated this volume.

B.R.B.
J.W.S.

Carleton University
Ottawa, Canada
March 1973

Introduction

SIR JOHN LAWRENCE

Twelve years ago it was difficult to find anyone interested in religion in the U.S.S.R. There were a few enthusiasts accustomed to sift every particle of evidence, and a larger number of religious people (Christians, Jews and Muslims) who sympathised with the believers in the Soviet Union but who had very little information about them. Knowledge of the other socialist countries was a little better but, by and large, there was general ignorance in the West concerning religious life in the Communist countries of Eastern Europe. This ignorance went with indifference. It was widely supposed, by the general public, that religion had been effectively suppressed and that what little remained was marginal. Moreover, many of the experts were only a little better informed than the general public. There were exceptions, but it would be fair to say that the academics, the journalists and the diplomats had failed to comprehend the continuing and increasing importance of religion for any realistic understanding of Eastern Europe. Atheist propaganda paid religious faith the compliment of taking it seriously but, in view of the air-torn character of some Communist propaganda, it was understandable that many Western observers failed to understand that this time the propagandists were genuinely disturbed at the continuing vitality of religious practice and beliefs which were totally incompatible with Marxism–Leninism.

Today the situation is transformed. There is abundant evidence about religion from every country in Eastern Europe, with the exception of Albania. This evidence needs careful sifting and assessment, but the general picture has become clear. It is always difficult to assess the importance of intangible factors in any country at any time. Today it would hardly be disputed that religion is a significant factor in the mental and moral climate of

every country in Eastern Europe; again with the probable exception of Albania. The almost universal disappointment with
Marxism–Leninism as a pseudo-religion has left a vacuum which
tends to be filled with elements from each people's past inheritance.
Without over-estimating the influence of religion on the course
of events, we now know that religion, whether Christian, Muslim,
Jewish or Lamaistic Buddhist, is an important element in that
inheritance.

The material now available on religion and atheism in the
U.S.S.R. and Eastern Europe is so copious that one would never
have time to read it all, even if *per impossibile* he knew all the
languages required. Even to read and digest all the material in
Russian might be more than one man could do. This material
consists partly of what is published in the Soviet Union, mainly
in the form of anti-religious propaganda and sociological analysis
such as that examined by Stephen and Ethel Dunn. It also consists of reports of court cases brought against religious believers,
and the publications of the Churches. These last are skimpy and
unilluminating in some countries, sometimes very interesting in
others, such as Romania. This printed material may be one-sided
and sometimes unreliable, but is supplemented by a mass of
samizdat literature, much of which eventually becomes available
in the West. Religious *samizdat* in the main gives the views of
those who are strongly opposed to the policy of the legally recognised Churches in collaborating with the Communist authorities.
The chapters of this book give ample reason for this dissatisfaction,
but it should be noted that Russian religious *samizdat* on the whole
reflects loyalty to the Soviet State, in spite of the Government's
religious policy.

The voice of those in the Soviet Union who would like to see
changes in the law and in its administration, but yet who continue
to work within the legally recognised Churches, is not heard. This
is a significant element and, in the view of some, the most significant element. Such persons, who have deliberately decided to
remain with the state churches, while at the same time remaining
critical of many things done (or not done) by their church leaders,
have reasons for not wishing to compromise their position by taking
part in *samizdat*. Yet the Soviet authorities will not print a
reasoned defence of this position since it is bound to contain at
least some criticism of them for having forced unpalatable

decisions on the churches in flagrant contradiction of the 'separation of Church and State' doctrine enshrined in Soviet legislation.

This critical gap in the evidence leads some outside observers to imagine a sharper polarisation between 'collaborating' state Churches and 'underground' Churches than really exists. In its extreme form this view is expressed as a distinction between 'apostate' official Churches and a 'true' Church which is entirely illegal in its operations. The truth is more complex. Completely underground church organisations exist, but, according to the available evidence, they do not seem to have a very large following. There is rather a continuum of infinite gradations between those who cut themselves off from Soviet society and worship in secret, and those leaders of the official Churches who fully conform, at least outwardly, to what is required by the authorities. There are many Christian communities which operate illegally for the sole reason that the State will not grant them the legal registration which they seek. And it was, after all, a priest of the legally authorised Russian Orthodox Church who baptised Stalin's daughter. In the Soviet Union everyone, from the highest to the lowest, breaks laws and regulations, so there is no way of knowing how much illicit work is carried on behind a façade of legality. There are undoubtedly some traitors and apostates in the state churches, but there are also loyal members of the legal churches at this moment in prisons as a punishment for Christian witness. Christians of all kinds meet in the concentration camps, and recognise each other as brothers. This would hardly be the case if there were a clear distinction between a legal apostate Church and a true Church operating underground.

So far, I have mainly referred to the Soviet Union, as the classical case of relations between religion and a Communist state. Something of the same applies throughout Eastern Europe, but the differences are great and seem to be growing. In Yugoslavia there is a degree of freedom of religion that must amaze an old Moscow hand, especially when one considers what was happening in Yugoslavia during the early stage of Communist rule in that country. Albania is the only country in the world where every overt manifestation of religious life appears to have been effectively suppressed. Peter Prifti shows that this is explained by special circumstances in Albanian history. However, the example of

Mother Teresa in Calcutta shows that an Albanian can still have a deep faith. In matters of religion, Eastern Europe shows an amazing variety of policies and conditions. The German Democratic Republic and Yugoslavia represent one extreme and Albania the other. In East Germany the Government makes good use of the social commitment of Christians by giving them positions of minor responsibility as foremen, shop stewards, or the like. In the Soviet Union any possibility that an avowed Christian should hold any socially responsible post remains unthinkable. Of course crypto-Christians do sometimes hold responsible positions and the Soviet authorities look the other way. However, if this became officially known, the authorities would feel obliged to intervene forcibly. In a word, the Church is forbidden to have any part in social work, and the prohibition is stringently enforced as a matter of principle.

Alexandre Bennigsen's all too brief chapter on Islam in the Soviet Union gives facts and figures which show that this subject is one of the greatest importance. On present trends, the population of Islamic origin will soon be a majority in the Soviet Union. It is difficult to discover how much Islamic belief persists, but it is beyond question that a 'social Islam' is immensely powerful and seems to be growing stronger. Dr Bennigsen speaks of an 'unofficial Islam'. This is paralleled by what one could call an 'unofficial Judaism' and an 'unofficial Christianity'. In these latter cases, besides the religion interwoven with superstition, there is a more intellectual form of 'unofficial Christianity', or 'unofficial Judaism', which can be very interesting.

J. M. Bochenski's chapter begins this book with an intellectual inquiry into the conflict between Marxism–Leninism and religion. This is necessary because *Marxism* in the general sense includes socialist 'doctrines which are, in fact, as diametrically opposed as, for instance, the Russian and Yugoslav versions'. Dr Bochenski is exclusively concerned with the Russian version, i.e. 'Marxism–Leninism'. He shows conclusively, to my mind, that there is a complete incompatibility between Marxism–Leninism and any form of religion. Marxism–Leninism was the original motive of Bolshevik hostility towards religion, and there is no question that the men who made the October Revolution were completely sincere when they tried to destroy religion altogether. But much water has flowed down the Volga since 1917. It is a matter of opinion as to how much of the original ideological impetus remains. My own judgement is that Marxist–Leninist ideology is now reduced to trace elements, though there are compelling practical reasons for pretending to believe in it. A fanatical hatred and fear of religion remains in some quarters, albeit without the support of the original ideological fervour.

Dr Bochenski's closely reasoned views on this matter do not prevent him from concluding that a dialogue between Marxism–Leninism and the Christian religion is possible; not only on 'secondary, mostly tactical problems such as fighting a common enemy', but also 'on quite basic grounds, if it is conceived as a spiritual clash of two faiths where each party tries to understand the other in view of eventually converting him to his beliefs'. I feel sure Dr Bochenski would not think the time is ripe for such a dialogue, but I believe that in principle he is correct. He adds that, for such a dialogue to be fruitful, the representatives of the religious faiths 'must be true believers of a transcendant religion and not partisans of that sort of watered-down religion in which the sole function of a believer is to improve the social structures'. I would only add that the experience of ecumenical discussion over the last sixty years within the Church, and also between Christianity and other faiths, is that dialogue is more useful when the partners go into it with the intention not so much of converting each other to the views they hold at the beginning, but rather to the views that they will hold at the end of the dialogue when they see more deeply into what they believe, as the result of the dialogue itself. I do not suppose that at the present stage there is much prospect for a useful dialogue between the Churches and the rulers of most of the East European countries, but I should be glad to be wrong. However, the time will come for dialogue, and the Churches will hold some trump cards.

Communism does work – up to a point – but not well enough to give great satisfaction anywhere in Eastern Europe. Whatever else may be said, it is incontestible that the Jewish and Christian religions produce a considerable number of men and women with an unusually strong sense of social obligation. If the Soviet Union and other countries of Eastern Europe could come to the point of doing on a large scale what the German Democratic Republic is already doing on a small scale (that is to enlist Christian initiative and responsibility in making the system work better) Communism would be distinctly nearer to attaining some of its ideals. At present many factors, not all of them ideological, make this impossible, but in due time a realistic dialogue might remove whatever difficulties are still genuinely ideological.

List of Contributors

ALEXANDRE BENNIGSEN. Directeur d'Etudes à l'Ecole Pratique des Hautes Etudes, Sorbonne, VIème Section. Professor of History, University of Chicago. Author of several works in English and French concerning the Muslims of the Soviet Union.

JOSEPH M. BOCHENSKI. Professor of Philosophy and Director of the Institute of East European Studies, University of Fribourg, Switzerland. Author of *Der sowjetrussische dialektische Materialismus* (1950). Editor of *Studies in Soviet Thought* and *Sovietica*.

BOHDAN R. BOCIURKIW. Professor of Political Science, Carleton University, Ottawa, Canada. Author of numerous articles in Canadian, American and European journals and symposia, on church–state relations, religion and atheism, and selected internal political problems in the U.S.S.R. Co-editor of Vol. 11 of *Ukraine: A Concise Encyclopaedia* (Toronto, 1971).

MICHAEL BOURDEAUX. Director, Centre for the Study of Religion and Communism, Kent. Formerly Research Fellow at the Royal Institute of International Affairs, London. Author of four books and numerous articles on religion in the U.S.S.R.

BRANKO BOŠNJAK. Professor of Philosophy, University of Zagreb, Yugoslavia. Author of numerous books and articles in Serbo-Croatian and German, including *Philosophy and Christianity* (1966) and *Greek Philosophical Critic of the Bible* (1971).

GEORGE H. BRAND. Assistant Professor of Political Science, Manhattanville College. Ordained in the Lutheran Church, Taught at the City University of New York and New York State University at Purchase.

MANOJLO BROĆIĆ. Member of the Yugoslav Institute of Social Sciences and scientific associate at the University of Belgrade. Specialist in the sociology of youth and in religion and secularisation. Author of numerous studies in these fields with special reference to Yugoslavia.

VINCENT C. CHRYPINSKI. Professor of Political Science, University of Windsor, Canada. Author of several studies on Poland including

chapters in *Polish Law Throughout the Ages,* ed. W. J. Wagner
(Hoover International Press, 1970) and *The Communist States in
Disarray, 1965–1971,* ed. Bromke and Rakowska-Harmstone
(Minneapolis, 1972).

BOGDAN DENITCH. Senior Fellow of the Research Institute on Com-
munist Affairs, Lecturer in the Department of Political Science
and in the Institute on East Central Europe, Senior Research
Associate in the Bureau of Applied Social Research, Columbia
University; Assistant Professor of Sociology, Queens College, City
University of New York. Author of numerous articles in American
and European journals. Editor of *Yugoslav Opinion-makers*
(Praeger, 1973), and author of *Social Change and Social Science in
Eastern Europe* (forthcoming).

ETHEL DUNN. Executive Secretary of the Highgate Road Social
Science Research Station, Berkeley, California. With Stephen P.
Dunn, author of *The Peasants of Central Russia,* plus articles on
the Soviet Far North, Central Asia and problems of Russian
religious dissidence.

STEPHEN P. DUNN. Lecturer in Anthropology at the Monterey
Institute of Foreign Relations, Monterey, California. Editor of
Soviet Anthropology and Archeology and *Soviet Sociology.* With
Ethel Dunn, author of numerous articles on directed cultural
change in the Soviet Union, and on comparative studies of religion.

WILLIAM C. FLETCHER. Associate Professor and Director of Slavic
and Soviet Area Studies, University of Kansas. Author of *A Study
in Survival* (New York and London, 1965), *Nikolai: Portrait of a
Dilemma* (New York, 1968), *The Russian Orthodox Church
Underground, 1917–1970* (London, 1971) and *Religion and
Soviet Foreign Policy* (London, 1972).

KEITH HITCHINS. Professor of History, University of Illinois. Author
of *The Rumanian National Movement in Transylvania, 1780–
1849* (Cambridge, Mass., 1969). Editor of *Rumanian Studies* and
Studies in East European Social History.

LESLIE LASZLO. Assistant Professor of Political Science, Loyola
College, Montreal. Author of a Ph.D. dissertation at Columbia
University on 'Church and State in Hungary, 1919–1945', and
several articles on Church–State relations in Hungary in English
and Hungarian journals.

JEAN K. LAUX. Assistant Professor of Political Science, University of
Ottawa. Research Associate and Assistant to the Director, Carleton
Institute of Soviet and East European Studies, 1970–72.

SIR JOHN LAWRENCE. Editor of *Frontier.* British Press Attaché in the
Soviet Union from 1942 to 1945. Founder and editor of the

Britanskii Soyuznik. Author of *A History of Russia* (Mentor Books), *Russians Observed* and other books.

WASYL MARKUS. Professor of Political Science at Loyola University in Chicago and Loyola Rome Center. Author of books and articles on Soviet federalism, nationalities policy and foreign relations of the U.S.S.R., including *L'incorporation de l'Ukraine subcarpathique à l'Ukraine soviétique* (Louvain, 1956), *L'Ukraine soviétique dans les relations internationales et son statut en droit international* (Paris, 1959), *Nationalities Policy of the U.S.S.R.* (New York, 1961; in Ukrainian). Co-editor of the *Ukraine: A Concise Encyclopaedia* (Toronto, 1971).

KATHLEEN E. MATCHETT. Graduate in Russian from the University of Cambridge, England. Research assistant at the Centre for the Study of Religion and Communism.

DAVID E. POWELL. Assistant Professor of Government and Foreign Affairs and Director of the Center for Russian and Communist Studies, University of Virginia. Author of articles on Soviet affairs in *Problems of Communism, American Political Science Review* and other journals.

PETER R. PRIFTI. Research Affiliate at the Center for International Studies, Massachusetts Institute of Technology. Author of a chapter on Albania in *The Communist States in Disarray 1965–1971,* ed. Bromke and Rakowska-Harmstone (Minneapolis, 1972).

MARIN PUNDEFF. Professor of History, California State University, Northridge. Author of *Bulgaria: A Bibliographic Guide* (New York, 1968), 'Bulgarian Nationalism' in *Nationalism in Eastern Europe,* ed. Sugar and Lederer (Seattle, 1969), plus numerous articles on Bulgaria in American and European journals.

MILAN J. REBAN. Assistant Professor of Political Science, North Texas State University. President, Southwestern Association for Slavic Studies. Author of several articles and reviews on Soviet and East European affairs.

JOSHUA ROTHENBERG. Lecturer in Contemporary Jewish Studies and Judaica Librarian, Brandeis University. Author of *An Annotated Bibliography of Writings on Judaism Published in the Soviet Union, 1960–1965* (Waltham, Mass. 1969), *The Jewish Religion in the Soviet Union* (New York, 1971) and various essays in anthologies and journals on Judaism in the U.S.S.R.

GERHARD SIMON. Fellow of the Bundesinstitut für ostwissenschäftliche und internationale Studien, Cologne, Germany. Author of *K. P. Pobedonoscev und die Kirchenpolitik des Heiligen Sinod 1880–1905* (Göttingen, 1969) and *The Churches in Russia* (London, 1972).

JOHN W. STRONG. Associate Professor of History, Carleton University, Ottawa, Canada. Managing Editor of *Canadian Slavonic Papers*. Editor of *The Soviet Union under Brezhnev and Kosygin* (New York, 1971).

PETER A. TOMA. Professor of Government, University of Arizona. Fulbright-Hays research scholar, Yugoslavia (1972–73). Author and editor of several books and articles including *U.S. and Communist Treaty Negotiations* (1972) and *The Changing Face of Communism in Eastern Europe* (1970).

1 Marxism–Leninism and Religion

J. M. BOCHENSKI

The purpose of this paper is to describe and analyse the basic Marxist–Leninist doctrines concerning religion.

In order to avoid the misunderstandings so common to discussion of Marxism–Leninism and religion, it will be necessary to explain every word in the stated theme. The concern is with *doctrines*, with theory only, while the practice, the actual religious policy, is completely outside the scope of this article. Religious policy, however, is so dependent on theory that it cannot be fully understood without an adequate knowledge of the theory. It has been well documented in a number of excellent Western publications which ought to be, if they are not, well known. Furthermore, only the *basic* doctrines will be examined. Much of the misunderstanding surrounding the problem of religion and Marxism-Leninism is due to the fact that a knowledge of even the most rudimentary assumptions of Marxist–Leninist theory is often lacking. In this regard it is useful to stress the very fundamentals out of which everything else follows.

Above all, the paper will not be concerned with 'Marxism' but exclusively with 'Marxism–Leninism', Few words in philosophy are as ambiguous as 'Marxism'.[1] It is true that there seems to be a common stock of economic and political terms denoted by that term but as far as *philosophy* is concerned the term 'Marxism' often refers to doctrines which are, in fact, as diametrically opposed as, for instance, the Russian and Yugoslav versions. It is thus necessary to reiterate that we are *not* concerned with Marxism in general, which would have no meaning in our context, but exclusively with *Marxism–Leninism*.

Yet even Marxism–Leninism is not a uniform doctrine. One

often hears about the ideological dispute between Russian and Chinese Marxists–Leninists. There have also been other trends, such as Trotskyism. But as there seems to be little difference between them in regard to religion, we shall deal exclusively with *Soviet*, i.e. *Russian* Marxism–Leninism,[2] in order to assure complete clarity, and especially to avoid being misled by some Western Communists who sometimes deviate from the basic doctrines for tactical purposes.

One sometimes finds a tendency to disregard Soviet doctrines and in particular Soviet philosophy. Many authors seem to believe that it is less relevant than, say, the Yugoslav, Italian or Polish kind of 'Marxism'. This is an error. Soviet Marxism–Leninism is, in reality, not only the theory of the most powerful Communist Party, not only the paradigm which the majority of the other Parties are trying to follow, but it is also the largest and most articulate school of philosophy in this camp. Soviet Marxism–Leninism is, in other words, leading not only as far as its influence is concerned but also in regard to its content and elaboration.

It is perhaps superfluous to add that Marxism–Leninism should in *no case* be identified with the doctrines of *Marx himself*. This is also very true regarding religious doctrine where one finds considerable differences between the two attitudes, in spite of the fact that Marxism–Leninism draws heavily from Marx's writings. To believe that a cursory reading of Karl Marx suffices to understand the Marxist–Leninist attitude towards religion is, to say the least, a rather childish assumption.

I

An accurate understanding of Marxist–Leninist doctrines concerning religion presupposes that its fundamental tenets are known. Contrary to what may be true in other systems, religious doctrines are not marginal to Marxism–Leninism. They belong to its very core. The bulk of this paper, therefore, will be devoted to a twofold analysis of Marxism–Leninism itself. First, it shall consider the role of the theory in the system. Second, the theory itself, i.e. Marxist–Leninist philosophy, will be examined from the relevant standpoint.

In approaching the belief system of Marxism–Leninism, one must first contend with a widespread opinion which seems to be caused by a sort of incorrigible parochialism among many Western writers. They seem to be incapable of understanding the attitudes of others because they insist on projecting personal attitudes and ideas on to the Marxists–Leninists. Consequently, they try to arrange Marxist–Leninist theory in a way consonant with their own principles. In particular, opinionated Western parochialism takes several forms.

First, many Western intellectuals are sceptics, i.e. they subscribe to *no* system of beliefs and, being parochial, they are not capable of understanding those who do. 'We do not attach great importance to any proposition,' they say, 'so that must also be the case with the Communists.' 'Their ideology is sheerly irrelevant.' 'It is but a set of ritual formulae adjusted to successive Machiavellian policies and nothing more.'

Second, that being the supposition, our intellectuals are also often unable to comprehend how someone can attach any importance to a world-view. 'Since we despise every sort of metaphysics the Communists, too, must be of the same opinion.' 'If they speak of such things none the less they remain irrelevant.' Only practical, or social, problems remain. Communism is no more than a social trend.

Third, a conclusion is drawn for the Marxist–Leninists with regard to religion. Religion is clearly a world-view, consequently, it cannot be taken seriously. One may combat it for practical and political motives but it is not worthy of a theoretical discussion. Every such discussion is a waste of time and, since we feel this way, the same must be true about the Communists. Not only is religion regarded as a trivial theoretical matter for the Marxists–Leninists, but also for Karl Marx himself.

The resulting interpretation of the Communist attitude towards religion is as follows: this attitude is an *incidental* matter for it is not connected to the core of Communism. It is purely a matter of *social* and *political* significance. Religion need not be taken seriously; it is a random phenomenon.

If one started with such assumptions it would be impossible to understand the Marxist–Leninist attitude towards religion. One would be faced again and again with acts that would remain inexplicable. In addition, continual frustration would be encountered in any attempt to have a dialogue with the Marxists–Leninists. Marxism–Leninism is, in fact, the opposite of this sort of scepticism.

To begin with, Marxism–Leninism is formulated as a living and forceful faith. Its true adherents *do believe something,* viz. propositions which are accepted as absolute truths. This has been explicitly repeated thousands of times in Soviet literature. Of course, one has to make a distinction between what the doctrine teaches and what men really do believe. Every group of believers has its weaknesses. The entire history of the great religions is proof of that. It is usually difficult to know what a man truly believes in his heart. But one may always observe his behaviour. And, as far as behaviour is concerned, an extraordinary fact is the thoroughness with which most Marxists–Leninists are true to their faith.

There is a story about the late Queen Mother of Belgium who somewhat liked the Communists. At one time she travelled to a Festival of Youth in Warsaw and was accompanied there by a Polish government minister. Having heard that many people attend church in Poland she said she would like to go to church herself. 'Majesty,' said the Communist official, 'it would be a great honour to accompany your Majesty.' 'You?' said the Queen. 'Yes, your Majesty. I am a Catholic, you know. It is true that I am not practising – but I am still believing.' 'But how is this possible, are you not a Communist?' 'Yes, your Majesty, practising but not believing.'

Though often repeated and perhaps true in some cases – especially true for the parties in Eastern Europe where every tendency to think otherwise than with Russia is suppressed by methods familiar from Hungary and Czechoslovakia – two remarks concerning that unbelief must be made. First, personal experience seems to show that leading men *do* believe. Second, practice, at least, makes the doctrine relevant as the example of the Polish minister shows.

Marxism–Leninism, though not primarily a social doctrine, is a metaphysical world-view. Its social doctrines are to be found in so-called 'historical materialism'. It is said to be an application of the more general laws of dialectical materialism to society and history. Now dialectical materialism which is an all-embracing world view – a *mirovozrenie* as they say – is *not* a social doctrine. It is a metaphysical view. Dialectical materialism is constantly said to be the general outlook, the theoretical foundation of the

Party. Without doubt, anti-metaphysically oriented Westerners dislike it, but to like or dislike a doctrine is one thing whereas the brute fact that some people think otherwise is another. And this is precisely the case with the Marxists–Leninists. Not only are they believers but believers of an all-embracing, absolutist world view.

Finally, contrary to what many Westerners think – including Karl Marx – the Marxist–Leninists do not consider religion to be irrelevant. For them it is a highly important matter. So important, in fact, that an enormous effort is concentrated on theoretical discussion of it.[3] This, of course, can be understood by one who knows what a living faith is. For a sceptic it will remain an utterly incomprehensible phenomenon.

II

Our last point leads to a remark concerning the second aspect of Marxism–Leninism – its basic content.[4] Specifically, it involves *two* very different sets of doctrines. This is externally manifest in the division of its philosophy into dialectical and historical materialism. It is not a mere exterior systemisation. As a matter of fact, there are two doctrines of different origin and relevance.

The first is a *metaphysical world-view. Roughly* speaking, this is a consistently developed metaphysics of enlightenment couched in Hegelian categories and spirit. It contains nothing peculiarly Marxian. Rather, it stems directly from Engels who inherited these doctrines from Hegel and the German Enlightenment. It may even be claimed, and often has been, that the formulation of this aspect is quite foreign to Marx in spite of the fact that he was a follower of the Enlightenment.

The second aspect, historical materialism, is, on the contrary, of Marxian origin. Although the influence of Engels and Lenin is apparent here, these doctrines seem to be true to the logic of Marx's system. This is the thoroughly social aspect of Marxism–Leninism.

Theoretically, in Marxist–Leninist literature, these two elements are interrelated in the following way. The first supplies the main content of the doctrine concerning religion. The latter explains its origin, its social function and allows for the formulation of tactical rules concerning religious policy. It is constantly stressed

that the second element is based logically on the first; that historical materialism consists simply in an application of the principles
of dialectical materialism to society and history.

III

The essentials of dialectical materialism are the following. The
world is the only reality; there is no other world above or alongside nature and, consequently, there is no God, no absolute spirit.
This unique world is *infinite* in several respects. It is, first, infinite
in space (properly infinite, not only unlimited). Second, it is infinite
in time, i.e. has no beginning and no end. Moreover, it is infinite
in profundity (depth) meaning that it contains within itself a
virtual infinity of 'forms of movement', i.e. forms of being up to
consciousness. To this threefold meaning of infinity a further
absolute character is added – causality. The world is uncaused
but itself is the cause of everything. Thus, this view is clearly
absolutist: there is an Absolute, Nature.

The second central tenet of dialectical materialism is the doctrine of *emergent evolution* inherited from Hegel. The world
contains nothing static, it is in continuous evolution towards new
stages. Evolution is not conceived mechanistically; it produces
ever new qualities. It is important to note that these qualities
are separated one from the other by 'dialectical leaps', by breaks,
so that they cannot simply be reduced to lower qualities. In the
process the world produces, at a certain time, consciousness which
again evolves to ever higher forms.

This is the third important point: there is consciousness in the
world but it does not figure from the beginning as with the theistic
views. It is, rather, a late result of evolution. Man is the only
point where the Absolute reaches consciousness. For this reason
the Marxist–Leninists claim that their materialism – which is
simply the denial of the spirit at the start of the process – is at the
same time *Humanism*; man is the only bearer of consciousness.

However, and this is a fourth essential doctrine of dialectical
materialism, consciousness is a product of matter, is carried by
matter and consists in being a 'copy' of matter. It is a sort of
superstructure, nearly an epiphenomenon of the physiological
processes. This doctrine is said to be, among others, the foundation
of a similar doctrine concerning society: all spiritual phenomena of

a society, i.e. the social consciousness, depend upon and are ultimately determined by the economic life of the same society.

And yet Marxism–Leninism has a very optimistic view of
consciousness, of human spirit. Consciousness can, in principle,
penetrate everything. There is nothing which would be unintelli-
gible. Using scientific methods confirmed by practice man can
know everything. There is nothing mysterious at all: *'das Rätsel
gibt es nicht'*, to use Wittgenstein's expression. Although consciousness does not create reality it knows reality and can guide
human action to dominate and transform the world and humanity
itself.

From this view of the world and consciousness a moral lesson
is derived: *Man's task is progress.* He should do consciously what
nature does without consciousness, i.e., foster evolution which
consists basically of a rationalisation, i.e. submitting nature and
society to reason. By accomplishing this task man becomes free
and can hope for the satisfaction of all his desires. Marxism–
Leninism does not preach a morality of personal happiness for
the individual; it gives to the individual an objective task, a task
which transcends his personal desires. Only when man is capable
of identifying those desires with the aims of Society – meaning, in
the last analysis, of the Absolute – can he really be happy. This
moral doctrine is, like the underlying metaphysics, completely
immanent, worldy. Every aim transcending Nature and Society is
rejected, as are all values which would not be directly linked with
the life of man in the world.

This is one side of the doctrine. The other has been rightly
called its *Promethean character* – man is the *only* conscious being
in Nature. He alone is responsible for progress. In the face of
brute natural and social forces he is called to transform the world
and himself in an unending heroic effort.

It is enough to understand this doctrine in order to see,
a priori, what the Marxist–Leninist theory of religion must logically be. It can be subsumed under three main propositions: first,
religion is a false, obsolete science; second, it is an equally false
metaphysics; and third, it preaches false moral values.

The Marxist–Leninists regard religion as a sort of pseudo-
science. They do not deny that it also comprehends a number of
emotional attitudes, but basically they see it as a set of propositions. These propositions are understood as being on the same

level as those of the natural and social sciences. In this perspective religion is, consequently, a false, obsolete, even absurd sort of science that can be refuted by modern empirical science (the only true science). Religion is also regarded as supplying a foundation for an absurd, in fact a magical, technique. It follows that only an obscurantist can be religious – even from that point of view alone.

Moreover, and by far more important, religion is also false metaphysics. It is dualistic (another name for transcendant) in that it admits a second world above and beyond the world of nature. It denies the possibility of a paradise on earth and talks only about the happiness beyond. Furthermore, religion distrusts human reason by preaching mysteries which are utterly inaccessible to human understanding.

Finally, religion carries a false set of moral values. It is individualistic, egoistic. It preaches personal and not social salvation; a salvation beyond rather than on earth. That being the case it prevents man from performing his only relevant duty on earth. Religion, it is true, will incorporate most of the current social precepts, but in such a way that they become oriented towards an illusory, transcendent world and are egoistically directed towards personal happiness. Above all, religion does not attribute to man his primacy since it admits a God and higher beings. It is thus not humanistic, but anti-humanistic. Religious morality is also anti-humanistic in another way: it deprives man of his Promethean vocation. It makes of him not the unique creator of history but a tool of a superior being.

IV

This paper has thus far considered only the first set of doctrines related to Marxist–Leninist theory of religion – the metaphysical world-view. The second set is incorporated within so-called historical materialism. Historical materialism, as has been stressed already, is concerned with the origin and social function of religion. There are two main points to historical materialism. First, that every form of social consciousness – morality, art, philosophy, religion – is a 'superstructure' over a 'basis', i.e. a certain set of social relations corresponding to processes of production. Given a certain set of relations a specific type of social consciousness will necessarily emerge. So religion is by no means an autonomous factor but simply a reflection of the economic life of a society.

The second point is that throughout the entire history of humanity prior to the Socialist Revolution relations of production were dominated by the class struggle, caused by the exploitation of one class by another. Society, then, has been completely disrupted by the class struggle and there are, consequently, as many types of social consciousness as there are antagonistic classes.

It is within the framework of this theory that the origin and social function of religion is actually understood by Marxist–Leninists. The basic contention is that religion is the superstructure of society in which there is exploitation. It is, in fact, the characteristic feature of such a society's superstructure. This is explained in the following way: religion plays an important role in such a society both for the exploited and the exploiter. As far as the former is concerned, his life is so horrible, his misery so great, that he craves after a consolation which only religion can offer. When Marx said that 'Religion is the opiate of the people' he seems to have meant that it is a type of sedative, a tranquiliser, made practically necessary by the hopelessness of life.[5]

But religion also plays a role in regard to the exploiter. On the one hand it helps to prevent the revolt of the exploited. 'Why make a revolution if life is short and happiness awaits us beyond the grave?' In that respect, religion is a powerful weapon helping the exploiter subdue his victims. On the other hand, it is subjectively necessary for the exploiter himself. He is somewhat, though confusedly, conscious of being an exploiter. Religion offers him the possibility of buying a cheap ticket for heaven in order to save his conscience.[6]

In a society where there is no exploitation religion will completely disappear; it will be unnecessary, have no function. A cruel joke circulated in Poland during the 1957 'thaw' asked: 'Why is there so much religion in Poland?' 'Why? Because the workers are so brutally exploited.' But once exploitation ceases every reason to be religious will disappear.

If so, religion should have long since disappeared in the Soviet Union, which has not only reached Socialism, but also, the first stage of Communism. This, however, is not a serious objection. Marxism–Leninism asserts that if forms of social consciousness are not fully autonomous, i.e. if they still have economic roots, they will possess a certain degree of autonomy or, let us say, inertia, which allows them to subsist for a time after their basis has been destroyed. In addition, the capitalists are supposed to foster religion in the Soviet Union from outside.

V

Two conclusions were drawn by Marx from these premises. First, that religion is socially harmful because it hinders the revolution, i.e. the progress towards the liberation of the exploited, by acting as a tranquiliser. Second, that religion is by no means a major factor in the liberation struggle; it is a superstructure which will disappear when its base is destroyed. The base should be attacked, not that which is constructed upon it.

This is the way Karl Marx looked at religion. Religion had been theoretically refuted by Feuerbach and its relevance was practically minimal in comparison to other hostile social forces. Nicholas Lobkowicz is probably correct in saying that religious believers seldom met with such a humiliating treatment as that inflicted on them by Marx. He did not consider them even worthy of attention.[7] They were simply dismissed as irrelevant.

However, Marx's relative indifference is not the attitude adopted by Lenin and subsequent Marxism–Leninism towards religion. While always repeating that religion is merely a superstructure and that only a bourgeois atheist can imagine the possibility of destroying religion by fighting it directly, Lenin, contrary to Marx, attributed a central importance to religion at the spiritual level. This emphasis has remained in Marxism–Leninism until the present day.

When arguing against any philosophical view Lenin tried to show, practically without exceptions, that religious motives are concealed behind it. He borrowed the elder Dietzgen's saying that philosophers are merely learned lackeys of the theologians. Once this has been shown Lenin could simply dismiss the other view. How? Because religion is supposed to be the main spiritual weapon of the bourgeoisie.

This attitude, so central to Lenin not only in *Materialism and Empirio-criticism,* but also in his letter to the editors of *Pod znamenem marksizma* in his later period, demands an explanation

– especially given its outright opposition to the Marxian thesis. A Marxist, J. Harper, once wrote a whole book on the subject[8] trying to explain the evident disagreement by the different social contexts in Russia and the West. Lenin's attitude, however, also displays some influence both of the Russian so-called nihilistic tradition and of his own personality. One thing is certain: Lenin considers religion to be highly important and treats it accordingly.

The central importance of religion for the ideological class struggle is also fully recognised in contemporary Marxism–Leninism, which in that respect closely follows Lenin. There exist in the Soviet Union a series of academic institutions headed by the Institute of 'Scientific Atheism' at the Academy of Social Sciences and a chair for the same at Moscow State University. A regular course in 'Scientific Atheism', i.e. on criticism of religion, is given in all Soviet institutions of higher learning, as witnessed by the great number of specialised textbooks. Thomas Blakeley has compiled a bibliography of hundreds of Soviet philosophical writings on the subject.[9] Since Khrushchev's well-known decree of 7 June 1954, there are frequent conferences related to religion and atheism, while the magazine *Science and Religion*, a monthly publication, has reached a circulation of 290,000 copies.[10]

Moreover, up to a few years ago, at least, the manner in which non-Communist philosophers were analysed by Marxists–Leninists was thoroughly Leninist. The 'classical analysis' was even applied to thinkers little committed to any religion, as Bertrand Russell, for instance. All were seen as lackeys of theologians who, at heart, attempted to make propaganda for religion.[11]

VI

In summary, Marxism–Leninism sees religion as a radically false, magical pseudo-science. It is also radically false, transcendent metaphysics. It carries with it a completely wicked morality. It is, at the same time, the chief ideological weapon of the exploiters in their fight against the liberation of mankind. There can be, as Lenin said, nothing more abominable than religion.

A long tradition stands behind that doctrine and attitude. First, there is the Enlightenment. Marxism–Leninism takes over the war cry of Voltaire: *'Ecrasez l'Infame'* – 'Destroy the Infamous Thing'. There is Hegel with his completely immanent view of the world as well as the entire tradition of materialism. Further, the moral tradition of the Humanists and that of the Russian Nihilists is important. Finally the heritage of Engels and Lenin with their belief that on the spiritual level nothing is so precious for the exploiters – and so harmful for the exploited – than religion. Alongside all these philosophical-historical traditions there is still the personality of the founder, Vladimir Il'ich Ulianov, with his intense personal dislike of anything religious.[12] It is probably not an exaggeration to say that never before in history had so many powerful traditions come together to form a single, central, dynamic attitude.

As mentioned above, Marxism–Leninism is mistakenly often understood to be a purely social doctrine. In that context Marxist–Leninist attitudes towards religion are all too often interpreted in the following way: the clergy is linked to the exploiters, to the capitalists; therefore, the clergy and religion must be combated. Were the clergy to behave better, were it only to take the side of the exploited, then the Marxist–Leninist attitude towards religion would certainly change.

It is perhaps superfluous to stress that such an interpretation hardly does justice to the Marxists–Leninists and even degrades their doctrine to a sort of superficial anti-clericalism. As a matter of fact, Marxism–Leninism is not only anti-clerical but anti-religious as well. The purer and more disinterested religion is, the more dangerous it becomes. A clergy which would express its solidarity with the proletarians against the capitalists would be, in one sense, far more dangerous than one committed to the defence of exploitation. For a saintly, selfless man may exert far more influence than an egotistical and immoral one. This is Lenin's doctrine and it is easy to see how consistent he is to his principles. For Lenin, not the clergy but religion itself is the enemy.

This principle is mitigated, it is true, by still another Leninist doctrine – the tactical principle of the outstretched hand. If a religious believer is willing to aid the Marxist–Leninist cause in overthrowing his own basis, the system of exploitation, why not enlist his support?[13]

There is, as one can see, some inconsistency in that respect and it is not the only inconsistency in Lenin's doctrine. At times Lenin taught that religion should be fought with spiritual weapons alone. In fact his followers have had frequent recourse to the so-called mechanical means: prison, administrative pressure, forced labour and even the death penalty, as a means to combat religion. Some explanation of the frequent omission of the principle of the outstretched hand must be sought.

It does not seem that such an explanation is forthcoming from the theory alone. Apparently an emotional attitude is present here. But it is still the theory, which, by presenting the manifold wickedness of religion, supplies a foundation for the emotional attitude.

VII

A few critical remarks concerning the theory of religion just exposed may be useful for clarification.

When the Marxist–Leninist doctrine concerning religion is considered from the point of view of research done over the past century, its antiquarian character is striking. Its basic tenets are simply taken over from the Enlightenment with all of the usual misunderstandings which have long since been exposed. Although Marxism–Leninism also contains original, Marxian features, all of these presuppose the philosophy of religion developed by the Enlightenment.

The central point, herein, is that religion is a type of human reaction to worldly evils. A peasant's sick cow may die and he is distressed. A worker sees the hunger and misery of his children. An intellectual learns about mass injustice and exploitation. All of this, coupled with a feeling of helplessness, produces the religious reaction. The basic element is fear: Man's fear of natural and, above all, social forces.

Now it is certain that in most cases religion does serve the function of providing an answer to worldly pains and evils. However, since the Enlightenment, this has not been its essence. Religion, in its most authentic sense, is not concerned with worldly evils. It is, rather, an answer to the so-called 'limiting situations': the necessary failure in everything we do: failure in communication, in love, or death – in short, the essential fragility and hopelessness of human existence. Suppose a man completely free of all worldly evils and still he will have to face these limiting existential situations. Religion, in its essence, is precisely a reaction to such situations.

Philosophers throughout the last one hundred years have taught that if religion is founded on fear, then the term 'fear' refers to something radically different than what is contained in expressions such as the 'fear of lightning', 'fear of imprisonment', and even 'fear of death'. The religious fear has a peculiar object called 'the divine', or the 'tremendous mystery' known to St Augustine and Otto. As long as a man has not experienced that fear, this peculiar relation to the Holy, he is not a religious man. Here again, the Marxist–Leninist doctrines concerning religion seem to be based on a total misunderstanding of the phenomenon at hand.

Moreover, to anyone who knows anything about authentic religious morality, the Marxist–Leninist analysis must appear simply ludicrous. Marxism–Leninism imagines that love of the divine is of the same sort and occurs at the same level as love of a neighbour. Quite obviously, it doesn't, nor does it exclude human love – on the contrary it is sufficient to mention the writings and life of Buddha or St Francis of Assisi.

It is also not true that religion deprives man of his uniqueness as a conscious factor in history. This misunderstanding arises from a similar confusion of levels. In fact, from an authentically religious point of view, as opposed to a magical one, on earth it is man alone who consciously builds the future and is ultimately responsible for it.

Again, religion does not necessarily divert men from their earthly tasks. All great religions have always claimed that every man has the right to devote himself exclusively to religious tasks. But the entire history of religions – from the tremendous social and economic influence of both Buddhist and Christian monasteries to the work of the Calvinists (as shown so well by Max Weber) – proves the importance of religious motives for social and economic tasks.

Should one conclude that if Marxists–Leninists free themselves from these misunderstandings and obtain some factual knowledge their attitudes towards religion will change?

It does not seem to be the case. For all that has been mentioned here is rather incidental to Marxist–Leninist theory. The basic doctrine is immanentism; it denies any transcendent order and therefore any value to religious belief. As long as one is firmly persuaded of the truth of such doctrines, no religion can be accepted.

The arguments produced to corroborate a denial are, to quote Bradley, 'bad arguments to prove what we believe on faith'. Faith, not argument is what counts.

VIII

There is nowadays much talk about the dialogue between religious believers and Marxists–Leninists, especially since many attempts at such an encounter have been made. Perhaps it might be useful to draw some conclusions concerning that dialogue on the basis of the previous outline of doctrine.

How great the difficulties are may be illustrated by the following historical comparison.

One learns from the diaries of officers who went to Tenochtitlan with Cortez that they found a wonderful city full of things they had never seen before, though some of them had been to Rome and Constantinople. Yet they found that the Aztecs practised mass ritual murder. It was reported that some 20,000 victims had been sacrificed a few days before the arrival of the Spaniards in the capital. Now among these Spaniards was a great man, Fray Juan de Zumárraga. Seeing all that splendour built on such inhumanity he came to the conclusion that this must be the work of the devil. He began preaching this conviction and under his leadership the Spaniards destroyed Tenochtitlan. They destroyed it so methodically that today anyone who wanders through the city has trouble finding even a single remaining wall. On that heap of rubble the marvel that is Mexico City was built.

There are few Christians today who would understand Fray Juan de Zumárraga and his soldiers. But a group exists today which strongly resembles those Spaniards: the Marxists–Leninists. Like the Spaniards they firmly believe something. They are convinced of the truth of their beliefs and their values. And they have shown themselves capable of destroying and building in conformity to that faith.

Let one imagine an Aztec and, for that matter, a sceptical, doubting Aztec, facing Fray Juan and entering into a dialogue with him about the sacrifices to the Gods; precisely the situation when some religious believers encounter the Marxists–Leninists.

The psychological difficulties are overwhelming. A striking two-fold attitude characterises most Marxists–Leninists; they are positively certain that they possess the absolute truth and, what is more, they are equally certain that those with whom they have to deal are more or less conscious agents of some dark powers, usually the Pentagon, Wall Street or an equivalent. It is clear that within such an atmosphere dialogue is difficult. Moreover, the Marxist–Leninst tactical principles should not be forgotten. These assert that one should try to win over the religious man for the Marxist–Leninist cause. The tactic of the outstretched hand is, it seems, ever present.

These are only minor difficulties. The central point is that a true believer of any great religion and a true Marxist–Leninist affirm diametrically opposed views in so far as the principal tenets are concerned, that is the very legitimacy of a religion.

This is not to say that a dialogue is impossible. It is often possible where it concerns secondary, mostly tactical problems such as fighting a common enemy. It is also possible on quite basic grounds if it is conceived as a spiritual clash of two faiths where each party tries to understand the other in view of eventually converting him to his beliefs.

However, in order that such a dialogue be fruitful several conditions must be fulfilled by the representatives of the religious faiths. For one, they must be true believers of a transcendent religion and not partisans of that sort of watered-down religion in which the sole function of a believer is to improve social structures. Then they have to know what Marxism–Leninism is and with whom they are dealing. Both conditions were often sorely lacking in dialogues already attempted. Had they been present the encounters might have been more fruitful.

NOTES

1. This ambiguity has been forcefully stated by the Yugoslav journal *Praxis* among others. See *Praxis* (International edition, 1965), No. 1.
2. The principal Soviet philosophical journals, *Voprosy filosofii* and *Filosofskiye nauki*, regularly carry articles on our subjects. Among specialised periodicals the following may be mentioned: *Nauka i religiya* (1959); *Ezhegodnik Muzeya istorii religii i ateizma* (Yearbook of the Museum of History of Religion and Atheism) (1957); *Voprosy istorii religii i ateizma* (Questions of History of Religion and Atheism) (1954).

   A good selection of basic texts is to be found in I. I. Brazhnik and F. I. Dolgin (eds.), *O religii. Khrestomatiya* (On Religion. An Anthology) (Moscow, 1963). From the extensive "scientific" literature the following may be quoted: *O spetsifike religii* (on the Specifics of Religion) (Moscow, 1961); I. D. Pantskhava (ed.), *Osnovnye voprosy nauchnogo ateizma* (Fundamental Questions of Scientific Atheism) (Moscow, 1962; new ed., 1966); I. P. Tsamerian (ed.), *Voprosy nauchnogo ateizma* (Questions of Scientific Atheism) (3rd. ed.; Moscow, 1964). A quite recent collective work V. V. Mshneviradze (ed.), *Religiyvya planakh antikommunizma* (Religion in the Plans of Anti-Communism) (Moscow, 1970), shows that the doctrine contained in the above is still rigorousl adhered to.

3. See below, end of section v.

4. *Osnovy markisma-leninizma* (Foundations of Marxism–Leninism) (2nd ed.; Moscow, 1962), 782 pp.; *Osnovy marksistskoi filosofii* (Foundations of Marxist Philosophy) (Moscow, 1959), 671 pp.; A. V. Makarov, A. V. Vostrikov and E. N. Chesnokov (eds.), *Dialekticheskii materializm* (Dialectical Materialism) (Moscow, 1960), 471 pp.; F. V. Konstantinov (ed.), *Istoricheskii materializm* (Historical Materialism) (Moscow, 1950) 747 pp.

5. The meaning of 'opiate' seems to be very different in Marx and Lenin.

6. 'Sotsializm i religiya', *Sochineniya* (Works) (5th ed.), Vol. 12, p. 142.

7. Nicholas Lobkowicz, 'Marx's Attitude Toward Religion', in *Marx and the Western World* (Notre Dame: University of Notre Dame Press, 1967).

8. J. Harper, *Lenin als Philosoph*, Biblithek der Rätekorrespondenz 1, s.l. (1936).

9. T. J. Blakeley, 'Soviet Writings on Atheism and Religion', *Studies in Soviet Thought*, No. 4 (1964), pp. 319–38; No. 5 (1965), pp. 106–13.

10. *Nauka i religiya* (1959). The circulation has been constantly increased: in 1962 (January) 125,000 copies were published; in 1963, 140,000; in 1970, 290,000 copies.

11. An earlier list of similar statements may be found in my 'Der bolschewistische Katechismus', *Schweizer Rundschau*, No. 48 (2 May 1948), pp. 237–44.

12. *V. I. Lenin ob ateizme i tserkvi* (V. I. Lenin on Atheism and the Church) (Moscow, 1969) contains all relevant texts. The most characteristic among them is the (first) letter to A. M. Gorkii of 13 (14?) January 1913. *Sochineniya*, Vol. 48, pp. 140f.

13. 'Sotsializm i religiya', p. 145.

2 Reflections on Religion

BRANKO BOŠNJAK

1. THE UNIVERSAL APPEAL OF RELIGION

The religious person experiences his existence in two ways. One is the worldly, terrestrial life and the other the uncertainty of what will come hereafter. Eschatological questions and concepts are the subject-matter of every religion. If it is the very nature of dogma that its contents remain unchanged, nevertheless historical and social developments have led to new conceptions. For example, the movement in Protestant theology, which is called the demythologisation of the Bible, is seeking for the modi of religiosity in the atomic age. One of the movement's spokesmen, R. Bultmann, is of the opinion that the contents of the Scriptures can be brought closer to contemporary human beings only by ridding them of their mythological veneer, that is by finding a language understandable to contemporary man. Karl Jaspers, in his polemics with Bultmann, has defended the myth as an element which enriches rational testimony.[1] A movement known as the New Theology attempts to find new interpretations for established contents. These modifications are very interesting, although they by no means negate the essentials of the faith. They are rather attempts to bring the traditional closer to man and to do this in such a manner that everyone has an opportunity to find himself.

Religion is thus linked with existentialism. Everyone contemplates himself. Why must man be sick, ill-tempered, worried, dissatisfied? And ultimately, why must man die? This is the absolute question with which every religion concerns itself. For the believer uncertainty begins at the boundary between life and death. Is everything over for him, or is he entitled to hope there is something more? Eschatology as contents and goal was, and remains, the foundation stone of every religion, irrespective of historic period.

In rationalist philosophy, the necessity of a rational critique of religion was emphasised in order to liberate mankind from the erroneous ideas of its religious faith. This critique was at once sharp and ingenious. None the less, religion, with all its dogmas, survived it. Marx, in contrast to rationalist atheists, advanced his critique of religion in a social and historical context and claimed that a successful criticism of religion could only be realised by social and revolutionary changes in society itself. A social act is required to deprive religion of its socio-political power. Once this power is lost, religion and the Church are left with only their existential, individualistic influence. For Marx, under changed social conditions, in which private property as a source of exploitation has been eliminated, religion would no longer have any grounds for existence as a substitute for formally unrealisable needs. Logically religions would then necessarily die out. But does this really occur?

From Egyptian necrology to the present-day New Theology and its various sects, religion has been the hope for mercy, reward and justice. When these cannot be achieved on earth, time and space will be found for them in heaven. This hope, *sub specie aeternitatis*, is the illusion which has represented psychological solace for the depressed. If there is a Being who sees and hears everything, then one must only be patient and nourish hope. Because of such a Being, one must be just, for although man can outsmart worldly laws, he can not outsmart those of God. This is how the Sophist Kritias explained the genesis of religion.

Marx teaches that the Socialist Revolution, through the realisation of new socialist relationships, in which private property has been eliminated as a source of exploitation, causes religion to lose the roots of its existence. In the new society man himself determines the manner and nature of his existence. The power of disposition over his products makes religion impossible, for man will no longer allow himself to be overcome by the illusive hope for a hereafter. He will understand that the real problem is the realisation of the whole contents in this world. Only then does history affirm itself as the true form of existence in human conditions. Religious concepts cease being the basis of society and the State, because nature and human praxis, in the real world of being, are explained by science. Religion as a form of social solace loses its purpose. Real life is subject to its own laws and its own purpose. This *logos* of activity is accompanied by even greater possibilities, because man tends to liberate himself from the entire ideology more than from the sphere of erroneous thought. Religion as a theory of the hereafter no longer contributes to the improvement of man's real existence. It has in effect banned itself from this world because it seeks its existence in something which is outside this world. The texts of later Marxist writers explain the problem of religion along similar lines.[2]

Following the Socialist Revolution the Church remains only as a church, a private institution, because new laws establish a complete separation of Church and State. Juridically, this is the only possible solution, and as a result of this separation, State and society become independent. The duality of legal systems is abolished. Religiosity remains the private affair of the believers. Man, liberated from the control of religion and the Church, becomes a free social being. From now on the laws of society are the only valid and true norms. But religion never regards itself as a mere private matter, and does not wish to abdicate its influence over life and society. The Church as an institution attempts to expand its sphere of influence, for it always demands that life in this world be a prerequisite for the eschatological future as the Church sees it. The Church has never denied this tendency. Socialist society does not give the Church the right to be a state within the State. The Church is merely permitted to remain a religious institution concerned with the problems of religion but not those of politics.

Socialist society is not a magic institution capable of abolishing all contradictions in society and history. Changed economic and social circumstances can merely create the objective conditions for humanising the relations between men. This however is neither an absolute certainty nor an automatic result. Even the abolition of private ownership is no guarantee against the development of a bureaucracy which can be as heartless as the private capitalist. The changes in the economic and political system simply do not have any automatic effects leading to positive results. Socialist society can have its own forms of alienation. Socialism represents merely a social possibility to humanise history. This does not occur on the basis of a mere declaration. For the realisation of the humanisation, complete freedom must be assured; a critical stance towards the whole of socialist reality must exist. This was hindered by the practice of Stalinism which created a fertile soil for a socialistic mystique, or the deification of the personality. This god-making corresponds to parousia in the Christian sense – God has returned to earth. Within the framework of this mysticism, a religious relationship (i.e. only faith and absence of criticism of the party and state leadership) was demanded.

Party and State were elevated to an infallibility corresponding to that of the Pope within the Catholic Church. The party purges were able to imitate the activity as well as the effects of the Inquisition. Thus it came to pass that under the banner of socialism, in place of criticism, a new religion with its cult of the personality was formed. This pseudo-religion represented a great danger for socialism. From the practice of Stalinist dogmatism it becomes apparent that not everything which was declared to be socialist was real socialism. That is why the question of death of religion in socialist society remains an open question. When socialist society under Stalinism developed its own worldly mysticism, how can the mysticism of the hereafter be successfully negated? It is essentially the same relationship, except that 'this-worldly' gods are closer to man, and thus more influential, than the 'other-worldly' gods. Changed world economics will never lead to the abolition of religion if this process of social development is not accompanied by the development of a scientific and critical consciousness.

For the future the problem is simple. Can religion exist and develop within socialist society? On the basis of the practice of socialism today can one state that religion is dying out? As a result of the Socialist revolution, the Church has been deprived of its economic and political influence. The law has made it impossible for the Church to maintain its former control of society, the State and life. However, being relegated to the private sphere does not endanger the continued existence of religion because religion can never be reduced to a purely socio-economic relationship, although it is in this relationship that it develops its most active influence. Every religion, by its nature, transcends the world of reality and turns to eschatology, i.e. to the doctrine of the last things. For this reason no social system can be an obstacle to religion as long as that religion by law has been relegated to the private sphere. For this reason the death of religion is not a quick and easy process. In Marxist philosophy, the phenomenon of religion is regarded as being far simpler than it is in fact.

In Marxism the phenomenon of religion belongs to the super-structure. None the less it has specific characteristics which differentiate it from other forms of ideology. Just as it is possible for various forms of philosophical thought to occur at the same time and under the same objective circumstances (which is itself proof of different forms of superstructure) so can the phenomenon of religion find its realisation in social or economic bases. Changes in the economic and social bases, as well as the general developments of the intellect and the passage of time, may be accompanied by changes in the interpretation of the contents of religious ideas. However, this is not to say that religion as a whole disappears. If religion were not bound to the individual's existential relationship to being, then changes in the base would lead to a complete change of this form of consciousness, as for example has been the case with the legal system. Laws are not created from *a priori* determination but they always generalise social facts and realities. That is why (unlike religious dogmas) juridical norms can frequently be changed. Religion uses dogma to protect itself against historical influence and social change. The content of dogma, for the most part, transcends reality and does not change with modifications of the base. To the believer, the religious content continues to be 'the only road of salvation' and of the 'eschatological relationship'. It is precisely because religion cannot be related exclusively to historical changes that it can continue to develop by virtue of its immanence. This means that religion as a form of ideology maintains its relative independence which protects it from the change in the framework of real life structure. Thus, e.g., the belief in resurrection is an eschatological relationship and has no relation whatever to the economics of a given society. This existential desire for resurrection cannot be negated by any historical reality, neither at the time the Apostle Paul testified before the Corinthians that it was evident that good Christians have to die the same as heathens, nor today in the era of space travel. It is necessary to take note of this when speaking of the superstructure, otherwise the entire problem is over-simplified. The fact that religion continues to exist is, however, no proof of its truthfulness. It is merely a manifestation that there are those who, in the hope for a life eternal, wish to insulate themselves from the inevitable realities of nature.

Within its eschatological realm the contents of religion in relationship to dogma remains immutable. Once faith is accepted as the revelation of God[3] it must not be changed. Contrary tendencies caused the Church to initiate measures as extreme as the Inquisition in order to be able to conduct successfully its struggle against those who doubted the dogma. The example of the Inquisition clearly shows that the Church has supported worldly matters much more than those of the next world. The bad conscience of the papacy cannot be denied. To the believer, dogma is equivalent to the belief in salvation and eternity. Irrespective of the epoch or the social system the Church maintains its eschatological dogmatic contents. In this respect even the atomic age is no exception.

Will this content die out in a society which has completed the Socialist Revolution? Following the elimination of the sociological roots of religion there remains this eschatological content for the Church *sub specie aeternitatis*. The dogma of the Holy Trinity, the Marxian dogma, the dogma of God-Man and the like must remain as valid today as they were two thousand years ago. Belief in the resurrection of Christ is as imperative to the beginnings of Christendom. Christians are required to believe this if they are to seek their reward and salvation in heaven. This part of the contents is never questioned (irrespective of the social system) as long as man considers himself an eschatological being. Simply because man is mortal, these questions concerning life and the purpose of life present a problem. The eschatological part of existence is incorporated in the individual's relationships to totality. When the sceptic Pyrrhon posed the problem as to the time of Socrates' death, he did so in order to point out how inadequate the concepts of beginning and end are. St Augustine wrote that death was the tearing off of life and that without life there could be no death (*De civitate Dei*, XIII, 10). The attitude to eschatology and to totality has two possible aspects. If man regards himself as a natural being then he is free of any illusions concerning the hereafter. History teaches us that along with theists there have always been atheists. Those who believe in God believe because they wish to be immortal. They do not regard death as a natural phenomenon or the end of their own being. Precisely because man is mortal, this eschatological wish can arise and be maintained independent of any social system.

With the statement that all power is derived from God (Romans 13, 1), the Church is given the opportunity to preserve its relative independence; to separate its teachings and its faith as much as possible from the 'worldly state'. According to St Augustine, all of mankind is divided into two groups. One group encompasses those whose model for life is man himself (i.e. those who do not accept the beliefs of the Church), and the other group contains those who model their lives on God. In a figurative sense, these two groups of human beings can be described as two states: the worldly and the heavenly (*De civitate Dei*, XV, 1). Accordingly a believer can be the subject of the heavenly state in any social system. The question is when does this heavenly kingdom in the human consciousness begin to die out? An answer can be found in the interpretation of the phenomenon of death, because death is the original source of every religion. If human life were eternal then man would have no need for a philosophy or a theology.

The problem of the death of religion cannot be related simply to the interrelationship of economic and social circumstances. As long as the fear of death, as well as the desire for immortality, continues to exist, there will be religion (irrespective of all the possible modi and systems by which it may manifest itself). Even Epicurus stated that the fear of death was a great obstacle to peace of mind (ataraxia). He explained death as the loss of the senses. Both good and evil for man are perceived through the senses. Thus the fear of death is illogical, for as long as we exist there is no death, and as soon as death has arrived we exist no longer.[4] Although true, the desire for individual immortality none the less remains. This desire can only be overcome by a *rational* relationship to being. As long as this is not achieved, religion will not die, but will continue to exist as an antithesis to death.

The rational relationship to existence consists of the realisation that man is a natural being, that he exists in the manner of all beings, and that he is subject to the general change in the world of being. It is clear that man is a mortal and that he must die. In the search for a further 'why' human thought finds no answer. There is no answer to the question why something exists, and nothing does not exist. This remains a mystery for man and he knows that there is no answer to it. His theological answers do not represent a solution, for then one would also have to answer the question who created God, and so on, *ad infinitum*.[5]

Man is not created by a purposeful activity in nature. *Therefore the question 'why has man been created?' can be answered in no way other than: 'for nothing'.* Being cannot be conceived as a new God for whom man is the fulfilment of his goals. Once the theological premise of God is eliminated, one is left entirely in the realm of being. Man too is a part of being and is within being. Man is the consciousness of being, and in man being becomes consciousness. Being becomes conscious of itself, or man thinks of being and thus also of himself. Thus man realises he is a tragic creature, that is to say he has the realisation of death. This leads to religion as a wish for overcoming death, and in life religion can be used as a solace for everything which causes man to suffer.

The question concerning the death of religion is related to the problem of whether myth or *logos* is the criterion of man's relationship to being. Myth upholds eschatology, *logos* rejects it. Myth cannot be consistent, and *logos* must be consistent.

In discussing myth and *logos,* Heidegger advanced the thesis that in Greek thought and culture myth was not destroyed by *logos.* He says: 'the religious is never destroyed by logic, always by the God withdrawing himself'.[6] How and why does a God withdraw? If myth had a greater power than *logos*, divinity would not withdraw itself, and as long as *logos* remained weak, myth would be very influential. It is the nature of myth to grow weaker because, as a result of its immanence, it must proceed towards its own negation. As soon as an attempt is made to investigate eschatology by means of *logos*, one finds that the eschatological area loses its very foundation. This has already been incisively noted and formulated by Lucian of Samosata. For his heroes of the underworld it is clear that not everything is happening according to *logos*, because if *logos* were to be applied then Hades would be deprived of the very foundation of its existence. In order to preserve Hades, *logos* must be excluded. This is a general principle valid for every form of eschatology. The divinity does not withdraw itself without reason. Christianity overcame antique mythology because it succeeded in including eschatology in the historical realm of human activity. Faith in salvation and the messianic idea fulfilled their concrete demand in actual practice as well. When one religion replaces another, this signifies a withdrawal of the divine into myth. This explains the origin of many different sects. The replacement of gods is a process which takes place on its own ground, i.e. within its own area of mythology.

The disintegration of religion cannot take place solely on religious grounds, because the very modi of religion remain religion. Even the possibility of a change of context (a change of dogma) does not represent a negation of religion as an eschatological relationship to being. This relationship can be disintegrated only with the aid of *logos*, or with the aid of the rational, i.e. the causualistic, conception of the world.

Why should God withdraw himself without an eschatological or a logical reason? If the withdrawal of God were also to signify a dissolution of the religious realm then the withdrawal must be regarded as the result of something that has preceded it.

Myth and *logos* are two modi of the relationship to being. *Logos* as causality can only have validity where man is prepared to listen to *logos*. Heraclitus said: 'If you do not wish to listen to me but rather to logos then it is reasonable to recognise that everything forms a unity' (*Fr.* 50). Those who are not prepared to listen to *logos* cannot be helped by *logos*. This is the case of religion which is based on: (1) the fear of death and (2) the wish for immortality. As long as these two modi of existential relationships continue to exist, religion will exist, irrespective of the modi and systems in which man lives. This would not be the case if *logos* (i.e. logical thought) had the force of natural laws. Being a primary foundation of thought, *logos* does not possess this force and, in spite of its effects, it is possible to live and think in contradiction to *logos*. Religion can continue to be an eschatological solace even when, on the basis of social and economic conditions, it has died as a social solace.

II. THE YUGOSLAV PRACTICE

In the 19th century the Marxist socialist movement declared religion to be a private matter of the believers, and that religion was not to be utilised in the creation of the social, political and historical events. This corresponded to the view that socialism, being a science, must develop as such. Religion, being a form of metaphysics, lost its claim to be the alpha and omega of society

In itself the principle of religion as a 'private affair' is easily explained, for man has the right to believe or not to believe. However, as soon as such a demand is applied to real life, it no longer remains simple. In this respect Lenin has differentiated between the State and the Party, by explaining that religion remained a

private matter as far as the State was concerned, but not as far as
the Party of the proletariat was concerned. The latter had the task
of leading the working people to irreligiosity, and such a task corresponds in principle to Marx's interpretation. In an editorial published in No. 179 of the *Kölnische Zeitung* in 1842, Marx wrote:

> As soon as a state contains several confessions enjoying equal
> rights, it can no longer be a religious state without offending
> particular religious confessions. It is the church which con-
> demns every adherent of another confession as a heretic,
> which makes every crumb of bread dependent upon faith,
> which has made dogma the link between individuals and the
> civic existence.[7]

In creating legal equality among all confessions, with no distinction based on the number of followers, the State elevated itself
above any affiliation to particular religions and their ideas. That is
the nature of the political emancipation of the State. The next
stage is the emancipation of man and his humanisation, or the
abolition of alienation which was once regarded as a necessity of
existence. In legally separating the religious communities from
the State, the socialist State does not regard itself as anti-religious
in its character or in its function, but merely as an irreligious
institution, in which religion is declared to be a private affair of
the believers. Atheism is the basis upon which religion is regarded
as a private matter in relation to the State and its function. From
the very fact that the irreligiosity of the State does not present an
obstacle to religion, it is evident that irreligiosity is not synonymous
with anti-religiosity, and thus in principle the separation of
Church and State can be beneficial by allowing a more independent activity of the former. The difficulties in Church–State relations arise because of the various interpretations of religion as a
private matter; for religion regards itself as a universal basis for
social and historical life, which in turn is regarded as merely
transitory by virtue of the higher goal pursued by religion, i.e.
the Kingdom of Heaven. By drawing eschatology into history,
as well as history into eschatology, the Church places itself above
society and State, and such a demand necessarily leads to conflicting tendencies and views, because the Church wishes to
preserve for itself the right to decide what is and what is not. (Cf.
Acts of the Apostles 15, 28.)

It is necessary to examine the question: How can religion be maintained as a private matter? As soon as believing individuals join together, they tend to strengthen their beliefs and spread them. For example, the learning of Esperanto is a private matter and nobody is required to speak or write this language. None the less when Esperantists unite they desire to exert a common influence and to convince others that their idea is necessary and useful. They have moved from the private into the public sphere. The case of religion is similar. When religion ceases to remain a domestic cult and begins to express itself through an organised church, the private matter takes on a special social dimension. A social dimension is an externally visible social manifestation which no longer is a private matter. It becomes a society within society, its relationships being juridically and legally regulated by the latter.[8] Religion also has an elaborate international organisation through which it attempts to make its effects felt in accordance with carefully considered criteria.[9]

Even if religion were to be officially declared a private matter in all countries of the world, it would not really be a private matter if it took on external organisational forms. When this situation exists in a few countries only, the solution of the problem becomes all the more difficult. In socialist society the Church has no political programme, and yet it tries not to limit spiritual questions to the sphere of eschatology but to apply them to everyday life, and to demand from its believers the application of practice adequate to this aspiration. This transference of the eschatological into the historical, or of the metaphysical into the material, clearly indicates that religion as a merely private matter does not exist and that even in its eschatology it is public, social and historical. Legally, private matters can be regulated, and juridically, religion really remains a private matter. The politicisation of religion must be avoided, although it would be quite difficult to draw precise boundary lines in this respect. As far as the juridical and political situation is concerned, the law declares religion to be a private matter. The law, however, is not capable of precisely solving the metaphysical part of the question. It follows that religion as a private matter organises itself as something public, in which eschatological questions are present as a form of ritual practice.

Thus religion both is and is not a private matter. Obviously this is a contradictory relationship. If religion regarded itself as a merely private matter then it would have to remain without its dogma, and an eschatology without dogma and organisation can be neither a movement nor a power. Since religion is characterised by both of these attributes, it is not, and also does not want to be, a mere private matter. The immanence of religious contents and goals do not lead to a private being, but to a desire for universality (*katholikos*). This relationship (private versus public) creates a situation in which eschatology attempts to seek affirmation, not merely as an absolute, but also as a historical need; as a necessity and reality in the sense of certain deeds and goals based on the conviction that religion is absolute truth. Religion represents itself as fulfilling a universal need and not as a private matter. In a society which has declared religion to be a private matter, these contradictions are always present. Juridically and legally, something which regards itself as absolute and universal is declared to be a private matter. The Church wishes to extend its influence, it wishes to collect all beings and to speak for all of them. In this sense the question asked by the theists – whose fault is it that there are atheists? – also becomes comprehensible. If religion were only a private matter, such a question would be impossible.

In the process of grouping religious individuals the transition, in a Hegelian sense, from quantity to quality is achieved. Whenever numerous people are united, the resulting group becomes a real force, and one which cannot be regarded with indifference by the State. Even the early organisation of Christians in the Roman Empire has shown that private matter becomes a state within a state. The Church has never ceased to be such a state within the State. It would be illusory to think that by legally declaring religion to be a private matter, this essential characteristic is abolished.

Within the spheres of individuality and ideas, philosophy can be regarded as a private matter, because philosophy does not offer any absolute certainty of its theses and does not appear as an organisation demanding absolute faith and obedience. In every philosophy the personality of the philosopher is present, and thus subjectivity is introduced. No philosophy can be explained purely on a basis of historical preconditions. It would be wrong to think that Marxism could have occurred without Marx, or that another Lenin could have easily appeared on the scene. To think along these lines would be the purest historical fatalism. It is the individuality of the philosopher which gives philosophy its special character. Philosophy, by its nature, is always individualistic, because that is how truth is achieved. The philosophy of Marxism becomes the philosophy of those who accept it as the goal of their life; but neither this nor any other philosophy offers eternity and the absolute, as do religions. From this the difference between free thought and dogma becomes evident. Religion, being by its very nature and intention a dogmatic conviction, cannot be a private matter. Philosophy, as individual thought, is and remains purely a private matter.

The Church, as an institution which regards itself as the representative and guardian of revealed truth, might object that the philosophy of Marxism in socialist countries has an institutional existence and protection and that therefore this philosophy is not a private matter. It is true that philosophy can dogmatise and institutionalise itself (just as religion has done) and become a 'state philosophy', or the sole philosophical answer within the framework of philosophy. Methodologically, philosophy can only be interpreted on the basis of philosophy, because the theory of philosophy is its practice (Marx). The dogmatisation of Marxism during the Stalinist epoch is by no means proof that this was Marxism. It becomes evident that the dogmatic model of thought (utilising institutionalised forms) wishes to be general, all-encompassing and uniform in its nature, and that in this aspiration it does not regard itself as a private matter. In such conditions philosophy does not become a form of dogmatism. However, there also exists creative Marxism as a constant critique and as a theory of revolution. Creative Marxism sees its goal as a pluralism of ideas. Its purpose and its actuality are in a constant dialogue with these ideas, which it must explicate. The nature of genuine philosophising is the interpretation of contemporary ideas on the level of contemporary events.

In Yugoslavia the philosophy of Marxism rather than religion is taught in schools in accordance with the law on the separation of Church and State. Marxism is thus forced upon all as the new selected faith, but everyone has the right to judge Marxism critically. Pupils in school have the right to freely express their opinions on any philosophy, including Marxism. Today it is clear that Marxism is not a uniform concept, and that within its various trends, both theoretical and practical, are apparent. In Yugoslavia there is a pluralism of ideas, both regarding possibility and reality, and this expresses itself in various forms of criticism. In contrast, a teacher of catechism would not allow dogmas to be explained in a manner different from the pronouncements of the Church, but instead would demand absolute faith in its teachings. This is also evident from the very definition of the word faith. The Apostle Paul says (Hebrews 11, 1): 'Now faith is the substance of things hoped for, the evidence of things not seen.' Philosophy can never make this claim and therefore remains a private matter; religion, because it is institutionalised, cannot.

This is the parting of ideas and ways at which the present dialogue between Christians and Marxists in Yugoslavia has arrived. A theologian from Ljubljana, in reviewing my book *Philosophy and Christianity,* posed the question: who is called upon to judge Marxism and who to judge faith? Marxism is to be judged by the members of the League of Communists. Only the Church is qualified to talk about faith. Where the Catholic faith is concerned, only the Catholic Church can speak. This would be in principle a co-existence of status as a theoretical relationship: Marxism to the Communists, and Church and faith to the believers.

Theological publications openly pursue the fundamental idea that without faith life has no purpose, and without the concept of God the world and life cannot be explained. Every theory and philosophy which attempts to solve these questions without accepting the revealed truth of God will necessarily find itself in a hopeless position, because human reason cannot grasp the mystery of the world and of man. There are many such publications, and they react to everything that happens in society from the religious and theological point of view. In churches lectures are given on how, and by what means, Marxism can lead the youth astray. Discussions concerning ideas of freedom, the abolition of alienation, the concept of a new future, etc., create the impression that in Marxism these things are all possible. But in replacing faith, Marxism has only shifted these problems on to the humane plane. According to the theological view, that is sufficient proof that Marxism cannot give man what he needs for life. Therefore religious education is the goal for the entire Church, and the expansion of religious activity remains its constant concern.

Through its institutions and publications, the Church also organises various kinds of social aid in the spirit of: 'Who is my neighbour?'

The dialogue between Marxists and Christians on theoretical questions is not conducted for the purpose of changing personal convictions. None the less the dialogue does help to contribute towards the creation of a possibly more tolerant attitude, which under present-day circumstances is both necessary and significant. A theologian could, for example, refuse to reply to the question: What in reality corresponds to the concept of God? Viewed logically nothing corresponds to this concept. This question would not confuse the theologian, for he would say that he believes that God exists, and that he adheres to what his faith teaches him. This is the sense in which a dialogue between a professor of theology and myself, concerning my book *Philosophy and Christianity,* took place in front of an audience of some 2,500. A newspaper in West Berlin published a report on this discussion and described it as an example of something which hitherto had not existed in socialist countries.

The theologian could not convert the Marxist in the course of this discussion, and the Marxist did not influence the theologian. In these cases no 'victory' is possible, because what takes place is a dialogue of ideas in which both parties exert a maximum effort to establish the validity of their position. This is the value of such discussions. It is important to know what theism stands for and what atheism offers. It is only natural that one cannot expect more from a person than he can offer. Schleiermacher's thesis concerning the *experience of cosmos as a religious feeling,* and Fichte's thought that everyone should have a philosophy suited to himself as a human being, indicate that the intellectual and individual differences between humans also manifest themselves in their differing application in reality.

If the Church ceased to regard itself as a political institution, the dialogue concerning ideas and life would be a novelty, which one could appreciate without reservation. In Yugoslavia, following the victory of the Socialist Revolution, questions concerning social development and life are part of a continuing debate. Religion must not be regarded as an idea which has already been defeated. In Yugoslavia this view was held for a long time, and thus philosophy has not devoted itself to the problems of religion and of religious influence. For some Marxists this was regarded as a chapter that had already been closed and doubts were expressed concerning the seriousness of those still wishing to devote themselves to these topics. It would be a complete illusion, however, to think that religion will die out now that the political and economic change of Yugoslav society has been achieved.

The discussion between theologians and Marxists encompasses many questions. If in school a religious pupil proclaims that God created the world in six days, the theologian would explain to him that he should not understand this as being literally six days. When the theory of evolution is advanced as an argument against the biblical story of the creation of man, the theologian would answer that unquestionably God created man, but would leave open the possibility that God desired a gradual development of man. The question of whether Muslims believe in the true God would cause the Catholic theologians to answer that they do believe in the true God, but that they do not know the entire truth concerning this God. They do not know all the things that Catholics know, such as the Trinity of God, or the human birth of God. In short they do not know the teachings of the Christian dogma, which is the entire truth. In this manner the theologians explain questions of dogma.

Believers are told that good deeds alone do not suffice and that a firm faith must constantly be professed. This is all the more necessary today because the ecumenical idea of Christian unity is regarded as a constant modus of church practice. In Yugoslavia this has a particular political significance. It now is quite natural for representatives of various confessions to visit one another, meet at various ecclesiastical festivities and keep each other informed concerning their experiences and successes. At the same time this creates a new type of attitude towards Marxism and atheism. The multiple theological views express themselves as a unit, with a uniform anti-Marxist position, in order to better resist the idea of atheism which represents the principal and common danger. The dialogue of Christians and Marxists is also interesting from a political point of view, because for both it deals with questions of theory and practice.

Legal possibilities are also carefully considered, and it can happen that a person must face a court of law as the result of expressing views concerning dogma. An instructive case was that of the young Slovene poet, Gajsek, who was charged by three Slovene bishops that in his poem 'Christ and the Mother of God', he had violated the religious feelings of believers. At first he was found guilty; but then he filed counter-charges, and a sharp public protest against this violation of his freedom of thought erupted. Ruling on his counter-charge, the court eventually found him not guilty. Nevertheless it is still not clear how the law can determine when the feelings of theists and atheists have been violated. In Zagreb the editorial board of the Church newspaper *Glas Koncila* conducted an investigation based on a number of letters sent to it by members of the audience of a seminar in which a lecturer in the field of political economy was said to have insulted the Mother of God by reportedly stating that Mary had given birth to an illegitimate child. It came out that he discussed this issue during an intermission and not in the course of his lecture. Consequently the editorial board of the paper chose not to regard this as an abuse of a university chair, but as a personal lack of taste and culture.

The idea of ecumenism has been strongly maintained in Yugoslavia. All religious communities have ceased to play a political role and instead are developing activities in the field of pastoral work. The ecumenical idea also has had a positive political effect, because it emphasises that human beings should unite and attempt to create a better future. The situation is very dynamic and various tendencies can now be distinguished within the Catholic Church.

In the Catholic Church, particularly in Croatia, a progressive group is active in attempting to bring about a democratic renewal of the entire life of the Church. This group issues several publications, the most influential of which are: *Glas Koncila* (The Voice of the Council) and the periodical *Kana*. The conservative group within the Catholic Church is not enthusiastic about this movement and attempts to safeguard its own position. Thus a lively polemic among believers is in progress from which it is clear that diverse European trends in theology are represented in Yugoslavia.

The position of the Serbian Orthodox Church is somewhat different because the Church is essentially national. According to canon law only one Church can be autocephalous in a state, and in Yugoslavia this was the Serbian Orthodox Church. A few years ago, however, the Macedonian Orthodox Church separated from the Serbian Orthodox Church and declared itself autocephalous. The Patriarch of the Serbian Church did not recognise this split, and the whole matter took on political significance. This issue has remained unresolved and the dispute is still smouldering.

In Yugoslavia religion remains a subject of scholarly interest. Our philosophers, for a number of years, have conducted research into the phenomena of religion and theism. The results show that religion does maintain itself in socialist societies and continues to lay claim to the entire human being. At Zagreb, in the University's Institute for Social Science Research, there is a section for post-graduate studies of atheism and religion. There, representatives of various confessions are among the lecturers, providing another example of co-operation between Marxists and theists. In the course of a lecture series, a member of the Secretariat for Non-Believers from Vienna was one of the lecturers. Such joint action has had public approval because the dialogue has achieved a broad basis. It is common for Marxists to address audiences of theologians, and theologians to address audiences of Marxists. Thus there is ensured an intellectual movement which has a positive present and an open future.

NOTES

1. Karl Jaspers and Rudolf Bultmann, *Die Frage der Entmythologisierung* (Munich, 1954), p. 118.
2. Anton Pannekoek, *Religion und Sozialismus, Ein Vortrag* (Bremen, 1906); Antonia Labriola, *La concezione materialistica della storia* (Rome, 1896); *Il materialismo storico e la filosofia di Benedetto Croce* (Turin, 1948); Ambrogio Domini, *Lineamenti di storia delle religioni dalle prime forme di culto alle origini del cristianesimo* (1959); Charles Hainchelin, *Les origines de la religion* (Paris, 1935). This book was first published under the pseudonym of Lucien Henry (Paris, 1935). The author has subsequently supplemented his original volume. Georg Klaus and Manfred Buhr (eds.), *Philosophisches Wörterbuch* (Leipzig, 1964); *Kratkii nauchno-ateisticheskii slovar* [Short Dictionary of Scientific Atheism] (Moscow, 1964).
3. The contents of revelation can never represent the basis for philosophy. Faith requires absolute certainty for its contents. Philosophy cannot relate to such a demand. This is in essence the difference between dogmatic and critical thought. That is why a critique of revelation becomes the prerequisite for every philosophy. For example Karl Jaspers in his analysis of the relationship of Catholicism and philosophy came to the conclusion that the decision must be made on the basis of thinking: either reason or Catholicism (p. 850). Jaspers states that the purpose cannot be the existence of a single authority for all of mankind. The general movement must not be cornered in a 'cemetery of universal authority' (p. 836). This is why the Catholic authority cannot be accepted. Everything must remain subject to criticism (p. 866). Reason does not permit authority to remain Catholic (p. 862). The truth cannot be usurped

by several human beings and institutions (Karl Jaspers, *Von der Wahrheit*, Munich, 1958). Naturally the theologians find sufficient cause to criticise Jaspers (for example Heinrich Fries, 'Karl Jaspers und das Christentum' in *Theologische Quartalschrift* [1952–53], pp. 257–87).

4. Epicurus' pupil and continuer Philodemos of Gadara in his work about death says the following: He who thinks that he will last forever is like those who would believe that glass and earthenware vessels can be flung against steel ones for some time without breaking. Epicurus' pupil Metrodoros said: All the good in mortality is mortal (Sen. Ep. 98, 9).

5. Herder (1744–1803) in his book, *Über die menschliche Unsterblichkeit* (1791), emphasises two concepts of immortality: the individual immortality of the soul or of the spirit is our hope which develops itself in our imagination, in the moral judgement and in the innermost human nature and it is neither a product of knowledge nor of experience. In contrast to this there is another immortality, that is the immortality of the name and of fame. That is this historical, poetic, or artistic immortality (E. Ermatinger, *Durch Aufklärung zur wahren Menschlichkeit*, Leipzig, 1932).

6. Martin Heidegger, *Was heisst Denken?* (Tübingen, 1954), quoted according to Walter Strolz, *Menschsein als Gottesfrage* (Pfullingen, 1965), p. 207.

7. K. Marx und F. Engels, *Werke* (Berlin, 1961), Vol. I, p. 102.

8. For Church–State relations in Yugoslavia, see Manojlo Broćić, 'The Position and Activities of the Religious Communities in Yugoslavia', below, pp. 351–67.

9. It is on the basis of such a *de facto* special position of the Church as a self-contained unit within society, that the Vatican is interested to find means for the regulation of its rights over the Church in spiritual questions with the individual states. Diplomatic relations between Yugoslavia and the Vatican were severed in 1952 because the Catholic Church regarded it as its duty to oppose the policy of the socialist society. Relations were restored on 25 June 1966 because of the positive change in the policy of the Vatican. The Church is a religious institution and as such enjoys its rights. The agreement between Yugoslavia and the Vatican is called a Protocol and it regulates these relations and enables the Vatican to direct the affairs of the Catholic clergy in Yugoslavia. In Part I, Point 2, the Protocol states *inter alia*: 'The government of the Socialist Federative Republic of Yugoslavia respects the competency of the Holy See in exercising rights over the Catholic Church in Yugoslavia in spiritual questions as well as in questions of an ecclesiastical and religious character to the extent that these are not in contradiction to the internal order of the Socialist Federative Republic of Yugoslavia.' In Part II, Point 1 it states: 'The Holy See confirms the principle that the activity of Catholic clerics in the exercise of their spiritual duties should take place within a religious and ecclesiastical framework and that accordingly they cannot abuse their religious and ecclesiastical functions for purposes which are actually political in character.' As is evident from the Protocol, everything has been clearly stated; but life keeps bringing up new questions which require not only legal interpretations but also analysis as to contents, in order to arrive at the true purpose and nature of events.

3 The Russian Orthodox Church in Council 1945–1971

MICHAEL BOURDEAUX and KATHLEEN MATCHETT

The life of the Russian Orthodox Church since the Revolution of 1917 has been marked by many difficulties, both atheist pressure from without and unrest within. The last few years have seen the emergence of a definite, although not organised, contemporary movement of dissent within the ranks of the Church. This will be dealt with in another chapter. The present chapter will concentrate on the Russian Orthodox Church in Council.

The strength of the Orthodox Church in the Soviet Union today cannot be accurately assessed due to the lack of proper data. Estimates of membership vary widely, figures depending in any case on the definition of membership, whether baptism into the Church, regular attendance at worship or personal faith. But there can be no doubt that the Orthodox Church continues to claim the allegiance of a significant percentage of the Soviet population.

The number of working churches may be estimated with greater probability. It is widely accepted that before the Khrushchev anti-religious campaign of 1959–64 there were some 20,000 Orthodox churches in the U.S.S.R. This campaign reduced the number by about half.[1] The present figure is estimated at some 7,000.[2] The number of clergy is probably lower, since in some areas a priest has to serve more than one church.

Theological training is available today in three seminaries (Moscow, Leningrad and Odessa) and two academies for higher study (Moscow and Leningrad). The Moscow theological schools are housed in the Trinity Monastery of St Sergius at Zagorsk, near the capital. This is a focal point of contemporary Russian Orthodox church life. The total student body for all the theological schools of the Orthodox Church probably does not exceed 500 at any one time.[3] It is evident that this is insufficient to meet the parochial need; there is also a theological correspondence course handling another 400–500 students.[4]

There seem to be no more than six monasteries still working in the Soviet Union. These are the Trinity Monastery at Zagorsk and the Pskovo-Pechersky Monastery, both in the Russian Republic; the Dormition Monastery near Odessa, summer residence of the Patriarch and home of the Odessa seminary; and the Pochaiv Monastery in Ternopil oblast, Ukraine; the Zhirovitsy Monastery in Belorussia, and the Holy Ghost Monastery in Vilnius, Lithuania. An unsuccessful attempt was made to close the Pochaiv Monastery at the beginning of the 1960s.[5] For women, there are seven convents in the Ukraine, one in Lithuania, one in Latvia, one in Estonia and one in Moldavia.[6]

All bishops of the Russian Orthodox Church are drawn from the 'black' or monastic clergy. In mid-1972 there were 57 bishops and four auxiliary bishops in office in the U.S.S.R., with a further six bishops and two vicar-bishops in foreign dioceses (excluding the Japanese Autonomous Church).[7] The Church is governed by the Holy Synod, consisting of eight members and headed by the Patriarch. *Ex officio* members of the Synod are the Metropolitan of Krutitsy and Kolomna, who is the Patriarch's deputy and 'Bishop of Moscow', the Metropolitans of Leningrad and Kiev, the heads of the Department of Foreign Relations and the Patriarchal Chancellery. The complement is made up by three bishops summoned by the Synod to sit for a term of six months.

Supreme administrative authority in the Church rests with the *Pomestny Sobor* (literally 'Local Council', but in fact a national assembly, as opposed to an 'Ecumenical Council'). A *Sobor* is a great event in the life of an Orthodox Church. The Orthodox Churches recognise seven Ecumenical Councils (325–787 A.D.) which have laid down Christian doctrine for the whole Church. A *Pomestny Sobor* is not binding on all Orthodox Churches, but constitutes a legislative and executive meeting for the Church in the relevant national area. Professor A. I. Georgiyevsky, a teacher at the Moscow Theological Academy, has described its function as follows:

Local Councils of the Russian Orthodox Church constitute the supreme organ of church government; as history bears witness, they have been called in connection with the need to settle questions arising in church life regarding legislative, judicial, administrative or other ecclesiastical matters. At the same time the Councils themselves have formulated their own scope of action, for there are no hard and fast rules of procedure for a *Pomestny Sobor,* although some have made use of precedents from previous Councils.[8]

Since the October Revolution, Russia has seen the commencement of two – and the conclusion of three – Russian Orthodox Local Councils. One was in session when the Bolsheviks seized power. Having lasted twelve months, it finally wound up in the autumn of 1918, due to lack of funds. The second Council took place at the beginning of 1945, and the third was held in the spring of 1971.[9] All three Councils included the election of a new Patriarch. Patriarch Sergii was elected by a Synod of Bishops (*Arkhiyereiskii Sobor*) in 1943. There was also a Synod of Bishops in 1961 which emended the church regulations laid down by the 1945 Council.

As one Western Orthodox observer has succinctly expressed it: 'One of the primary purposes of a *Pomestny Sobor* is to adjust to a changed world.'[10] In the case of the 1945 *Sobor,* the change was dramatic. This *Sobor* was the first to open its deliberations in an avowedly atheist environment. Yet it was far from being a hole-in-the-corner event, and the reasons for this are not hard to find.

Since the October Revolution, the Russian Orthodox Church had had severe difficulties with the Soviet authorities. Under Patriarch Tikhon, there had been open conflict, at least until 1923. A final compromise agreement was then reached by Metropolitan Sergii in 1927, which to this day underpins Church–State relations in the U.S.S.R., but this compromise was followed by the unrelenting terror under Stalin which decimated the visible Church. During the Second World War massive loss of life among the Soviet population necessitated the mobilisation of maximum popular support behind the leadership. Thus on 4 September 1943 Stalin saw fit to summon the three leading figures of the Russian Orthodox Church to a private audience. The next day, *Izvestiya* reported that permission had been granted to the Church for the election of a Patriarch (the office having been vacant since the death of Patriarch Tikhon in 1925). Metropolitan Sergii was elected and enthroned on 12 September but died in May of the following year, leaving the church administration in the hands of Metropolitan Alexii (Simansky).

Sergii's death necessitated the calling of a full-scale *Pomestny Sobor* for which many preparations went on beforehand. On 21 November 1944 Metropolitan Alexii convened an episcopal synod to discuss the situation, and on 31 January 1945 the *Sobor* itself opened with great pomp and splendour. It differed from previous Local Councils by having a large number of guests both from inside and outside the Soviet Union. With financial support from the Government (the head of the Government's Council for Russian Orthodox Church Affairs took a large part in the formalities), and lasting a mere three days, it offered a striking contrast to its predecessor in 1917–18.

Before the lavish ceremonies of the enthronement of the new Patriarch, the *Sobor* devoted itself to legislative matters and passed a new church statute, sometimes called the 'forty-eight paragraphs'. This statute, divided into sections headed 'Patriarch – Holy Synod – Dioceses – Parishes', set out at these various levels the role and possibilities of the Church. Although most of the repressive 1929 legislation remained in force, an unpublished decree of 1945 restored to the Russian Orthodox Church the rights of a person at law, with some qualifications. This decree must, however, have been retracted later.[11]

Metropolitan Alexii was unanimously elected Patriarch (there was no other candidate), by open vote, and enthroned on 2 February 1945. He proceeded to lead a renaissance in Russian Orthodox church life, particularly in the theological schools, where his memory is still especially honoured.

The relative relaxation of official state policy towards religion during and after the Second World War did not last. After the death of Stalin, and with Khrushchev's rise to power, a new wave of persecution burst upon the churches. Perhaps Khrushchev, under attack for his controversial policies in other spheres, hoped that in this area he could show the iron fist without troublesome reaction. If this surmise is true, it is apparent that he made a severe miscalculation. By 1965 it was obvious that the atheist campaign was producing results opposite to those intended. Reviewing the drastic measures which the Government had inspired local authorities to take in towns and villages throughout the country, Ukrainian atheist, G. Kelt stated in August 1965:

> Insults, violence and the forcible closure of churches not only fail to reduce the number of believers; such measures even tend to increase their number, to make clandestine religious groups more widespread and to antagonise believers against the State.[12]

To the casual observer, the anti-religious campaign of the Khrushchev period may appear to have been an unsubtle undertaking which misfired. Yet, upon closer inspection, it is easy to see that it had another side, the long-term effects of which could well be more damaging to the Church. This is not the first time in Soviet history that there has been a subtle underlay beneath a carpet of violence. The less obvious side of the policy of the early 1960s was legislative. There were new state decrees invoking harsher penalties and making the range of punishable religious offences more ill-defined and therefore easier to bring before the courts – especially the new Article 227 of the Penal Code.[13] Far worse, from the viewpoint of the Churches, was the enactment of new church regulations, which gave the impression to many Soviet believers that religious leaders were conniving in the downfall of their own Church. The fact that similar measures were rushed through by Baptist leaders and by the Orthodox bishops a year later (1961) made it obvious that the same state policy loomed immediately behind all these similar events. Indeed, the influence of the state authorities upon the 1961 Synod of Bishops was directly admitted by the official publication of the Orthodox Church in an unusually revealing paragraph:

> In April of this year the Council for Russian Orthodox Church Affairs informed us that the Council of Ministers of the U.S.S.R. had again drawn attention to the fact of repeated violations by the clergy of the Soviet legislation on cults and had pointed to the necessity of introducing proper order into parish life, specifically in the question of restoring the rights of the executive organs of the church communities in the financial and economic sphere, in accordance with the legislation on cults.[14]

In the case of the Baptists, the new legislative measures were never presented to the Church for even the pretence of a discussion. The new orders were circulated only among the senior presbyters (district superintendents). The Orthodox bishops did at least meet together to put a rubber stamp on the decisions. In the canon law of the Russian Orthodox Church, however, a Synod of Bishops does not have any legislative status. Only a *Pomestny Sobor* – consisting of an elected priest, an elected layman, and the bishop from each diocese – has this status. The decisions taken on 18 July 1961 by the Synod of Bishops were thus claimed to be only temporary, requiring ratification by a future full *Sobor*. Metropolitan Sergii's compromise agreement with the State in 1927 was also expressly stated to be subject to ratification by a future *Pomestny Sobor,* but neither of the two subsequent Councils in fact paid any attention to this important matter. As there was no *Sobor* after the 1961 Synod of Bishops until 31 May 1971, the intervening decade was one of tension in Church–State relations – a tension which even now has not been resolved.

The central feature of the controversial 1961 Synod was the removal of the parish priest from all administrative authority in his own church. The fourth section of the church statute of 1945, that dealing with the parishes, was completely revised. Although the *Journal of the Moscow Patriarchate*, in its reports on the 1945 Council, had failed to print the text of this important statute, it did later appear in the 1946 church calendar for the use of the clergy. One should particularly note the paragraphs which dealt with the parishes. Paragraph 40 of the church statute of 1945 stated: 'The incumbent of the parish as a result of his functions is an inalienable member of the parish society and he is the president of its executive organ, the church council. This consists of four members. . . .' Paragraph 41 said that 'The executive body of the parish society is under the immediate guidance and supervision of the incumbent of the church. . . .' After the 1961 Synod of Bishops, the parish priest merely 'translates into reality the *spiritual guidance* of his parishioners. . . .' No longer is he designated president or even a member of the executive body, the church council, while the latter 'does not interfere with the Divine Services. . . .' From holding the reins, the parish priest was thus forced to become an employee of his own executive committee, the membership of which (according to the secular legislation) could in turn be vetoed by the local *soviet*.[15]

It may well be argued that the position of the parish priest as laid down in the 1945 church statute actually contravened the 1929 legislation on religion. Although the latter did not directly state that the parish priest could not be a member of the executive body, it clearly implied that his sphere of activity was separate and concentrated on the non-administrative side of parish life, as decreed in 1961. This appears to be the significance of the statement quoted above from the Orthodox journal on complaints from the State about the conduct of church life – although at the same time the 1945 church statute could not have been enacted without state approval. What is certain is that the churches, without the parish priest to defend them administratively against threats of closure, shut their doors by the thousands all over the Soviet Union. The process was halted only by the fall of Khrushchev in 1964. However, this process had already begun before the 1961 Synod of Bishops, so it is not quite accurate to trace back all the woes of the Church to this particular event. It merely facilitated something that was going to occur anyway.

In attempting to evaluate the role of the bishops in 1961, we are fortunate in having access to an eye-witness, though anonymous, account of the Synod, circulated in the Soviet Union in *samizdat* (self-published) form. The author of the document[16] does not talk of physical intimidation, but rather of psychological pressures.

It was already known that there had been certain 'irregularities' in the convening of the Synod. Archbishop Yermogen (Golubev), in his *samizdat* article, 'The Fiftieth Anniversary of the Restoration of the Patriarchate',[17] had commented somewhat wryly that the mode of convening a Synod of Bishops by telegram had been unknown to the Church Fathers. Furthermore, some of the most active bishops were removed from the scene beforehand and their court cases were widely reported in the Soviet press – an intimidating signal to others. Archbishop Yermogen himself was prevented from attending.

The bishops summoned by the Patriarch assembled at the Holy Trinity Monastery, Zagorsk, the day before the Synod. When they arrived, they did not even know that there was to be such a meeting – yet they obediently played their roles. When they took their places in the hall, the anonymous eye-witness reports:

Behind them there was a very small table at which there sat three men dressed in civilian clothes. They were well known to each bishop. They had assistants locally, in every diocese – special representatives of the department on religious affairs. These representatives in the dioceses were terrifying and implacable. They had the power to 'bind and to loose', to debar priests from office and to deprive them of the priesthood. And if the representatives were terrifying, how much more so were these three sitting quietly behind the bishops! They sat behind, but their eyes literally penetrated like drills into the bishops whose backs were turned to them. They were silent and apparently had no intention of speaking, yet their silence was eloquent.

They had come here so that their very appearance should force the bishops to yield the Church's ground and to aid the destruction of the Church itself. Everyone understood this well. Everyone knew within himself moreover that even if he should play the hero and speak out in opposition, he would not find general support, thus only putting a noose around his own neck and let down the Patriarch.

The three sat in silence, not even speaking to each other. Their faces were serious. Would the bishops be completely obedient? Would not some fanatic step out of line and make a speech defending episcopal and clerical rights? Would not someone refer to canons or traditions? Would not someone cry that it was suicide to accept all these new measures removing authority from the priests and handing it over to lay people? They sat in silence and their faces were strained – the tension you see on the face of a ringmaster in a circus when he looks at the animal performing at his command. Will it be able to obey everything or will it fail and spoil the act?[18]

Felix Karelin is a Russian Orthodox layman closely involved with the current movement of independent thought in the Church. Speaking more recently of the role of the bishop in the Russian Church today, he writes:

Here is the bishop triumphantly celebrating divine worship. Everything trembles before him! He is surrounded by a gleaming retinue of assistant clergy. . . . But here is the bishop outside the church, in the world, and suddenly everything had

changed! . . . I am speaking about an inward degradation –
about fear. The bishop, just now commanding the fire and
thunder of the divine service, now trembles before a common
official. How can the human soul bear such a terrible
polarisation?[19]

In the case of the 1961 Synod, although the bishops met in
church buildings, it is clear that they were very much under official
scrutiny and virtually fulfilling an official act. In an area where
one knows almost nothing of the personal characteristics of the
key figures, the anonymous document described above from someone so close to, and frank about, the events described is unique.

Of particular interest are his portraits of Alexander Fyodorovich
Shishkin[20] and Anatolii Vasilevich Vedernikov, authors of the
two 'keynote' speeches at the Synod. It should, however, be
emphasised that this may well be the view of one man only, representing a highly personal and critical assessment. The internal
information it gives has not been corroborated. However, where
gaps in our knowledge are so extensive, it is worth reporting at least
something of what it contains. The anonymous author asks why
Shishkin had turned up here at the Synod of Bishops, and he
continues:

> The reason was, of course, that neither the Patriarch nor
> Pimen could compose the requisite speech and document.
> . . . Shishkin had composed the speech which Archbishop
> Pimen now had to read. He had long ago also worked out
> the resolution which the Synod now has to pass, but he had
> not of course basically formulated it. This had been done by
> the three who were sitting behind at the separate table.
> These three had long ago 'chewed over' (if one may put it so)
> the contents of the resolution for the Synod of Bishops of the
> Russian Orthodox Church and had reflected upon how to
> strangle the Church. In that first stage everything was
> conducted in complete secrecy. Shishkin worked out the
> resolution in literary form and handed it over to Pimen and
> the Patriarch. . . . At this final stage the resolution
> setting out to deprive the Russian Orthodox Church of
> all its administrative rights was supposed to become fully
> public.

> Shishkin had once been a luminary of the Living Church,

a collaborator with Metropolitan Nikolai Platonov of that Church who later renounced God and the Church; he is now a leading figure on the staff of the Leningrad Theological Academy (teaching the Soviet Constitution and Fundamental Theology). At the same time he is choirmaster at the Metropolitan's Nikolo-Morskoi Cathedral, a member of the Foreign Relations Department of the Moscow Patriarchate, editor-in-chief of the *Journal of the Moscow Patriarchate* and a trusted individual who is sent on various foreign missions.[21]

The Patriarch's speech was composed, the anonymous writer says, by Anatolii Vasilevich Vedernikov, who had formerly controlled the *Journal of the Moscow Patriarchate* under Metropolitan Nikolai (who had been deposed the previous year and was shortly to die in obscure circumstances). Vedernikov's fortunes had allegedly declined, and he was trying to climb back into a position of authority. The writer describes the contrasting characters of the two men, and the rivalry between them, in considerable detail.

Everything at the Synod went according to plan. The assembled company listened to the speeches impassively. According to the official account in the *Journal of the Moscow Patriarchate,* the bishops heard Archbishop Pimen state unambiguously that 'the time has come concretely to limit the rights and duties of the parish priests'.[22] No voice spoke out in opposition and there was no debate. For the next three years the Russian Orthodox Church gave the appearance, to some observers at least, of having connived at its own downfall.

While a similar intrusion of the State into the affairs of the Baptist Church caused an immediate and nation-wide outcry within the Baptist ranks, there was no organised opposition resulting from the events of 1961 in the Russian Orthodox Church. It was left to individuals to speak out, protesting their loyalty to the Patriarch, but yet calling with increased insistence for a properly-constituted *Sobor* to discuss reform of the 1961 regulations.

No successor to Patriarch Alexii, already in his eighties in 1961, could be elected without the calling of a *Sobor*. Alexii's death in April 1970 finally presented the State with a choice: to forbid the election of a successor (as during 1925–43) or run the risk of an assembly where someone might speak out against the decision of 1961 and rally the opposition. The first alternative would have demonstrated to the whole world that there was no freedom of religion in the U.S.S.R. The second, though risky, was obviously considered preferable. A new Patriarch was needed who would maintain the new (post-1961) *status quo,* and who could command enough loyalty within the Church not to fan the flames of opposition. Such a man was found in Metropolitan Pimen (Izvekov). He had done what was required of him in 1961 and his subsequent rise to an even higher position of trust had not been marred by any false steps. The government Council on Religious Affairs probably considered this an easier part of the proceedings to engineer than the suppression of debate on the 1961 regulations. At the same time, many observers characterise Pimen as a man of genuine humility and one who never desired the office of Patriarch.

The long (and uncanonical) gap of thirteen months between the death of Patriarch Alexii and the election of a successor was used by the State to ensure unanimity on the question of Pimen's election and to occlude any debate on the other issue by the 'loyal oppositon' (one uses the phrase in contrast to the other offshoots of the Russian Orthodox Church which have severed their connections with the Moscow Patriarchate at various times). Twelve of the thirteen trump cards lay in the hands of the State. The thirteenth was the pen of a few determined individuals who, reckless of personal liberty, were resolved to circulate their point of view (opposed to the results of the 1961 Synod) to as many people as possible.

The earlier initiatives in this direction by Archbishop Yermogen and by Fathers Nikolai Eshliman and Gleb Yakunin are well known, as is the price (dismissal from their posts) which they were forced to pay. Several churchmen zealously took up the same cause during the interregnum. The most far-reaching proposals were expounded by the monks, Georgii Petukhov, from Zagorsk, Varsonofii Khaybulin, from the Vladimir oblast, and the layman, Pyotr Fomin, from Moscow. They addressed a letter, now published in the West,[23] to all bishops of the Russian Orthodox Church. The writers begged the bishops to request the following from the Soviet Government:

(1) to restore the rights of a person at law with full legal entitlement to the Russian Orthodox Church, to its leadership, its diocesan administrations, monasteries and parish executive committees;

(2) to work out precise legislation on the rights and duties of the officials of the Council on Religious Affairs under the Council of Ministers of the U.S.S.R.;

(3) to work out precise legislation on the monasteries of the Russian Orthodox Church, to restore limited autonomy to them – absolutely essential for the spiritual sustenance of monasticism in accordance with the Canons of the Holy Church;

(4) to allow children to be taught the catechism upon request;

(5) to reopen the theological seminaries and courses which were formerly operative for the preparation of cantors and choirmasters;

(6) to set up a printing press with Old Slavonic and Russian type under the control of the Moscow Patriarchate and other Patriarchal departments and to open a larger subscription list for church publications;

(7) to reopen churches in Gorky and other towns and villages where they used to be before closure in 1956–66;

(8) to reopen the Kievo-Pecherskaya Lavra and the Vvedensky Convent;

(9) to reopen the convent at Borodino, Moscow Region (in accordance with the wish of His Holiness, Patriarch Alexii, of blessed memory).

The appeal ended with a call to annul the 1961 regulations. Never before has such a call for basic changes in state law come from an Orthodox source.

An even more eminent signatory to a series of unpublished appeals written to Metropolitan Pimen at various times during 1970 was Archbishop Venyamin of Irkutsk, a man who had borne the brunt of state pressure in the early 1960s, and who in spite of this was still in office ten years later. His proposals were far less radical than those of the nine-point document quoted above. They concentrated (perhaps with a more practical hope of fulfilment) upon the restoration of the parish priest to his pre-1961 administrative position, although with a superior formulation of the technical ecclesiastical legislation than in the defunct 1945 version.

Archbishop Venyamin was not the only headache to those responsible for the staging of the 1971 *Sobor*. To judge by recent events, they must have been even more concerned about Archbishop Pavel (Golyshev), then of Novosibirsk. Archbishop Pavel was educated in Paris, but after World War II voluntarily went to the U.S.S.R. and offered his services to the Russian Orthodox Church. At first he taught in the Leningrad Theological Academy. He was made a bishop in 1957 and served in a number of dioceses before that of Novosibirsk and Barnaul. Novosibirsk is near the new city of Akademgorodok which is dedicated to scientific study and is a vital centre of intellectual activity in the Soviet Union. The Holy Synod would deliberate carefully before appointing a bishop to this important diocese, and indeed Archbishop Pavel is reported to be a man of high spiritual and pastoral qualities.

From a letter he wrote in February 1972[24] it is known that his ministry in Novosibirsk was unlikely to please the authorities. Archbishop Pavel obviously exercised a genuine pastoral ministry and refused to yield to any unlawful atheist pressures. When the *Pomestny Sobor* opened he was not among those present. The above-mentioned letter speaks of a provocation by the local official of the Council on Religious Affairs, which may have been the reason for his non-appearance.

On 2 February 1972 Archbishop Pavel was demoted from Novosibirsk to Vologda, in his own words, 'a very insignificant diocese with only 17 parishes'. It was after this that he wrote the letter already referred to. In it he requested to be allowed to retire and return to Paris. On 11 October he was in fact 'released from all his duties' and sent into retirement, but not outside the Soviet Union. It may be surmised that the Soviet authorities feared what he might reveal to foreign inquirers about the methods used by Soviet officials in their dealings with the churches. At any rate, Archbishop Pavel, like Archbishop Yermogen before him, has been removed from the public scene and from any immediate possibility of becoming a focal figure for dissent.

As might have been expected, the one trump card in the hands of the 'loyal opposition' was not powerful enough (whether expressed in the moderate tones of Archbishop Venyamin or in a more demanding way by the authors of the nine-point letter) to make any visible impression on the unyielding policy of the State. When the *Sobor* met on 30 May 1971, state control was apparently absolute. The Government, with the physical power of control in its hands, had been able to use the 13-month period since Alexii's death to better purpose than the determined would-be reformers. Nevertheless, the State felt a sufficient danger to resort to force to gain its ends – a tactic which in the past has produced the opposite effect to that intended.

Anatolii Levitin-Krasnov, an outstanding lay voice in the Russian Orthodox Church, who had become identified with the general (secular) human rights movement in the Soviet Union, was imprisoned on 8 May 1971. This was an open threat recalling the imprisonment of Iosif Bondarenko, the Baptist, announced in the Soviet press on the day that the Baptist Congress of 1966 opened.[25] The message to both assemblies was clear: those who try to institute reform end in gaol.

The 1971 *Sobor* was an outwardly impressive event. Held in the Trinity Monastery of Zagorsk, and accompanied by long services in the monastery churches, it had a membership of 236 (233 were actually present) with 74 high-ranking guests from inside and outside the U.S.S.R. Its main task was the election of the new Patriarch – in effect the confirmation in office of Metropolitan Pimen who had been *locum tenens* since the death of Alexii. But a number of other important decisions and recommendations were made.

The *Sobor* was actually preceded (two days earlier) by a meeting of bishops only, from which other participants in the Council proper were rigorously excluded. The convening of this group to make major decisions ahead of time nullifies the one factor which makes a *Sobor* so notable among modern instruments of ecclesiastical government – its representatives, including as it does a layman and a priest (in theory elected) from each diocese, as well as the bishop. Nicolas Lossky, however, a non-Soviet member of the *Sobor* officially representing dioceses of the Moscow Patriarchate outside the Soviet Union, and author of an interesting and detailed article on the Council,[26] justified this episcopal meeting by stating that it was the only occasion during the whole week when anything remotely resembling freedom of speech was possible.

There is little to say about the election of Metropolitan Pimen as Patriarch (he was the only candidate). Although there was no debate, no pretence of following the canonical procedure for such an election, at least the bishops were individually able to state to the *Sobor* that their dioceses were voting for Pimen. Archbishop Basil (Krivoshein) of Brussels and Belgium, in an interview given after his return from the Council, described the voting as the manifestation of 'a great and profound spiritual unity among the Council members'.[27] The initiative for the election thus came from the Church, and not from the State. Such a result, coming by secret ballot, would have been even more effective. Lossky surmises that such a ballot was refused because the State could not allow the Church a concession which it had never made to ordinary citizens in a political election. At the same time, he does make the following assessment of the actual election:

> Everyone nominated Metropolitan Pimen. But it must be noted that, contrary to what one might think, this rather long and uniform procedure, far from becoming a predetermined masquerade, gave the impression more and more of a ceremony full of real dignity and an expression of real unanimity on the person of Metropolitan Pimen, the only man at the present time capable of carrying out the difficult office of Patriach of Moscow.[28]

One of the decisions of the Council on which such impressive unanimity was not reached was the approval of the 1961 'reforms'. It is probable that the strongest expression of doubt came from the non-Soviet members, although they had apparently decided that a definite intervention would be inopportune. Archbishop Basil of Brussels, in the above-cited interview, had this to say about the discussions:

> The Council did not by any means ignore the problem of the decisions of the 1961 Synod of Bishops concerning the statute on the parishes. They were discussed at length in the episcopal synod preceding the Council, as well as in the Council itself. Few people affirmed that they were ideal or that they did not contradict church canons. The majority of speakers gave assurances that there had not been the disastrous consequences which might have been feared; the

wisdom of the priests and the piety of the laity had neutral-
ised the defects and most importantly [the main argument]
these regulations corresponded exactly to the Soviet legislation of 1929 on religion. Therefore any refusal to approve
them or even any initiative to modify them would be
considered by the civil authorities as an act hostile to the
Government. It was not in the Church's interest, speakers
said, to allow its relations with the State to deteriorate over
a question not directly concerning the faith. Besides, any
attempt at modification would be impossible at the present
moment. The Government would not co-operate. Also,
ecclesiastical legislation cannot contradict civil legislation,
not only in the Soviet Union, but anywhere in the world.
When the Church reaches better times, the whole problem
can be reconsidered.

At the episcopal synod, a tiny minority nevertheless put
the opposing view that it was impossible in all conscience
to approve decisions which were contrary to the traditional
canonical structure of the Orthodox Church and which
threatened the unity of its ecclesiastical government, centred
on the person of the bishop whose representatives, in the
form of the parochial clergy, embraced the whole life of the
Church, both spiritual and material. Certainly, the earlier
regulations of 1945 were guilty of giving excessive power to
the clergy and excessively limiting the place given to the
laity in ordering the material well-being of the parishes. . . .
One should seek out a middle way between the two extremes
which would safeguard the position of the priest in the
administration of the parishes, while leaving the direction
of material things to the laity, still under the surveillance
of the clergy. These propositions were still considered unrealistic by the bishops who spoke at the episcopal synod, but it
should be noted that a considerable number of them (including some of the most venerated and experienced) kept silent
throughout the whole debate on the 1961 regulations.[29]

Thus despite some pressure to the contrary, the 1961 regulations
were confirmed.

Another important act of the *Sobor* on which complete agreement was evident was the confirmation of a decision taken by

the Holy Synod already in 1929, to annul the excommunication by the Russian Orthodox Church of the Old Believers. This schism had taken place in the seventeenth century and the intervening centuries had seen much tension and persecution. But a new spirit had since prevailed, at least at official, leadership level, possibly emanating from a solidarity of experience under Soviet rule. It is perhaps strange, therefore, that only one Old Believer dignitary attended the Council, Archbishop Pavel of Novozybkov, Moscow and All Russia.

The Council also confirmed previous decisions of the Holy Synod in the granting of autocephaly to the Orthodox Church in Poland (1945), Czechoslovakia (1951) and America (1970), as well as of autonomy to the Orthodox Church in Japan (1970). This apparently straightforward approval actually conceals a difficult controversy with the Patriarchate of Constantinople. Primacy of honour in the contemporary Orthodox world belongs to the Patriarchate of Constantinople, but this is being disputed by the Moscow Patriarchate, for example in such granting of autocephaly. The late Patriarch Athenagoras was wholly dignified in his attempt to resist this struggle, waged by one side only, but such decisions taken by Moscow continue to cause extreme tension. The recent moves in America and Japan are especially important for the foreign policy of the Moscow Patriarchate.[30]

Another critical point, on which the Council failed to obtain complete accord, was the proposal that a final condemnation be made of the Russian Orthodox Church outside of Russia (with headquarters in New York). Vigorous protest against such a move was made above all by the Western delegates led by Archbishop Antony (Bloom) of Surozh, Exarch of Western Europe and resident in London. Nicolas Lossky, quoted above, also spoke out on this issue. The voices raised in dissent did not condone the activities of the Church Abroad, but called for a sensitive approach dictated by pastoral situations. In the end the question was referred to the Holy Synod for further discussion. Such a condemnation of émigré Orthodox activity would also have involved the autocephalous Ukrainian Orthodox Church in America.

There was unanimous approval for another decision which in the opinion of many observers of the Russian Orthodox scene merited a very different approach. This was the confirmation of the liquidation of the Eastern-Rite Catholic Church in the

Western Ukraine and the forced conversion of its adherents to Orthodoxy. This took place in 1946-49 and was the cause of considerable persecution and suffering. The Eastern-Rite or 'Uniate' Church, as it is commonly called, continues to exist chiefly in Galicia, illegally and therefore under conditions of extreme hardship. Nevertheless Soviet press articles (mainly Ukrainian) and a small amount of *samizdat* literature testify to its continuing vitality. The subject of the suppression of the Uniate Church in the Soviet Union appears to be a complete taboo in the recently developing relations between the Moscow Patriarchate and the Vatican. The presence of Cardinal Willebrands at the 1971 Council does not appear to have inhibited the Orthodox leadership in the taking of this decision.

Finally, the other main area in which a degree of concern was evident regarding the activities of the Holy Synod in the period 1945–71, which were to be ratified, was that of the peace movement. Some delegates were apparently unhappy at the definite political bias evident in the involvement of the Moscow Patriarchate in this sphere, but such criticism as there was clearly found no concrete expression in the resolutions of the Council.

During the Council sessions, the main speakers talked at length and in stilted fashion, with the desired result that the participants listened with 'a receptivity that was passive, indifferent, or even somnolent' (Lossky[31]). At six p.m. on 1 June, after an exhausting day of speeches from the floor, Metropolitan Filaret of Kiev hastily read three typed pages of resolutions which no one had the chance to see. They included putting the seal of approval on the 1961 regulations. Metropolitan Nikodim called for their adoption, but this was quickly contested by Lossky. Nikodim appeared to make a partial concession, saying that the text had been adopted 'by a majority'. Press releases nevertheless claimed unanimity and Lossky was refused permission to see the text itself. When it was finally made available to delegates on 6 June it had been further hardened – especially on point 4, regarding condemnation of the Russian Orthodox Church outside of Russia.[32]

What, then are the implications of the 1971 Local Council for the future? The 'loyal opposition', having been completely rebuffed and treated as though it did not exist, may well become less loyal. Several recent documents suggest that the ground swell of opposition to the present *status quo* in Church–State relations is rising. Not only are writers becoming more outspoken, but the various viewpoints they express tend to become more and more opposed to the accepted position of the Moscow Patriarchate. The rebuff at the 1971 *Sobor* may force more people to turn against the Moscow Patriarchate. This would render the State's control less secure than it is now.

Finally, what are the real feelings within the hierarchy itself? This is an essentially unanswerable question. Despite official publications (admittedly paltry in scope and circulation) all official statements on behalf of the Church are subject to constant censorship, both external and internal. An interesting example of this is given in the occasional interview given by Russian churchmen to foreign journalists, and reprinted in the *Journal of the Moscow Patriarchate*. Particularly striking is an interview by a Czech editor with Patriarch Pimen printed in the *Journal* for December 1971.[33] Although the Czech editor put some very leading questions on church statistics and Church–State relations, the Patriarch parried them with a skill undoubtedly born of years of experience.

It is natural that the Patriarch would be more open to a member of his own Church, even a member from abroad. Nicolas Lossky describes the events of 6 June when the *Sobor* broke up:

> The Council really ended on June 6, the day of Pentecost, when after the meal every member personally took his leave of the Patriarch. The atmosphere of this reception in the patriarchal apartments of the monastery was again full of dignity and simplicity. The Patriarch said hardly anything, he just smiled and thanked his guests. When I came to him, he asked for my prayers and for the prayers of those I represented. Behind these few words, I felt that I was hearing the voice of a spiritual man who, in his own way, was carrying the cross of the Russian Church.[34]

NOTES

1. N. Yudin, *Pravda o Peterburgskikh Svyatinyakh* (The Truth about the Petersburg Shrines) (Leningrad, 1962), p. 8. See also letter from the priests Eshliman and Yakunin to Mr Podgorny, 15 December 1965, in M. Bourdeaux, *Patriarch and Prophets* (London, 1970), p. 191.
2. The figure of 7,500 churches is given, for example, by E. I. Lisavtsev in his

book *Kritika Burzhuaznoi Falsifikatsii Polozheniya Religii v SSSR* (The Critique of the Bourgeois Falsification of the Position of Religion in the USSR) (Moscow, 1971), p. 9.

3. The question of statistics for the theological colleges is examined by G. Simon in his book *Die Kirchen in Russland* (Munich, 1970), pp. 101–2. To appear in English as *Church, State and Opposition in the U.S.S.R.* (London, 1973).

4. *Bratsky Vestnik*, No. 6 (1968), p. 21. A German Baptist delegation visited Zagorsk in April 1968 and reported a figure of 430 students following this course.

5. See Bourdeaux, *op. cit.*, pp. 97–116.

6. Cf. *Pravoslavny visnyk* (Kiev), 1971–72.

7. For a complete list of bishops as of mid-1972, see G. Simon, *Church, State and Opposition in the U.S.S.R.*, Chapter IV, revised footnote 13.

8. *Zhurnal Moskovskoi Patriarkhii* (hereafter *Zh.M.P.*), No. 2 (1971), p. 18.

9. There were also two so-called Local Councils held by the schismatic Living Church in 1923 and 1925, but these have not been recognised by the Russian Orthodox Church.

10. W. B. Stroyen, *Communist Russia and the Russian Orthodox Church 1943–1962* (Washington, 1967), p. 43.

11. See M. M. Persits, *Otdeleniye Tserkvi ot Gosudarstva i Shkoly ot Tserkvi v SSSR (1917–1919 gg)* (The Separation of the Church from the State and of School from the Church in the U.S.S.R., 1917–1919) (Moscow, 1958), p. 120. It is evident, however, from the document written by Petukhov and others (see pp. 47–8), that this was later suspended. Certain tax concessions were also made to the Church in 1946.

12. *Komsomolskaya pravda*, 15 August 1965.

13. See *Vedomosti Verkhovnogo Soveta RSFSR* (Gazette of the Supreme Soviet of the R.S.F.S.R.), 24 March 1966, pp. 219–20. Article 227 is printed *ibid.*, 26 July 1962.

14. *Zh.M.P.*, No. 8 (1961), p. 6.

15. Russian texts of the basic 1929 Law and associated decrees are published in N. Orleansky, *Zakon o Religioznykh Obyedineniyakh RSFSR* (Law on Religious Associations of the R.S.F.S.R.) (Moscow, 1930) (reprinted by Gregg International Publishers, Farnborough, England, 1971). An English translation of the basic law and rules of application is printed in Stroyen, *op. cit.*, pp. 121–35. The Russian text of the 1945 church statute was published in *Pravoslavny Tserkovny Kalendar na 1946 God* (The Orthodox Church Calendar for the Year 1946) (Moscow, 1946), pp. 58–60. An English translation is given in Stroyen, *op. cit.*, pp. 136–40. Russian text of revised 1961 statute appears in *Zh.M.P.*, No. 8 (1961), pp. 5–17; English translation in Stroyen, *op. cit.*, pp. 141–3.

16. As yet unpublished document; 35 typewritten pages.

17. Dated 25 December 1967. Russian text in *Vestnik Russkogo Studencheskogo Khristianskogo Dvizheniya* (Herald of the Russian Student Christian Movement) (hereafter *Vestnik RSKhD*), No. 86, pp. 75–7. English extracts in Bourdeaux, *op. cit.*, pp. 244–7.

18. See note 16.

19. Russian text in *Vestnik RSKhD*, No. 103, pp. 160–72; this quotation pp. 169–70. English translation in *Eastern Churches Review*, Spring 1973.

20. Shishkin died on 15 July 1965.

21. See note 16.

22. *Zh.M.P.*, No. 8 (1961), p. 11.

23. *Vestnik RSKhD*, No. 99, pp. 42–4.

24. *Ibid.*, No. 103, pp. 173–4.

25. *Pravda Ukrainy*, 4 October 1966, p. 4.

26. *Contacts* (Paris), No. 4 (1971), pp. 359–85.
27. *Episkepsis* (Geneva), 20 July 1971, pp. 9–15; this quotation, p. 13.
28. Lossky in *Contacts, loc. cit.*, p. 373.
29. *Episkepsis, loc. cit.*, pp. 11–12.
30. On this subject, see a new book by W. C. Fletcher, *Religion and Soviet Foreign Policy* (London, 1973).
31. Lossky, *loc. cit.*, p. 368.
32. *Ibid.*, pp. 370–71.
33. *Zh.M.P.*, No. 12 (1971), pp. 5–8.
34. Lossky, *loc. cit.*, p. 377.

4 Religious Dissent and the Soviet State*

Bohdan R. Bociurkiw

POLITICAL DIMENSIONS OF RELIGIOUS DISSENT

A traditional definition of religious dissent, denoting disapproval of or difference from an established religious doctrine or ecclesiastical authority, cannot be well adapted to Soviet conditions unless one conceives of the Communist doctrine and the Party authority as occupying the position once reserved for the established religion and Church, and therefore treats all *religious* teachings and organisations in the U.S.S.R. as manifestations of dissent. For the purposes of this discussion, religious dissent in the U.S.S.R. may be defined as an overt repudiation of the existing relationship between institutional religion and the Soviet State, involving an explicit or implicit challenge to the legitimacy of the norms and structures governing this relationship.[1] While narrower in scope than the traditional notion of dissent, this definition allows one to bring into the discussion Lithuanian Catholic and Jewish dissenters, Ukrainian Uniates (Greek Catholics) and other religious groups 'banned' on political grounds in addition to the Orthodox and Baptist dissenters. It also reflects the inevitable 'politicisation' of religious dissent in the U.S.S.R. resulting from the far-reaching involvement of the political authorities in the conduct of internal affairs of all officially recognised ('registered') religious groups, including the determination of the groups' statutes and selection of their leaders. Conceived in these terms religious protest may be considered as a distinct sub-category of the larger phenomenon of political dissent, with which it shares a demand for the rule of law

---

* This is a revised and updated version of a paper presented on 22 October 1971 at the McMaster Conference on Dissent in the Soviet Union, organised by the Interdepartmental Committee on Communist and East European Affairs of McMaster University, Hamilton, Canada.

in the Soviet Union – a demand which, if realised, could only mean an end to the Party dictatorship in the U.S.S.R.

As for the Soviet regime, it has from its very beginning viewed religion as a political problem, religious doctrines as hostile ideologies, and churches and sects as competing with the Communists for influence over society and 'objectively' obstructing the process of 'Communist construction'. On the other hand, once the governmental authorities and the police established effective controls over the 'registered' religious organisations and approved their statutes and leadership, religious dissent could not but be seen as a threat to Soviet control over religious organisations. Hence the paradoxical situation of Soviet support for the Churches recurring at different stages of Church–State relations in the U.S.S.R.: a massive intervention of the Soviet administration and police to suppress the dissenting 'Tikhonites' on behalf of the 'Living Church' and other Renovationist groups in 1922-23; repressive measures taken against the ecclesiastical opponents of Metropolitan Sergii after his compromise with the regime in 1927; governmental enforcement of the 'reunion' of the Ukrainian Uniates with the Russian Orthodox Church since 1945-46; and, in the post-Stalin era, official harassment and repression of the dissenters within the Russian Church and among the Evangelical Christians–Baptists. In effect, as Levitin-Krasnov has noted, one finds in the Soviet Union a 'strange paradox: a state church within a system of an atheist state' – a situation which casts the Communist regime in the role of a protector of 'established' faiths against their own dissenters and schismatics.

Religious dissent in the contemporary U.S.S.R. is represented by three 'generations' of dissenters corresponding roughly to three distinct periods in Soviet church policy. The 'oldest' category consists mainly of the remnants of those elements of the Russian Orthodox Church which refused to accept Metropolitan Sergii's declaration of 1927[2] and which have since considered the 'official' Church as devoid of divine grace and dominated by the 'enemies of Christ'. This surviving Russian Orthodox underground movement has been known as the 'True Orthodox Church', and more recently, as the 'True Orthodox Christians'.[3] The 'middle generation' of religious dissent consists of those groups which were in effect 'outlawed' since World War II because they were considered 'bourgeois nationalist' or 'anti-Soviet' (e.g. the Uniates in the

Western Ukraine[4] and the Jehovah's Witnesses[5]), as well as of several factions which split away from their respective religious groups after the latter accepted Soviet conditions of 'legalisation', including changes in their doctrine or practices, merger with other denominations and extensive governmental controls (e.g. the Pentecostalists[6] and Adventists-Reformers[7]). The 'youngest generation' of dissenters which, undoubtedly, has been influenced both by the earlier dissent currents and by the general intellectual ferment in the post-Stalin U.S.S.R., dates from the massive anti-religious campaign instigated by Khrushchev's regime during 1959–64 – the campaign which resulted in the closing of more than half of all houses of worship and of the overwhelming majority of monastic and theological institutions in the country.[8] This latest wave of dissent emerged first from the ranks of the beneficiaries of Stalin's 'New Religious Policy' – the Russian Orthodox Church and the Evangelical Christians–Baptists – who have, more recently, been joined by protesters from several other religious groups, including the Roman Catholics in Lithuania and the Jews.

There were two immediate stimuli to the rise of this last wave of religious dissent. One was the gross violations of legality perpetrated by the authorities in the course of the anti-religious campaign, and especially their use of the very government agencies designed to enforce Soviet laws on religion – the Council for the Affairs of the Russian Orthodox Church and the Council for the Affairs of Religious Cults.[9] The other stimulus for Orthodox and Baptist protesters was the apparent failure of the ecclesiastical leaders – the Moscow Patriarchate and the All-Union Council of the Evangelical Christians–Baptists, respectively – to defend the legal rights of their churches, a failure which the dissenters interpreted either in terms of the leaders' timidity and moral weakness, or even as a sign of their 'collusion' with the atheist authorities. In fact, the strategy adopted by the regime in the 1959–64 anti-religious campaign was bound to compromise the 'loyal' church leaders as they were pressured by the authorities (often through confidential *oral* orders) to provide a semblance of 'legality' by 'voluntarily' abandoning some of their rights, restricting their activities and reducing the number of their congregations, monastic institutions and theological schools.[10]

This was not an unprecedented situation – witness the violent anti-religious campaign of 1929–30 and Metropolitan Sergii's press interviews in February 1930 denying any past or current persecution of religion in the U.S.S.R.[11] It was, however, symptomatic of the changing mood of Soviet society during the post-Stalin era – with the general weakening of fear and of the sense of isolation and political inefficacy – that the dissenters did not resign themselves to passive opposition or retreat into the 'catacombs', but rather chose to challenge openly the legality of the regime's anti-religious measures through public protests and confrontations with the authorities designed to attract maximum publicity for their cause at home and abroad. At first the protest took the form of petitions to the authorities, letters to the press, and delegations dispatched by the believers to plead before the governmental and ecclesiastical authorities. Frustrated in their appeals to 'socialist legality' and unable to secure any meaningful response from their own church leaders, the believers subsequently turned to more desperate measures of self-defence by physically blocking the closing of churches and monasteries, staging demonstrations and courting beatings, arrests, fines and prison sentences through acts of civil disobedience to what they believed to be illegal orders of Soviet officials.

FERMENT WITHIN THE RUSSIAN ORTHODOX CHURCH

The first manifestations of dissent within the Russian Orthodox Church date from the early stages of Khrushchev's anti-religious campaign. As early as 1958 the first *samizdat* writings of Anatolii Levitin, who was soon to emerge as the leading lay spokesman for Orthodox dissenters,[12] appeared under a pen-name 'A. Krasnov'. In September 1960 Metropolitan Nikolai (Yarushevich) co-architect of the 1943 'concordat' between the Patriarchate and the regime and until then the Church's leading political spokesman, was reportedly forced to submit his resignation for taking an 'independent stand' in the face of mounting anti-religious pressure from the State.[13] His compulsory retirement highlighted a purge of bishops who refused to join the Patriarch in supplying the regime's attack on the Church with a semblance of 'legality' by 'voluntarily' reducing the latter's autonomy[14] and abolishing 'superfluous' parishes, monasteries and seminaries.[15] In the course of the next few years, several other bishops were removed from their sees and the most 'obstinate' ones were sentenced in well propagandised trials for alleged violations of Soviet laws.[16] While the Church's new political spokesmen joined the Government in denying any persecution of religion in the U.S.S.R., intimidated bishops (with few notable exceptions[17]) turned deaf and blind to desperate pleas from their clergy and believers.[18] Abandoned by their bishops, the believers spontaneously rallied to the defence of their churches and monasteries by sending petitions and delegations to the Patriarchate and the Government authorities or by physically blocking the closing of some churches (e.g. the Kievan church of St Andrew in 1961[19]). When the authorities undertook to close the Pochaiv Lavra in the Ukraine, the faithful joined the monks in defending the monastery and addressed frantic appeals for help to foreign churchmen and statesmen – an action which evidently frustrated the Government's plans to close this famous shrine.[20]

Khrushchev's overthrow in the autumn of 1964 and the subsequent abatement in the anti-religious drive evidently emboldened the dissenters. In the summer of 1965 – towards the very end of the short-lived post-Khrushchev 'thaw' – a delegation of eight bishops headed by Archbishop Yermogen (Golubev) of Kaluga presented Patriarch Alexii with a declaration challenging the legality of the 1961 Synod of Bishops and demanding the repeal of the Synod's decision limiting the rights and duties of the clergy and parish councils.[21] The Patriarchate's response, after Yermogen refused to renounce the declaration, was to send him, in November 1965, into a forced 'retirement' at a distant monastery – an action reportedly requested by the Council for the Affairs of the Russian Orthodox Church.[22]

Archbishop Yermogen's case catalysed forces of dissent within the Orthodox Church. Reacting to his dismissal, two Moscow diocesan priests, Nikolai Eshliman and Gleb Yakunin, addressed, in November, open letters to the Chairman of the Supreme Soviet Presidium, N. V. Podgorny, and Patriarch Alexii. In their petition to Podgorny the two priests accused the Council for the Affairs of the Russian Orthodox Church of 'systematic violations of the laws on the separation of Church from the State and a systematic obstruction of the performance of religious rites', supplying a lengthy and detailed list of illegal acts of the Council officials. The letter called upon the Government to investigate and to condemn these acts and to restore to the Russian Church all its churches, monasteries and seminaries closed in the course of Khrushchev's anti-religious campaign.[23] In their second letter, Eshliman and Yakunin supported Archbishop Yermogen's arguments against the 1961 Synodal resolution and supplied a detailed account of recurring governmental violations of the Soviet legislation on religious cults. They pleaded with the Patriarch to abandon 'fruitless and pernicious tactics' of 'unconditional subordination – to secret dictates of the atheistic officials' and urged him to take immediate steps toward the restoration of canonical order within the Church and the normalisation of Church–State relations in line with their constitutional separation.[24]

The Patriarch responded in December 1965 with a resolution accusing the two priests of violating the peace of the Church.[25] When their letters were published abroad, Eshliman and Yakunin were suspended, in May 1966, and two months later the Patriarchate enjoined all diocesan bishops

> to give strict attention to suppressing personally and with utmost severity the harmful efforts by certain individuals to destroy the peace of the church and to discredit the highest ecclesiastical authority in the eyes of the clergy and laity. The dissemination of all sorts of 'open letters' and articles must be definitely stopped.[26]

The combined efforts of the Patriarchate and the reorganised Council for Religious Affairs[27] failed to check a surge of support for the courageous stand taken by the two priests. In June 1966 a group of believers from the city of Kirov (Vyatka) led by Boris Talantov, addressed an 'open letter' to the Patriarch and 'all the believers', endorsing 'fully and completely' the Eshliman-Yakunin letters and substantiating the priests' charges with a long list of hardships and reprisals suffered by the Kirov believers for defending their legal rights.[28] Subsequent letters and articles by Talantov further elaborated on the joint efforts of the Patriarchate and the local police to suppress the protests of the Kirov laymen.[29] Along with other accounts of lawlessness in the official treatment of individual parishes and churchmen,[30] there appeared letters and treatises by 'retired' Archbishop Yermogen which further revealed the extent of state domination over the internal affairs of the Church, rejected the legality of the 1961 Synod, and set out canonical requirements for a valid *Sobor* (questioning, by implication, the validity of the 1943 and 1945 *Sobors*).[31]

The strongest defence of the priests' cause came from Anatolii Levitin-Krasnov who rejected the Patriarch's charges against Eshliman and Yakunin and threatened that 'we shall never recognise these priests as unfrocked and shall never recognise that the Patriarch's decision or decree carries any weight'.[32] In a series of essays, petitions and letters, Levitin-Krasnov sharply attacked the servility, timidity and self-seeking of the Orthodox hierarchy which, more than the Communist persecution, he saw as the cause of the Church's 'illness':

> The Church has found itself under the domination of atheists acting as complete dictators over the priesthood, appointing to posts people (sometimes complete unbelievers) who toady to them and are bossing the Church as they like . . . ; it is Patriarch Aleksiy who has been countenancing it all in clear violation of the Soviet Constitution, who has been covering up unlawful actions by remaining silent, by bewildering or confusing people with his lying refutations . . . , by frustrating all attempts to rectify mistakes and by punishing honest priests who defend the Church. It is with the protection of his authority that anonymous characters, by exploiting their shady connections, have pushed themselves forward into exalted bishoprics. It is he who is betraying the Church to the godless.[33]

Together with Boris Talantov[34] and a Pskov clergyman, Sergii Zheludkov,[35] Levitin-Krasnov has taken a stand on broader issues of civil rights, political freedom, national equality and resistance to illegal acts of the K.G.B., procuracy and the courts. Levitin-Krasnov became the chief link between Orthodox dissent and the civil rights movement and joined, in May 1969, the 'Initiative [Action] Group for the Defence of Human Rights in the U.S.S.R.'[36] adding his signature to the Group's several appeals protesting violations of human rights in the Soviet Union, as well as the continuing Soviet occupation of Czechoslovakia.[37] In 1970, following his release from an eleven-month-long 'preliminary im-

prisonment', Levitin-Krasnov summed up the position of the
Orthodox dissenters in the following words:

> First of all, there is no extremist group in the Orthodox
> Church.[38] There is simply the Orthodox Church and nothing
> more. It all demands one thing: a precise observance of the
> existing constitution which speaks of the separation of church
> from the State, of freedom of conscience, and of freedom to
> perform religious rites. However, this constitution is being
> violated, for how can one reconcile with freedom to perform
> religious rites – the closing of ten thousand churches during
> the period from 1958 to 1964? . . . Or the closing during that
> very period, of a series of monastic communities, theological
> seminaries, etc.? How can one reconcile with that article of
> the constitution the facts of barbaric violence and arbitrari-
> ness towards the Pochaev monks? The *entire* Russian Ortho-
> dox Church was filled with indignation by these [events] . . .
> How to reconcile with the separation of the Church from
> the State . . . the obligatory registration of all priests, the
> impossibility of appointing, without sanction of a government
> official, a single servant of cult, from the patriarch to psalm-
> singer? How to reconcile with the principle of the separation
> of the Church from the State the obligatory registration of
> baptisms, with an obligatory inspection of passports of
> parents and godfathers, with the submission of the lists of the
> baptised to the rayon executive committees, etc.? . . . utilising
> my constitutional right to freedom of speech, I have called
> in my articles for the abolition of these practices which
> contradict the constitution.[39]

Despite the arrest and trial of Levitin-Krasnov on the eve of
the national *Sobor* of the Russian Orthodox Church (30 May–
3 June 1971), the timing of these repressive measures was calculated, it seems, to dissuade other dissenters from interfering with
this carefully staged gathering – several petitions were addressed
to the *Sobor* organisers or participants, requesting changes in the
Patriarchate's policy. Two clergymen and a layman from the
Moscow diocese appealed to the *Sobor* to 'remove the difficulties
presently experienced [by the Church]', and to request from the
Government the reopening of the suppressed theological seminaries, monasteries and parishes, the permission to offer religious

instruction to children, and the curtailment of arbitrary activities
of plenipotentiaries of the Council for Religious Affairs.[40] Another
petition attacked Metropolitan Nikodim and several other Patriarchate spokesmen for their quasi-theological rationalisations
of the Patriarchate's political activities abroad.[41] Even at the
closed bishops' conference preceding the *Sobor,* several bishops
demanded that the *Sobor* repeal the Church's controversial 1961
ruling banning the priests from membership on the parish executive organs – a decision which, they felt, 'contradicts the canonical,
traditional structure of the Church and violates the integrity of
ecclesiastical administration'.[42] No action was taken at the *Sobor*
on any of these grievances, though subsequent resignation of
Metropolitan Nikodim from the chairmanship of the Patriarchate's Department for External Ecclesiastical Relations might
have been affected by the bishops' criticism of 'political aspects'
of the Church's 'activities in the defence of peace'.[43]

THE BAPTIST DISSENT MOVEMENT

While dissent within the Russian Orthodox Church has been of
greatest political significance both in terms of the strength of the
Church and the ties forged between the Orthodox protesters and
the dissident Soviet intellectuals, by far the best organised and
most active of the contemporary protest movements in the U.S.S.R.
has developed since the early 1960s among the much less numerous
Evangelical Christians–Baptists (E.C.B.). It emerged as a grass-
roots reaction to the 1960 revision of the Church's statutes by its
All-Union Council (A.U.C.E.C.B.) and to its 1961 'instruction'.
Inspired, no doubt, by the same governmental pressure as the
controversial 1961 Synodal resolution in the Orthodox Church,
these documents 'voluntarily' surrendered some of the limited
rights held by the E.C.B. under the Soviet law.[44] In August 1961,
the dissenters formed an 'Initiative [Action] Group for the Convening of an Extraordinary All-Union Congress of the Evangelical Christian–Baptist Church in the U.S.S.R.' (hence the
movement's popular name *initsiativniki*) which has since attempted
to secure governmental recognition and permission to convoke
a national Congress in order to unseat the 'opportunist'
A.U.C.E.C.B. and restore the original 'Leninist' guarantees of
religious freedom in the U.S.S.R. Failing to overcome the hostility
of the authorities, the *initsiativniki,* led by Presbyters A. F.

Prokofyev, G. K. Kryuchkov and G. P. Vins, proceeded towards a complete break with the 'official' E.C.B. organisation by 'excommunicating' the All-Union Council. They then formed a rival ecclesiastical centre known, since September 1965, as the 'Council of Churches of the Evangelical Christians–Baptists' (C.C.E.C.B.).[45]

The grievances of the dissident Baptists closely anticipated those of the Orthodox dissenters: the perversion of the constitutional separation of the Church from the State into a virtually total state control over the Church; the illegal use of the Council for the Affairs of Religious Cults and of the K.G.B. to fill the leading positions in the Church with individuals willing to collaborate with them in the gradual liquidation of the Church; and governmental repressions against the opponents of the church leadership.[46] In the words of the movement's 1963 appeal to Khrushchev,

> all doubts have now been removed that the church which should be separated from the state, is completely under the illegal control of various state authorities. Apostate ministers have entered into illegal deals and collaboration with government bodies and the K.G.B., who have thus been granted both clandestine and unconcealed access into the Church.[47]

However, unlike the Orthodox dissenters who have been careful to adhere to the letter of Soviet law and who stopped short of setting up an organised movement (both to maintain their claim to 'legality' and to escape the opprobrium of 'schismatics'), the *initsiativniki* not only demanded a revision of Soviet legislation on religion, but soon adopted a tactic of a deliberate violation of the most discriminatory provisions of this legislation to dramatise, by confrontation with the authorities, the inherent injustice of these provisions and their incompatibility with the 'Leninist' 1918 Separation Decree, the Constitution, and the Universal Declaration of Human Rights. The most important programmatic document of the E.C.B. dissenters – an appeal addressed on their behalf by Kryuchkov and Vins to L. I. Brezhnev on 14 April 1965 – having carefully analysed the changing Bolshevik application of the principle of 'freedom of conscience', summed up the predicament of the dissident Baptists in the following words:

> . . . many hundreds of believers have been illegally deprived of their freedom, they are in prison, in concentration camps

and in exile, while some have died a martyr's death; the children of believers have been taken from them, thousands of E.C.B. communities have no legal status, their meetings take place in private houses, where there is only room for 23–30 per cent of the members of the congregation; moreover, even in these conditions, believers cannot gather in peace, because often these meetings of faithful are dispersed by the regular and auxiliary police and the houses are confiscated.[48]

The *initsiativniki* leaders pleaded with Brezhnev to take steps in the direction of greater legal scope for religious activities, and in particular

(1)   to re-establish the meaning of the decree 'Concerning the separation of church from the state' and its previous objective interpretation (in its practical application);

(2)   to repeal the resolution of the All-Union Central Executive Committee and Council of People's Commissars made on 8 April 1929, 'Concerning religious societies', because it contradicts the spirit and letter of the basic legislation of the decree, and also annul all instructions and resolutions which contradict the decree;

(3)   to give maximum clarity and precision of formulation to the article on freedom of conscience in the Constitution now being worked out by you, so that the clause contains a guarantee of true freedom of conscience, i.e. to include freedom of religious propaganda, without which there can be no question of true freedom of conscience.[49]

The Government's response to the dissident pleas was to offer some concessions to the 'loyal' A.U.C.E.C.B. to strengthen its hand *vis-à-vis* the *initsiativniki*. But when it failed to entice the dissenters back into the fold, in 1966 the authorities resumed repressive measures against the E.C.B. Council of Churches.[5]

Despite mounting administrative harassment and police repressions which, by the late 1960s, decimated the leadership of the Council of Churches, the dissidents succeeded in building up a dedicated following within some 'registered' and especially within the more numerous 'unregistered' E.C.B. congregations[51] throughout the U.S.S.R., attracting to their ranks significant numbers of young converts. For over a decade the *initsiativniki* have been disseminating *samizdat* documents, polemical essays, collections of religious poetry and sermons, hymnbooks, as well as their clandestine periodicals *Vestnik spaseniya* (The Herald of Salvation) and *Bratsky listok* (Fraternal Newsletter). They have been holding 'unauthorised' public religious ceremonies and processions; convening 'underground' meetings, congresses and youth conferences, and organising religious instruction classes for children and youth. With over 150 of the dissident Baptists imprisoned during 1961–63, a unique organisation called 'Council of the E.C.B. Prisoners' Relatives in the U.S.S.R.' was formed in February 1964. It assumed the tasks of collecting and disseminating information on the imprisoned dissenters and on children taken away from the E.C.B. parents, as well as of petitioning the Government for a review of all court cases involving the dissenters and the return of their children to parental homes.[52] Although some of its leaders were subsequently arrested – most notably its chairman, L. M. Vins, mother of the twice-sentenced secretary of the C.C.E.C.B. – the Council has effectively continued its work, becoming indeed the main source of information about the Soviet repressions against the movement.[53]

A measure of the Baptist dissenters' determination and organisational skill was the establishment, in 1971, of their own underground publishing house 'Khristiyanin' (The Christian) which assumed the printing of the C.C.E.C.B. appeals and periodicals and published the gospels and a book of psalms.[54]

THE OTHER CURRENTS OF RELIGIOUS PROTEST

In recent years more evidence appeared about ferment in other 'legally' existing religious organisations. In virtually every case manifestations of dissent have been provoked by the governmental interference with internal affairs of these organisations, including infiltration of the ecclesiastical administration by police informers, closing of churches, arbitrary restrictions on the training and activities of the clergy, or the removal of 'obstinate' priests. Early in 1969, an unsigned protest reached the West, accusing the Soviet authorities of interference with the internal affairs of the Old Believers, including the removal of one of the remaining four bishops, placement of a K.G.B. informer in the key position of secretary to the Archbishop of Moscow and All Rus', as well as harassment of the Old Believers' clergy and faithful.[55]

Since 1963 a series of protests have been addressed to the bishops and the Soviet authorities by the Roman Catholic clergy of Lithuania (the only predominantly Catholic republic in the U.S.S.R.)

On 12 December 1963 sixty-three priests of the Vilkaviskis diocese wrote to all Lithuanian bishops expressing concern over the 'abnormal situation' in the theological seminary.[56] In January 1969 two priests of the same diocese complained to the Government about severe restrictions imposed on admissions to the Kaunas theological seminary – the only one in Lithuania – with the resulting catastrophic shortage of clergy condemning the Church to slow death.[57] After they had been removed by the authorities for trying to enlist for their action the support of the remaining bishops and diocesan administrators, an elaborate appeal was sent in August to Kosygin by some forty priests of the Vilnius archdiocese. This document catalogued the grievances of the Lithuanian Catholics, such as the removal from office of all but two bishops, the blocking of the construction of new churches, prohibition of the priestly retreats, the imposition of severe penalties on the clergy offering any religious instruction to children, and interference with the performance of rites, especially confirmation. There was also the familiar complaint about the conspiratorial practices of the Council for Religious Affairs representatives.[58] The most acute issue has become the increasingly restrictive interpretation placed by the authorities on the active participation of minors in religious services and the examination of children's religious knowledge by the clergy prior to the rites of first communion and confirmation. In 1970 a large number of the Lithuanian clergy protested against the sentencing of the priest Antanas Seskevicius for such a pre-communion examination.[59] In the same year sixty-one clergymen of the Vilnius archdiocese petitioned Brezhnev for the return of the exiled bishop Steponavicius to the local see.[60]

The most elaborate statement of the Lithuanian Catholics' grievances appeared in the autumn of 1970 in a letter addressed by fifty-nine priests of the Vilkaviskis diocese and endorsed by the clergy of the Vilnius archdiocese. Significantly, this document aimed its criticisms not only at the arbitrary and illegal restrictions imposed upon the Lithuanian Catholics by the authorities, but also at the hierarchy for failing to speak out in defence of the Church's legal rights.[61]

Throughout 1971 administrative harassment, police and court repressions against the Roman Catholics continued. In November 1971 the priests J. Zdebskis and P. Bubnys were sentenced to one year's imprisonment each for religious instruction of children.[62] Several protest petitions with over 4,500 signatures were addressed to various government institutions but the only answer received came in the form of intensified repressions against believers.[63] In December 1971 and January 1972 17,054 Lithuanian Catholics signed a memorandum to Brezhnev reiterating their grievances and calling upon the authorities 'to secure for us the freedom of conscience which is guaranteed by the Constitution of the U.S.S.R. but which until now is absent in practice'.[64] Forwarding this petition through the Secretary General of the United Nations, its signatories complained to Kurt Waldheim about Soviet discrimination against believers and the continuing police repressions against protesters.[65]

The Uniates of the Western Ukraine who had been driven underground as a result of the forcible 1946 'reunion' of the Ukrainian Greek Catholics with the Russian Orthodox Church[66] have posed an especially complicated problem to the regime. Enjoying massive support among the believers in Galicia, as well as from the strong Ukrainian Catholic diaspora in the West, the Uniates have survived, despite repeated repressive measures, both within the formally 'Orthodox' Church (so-called 'secret' Uniates) and as an 'illegal' Church with a succession of its own bishops and a network of secular and monastic clergy combining their worldly occupations with clandestine religious rites performed in private homes, at cemeteries, and even in the officially 'closed' churches.[67] Closely identified with Ukrainian national aspirations, the Uniate underground has been considered a threat to both the Russian Orthodox Church and to Soviet rule in the Western Ukraine. An even more extreme position *vis-à-vis* the Soviet State–Church alliance has been taken by a Uniate sect of *Pokutnyky* ('Penitents'), dating from 1956,[68] which combines radical nationalist views with a total repudiation of the Soviet system. According to the dissident *Ukrainsky visnyk*, members of this sect refuse to serve a state other than the Ukrainian one and accept the consequences as 'punishment for the national misfortune of the Ukraine'.[69]

The grievances of the Uniates were summed up in a petition addressed, in March 1966, to the Procurator General of the U.S.S.R. by a Uniate priest, H. Budzynovsky, who had been sentenced twice before for his refusal to 'convert' to the Russian Orthodox Church. The Soviet regime, charged Budzynovsky, followed in the steps of Tsar Nicholas I in forcing the 'reunion' of the Ukrainian Greek Catholic Church with the Russian Church, in clear violation of the constitutional separation of the Church from the State and other legal guarantees of 'freedom of conscience'. The so-called 'Lviv *Sobor*' of 1946 was illegal in terms of both Catholic *and* Orthodox canons and it was in fact convened by the Soviet Ukrainian Government which continues to apply police and judicial repressions against the Uniate clergy who do not recognise that *Sobor*. 'The Orthodox Church does not exist as a unified entity', pointed out Budzynovsky, 'but rather is made up of individual national churches . . . only the Ukrainians have no Ukrainian Orthodox Church. In the Ukraine, the Russian Church rules, with all the consequences which result from such a situation.'[70]

The Government authorities have been ignoring repeated peasant requests for official permission to have Uniate church services in their villages.[71] Recently, *Ukrainsky visnyk* reported on the renewed persecution of the Greek Catholic Church since the autumn of 1968. It suggested the involvement of the Russian Church in this campaign, adding that the Patriarchate had ordered a purge of former Uniate priests from leading positions in the Orthodox Church.[72]

The interrelationships between religion and nationality has been especially close among the Armenians, Muslims and the Jews. While there seems to be no evidence of organised religious dissent in contemporary Armenia, a number of Soviet sources have admitted to the large number of 'unregistered' Muslim religious communities, wandering mullahs, 'unauthorised' pilgrimages to 'holy places', and in particular, the spreading tendency to consider Islamic traditions as part of national culture.[73]

Despite the far-reaching secularisation of Jewry in the European part of the U.S.S.R. (within the pre-1939 borders), Jewishness and Judaism have remained interconnected, especially since the suppression, by the end of 1948, of all *secular* Jewish institutions. This interconnectedness of religion and nationality has evidently been intensified by the anti-Zionist and anti-Israeli overtones of the official anti-Judaic propaganda which on occasions relapsed into crude anti-Semitism. Similarly, anti-Zionist propaganda has attacked Judaism as a 'nationalist' and Israel-oriented, if not potentially subversive, faith.[74] Accordingly there has been little evidence of a 'purely' religious dissent among the Soviet Jews, with religious grievances usually appearing along with demands for equal treatment of the Jews with other nationalities[75] and/or as a motive for the intended emigration from the U.S.S.R. The best known case of such a religiously inspired attempt to emigrate to Israel was that of the eighteen Jewish families from Georgia whose petition was transmitted by Israel to the United Nations in November 1969.[76] This intertwining of national and religious consciousness has expressed itself during the past decade in demonstrative assemblies of the young Jews at the Moscow synagogue for the annual 'Rejoicing of the Law' festivities – periodic 'reaffirmations' of their Jewishness.[77]

RELIGIOUS FERMENT AND POLITICAL DISSENT

The overlapping of religious protest with the national and civil rights movements, although most noticeable among the Soviet Jews, has also been characteristic of the Uniate and the Orthodox dissenters. The Uniate cause has been adopted by the more nationalist wing of Ukrainian dissenters, best represented by the twice sentenced young history lecturer Valentyn Moroz. In his *Khronika oporu* (Chronicle of Resistance), Moroz (an Orthodox by birth) wrote:

> The Uniate movement has grown into the spiritual body of Ukraine and becomes a national symbol. . . . Russia, having gained Ukrainian lands from Poland soon makes Orthodoxy into a weapon of russification. . . . The [Uniate] Church has grown into the cultural life so deeply that it is impossible to touch it without damaging the spiritual structure of the nation. . . . One must understand that a struggle against the Church means a struggle against culture. . . . It is impossible to break people, to make slaves out of them, until you steal from them their holidays, until you destroy their traditions, and until you trample over their temples. . . . The classical

swindle is to declare the spiritual riches of a nation 'useless things of the past', 'opium of the people'.[78]

An editorial statement in the October 1970 issue of *Ukrainsky visnyk*, while claiming equal respect for the autocephalous Ukrainian Church, reaffirmed its position towards the Uniate Church: 'Religious persecution, including the wanton liquidation of the Greek Catholic Church by the henchmen of Beria, was illegal and unconstitutional' and it therefore will be commented upon by the *Visnyk* which will cover all violations of legality in the Ukrainian S.S.R.[79] It is, however, significant that little attention and hardly any sympathy has been shown by the Ukrainian dissenters to the numerous *initsiativniki* in the Ukraine, possibly due to the sectarians' insensitivity to Ukrainian national aspirations. As for the Jehovah's Witnesses, Moroz characterised them, in 1970, as 'our fiercest enemies, the most reliable agents of Russification, because having become a Jehovah's Witness a Ukrainian turns hopelessly indifferent to the nationality problem.'[80]

While the regime's persecution of dissident Baptists and other 'illegal' religious groups, as well as all other forms of religious discrimination, have been condemned by spokesmen of the civil rights movement, the largely working-class *initsiativniki* have remained aloof from the struggle for the general democratisation of the Soviet system. In their pronouncements and appeals the sectarian dissidents have evidently shown no concern for the plight of the traditional churches against which they have been competing in their proselytising activities. While their indifference to the nationality problem has antagonised the nationalist dissenters, their radical tactics, including acts of civil disobedience and confrontations with the police and *druzhinniki*, tended to alienate the civil rights advocates with their emphasis on the observance of 'Soviet legality'.

The Orthodox dissenters, drawn mainly from the ranks of the Church's clergy and lay intelligentsia, have in time developed the closest links with the civil rights movement, especially through Boris Talantov and Anatolii Levitin-Krasnov. Of singular importance has also been the identification with Russian Orthodoxy (though not with the present leadership or policy of the Church) on the part of such leading representatives of intellectual dissent as Andrei Sinyavsky, Alexander Solzhenitsyn and Yurii Titov. The somewhat obscure case of the All-Russian Social-Christian Union for the Liberation of the People – liquidated by the Leningrad K.G.B. in 1967[81] – illustrated the overlapping of Orthodoxy and political opposition. On the other hand the Russian Orthodoxy tradition is being 'rediscovered' by the legal patriotic Russian youth circles and clubs.[82]

The Orthodox dissenters have justified their support for the 'democratic movement' by demands of 'Christian conscience'. In his 1968 open letter a Pskov priest, Sergii Zheludkov, called upon Professor J. Hromadka of Prague, President of the Christian Peace Conference, and a number of ecclesiastical figures abroad, to consider the fate of Anatolii Marchenko and other persecuted dissenters:

> They have merely sought to give effect to some of the human rights proclaimed back in 1948 by the United Nations. And these are human rights which at the same time constitute a man's religious duty. A Christian is bound before God to be a whole man, a free man – free to think, not to be untruthful or to act deceitfully either towards himself or towards others. To persecute a person for exercising his freedom of personal peaceful beliefs, the freedom to express the truth – is Caesar attempting to take [away] something which is God's. It is essentially a crime against humanity, against the free and sacred humanity bestowed upon him by God in Christ, Our Lord. The above named Marchenko and other unknown representatives of the Russian intelligentsia are today suffering in the 'severe regime' conditions on behalf of that Christian principle.[83]

This developing sense of interdependence between the religious and political dissent currents was best epitomised in the appeal addressed by thirty-two citizens (including some leading spokesmen for the 'democratic movement') 'To Public Opinion in the Soviet Union and Foreign Countries', following Levitin-Krasnov's arrest in September 1969. In this document they defended Levitin as the one who understood that

... freedom is indivisible and there cannot be religious freedom if basic human rights are violated. In the post-Stalin
years, he was the first religious leader in our country who
realised this truth and raised his voice in defence of civil
rights and in defence of men who fell victims of the struggle
for civil rights.[84]

In February 1971 a leading member of the dissident Committee
for Human Rights, V. N. Chalidze, intervened with the patriarchal
locum tenens Pimen on behalf of the believers of the town of
Naro-Fominsk who, for forty years, have been petitioning the
authorities for permission to open a church in their town.[85] In
his letter Chalidze derided the united front of the Patriarchate
and the regime in turning down the believers' demands: 'Once
the authorities do not agree to open the church, it means that [the
believers' request] does not please God either . . . I, a layman, see
in this only the fact that the believers have been rejected by their
pastor.'[86]

On 9 April 1972 Alexander Solzhenitsyn raised his voice in
protest against the complacency of the Moscow Patriarchate in
the face of the continuing destruction of Orthodoxy. In his 'Lenten
Letter' to the new Patriarch Pimen, Solzhenitsyn upbraided him
for ignoring the pleas of the priests Eshliman and Yakunin, Archbishop Yermogen of Kaluga and the Vyatka believers and for
using ecclesiastical sanctions against the protesters. The Patriarchate's 'voluntary internal enslavement', he observed, 'is
amounting to self-destruction':

> For every working church there are twenty churches which
> have been demolished and destroyed irrecoverably and
> twenty abandoned and desecrated. . . . Even a copy of the
> gospels is nowhere to be had. . . . The entire administration
> of the Church, the appointment of parish priests and bishops
> (including those who commit outrages with the aim of
> making it easier to deride and destroy the Church), every-
> thing is controlled by the Committee [Council] on Religious
> Affairs just as secretly as before. Such a church, directed
> dictatorially by atheists, is a sight which has not been seen for
> two millennia. All the property of the Church has been
> surrendered to their control, as well as the use of the church
> funds . . . the priests are deprived of their rights in their

parish, remaining entrusted solely with the holding of services. ...[87]

Condemning the tactics of 'preservation' of the Church 'by lying', Solzhenitsyn invoked the memory of the Church's not-too-distant 'martyrdom worthy of the first centuries of Christianity' and appealed to the Patriarch to reassert the Church's independence from the atheist State.[88]

THE STATE AND THE DISSENTERS

The Soviet Government which once, during the first years of its existence, followed a policy of *divide et impera* against the hostile Orthodox Church and several other denominations – playing up the lower clergy and laymen against the episcopate and encouraging internal dissent and schisms – has firmly embraced, since World War II, a new role as the protector of the ecclesiastical *status quo*. After most of the churches accepted Soviet conditions of 'normalisation', including extensive governmental controls over their internal activities, Khrushchev's anti-religious campaign brought about an end to this paradoxical pattern of 'symphony' between the Churches and the atheistic State, undermining the credibility of the 'loyal' church leaders who failed to rise in defence of their flock in the face of a new wave of religious persecution.

The emergence of dissent in the ranks of the Russian Orthodox Church and the Evangelical Christians–Baptists, and the increasing ferment within several other religious groups as well as activisation of the Uniate Church and other 'underground' groups, presented the regime with a serious challenge not only to its church policy but also to internal security, especially in view of the possible confluence of religious dissent with the civil rights and nationality rights movements. The initial Soviet response to this combined challenge was to attack the earliest and seemingly most serious manifestations of religious dissent – the E.C.B. *initsiativniki* movement – by slandering, harassing and finally arresting its leaders and activists.[89] At the same time, some concessions were offered to the 'loyal' A.U.C.E.C.B. It was allowed to hold a congress in 1963 and to withdraw some of the 'self-imposed' restrictions (contained in the 1960 statute amendments and the 1961 'instruction') in order to attract the more moderate dissenters back into the 'official' E.C.B. organisation.

The failure of this strategy became obvious by 1964. Another approach was tried both by the authorities and the A.U.C.E.C.B. during the brief 'thaw' following Khrushchev's ouster, when a number of *initsiativniki* were reportedly released from imprisonment.[90] Significantly, not a single E.C.B. dissenter was arrested during 1965.[91] However, the dissidents' requests, submitted in the April 1965 memorandum by Kryuchkov and Vins, were evidently found unacceptable by the Government. In September 1965 the leaders of the E.C.B. dissenters were at last received by Anastas Mikoyan, then Chairman of the Supreme Soviet Presidium, but his promise to investigate their complaints did not improve the position of the dissenters.[92] That very month the *initsiativniki* held an All-Union Conference in Moscow which completed the break with the A.U.C.E.C.B. by establishing a rival body – the Council of Churches of the E.C.B.[93] The subsequent intensification of dissident pressure on the Government authorities to legalise the C.C.E.C.B. and to 'register' its congregations, which the authorities refused to do, led in time to public demonstrations which culminated, in May 1966, in massive confrontations in Rostov on Don, Moscow and Kiev.[94]

In the meantime the arrests of Sinyavsky and Daniel in Moscow and of a large number of dissident intellectuals in the Ukraine[95] signalled an end to the post-Khrushchev 'thaw'. The toughening of the regime's reaction to political dissent could not but affect its treatment of religious dissidents as well. Recent manifestations of dissent, now coming from the Russian Orthodox Church as well, added urgency to the problem of tightening administrative and legal controls over religious activities. In December 1965 the two governmental agencies for the Russian Orthodox Church and other denominations were merged into a single Council for Religious Affairs under Vladimir Kuroyedov, who announced that the new Council was given 'a much greater role to play and greater responsibility in controlling observance of the laws on the cults', as well as 'correspondingly greater powers'.[96] In March 1966 the republican legislation on religious cults was amended to impose more severe prison sentences and higher fines for the 'violation of the laws on the separation of the Church from the State'.[97] The new *corpus delicti* evidently aimed at the activities of religious dissenters by classifying as criminal activities 'the preparation for purposes of mass dissemination or the mass dissemination of handbills, letters, leaflets and other documents making appeals for the non-observance of the legislation on religious cults', as well as 'the organisation and holding of religious meetings, processions and other [religious] cult ceremonies disturbing public order'.[98] In September an amendment to Chapter Nine of the Russian Criminal Code expanded the definition of 'crimes against administrative order' to deal with all overt manifestations of dissent. Punishment of up to three years imprisonment, of up to one year 'correctional labour', or a fine of up to one hundred roubles was now imposed for

> the systematic distribution in *verbal form* of clearly false fabrications discrediting the Soviet state and public order, as well as the preparation or distribution in written, printed *or other form* of compositions of such content. . . . (Article 190-1).

Another section imposed severe penalties for

> the organisation of, as well as active participation in, group activities which rudely disturb public order or which are accompanied by evident disobedience to legal demands of government representatives or result in the disturbance [of the operation of] the transport, state or public institutions or undertakings . . . (Article 190–3).[99]

The authorities thus served a clear notice that they will resort to criminal proceedings against the opponents of the *status quo* in Church–State relations, with most of the future trials of religious dissenters to be based on either or both subsections of Article 190 cited above.

At the same time, the Government offered further concessions to the 'loyal' Baptists to strengthen their hand against the dissenters. In October 1966 the A.U.C.E.C.B. was allowed to convene an All-Union Congress which produced a new constitution for the Church providing for a more representative All-Union Council and more autonomy to local congregations.[100] 'Several tens' of E.C.B. churches were 'registered' by the authorities during the following year and new editions of the Bible (20,000 copies) and of the hymnbook (26,000) were published during 1968. In the same year, the A.U.C.E.C.B. was permitted to start two-year correspondence courses for some 100 preachers.[101]

The tactics pursued by the regime with regard to the dissident Baptists during the same period combined more severe repressions against the 'recalcitrants' with token concessions for the 'moderate' elements in the C.C.E.C.B. ranks, evidently in the hope of attracting the latter back into the 'official' E.C.B. organisation. After some abatement in repressions during 1967, the number of arrests of the *initsiativniki* markedly increased during 1968 (50 arrests) and 1969 (62).[102] The 'First All-Union Conference of Relatives of Imprisoned Members of the Church of Evangelical Christians–Baptists', which met illegally in November 1969, described the plight of the dissidents in the following terms:

> ... From 1961 to this date [November 1969] more than 500 brethren have been arrested and imprisoned, chiefly ministers of the church, presbyters, preachers. . . . In many cities and towns, e.g. Odessa, Chelyabinsk, Frunze, Brest, Gomel, Kiev, etc., houses of prayer were seized and private homes where worship had been held were confiscated. . . . Worship services were fiercely disbanded by the authorities, in many places accompanied by beating of believers, e.g. in Krivoi Rog, Zaporozhe, Chelyabinsk, Sverdlovsk, Vladivostok, and other cities and towns. . . . A great many searches of believers are accompanied by arrests for 15 days. . . . Fines have been decreed. During these years they have totalled hundreds of thousands of roubles. . . .
>
> Our children are in hard circumstances. They suffer interrogation by the state attorneys and the police on questions concerning their religious upbringing; they are forced to be witnesses at trials of their parents. . . . For praying at bedside and for witnessing for Christ they are thrown into solitary confinement, deprived of food parcels and of family visits. . . . They are deprived of the right to have and to read the Bible. They are subject to all kinds of repressions and constant interrogation, with the proposals that, by abjuring, they could get conditional freedom. . . . Our relatives who return on completion of their prison terms are immediately threatened by the authorities with demands that they cease religious activities, with the threat that if they do not they will be thrown into prison again.

E.C.B. believers are systematically subjected to falsehoods

on the radio and in the press, where the most refined imaginations link us with vile criminals and immoral persons. . . .[103]

By the end of 1969, the 'official' A.U.C.E.C.B. made another attempt at 'reunification' of the 'schismatic brethren', with clear support from the authorities. Despite Kuroyedov's recent press attack on the *initsiativniki,* warning that they 'have begun to cultivate the idea of seeping into the governing organs of the Baptists quietly',[104] the A.U.C.E.C.B. held a meeting on 4 December with several dissident leaders who had recently completed their terms of imprisonment. Though the A.U.C.C. failed to secure a joint condemnation of the recent 'illegal' All-Union Conference of the Prisoners' Relatives and its appeal 'To the Christians of the Whole World',[105] the two sides evidently produced a 'Draft of a Joint Appeal' for unity which was to be ratified by both the 'official' E.C.B. and the dissident C.C.E.C.B.[106] Possibly in anticipation of 'reunion', the Soviet authorities now promptly granted the long-standing dissident request for permission to hold an All-Union Conference of the C.C.E.C.B., which was held at Tula on 6 December, almost simultaneously with the Moscow All-Union Congress of the 'official' E.C.B. Attended by some 120 dissident ministers, the Tula Conference failed to consider the 'Draft of a Joint Appeal' or to condemn the All-Union Council of the Prisoners' Relatives; but it called upon the C.C.E.C.B. congregations to 'register' with the Soviet authorities under the terms of the existing Soviet religious legislation and appealed to the Government to allow the elected leaders of the C.C.E.C.B. to perform their spiritual duties without obligation to take up secular employment. Hundreds of applications for 'registration' were soon submitted by the *initsiativniki* to the appropriate government agencies.[107]

Before long it became clear that this new attempt to split the Baptist dissident movement and attract the 'moderates' into the 'official' E.C.B. organisation had failed. The authorities not only refused to 'register' the C.C.E.C.B. congregations but intensified repressions against them, confiscating the houses in which they met. Retroactively, the Council for Religious Affairs declared the Tula Conference illegal.[108] Dissident presbyters were refused recognition as 'servants of cult' and threatened with prosecution as 'parasites'; some of the C.C.E.C.B. leaders felt compelled to go underground.[109] With about thirty-four of the dissident leaders arrested during 1970, the total of imprisoned C.C.E.C.B. leaders reached 156 by January 1971. By April 1971 thirty-one more arrests were reported.[110] In the words of a message addressed 'To All Christians of the World' by the Second All-Union Congress of Relatives of the E.C.B. Prisoners in December 1970,

> . . . the situation of the Church in the U.S.S.R. becomes more and more difficult. . . . The harassment and persecution of believers increase every day. . . . The *aim* of the atheists is clear to us – to destroy the Church by any means, to destroy belief in God. This poses a threat not only to us and the future of our Church, but also to the universal Church and all believers.[111]

Meanwhile, while offering some concessions to the Russian Orthodox Church in the Ukraine,[112] the regime has intensified its repressions against the 'underground' Ukrainian Greek Catholic (Uniate) Church since the autumn of 1968. In October of that year the police searched dwellings of a number of the 'illegal' Uniate priests, eleven in Lviv alone, confiscating all religious articles and books. Two of the priests – Rev. Horodetsky of Lviv and Rev. Bakhtalovsky of Kolomyya – were arrested and, in January 1969, the authorities imprisoned the underground bishop of the Church, Vasyl Velychkovsky. During 1969, as the propaganda media opened a concerted campaign against the Uniates,[113] searches and interrogations assumed a mass scale throughout the Western Ukraine. In October the Lviv court sentenced Bishop Velychkovsky to three years' imprisonment under Article 187-1 of the Soviet Ukrainian Criminal Code. Similar sentences were imposed on the priests Horodetsky and Bakhtalovsky.[114]

From 1969 on, the regime extended police and judicial repressions to some leading Orthodox dissenters, especially those involved in the general 'democratic movement'. In June 1969 Boris Talentov was arrested in Kirov and sentenced, in September, to two years' imprisonment for writing letters and articles 'slandering' the Soviet system. He died in January 1971 in the Kirov prison.[115] In September 1969 the K.G.B. arrested Anatolii Levitin-Krasnov only to have him released after eleven months.[116] He was, however, rearrested and tried in May 1971 on charges of 'slandering' the

Soviet system and 'inciting servants of the Church to violate the law on the separation of the Church from the State', as well as signing a series of appeals and petitions. Sentenced to three years of 'ordinary-regime camps' and one year of 'correctional labour', Levitin-Krasnov summed up his *credo* in his final address to the court:

> I am a believing Christian. But the mission of Christianity consists in more than going to church. It consists in putting the behests of Christ into practice. Christ called upon us to defend all who are oppressed. That is why I defend people's rights, whether they be Pochaev monks, Baptists or Crimean Tatars, and if opponents of religion should some day be subjected to persecution, I shall defend them too. . . .[117]

Following the trial, the Initiative [Action] Group for the Defence of Human Rights in the U.S.S.R. appealed to the U.N. Human Rights Commission, Pope Paul VI and the *Sobor* of the Russian Orthodox Church to intercede on behalf of Levitin-Krasnov.[118]

Repressions against Orthodox dissenters did not cease with Levitin-Krasnov's trial. In December 1969 the authorities arrested Rev. Pavel Adelgeim of Kagan, Uzbekistan, with the local press slandering the accused priest.[119] Throughout 1969 and 1970 extra-judicial repressions were applied against believers demanding registration of congregations and the reopening of churches (e.g. in Naro-Fominsk and Gorky[120]) or defending their churches from being closed by administrative fiat. Dwellings of a number of dissidents were searched by the police, including that of the priest Gleb Yakunin,[121] and, at least in one case, a lay proselytiser of Orthodoxy was placed without trial in a psychiatric ward.[122]

The rising wave of repressions has dissipated the early hopes for the Government's return to legality in its treatment of believers' grievances. The recent religious dissent documents, as has been noted by William Fletcher,

> are permeated with resignation, if not despair, and partici-pants in the movements now act not so much in the hope of changing the situation but in a defiant resolution to live according to their convictions regardless of the consequences, fully willing to be arrested if necessary.[123]

The general intensification of the Soviet persecution of religious dissenters since 1966 reflects the larger process of the gradual 're-Stalinisation' of the post-Khrushchev regime. The latter has evidently been growing more and more insecure in the face of the internal opposition which it is now viewing, in the context of the rehabilitated 'two-camp theory', as 'objectively', if not 'subjectively', an instrument of 'reactionary forces of the West' used for the purposes of 'ideological subversion', 'anti-Communism' and 'anti-Sovietism'.[124] While thus claiming that religious dissenters are not prosecuted for their religious convictions but only for 'violating Soviet laws' or 'abusing' the rights granted to institutional religion, the Government has displayed an increasing contempt for its own constitutional and procedural safeguards against administrative arbitrariness and police terror. Capable as they are of a much more thorough suppression of overt religious dissent, the authorities have nevertheless relied on selective application of terror, giving preference to a much wider use of extra-judicial, administrative and economic sanctions against the rank-and-file dissidents. Among the political considerations restraining the hand of the regime, of some importance could be the fear of a further radicalisation and politicisation of religious dissent and its merger with the larger currents of political opposition. At the same time, the authorities are, no doubt, mindful of the virtually instant publicity given to cases of religious persecution in *samizdat* and – through *samizdat* – in foreign communications media, tarnishing the carefully cultivated external image of the present Soviet regime. Moreover, through Western broadcasts in the languages of the Soviet peoples, the plight of the dissenters has become known to numerous Soviet listeners of foreign radio. This inability to suppress publicity about its treatment of dissenters may well serve as another restraint on the Soviet Government.

On the surface it seems that little has been achieved by the dissenters apart from reawakening the social conscience of the clergy and believers, revealing to the world the carefully concealed state-domination of the 'loyal' Churches and sects in the U.S.S.R., and exposing the persecution of opponents of such perversion of Soviet guarantees of 'freedom of conscience'. Any basic changes in the Soviet treatment of religious dissenters may have to wait for the inevitable and no-too-distant generation change at the top of the Soviet political system which may perhaps result in another de-Stalinisation phase. In the meantime the real beneficiaries of religious dissent appear to be the 'loyal', officially 'registered' religious groups which have had to be given some concessions by the regime to strengthen their position *vis-à-vis* the dissenters.

NOTES

1. This notion of religious dissent in the U.S.S.R. appears to be shared by the principal works on the subject: J. C. Pollock, *The Christians from Siberia* (London, 1964); D. Konstantinov, *Religioznoye dvizheniye soprotivleniya v SSSR* (Religious Resistance Movement in the U.S.S.R.) (London, Ont., 1967); M. Bourdeaux, *Religious Ferment in Russia: Protestant Opposition to Soviet Religious Policy* (London, 1968); and *Patriarch and Prophets: Persecution of the Russian Orthodox Church Today* (New York, 1970); P. Reddaway, 'Freedom of Worship and the Law', *Problems of Communism*, July–August 1968, pp. 21–9; W. C. Fletcher, 'Religious Dissent in the USSR in the 1960s', *Slavic Review*, Vol. 30, No. 2 (June 1971), pp. 298–316, and his *The Russian Orthodox Church Underground, 1917–1970* (London, 1971). See also M. Bourdeaux (ed.), *Faith on Trial in Russia* (London, 1971); S. Durasoff, *The Russian Protestants: Evangelicals in the Soviet Union, 1944–1964* (Rutherford, N. J., 1969); R. Harris and X. Howard-Johnston (eds), *Christian Appeals from Russia* (London, 1969); *Kampf des Glaubens* (Bern, 1967); A. Martin, *Les Croyants en URSS* (Paris, 1970); G. Simon, *Die Kirchen in Russland* (Munich, 1970); N. Struve, *Christians in Contemporary Russia* (New York, 1967); N. Theodorowitsch, *Religion und Atheismus in der UdSSR* (Munich, 1970); and R. Ronza (ed.), *Dissenso e contestazione nell'Unione Sovietica* (Milan, 1970).

2. For the background and analysis of Metropolitan Sergii's loyalty declaration of 16–29 July 1927, see W. C. Fletcher, *A Study in Survival: The Church in Russia, 1927–1943* (London, 1965), Chs 1–2.

3. The most extensive discussion of these movements appears in Fletcher, *The Russian Orthodox Church Underground*, Chs VII and VIII.

4. On the liquidation of the Uniate (Greek Catholic) Church in the Western Ukraine, see this writer's 'The Uniate Church in the Soviet Ukraine: A Case Study in Soviet Church Policy', *Canadian Slavonic Papers*, Vol. VII (1965), pp. 83–113.

5. See E. M. Bartoshevich and E. I. Borisoglebsky, *Sviditeli Yegovy* (Jehovah's Witnesses) (Moscow, 1969).

6. The so-called *pyatidesyatniki-voronayevtsy*; see A. T. Moskalenko, *Pyatidesyatniki* (The Pentecostalists) (Moscow, 1966), esp. Ch. 2.

7. See W. Kolarz, *Religion in the Soviet Union* (London, 1966), pp. 326–7.

8. See this writer's 'De-Stalinization and Religion in the USSR', *International Journal*, Vol. XX, No. 3 (Summer 1965), pp. 312–30; and 'Religion in the U.S.S.R. after Khrushchev' in J. W. Strong (ed.), *The Soviet Union under Brezhnev and Kosygin: The Transition Years* (New York, 1971), pp. 135–6. Drastically reduced totals of churches or congregations for individual religious groups are shown in *Spravochnik propagandista i agitatora* (A Reference Book of Propagandist and Agitator) (Moscow, 1966), pp. 149–50 (cited in *Research Materials on Religion in Eastern Europe*, Vol. II, No. 10 [October 1969], p. 1).

9. The legislation setting out the organisation, powers and responsibilities of the two Councils was not published for general use; the relatively most extensive

description of the Councils' role appears in A. Kolosov, 'Religiya i tserkov v SSSR', (Religion and the Church in the U.S.S.R.) in *Bolshaya Sovetskaya Entsiklopediya* (Greater Soviet Encyclopaedia), Vol. 50: *S.S.S.R.* (Moscow, 1948), cols 1775–90.

10. See 1965 open letters of priests N. Eshliman and G. Yakunin reproduced in *A Cry of Despair from Moscow Churchmen* (New York, 1966) as well as the relevant E.C.B. documents in Bourdeaux, *Religious Ferment in Russia*, esp. Ch. 2.

11. *Pravda*, 16 and 19 February 1930.

12. See A. Levitin-Krasnov's 1966 'autobiography' in Bourdeaux, *Patriarch and Prophets*, pp. 255–63.

13. A. Levitin-Krasnov, 'With Love and Anger', *ibid.*, pp. 275–88. Cf. W. C. Fletcher, *Nikolai: Portrait of a Dilemna* (New York, 1968), Ch. 10.

14. Note a 'resolution' of the 18 July 1961 *Sobor* of Bishops surrendering priests' authority over the administration and economic and financial affairs of the parishes, which was opposed by at least three bishops (*Zhurnal Moskovskoi Patriarkhii*, No. 8, 1961, pp. 5–17). For an elaborate critique of this 'resolution', see Eshliman–Yakunin letter to the Patriarch in *A Cry of Despair*, pp. 5–42.

15. *Ibid.*, pp. 11–13. Cf. Boris Talantov's account of the closing of Orthodox churches in the Kirov *oblast*, in Bourdeaux, *Patriarch and Prophets*, pp. 125–52.

16. Among those tried by Soviet courts were Archbishops Yov (Kresovych) of Kazan, Venyamin of Irkutsk and Andrei (Sukhenko) of Chernihiv.

17. One known exception was Archbishop Yermogen of Kaluga who refused to approve the closing of any church in his diocese and was therefore removed from his Tashkent and Kaluga sees on demand of the government authorities (see his 1968 letter to Patriarch Alexii in Bourdeaux, *Patriarch and Prophets*, pp. 248–54).

18. See *ibid.*, pp. 125–52, as well as the account of the repeated attempts of liquidation of the Pochaiv monastery during 1961–65 (*ibid.*, pp. 98–116).

19. Reported by a group of French travellers who visited Kiev in 1961 ('Temoignages sur l'U.R.S.S. actuelle [1957–1961]', Paris, n.d., p. R-2).

20. Bourdeaux, *Patriarch and Prophets*, pp. 97–118.

21. See *ibid.*, pp. 221–3, 245–7, 317.

22. *Ibid.*, pp. 223–39.

23. *A Cry of Despair from Moscow Churchmen*, pp. 5–42.

24. *Ibid.*, pp. 42–53.

25. Bourdeaux, *Patriarch and Prophets*, pp. 223–5.

26. *Ibid.*, pp. 229–30.

27. In December 1965 the Council for the Affairs of the Russian Orthodox Church and the Council for the Affairs of Religious Cults were merged together into a Council for Religious Affairs, under Vladimir Kuroyedov. The legislation setting out the organisation and frame of reference of the new Council was not made public.

28. Bourdeaux, *Patriarch and Prophets*, pp. 237–8. For a partial text of the original letter sent by Talantov and other Kirov laymen to Patriarch Alexii, see *Vestnik Russkogo Studencheskogo Khristianskogo Dvizheniya* (Herald of the Russian Student Christian Movement), No. 83/1 (1967), pp. 29–64.

29. Bourdeaux, *Patriarch and Prophets*, pp. 153–4; Talantov's 'Complaint' to the Procurator-General of the U.S.S.R. is reproduced in *Problems of Communism* (July–August 1968), pp. 111–12.

30. See, in particular, a letter from 'the Orthodox Christians of Russia, the Ukraine, and Belorussia', sent in February 1964 to the Odessa meeting of the Executive Committee of the World Council of Churches, reproduced in

Situation des Chrétiens en Union Sovietique II: Dovuments (Paris, 1965), pp. 10–13; and Bourdeaux, *Patriach and Prophets*, pp. 161–77, 305–20.

31. *Ibid.*, pp. 239–54; and *Vestnik RSKhD*, No. 86/IV (1967), pp. 66–80.
32. Bourdeaux, *Patriarch and Prophets*, p. 283.
33. A. Levitin-Krasnov, 'Listening to the Radio', *Problems of Communism* (July–August), 1968 pp. 108–9.
34. See, e.g., Talantov, 'Sovetskoye obshchestvo 1965–1968' (Soviet Society, 1965–1968) *Posev*, No. 9 (1969), pp. 35–41.
35. S. Zheludkov, 'K razmyshleniyam ob intellektualnoi svobode. Otvet akademiku A. D. Sakharovu' (With Regard to Reflections on Intellectual Freedom. A Reply to A. D. Sakharov), *Vestnik RSKhD*, No. 94/IV (1969), pp. 46–57.
36. See A. Krasnov, 'Moye vozvrashcheniye' (My Return), *Grani*, No. 79 (1971), p. 25.
37. See the Group's statement 'Chto takoe Initsiativnaya gruppa?' (What is the Action Group?), *Posev*, Vol. 26, No. 11 (November 1970), pp. 8–9; cf. this writer's 'Political Dissent in the Soviet Union', *Studies in Comparative Communism*, Vol. 3, No. 2 (April 1970), pp. 82–3, and appended Documents 5–8 (pp. 114–19).
38. Levitin-Krasnov denies here an allegation made by a 'commission of experts' which was called by the Procuracy to 'analyse' his writings: 'The author belongs to an extremist group which exists in the Russian Orthodox Church. This group pursues the following ends: an unlimited religious propaganda, abolition of all laws regulating the performance of religious rites, religious education (including the opening of Sunday schools), and prohibition of anti-religious upbringing' ('Moye vozvrashcheniye', *loc. cit.*, p. 71).
39. *Ibid.*, pp. 72–3.
40. A letter of the priest Georgii Pyetukhov (Zagorsk), hierodeacon Varsonofii Khaybulin (Gorokhovets) and layman Petr Fomin (Moscow). See G. Rar, 'Tserkov v Rossii yest i spasayet' (The Church in Russia Exists and Saves), *Posev*, No. 11 (1971), p. 44.
41. *Ibid.*, p. 45. Priest Nikolai Gaynov of the Moscow diocese, who co-authored this petition with several laymen, was subsequently suspended by the Patriarchate.
42. Interview offered by Archbishop Vasilii (Krivoshein) of Brussels and Belgium to the Geneva bulletin *Episcepsis* (July 1971), cited *ibid.*, No. 10 (1971), p. 20.
43. *Ibid.*
44. See Bourdeaux, *Religious Ferment in Russia*, Ch. 2.
45. L. N. Mitrokhin, *Baptizm* (Moscow, 1966), pp. 80–83.
46. Cf. *ibid.*, pp. 88–9. See also Bourdeaux, *Religious Ferment in Russia*, pp. 53–62.
47. *Ibid.*, p. 54
48. *Ibid.*, pp. 111–12.
49. *Ibid.* p. 112. The law in question was a republican (RSFSR) and not an All-Union statute.
50. In 1966 alone, Soviet authorities arrested 40 leading *initsiativniki*.
51. Mitrokhin, *op. cit.*, pp. 88–9. According to an appeal from the Second All-Union Congress of the E.C.B. Prisoners' Relatives, out of 5,000 congregations, only one-third was 'registered' and incorporated into the A.U.C.E.C.B. (unpublished appeal 'To All Christians of the World' adapted by the Second All-Union Congress in Kiev on 12 December 1970, p. 3).
52. Bourdeaux, *Religious Ferment in Russia*, pp. 88–9.
53. See, in particular, the documents reproduced in *Religion in Communist Dominated Areas* [hereafter *RCDA*], Vol. VII, Nos. 3–4 (1968), pp. 21–43, and Vol. IX, Nos 3–4 (1970), pp. 13–17; as well as a mimeographed 'Collection

88　　*Religion and Atheism in the U.S.S.R. and Eastern Europe*

of Documents' of the Second All-Union Congress of Relatives of E.C.B. Prisoners in the U.S.S.R., Part I (December 1970).

54. *Posev*, No. 10 (1971), p. 12.
55. *Posev*, March 1969, p. 5. The document in question refers to the largest of the Old Believer groups, the 'Church of the Byelo-Krinitsa Concord' headed by the Archbishopric of Moscow and All Rus'.
56. See the October 1970 'Lettera di sacerdoti lituani ai loro vescovi', *Russia Cristiana*, No. 123 (May–June 1972), p. 61.
57. *A Chronicle of Current Events*, No. 18 (5 March 1971) (London, 1971), pp. 136–7.
58. For the Vilkaviskis diocesan priests' appeal to Lithuanian bishops and administrators, see *East West Digest*, No. 6 (1970), pp. 180–81.
59. The appeal from the forty Lithuanian priests is reproduced in *RCDA* Vol. IX, Nos 5–9 (1970), pp. 34–6.
60. See C.S.R.C., *Documentation Service on Religion in the Soviet Union*, Nos 9–10 (August 1971), pp. 6–7, espec. item 287.
61. 'Lettera di sacerdoti lituani', *loc. cit.*, pp. 56–63.
62. *Ibid.*, pp. 74–7.
63. 'Al Segretario generale dell 'ONU', *ibid.*, p. 66.
64. 'Memorandum dei cattolici lituani al Segretario generale del PCUS sotto-scritto da 17,054 persone dicembre 1971 – gennaio 1972', *ibid.*, pp. 64–5.
65. 'Al Segretario', *loc. cit.*, pp. 65–6. Since early 1972, Lithuanian Catholic dissenters have been publishing a clandestine quarterly, *Chronicle of the Catholic Church in Lithuania*. Similar in style and tone to the now suppressed organ of the Ukrainian dissent movement, *Ukrainsky visnyk*, the Lithuanian *Chronicle* has supplied extensive information and documentation on the Soviet violations of the constitutional guarantees of religious freedom the official harassment of the Roman Catholic clergy and faithful, large-scale mani-festations of religious and national protest in Lithuania and the regime's persecution of the Lithuanian dissidents. Nine issues of *Chronicle* had appeared by early 1974.
66. *A Chronicle of Current Events*, No. 18 (5 March 1971), p. 136.
67. See this writer's 'In the Catacombs: The Church in Western Ukraine.' *Tablet*, 16 April 1966, pp. 444–5; M. P. Mchedlov, *Katolitsizm* (Moscow, 1970), pp. 242–6; T. Myhal, 'Kryvavi mify' (The Bloody Myths), *Vitchyzna*, No. 10 (1970), p. 179; and *Ukrainsky visnyk* (Paris, 1971), pp. 56–71.
68. A hostile account of the sect's genesis and activities appears in Ye. Pryshchepa, 'Lyk uniyatskoho dushpastyrya' (The Face of a Uniate Pastor), *Lyudyna svit*, No. 11 (1968), pp. 36–9.
69. *Ukrainsky visnyk*, No. 3 (October 1970 [mimeographed]), p. 60.
70. *Ukrainsky visnyk*, No. 1 (January 1970), pp. 64–71.
71. *Ibid.*, p. 63.
72. *Ibid.*, pp. 59, 63.
73. M. Kryukov, 'Myuridy poluchayut otpor', *Pravda*, 29 March 1970. See also Fletcher, 'Religious Dissent in the U.S.S.R. in the 1960s', *loc. cit.*, pp. 306–8; and G. Wheeler, 'National and Religious Consciousness in Soviet Islam', in M. Hayward and W. C. Fletcher (eds.), *Religion and the Soviet State: A Dilemma of Power* (New York, 1969), pp. 187–98.
74. See, in particular, T. Kichko, *Yudaizm bez prykras* (Judaism Without Embel-lishments) (Kiev, 1963). Cf. J. Rothenberg, 'Jewish Religion in the Soviet. Union', in L. Kochan (ed.), *The Jews in Soviet Russia since 1917* (London, 1970), pp. 177–8.
75. Cf. *samizdat* document 'Yevreiskii vopros v SSSR (Tezisy)' (Jewish Question in the U.S.S.R. [Theses]), *Posev*, 7th special issue (March 1971), p. 63.

76. *New York Times*, 11 November 1969. Some of the Georgian Jews subsequently decided to return to the U.S.S.R.
77. See R. Cohen (ed.), *Let My People Go* (New York, 1971), Ch. 1.
78. V. Moroz, *A Chronicle of Resistance in Ukraine* (Baltimore, 1970), pp. 2, 5, 6.
79. *Ukrainsky visnyk*, No. 3 (October 1970), pp. 86–7.
80. V. Moroz, 'Sered snihiv' (Amidst the Snows), *Suchasnist*, No. 3, (1971), p. 76.
81. See *Posev*, Bol. 27, No. 1 (January 1971), pp. 38–43; *Khronika tekushchikh sobytii*, No. 1(4) (30 April 1968), reported in *Posev*, 1st special issue (August 1969), pp. 12–13; and *Khronika*, No. 19 (30 April 1971), reproduced in *A Chronicle of Current Events* (London, 1971), pp. 180–2.
82. Cf. J. Harris, 'The Dilemma of Dissidence', *Survey*, Vol. 16, No. 1 (78) (Winter 1971), pp. 120–22.
83. *Russkaya mysl* (Paris), 26 June 1969. See also his 1968 letters to Pavel Litvinov in K. Van het Reeve (ed.), *Dear Comrade: Pavel Litvinov and the Voices of Soviet Citizens in Dissent* (New York, 1969), pp. 155–62, and to the Central Committee of the C.P.S.U. in *Novoye Russkoye Slovo*, 2 December 1968.
84. *Khronika tekushchikh sobytii*, No. 5(10) (31 October 1969), reproduced in *Posev*, 3rd special issue (April 1970), p. 8.
85. According to *Posev* (No. 11, 1971, p. 11), 1,432 believers from Naro-Fominsk petitioned the Presidium of the Russian Supreme Soviet, complaining about persistent refusal of the lower government organs to allow the requested registration of an Orthodox parish in the city.
86. *Ibid.*, Vol. 27, No. 5 (May 1971), p. 8.
87. Alexander Solzhenitsyn, *A Lenten Letter to Pimen, Patriarch of All Russia* (Minneapolis, 1972), pp. 7–8.
88. *Ibid.*, p. 8.
89. See Bourdeaux, *Religious Ferment in Russia*, Chs 6 and 7.
90. *Ibid.*, p. 95.
91. As shown by the examination of Bourdeaux's list (*ibid.*, pp. 211–29) and the October 1970 list of 167 imprisoned Baptists circulated by the Council of the E.C.B. Prisoners' Relatives.
92. See an account by a delegation member in V. I. Kozlov, *A Criminal Becomes a Christian in a Russian Prison* (Heightside, 1971), p. 8; as well as Bourdeaux, *Religious Ferment in Russia*, pp. 115–16.
93. P. Ya. Stepanov, *Pro suchasnyi pozkol sered Yevanhelskykh khrystyyan-baptystiv* (About the Contemporary Schism among the Evangelical Christians–Baptists) (Kiev, 1967), pp. 8–9.
94. See Bourdeaux, *Religious Ferment in Russia*, pp. 117–24, 131–5. The confrontation in Moscow involved a 'sit-in' of some 500 C.C.E.C.B. delegates by the building of the Party Central Committee on 16–17 May in a vain attempt to obtain an interview with L. I. Brezhnev.
95. See M. Hayward (ed.), *On Trial: The Soviet State versus 'Abram Tertz' and 'Nikolai Arzhak'* (rev. ed.; New York, 1967); and V. Chornovil, *The Chornovil Papers* (Toronto, 1968).
96. *Izvestiya*, 30 August 1966.
97. See the Resolution of the Presidium of the Supreme Soviet of the R.S.F.S.R. 'O primenenii stati 142 Ugolovnogo kodeksa RSFSR' (On the Application of Art. 142 of the RSFSR Criminal Code), *Vedomosti Verkhovnogo Soveta RSFSR*, No. 12 (24 March 1966), p. 220; as well as the Presidium's decree 'Ob administrativnoi otvetstvennosti za narusheniye zakonodatelstva o religioznykh kultakh', *ibid.*, p. 219. Identical legislation was adopted by other Union Republics.
98. *Ibid.*, p. 220.
99. The Decree of the Presidium of the Supreme Soviet of the R.S.F.S.R.

(duplicated by other Union Republics) 'O vnesenii dopolneniya v Ugolovnoi kodeks RSFSR' (On the Amendment to the RSFSR Criminal Code), *ibid.*, No. 38 (22 September 1966), p. 819.

100. See Bourdeaux, *Religious Ferment in Russia*, pp. 172–182.
101. *RCDA*, Vol. VII, Nos 21–22 (15–30 November 1968), p. 194.
102. Only 5 *initsiativniki* were reportedly arrested in 1967. The data for the years 1967 to 1969 have been supplied by the Council of the E.C.B. Prisoners' Relatives. From January to 10 October 1970, 31 C.C.E.C.B. activists have been arrested.
103. *RCDA*, Vol. IX, Nos 3–4 (February 1970), pp. 13–17.
104. *Izvestiya*, 18 October 1969.
105. *Bratsky vestnik*, No. 2 (1970), cited in *RCDA*, Vol. X, Nos 3–6 (February–March 1971), p. 40.
106. *Bratsky vestnik*, No. 5 (1970), cited in *RCDA*, Vol. X, Nos 7–8 (1971), p. 57.
107. *Ibid.* See, in particular, a mimeographed background paper by M. Bourdeaux, 'Russian Baptists: The Facts (1968–1970)' (9 July 1970), produced by the Centre for the Study of Religion and Communism, pp. 4–6; and M. Bourdeaux and A. Boiter, 'Baptists in the Soviet Union (1960–1971)', Radio Liberty Research Paper, No. 47 (1972), pp. 7–8.
108. Kozlov, *op. cit.*, pp. 9–10.
109. Bourdeaux, 'Russian Baptists', pp. 5–6; see, in particular, a declaration addressed to Soviet leaders by the Council of the E.C.B. Prisoners' Relatives on 10 October 1970; and 'Srochnoye soobshcheniye' of the Council of the same date.
110. Bourdeaux and Boiter, *loc. cit.*, p. 10.
111. Appeal 'Vsem khristianam mira' (To All Christians of the World) from the Second All-Union Congress of the E.C.B. Prisoners' Relatives dated 12–13 December 1970, at Kiev.
112. See this writer's 'Religion in the U.S.S.R. after Khrushchev', *loc. cit.*, pp. 148–9.
113. *Ukrainsky visnyk*, No. 1 (1970), pp. 59–62. For samples of anti-Uniate propaganda, see, in particular, S. Danylenko, *Shlyakhom hanby i zrady* (Along the Path of Shame and Treason) (Kiev, 1969); V. Dobrychev, *U tini svyatoho Yura* (In the Shadow of St George's Cathedral) (Lviv, 1970); and *Lyudyna i svit*, 1969–71, *passim*.
114. *Ukrainsky visnyk*, No. 1 (1970), pp. 61–2; for an official account of Velychkovsky's trial, see M. Byelinsky, 'Yuda. Iz zalu suda', *Vilna Ukraina* (Lviv), 14 December 1969. After serving his sentence, Bishop Velychkovsky was allowed to leave the U.S.S.R.
115. Talantov's obituary appears in *A Chronicle of Current Events*, No. 18 (5 March 1971) (London, 1971), pp. 141–2.
116. Levitin-Krasnov, 'Moye vozvrashcheniye', *loc. cit.*
117. See report of the trial in *A Chronicle of Current Events*, No. 20 (2 July 1971) (London, 1971), pp. 234–7.
118. See *Posev*, Vol. 27, No. 8 (August 1971), p. 6.
119. *Khronika tekushchikh sobytii*, No. 2(13) (30 April 1970), cited in *Posev*, 4th special issue (June 1970), p. 39; cf. *Pravda vostoka*, 12 and 26 July 1970.
120. *A Chronicle of Current Events*, No. 20 (2 July 1971), pp. 246–8.
121. *Khronika tekushchikh sobytii*, No. 2(13) (30 April 1970), cited in *Posev*, 4th special issue (June 1970), p. 16. For a complete text of the Gorky letter, see 'An Appeal from the Orthodox in Gorky', *Eastern Churches Review*, Vol. II, No. 4 (Autumn 1969), pp. 419–22.
122. See G. M. Shimanov, *Notes from the Red House* (Montreal, 1971).
123. Fletcher, 'Religious Dissent in the USSR in the 1960s', *loc. cit.*, p. 316.
124. Cf. A. V. Belov and A. D. Shilkin, *Ideologicheskiye diversii imperializma i religiya* (Ideological Diversions of Imperialism and Religion) (Moscow, 1970).

5 Islam in the Soviet Union

The Religious Factor and the
Nationality Problem in the
Soviet Union

ALEXANDRE BENNIGSEN

Today the Soviet Union counts some forty million people belonging to different social groups – nations (*natsiya*) or sub-nations (*narodnost*) – which before the Revolution were part of the Muslim religions and cultural *Umma*. One Soviet citizen in five has a Muslim background. The U.S.S.R. is the fourth largest Muslim state in the world.

What is the current meaning of the expression 'Moslem' in the Soviet Union? Does it still have a religious, or only a cultural and political, meaning? Officially this expression is never used by the Soviet administration, but Soviet ethnographers, sociologists and historians continue to employ it.

Before the 1917 Revolution, the distinction between religion and culture had no meaning whatsoever. The Muslim peoples of Tsarist Russia, 80 per cent of whom were Turks, were not fully aware of belonging to a 'nation'. 'Azeris' (Azerbaidzhani), 'Tatars', 'Uzbeks', 'Kazakhs', these expressions were never used by the Moslems themselves – neither by the masses nor by the intelligentsia. The masses never went beyond a tribal or a religious consciousness – tribal if they were nomads, religious if sedentaries. The intelligentsia had an extended consciousness of belonging to a 'pan-Turkic', or to a 'pan-Islamic' community – but not to a restricted, modern nation.

The majority of Soviet Muslims belong to the *Sunni* branch of the Hanafi school (the only exception being the Daghestanis who belong to the Shafei School). There is a *Shii* (*Imami* – 'Twelvers') minority: some three million, mostly Azeris, and a small group of

Ismaïlis (less than 50,000) in the Pamirs. Some Bahaïs live in the cities of Central Asia and in Astrakhan.

When speaking of Islam, it is necessary to consider two different aspects: (1) The official aspect, the legal position of the religion; and (2) its psychological or political aspect, the 'Muslim way of life' and its impact on the Russian-Muslim relationship and on the problem of national consciousness.

THE OFFICIAL POSITION OF ISLAM

There exists in the Soviet Union a legal structure for the Muslim religion, created in 1941. When the war broke out Stalin was looking for support among the believers in the population and the result was the signature of a 'concordat' with Rassulaev, the *mufti* of Ufa, and the creation of four 'Spiritual Administrations' (*Nizarat*) for Soviet Muslims – a step similar to the re-establishment of the Russian Orthodox Patriarchate. However, there is a great difference between the Muslim religion and Russian Orthodoxy. A Christian Church cannot exist without an official hierarchy, while the Muslims may perfectly well do without one. Islam is a religion without clerics, and there is no intervening middleman between the believers and God. So the four Spiritual Administrations are not religious but *administrative* bodies. They are not supposed to direct spiritual life, but to control the Muslim community for the benefit of the Soviet power (a parallel with the Spiritual Administration of Orenburg created by Catherine II in the eighteenth century which played a dubious role, being half a police and half a religious administrative body).

The four Spiritual Administrations are: the *Ufa muftiat* (Sunni) for European Russia and Siberia, using Kazan Tatar as its official language; the *Tashkent muftiat* (Sunni), the most important of the four, covering all of Central Asia and Kazakhstan and using the Uzbek language (its chairman, Mufti Ziauddin Babakhanov, often plays a pre-eminent role in Soviet foreign politics); the *Buynaksk muftiat* (Sunni), for Daghestan and the Northern Caucasus, using the classical Arabic language; the *Baku Directorate* (mixed Sunni and Shii). Its authority covers the Trans-Caucasian Sunni communities and the entire Shii population of the Soviet Union. The chairman is the Shii *Sheikh-ul Islam*. The vice-chairman is the Transcaucasian Sunni *mufti*. The official language is Azeri.

Different heterodox sects, such as the Ismaïlis, the Bahaïs, the Yezidis and the Alli-Ilahis of Trans-Caucasia have no recognised administration.

Nothing is known abroad of the internal life of these four bodies. It seems to be limited to the maintenance of the cult in some rare 'working' mosques. There are no *Shariyat* courts to control the Muslim community's legal life, no *waqf* to administer and only very limited publishing activity. During recent years one Koran was published in Tashkent and perhaps another in Ufa, and one religious calendar was also published in Tashkent. There is no other spiritual literature, except for a new journal, *The Muslims of Soviet Union,* in Uzbek (Arabic script), launched recently in Tashkent. Teaching activity is also strictly limited. There is only one *medressèh,* the *Mir-i Arab* of Bukhara, with some hundred students, divided between five or six years, and a rather low level of instruction. It trains readers of the Koran and preachers (*Khatib*), but does not educate real doctors of theology (*Ulema*) or doctors of law (*Kadi, mufti*). Every year between five and ten of the best students completing their studies are sent to the Al-Azhar University in Cairo.

Observers disagree about the number of 'working mosques' in the U.S.S.R. It seems to be very low; probably not more than 400 of 500 altogether (for a total population of some 40 million). The Administrations have also under their control the official clergy, 'the registered mullahs' whose number is probably less than 5,000 (against more than 50,000 before 1917). These are generally old, pre-revolutionary, intellectual survivors of Stalinist purges, with a small number of young graduates from *Mir-i Arab.*

The private or public expression of the Muslim faith is more difficult to appreciate and here one must distinguish between 'official' Islam and what may be called 'unofficial' or 'underground' Islam.

OFFICIAL ISLAM

Here too one must distinguish between private and public life. The private expression of faith is virtually impossible to measure. The individual behaviour of a believer is based on five 'pillars of faith' (*arkan ud-din*), which in theory every believer is compelled to observe. These are:

1. The *zakat:* the legal alms of ten per cent of one's income for the benefit of the poor; it is forbidden by Soviet law.
2. The *hadj,* the pilgrimage to Mecca: this too is nearly impossible as there is but one chartered flight a year, carrying only about thirty or forty pilgrims.
3. The *Uraza* or *Sawn,* the fasting of the month of Ramadhan which is not forbidden officially but is strongly attacked by anti-religious propaganda and its observance is practically impossible outside rural areas, where it seems to be still observed.
4. The *Salat,* the private prayer five times a day. This demonstration is less and less frequently performed anywhere in the Muslim world except in rural areas.
5. The *Shahada,* the profession of faith in one God and in Mohammed, his Prophet, is done by the believer in the secrecy of his heart and thus eludes the control of the authorities.

The public expression of faith may be estimated by the number of believers attending the public, Friday *salat* in mosques, or else by the number of believers present at the great Muslim festivals. Here the testimonies of different observers are conflicting. It seems, on the one hand, that even the largest mosques are almost entirely deserted at the ordinary Friday prayer, with only two or three hundred believers, mostly old men; the only exception being in Azerbaidzhan where Shiism maintains a stronger hold on the believers.

On the other hand, it is obvious that the great Muslim festivals, such as *Aïd al-Kebir* (sacrifice of the Prophet Ibrahim) or the *Aïd al-Fitr* (breaking of the feast of Ramadhan), have a powerful attraction for the Muslim population. Thousands of people assemble, even if they do not observe religious prescriptions. For those who do not practise their religion any more, these festivities are part of national traditions. The enormous crowds (10,000 to 20,000 persons) during the great religious festivals have been noticed by foreign visitors everywhere, in Tashkent, Moscow, Baku and Alma-Ata.

UNOFFICIAL ISLAM

'Unofficial Islam' is the entire body of different organisations, customs and practices which completely escape the control not only of the official Directorates, but also of the Soviet authorities. It appears much stronger than 'official' Islam.

There is a common trend in all religions in the Soviet Union. The official Churches – either Christian or Islamic – hard pressed by the anti-religious activities and propaganda, are, since the Revolution, steadily losing ground. Their hold on the masses is becoming weaker. The position of the official Church is replaced not so much by the official materialist atheism as by a sort of *'Erzatz* religion', 'popular religion', the roots of which go far back to the pre-Islamic tradition (or pre-Christian for the Orthodox Church).

The Orthodox Church knows this phenomenon in the reappearance of innumerable radical-extremist sects, 'Red Dragon', apocalyptic groups which totally reject both the Soviet regime and the official Russian Church, compromised as it is by co-operation with this 'Anti-Christ' state.

In Islam, there are no new heterodox sects and the 'popular' religion is not opposed to official Islam. It is rather a 'parallel religion', a kind of substitute religion, which may be perfectly orthodox, but which also may in its extreme wing, relapse into Shamanism.

Thus, because of the lack of official clerics, their place is taken more and more by unofficial, 'unregistered' mullahs – people with some knowledge of Arabic, who escape control by the Directorates and who perform the familial rites, weddings, circumcision, burials. As the Bukhara *medressèh* is unable to supply necessary clerics, there are, especially in the Caucasus (Daghestan and Chechenia), numerous 'underground mekteps', where unregistered mullahs, often members of a Soufi Brotherhood, are teaching Arabic and prayers. In the same way, instead of 'official' working mosques controlled by the Administration (*Nizarat*), there are 'unofficial' uncontrolled ones, which are much more numerous. According to a recent article in the Azeri (Azerbaidzhani) *Kommunist*,[1] seven *non-official* mosques have recently been built (at the expense of the local Kolkhoz, that is at the State's expense) in the district (*rayon*) of Jelalabad.

According to the same article a traditional, sacred Shii mystery-play ('The Death of Imâm Hüseyin') was recently shown in an Azeri village with more than 5,000 people attending.

Further from pure Islam, are the Soufi *tariqa* ('Brotherhoods'). They are strictly forbidden by law, but according to the Soviet press they are still extremely active, especially in Northern Caucasus (Chechenia, Daghestan). Since the war new *tariqa* have appeared, mostly related to the old Naqshbandiyya. Their practice, such as the public performance of the *zikr,* is often mentioned in the Caucasian press. Still further from Muslim orthodoxy is the cult of different holy places, tombs (*manazar*) of more or less mythical saints (*pîr*), generally situated on sites of pre-Islamic, Zoroastrian or Christian cults. This is an *Erzatz* substitute for the impossible *hadj.* Some of the holy places are famous and attract huge crowds (thousands and even tens of thousands), for example Mount Süleyman in Kirghizia.

Such are the two aspects of official and non-official Islam. However, there is a third aspect of the Moslem religion, which is certainly the most important. It is what one may call 'the Muslim way of life'. It is a broad subject, impossible to analyse in a brief chapter, and therefore attention will be devoted only to the religion's influence on family life and on national consciousness.

The most important event in a young Muslim's life is circumcision. This practice is not forbidden officially by Soviet law, but is constantly denounced in anti-religious propaganda. It is the only clear external sign of belonging to the community of the faithful and the only way to distinguish them from the 'Infidels'. According to Soviet sources circumcision is still practised by almost 100 per cent of the Muslims – including those who are officially beyond the pale of Islam (members of the Communist Party), and is generally presented as a 'hygienic' measure and sometimes even as a 'national tradition'.

The second important event is the wedding. Before the Revolution, a Muslim marriage was governed both by the *shariyat* – the Koranic law – for sedentaries, city-dwellers, the middle and upper classes – and by the *adat* – the customary law for the nomads and some sedentaries (in the Northern Caucasus).

The *adat* had a certain number of customs, traditions and taboos concerning marriages, such as: (a) endogamy among the Turkmens and the North Caucasian Mountaineers; (b) exogamy among the Kazakhs, the Kirghiz and the nomad Uzbeks. Other restrictive customs were designed to protect the clan, the tribe, or the joint family; for example *Kalym* or the buying of a bride (the husband had to compensate the bride's joint family for the loss of a working unit). Another example would be the *Kaytarma,* a vestige of a matriarchal marriage, obliging the husband to live and work in his wife's family. Another example would be the *amengerstvo* or levirat, a custom designed to keep women with the joint family.

Fifty years after the Revolution, what remains of the different *adat* rules concerning marriage, according to the Soviet press?

The *Kalym* is still observed in some rural areas, but it is considered as a sort of second dowry (*mahr*). The *Kaytarma* and the *amengerstvo* are dying out quite rapidly. The exogamous and the endogamous taboos are still observed in rural areas, and sometimes even in the cities.

If the *adat* rules are dying out, the purely Muslim, *Shariyat* rules are still very much observed. According to the *Shariyat* law, a Muslim can marry a woman belonging to the *Ahl al-Kitab* ('The Peoples of the Books' or those who have received the true revelation, i.e. Jews, Christians and Sabeans). In this case the wife may even remain non-Muslim. The contrary, the marriage of a Muslim woman to a Christian or a Jew, was strictly forbidden by the *Shariyat.* Today it seems that Soviet Muslims, even when officially they have a materialist and atheist outlook, still follow closely the rules of the *Shariyat* law.

The marriage between a Muslim and a *Ahl al-Kitab* girl, rare before the Revolution, is still an exception. The marriage between a Muslim girl and a non-Muslim is still considered practically impossible, and in such a case the Muslim girl would be ejected from her community. According to a recent Soviet source, among the mixed marriages registered in Turkmenistan during the last fifty years not a single marriage involved a Turkman girl with a Russian. To appreciate correctly this situation one must keep in mind that the rejection of mixed marriages comes from the Muslims and not from the Russians.

Islam is a religion without a clerical hierarchy, where faith can live and survive without any public or even private observance. The part played by spiritual leaders or religious institutions is secondary. As a consequence, Islam is certainly better suited to resist external pressure than Christianity. In this Islam is similar to Judaism, another religion without a clerical hierarchy.

One can also ascertain that, at least among the masses, the

weakening of the official religious structure is partly compensated by the appearance of a new phenomenon; the emergence of popular half-Islamic, half-Shamanic practices, which elude official control and which are the greatest obstacle to a Russian-Muslim biological or cultural symbiosis.

A second conclusion would be that the 'Muslim way of life' is still strong. Two manifestations, circumcision and marriage, have been mentioned, but there are many others which are often denounced by the Soviet press: for example, the Muslim burial and the existence of purely Muslim cemeteries where all are buried who supposedly belonged to Islam, including members of the Communist Party; sex segregation and a 'feudal' attitude towards women also persist in Muslim regions.

It seems that whether or not Islam is losing its meaning as a religious cult or as a philosophical doctrine, it maintains its social hold and remains the basis of *national self-determination*. It is still a social bond of union which enables the Muslims to differentiate themselves from the Russians. Those who have visited Central Asia may have observed the total segregation of Russians, as well as other Europeans, and Muslims. It is significant that the Christian Turks (Chuvashes, Yakuts, Altayans) are grouped with the Russian population. Segregation thus is not ethnic nor intellectual but religious, and this segregation is encouraged by the Muslims, not by the Russians.

Numerous recent Soviet articles confirm the confusion between religion and national consciousness among Soviet Muslims. A recent inquiry carried out in the native quarter of Tashkent(The Yangi Hayat) is revealing in this connection.[2] It shows that the majority of men and women aged fifty-five and over are believers, although only ten per cent of them scrupulously observe religious rites or regularly attend the Friday prayers in the mosque. Even those who are atheists or indifferent to religion turn to it again when they reach the critical age of fifty-five. They are motivated by loyalty to tradition and even more by national spirit, as well as by the desire not to be excluded from the community of the faithful. The replies obtained by the investigators are particularly significant: 'I am a believer because as an unbeliever I should be a public laughing stock'; and 'I believe because my parents were believers and because one cannot go against one's parents'; and even (and this was the most typical answer) 'I am a believer because I am a Muslim'. This last reply shows that for the Muslims of Central Asia the term Muslim continues to have a meaning which is as national as it is religious.

Another revealing article by a Kirgiz anti-religious propagandist, Doryenov, appeared recently in *Nauka i religiya*[3] 'Am I a Muslim?' Doryenov explains that he was lecturing to a group of Kirghiz Komsomol members, all supposedly atheists, about the reactionary character of Islam. After the lecture, the Komsomol members asked the lecturer whether he was a 'Muslim'. The lecturer, completely disgusted by such a question, replied that being an official atheist he obviously could not be a Muslim. The listeners appeared shocked and astonished: 'How dare you say that you are not a Muslim – you who are a Kirghiz?' For them a Kirghiz has to be *ipso facto* a Muslim. In the same article Doryenov explains that completely atheistic Muslim intellectuals who do not observe religious rituals still consider themselves as 'Muslims' and that the term 'Muslim' is still commonly used in all Soviet Islamic republics – there is even a new expression: the 'non-believing Muslims'.

It is also necessary to mention the attitude of the Soviet authorities towards the Islamic religion.

(a) The Muslim religious authorities are totally loyal to the regime. There are no hints of any opposition to the regime by the 'official' clerics.

(b) It is very likely that non-official Islam, particularly the *tariqa,* is strongly in opposition to the regime.

(c) The Soviet Government very skilfully uses the official Muslim hierarchy. The Muftis, heads of the four Spiritual Administrations, are often seen abroad at different congresses and are sponsored by the Soviet regime.

(d) Since the death of Stalin, the Soviet regime has conducted a steady and massive anti-religious propaganda campaign against Islam. For example, in Usbekistan alone, according to an editorial in the journal *Uzbekistan Kommunist,*[4] entitled 'Necessity to Intensify the Anti-religious Activity', 42,000 lectures on scientific atheism were delivered in 1969–70. There are in addition, twenty-nine People's Universities for atheism and 218 atheistic schools with 3,000 students.[5]

In spite of this gigantic effort, Soviet authorities are constantly complaining of the low quality of anti-religious propaganda. It is dull, boring and totally inefficient, even by normal Soviet standards. Generally it is simply a re-interpretation of the pre-revolutionary anti-Muslim literature by Kazan missionaries and the results of this propaganda are, according to the Soviet press itself, nil. Recently *Uzbekistan Kommunist* stated that there is even a revival of interest in religion among the young generation and that religion (Islam) is making inroads into the Komsomol and the Communist Party.[6]

Should one accept this Soviet conclusion? Yes and no. According to this author's personal observations, the majority of Soviet Muslim intellectuals are 'atheists', or have at least a materialistic outlook. They do not observe the rites and they do not believe, but (1) they remain impregnated with Islamic culture; and (2) they maintain a specific way of life which isolates them from their Russian 'Elder Brothers' and renders difficult or even impossible any biological symbiosis between the Muslims and the Russians. At the same time their attitude towards their traditional religion is becoming more and more positive. One often finds a direct refusal to fight Islam, which is similar to Sultan Galiev's attitude in 1920 – he considered Islam as the most progressive religion. In 1968 the Government of the Tadzhik Republic refused to let an anti-religious (anti-Islamic) film be shown in Tadzhikistan because it was injurious to the national feeling of the Tadzhik people.

NOTES

1. Azeri *Kommunist* (Baku), 4 September 1970.
2. Irbutov, 'V Mahale Yangi Hayat', *Nauka i religiya* (December 1965).
3. Doryenov, 'Am I a Moslem?', *Nauka i religiya*, April 1967.
4. 'Necessity to Intensify the Anti-religious Activity', *Uzbekitan Kommunist* (Tashkent), June 1970.
5. *Ibid.*
6. *Uzbekistan Kommunist*, June 1970.

6 Religion and Nationality: The Uniates of the Ukraine

VASYL MARKUS

The close relationship between organised national religion and nationality is striking in the East European socio-cultural context. Many religious denominations acquired national designations, e.g. Hungarian Church (Calvinists), Polish (Roman Catholic), German (Lutheran), Ruthenian or Ukranian (Uniate, i.e. Catholic Church of Byzantine–Slavonic Rite), etc. In certain cases the religious–ethnic identity has been so prevalent that ethnically different communities of the same religion were considered by common people as also being religiously different.[1]

Eastern Christianity in its two denominational manifestations – Orthodox and Catholic – has become the national religion in the Ukraine, differentiating the native society from past and present dominating nationalities and/or state powers, whether Polish, Russian (at least in the case of the Uniates) or Austro–Hungarian.[2] Practically all serious Ukrainian historians, from conservative Vyacheslav Lypynsky to socialist-populist Mykhaylo Hrushevsky, concur in attributing to the Church the pre-eminent role in the cultural, social and political development of the nation.[3] To a greater extent than elsewhere, religion in the Ukraine has been a nation-building factor. The Ukrainian Cossack political-military organisation in 16th–18th centuries closely identified itself with the Ukrainian Orthodox Church, although the common Orthodox religion which they shared with the Russians was partly instrumental in the political orientation of Cossack leadership towards the 'Orthodox Tsar of All Russia'. Ukrainian Cossacks proudly referred to themselves as the 'defenders of the Orthodox faith'.

When the Church lost its autonomous status and national

character, as in the case of the Orthodox Church in the Russian-ruled Ukraine from the second half of the 18th century, the concept of nationality was emptied of its dynamic content. Before long the Church in the Ukraine, subjected to the centralized rule of St Petersburg, became an instrument of Tsarist autocracy and Russification. The 20th-century movement for church reforms in the Ukraine aimed not only at emancipation from secular rule but also at the Ukrainianisation of the Church, in other words, at its de-Russification. Hence the establishment of the Ukrainian Autocephalous Orthodox Church in 1919–21 which was liquidated by the Soviet regime when its continuous development threatened the designs of Stalin's nationalities policy.[4]

The Uniate Church in the western regions of the Ukraine initially had the possibility of becoming a bridgehead for Polish influence, including cultural Polonisation of the Ukrainian élite. However, due to complex social, political and psychological circumstances, it has fulfilled quite an opposite function.[5] In the Austrian part of the Ukraine, since the end of the 18th century, the Ruthenian (Ukrainian) Church undertook the role of the national catalyst – particularly in the national-cultural revival during the 19th and 20th centuries. Western Ukrainians, termed ironically by Poles as the *naród chłopów i panów* (the people of the priests and peasants), underwent, in the last 150 years, a process of radical transformation into a political nation with strong nationalistic undercurrents, manifested to a great degree through the Ukrainian Catholic (Uniate) Church.

Ruling powers, made apprehensive by the emergence of a Ukrainian political movement, autonomist or separatist, directed their moves against the Ukrainian Church. They recognised that if the native Church with its Ukrainian–Byzantine rite could be taken from the people, or at least weakened in its components, the Ukrainians would become an easy target of Russification, Polonisation, Slovakisation, or eventually, of any type of assimilation in the countries of Ukrainian diaspora. Valentyn Moroz, a young Ukrainian historian, sentenced in 1970 to fourteen years' imprisonment and exile in the U.S.S.R., wrote:

How often in history has religion saved a nation! Particularly, in the situations when change of religion was equivalent to the change of nationality. In a number of villages of Kholm

region the Ukrainians spoke Polish. But they remained
Ukrainians as long as they belonged to the Ukrainian religion
and Church. Likewise, a Polish family in a Ukrainian village
in Zhytomyr region or in Podillya throughout the centuries
remained Polish (without even knowing the Polish language)
as long as they were Roman Catholic.[6]

Several interrelated factors, causes and consequences, may be
singled out to explain the religion-nationality coalescence in the
Ukraine, past and present. Historically, at least during the period
of the Ukraine's political self-assertion, there has been little if
any conflict between the native Church, society and political
power structure. Despite the Byzantine origin of Kievan Christianity, the Kievan State (Rus'–Ukraine) was one of the few
medieval states in Europe where the Church–State relationship
was quite harmonious, i.e. without the dominance of one power
over the other. The Ukrainian-Ruthenian aristocracy was de-
nationalised in the course of the 16th–17th centuries as a result
of the loss of political autonomy and subsequent embracement of
Roman Catholicism and Polish culture by aristocrats. In the
Polish-ruled part of the Ukraine, for a long time, the only spokesmen and representatives of the Ukrainian people were members
of the church hierarchy and other leading churchmen ('spiritual
princes').

Moreover, the Ukrainian lower clergy fully shared the fate of
the people as many of them were at the bottom of the social ladder
in the feudal state of Poland–Lithuania. Married clergy with large
families, although a distinct social class, continuously remained
an organic component of Ukrainian nationality. The sons and
daughters of priests constituted in the 19th and 20th centuries the
class of populist intelligentsia, the prime movers in national revival. Thus, under the most strenuous conditions of national
existence (complete loss of political autonomy), the native religion
remained the last refuge of ethnicity, and as such has become the
vehicle of national renaissance. It was the spiritual source and
institutional framework of cultural, literary and artistic creativity,
so indispensable in modern nationalism.

In at least two stages of the East European nation-building
process (ethnic awakening, cultural self-assertion, the drive for
political self-determination), the rule of religion was primordial

and politically indispensable. The almost complete absence of the Orthodox clergy in the initial stages of the national movement in the Eastern Ukraine (under Russia) resulted in its relatively late emergence and in its general weakness until the Revolution of 1917. Similarly, among the Byelorussians, the national awakening during the 19th and 20th centuries was delayed due, among other factors, to the absence of nationally inspired clergy. It seems that the early liquidation (1839) of the Uniate Church in Byelorussia had a negative effect on the development of the Byelorussian national movement.[7]

SOVIET RELIGIOUS POLICY *vis-à-vis* UNIATES
SINCE 1945

In the light of these observations, it is obvious why Soviet policy-makers were seriously preoccupied with the problem of religion and nationality in the Ukraine. Their policy resulted in the forceful liquidation of two intrinsically national churches during the first thirty years of Soviet rule in the Ukraine.

The Ukrainian Autocephalus Orthodox Church (U.A.P.T.s), headed by Vasyl Lypkivsky, was destroyed by the Soviet authorities in the 1930s. The Autocephalous Church under Metropolitan Polikarp Sikorsky, revived during the German occupation in 1942–44, was also suppressed after the Soviet recapture of the Ukraine and displaced by the official Russian Orthodox Church.[8]

The Uniate Church in the Western Ukraine[9] presented the Soviet regime with more difficult problems. In 1944–45, when the Soviets incorporated the West Ukrainian *oblasti* into the Ukrainian S.S.R., there existed a well-organised religious community of over four million faithful, an entire hierarchy and a Western-educated, nationalistic clergy numbering almost three and a half thousand. The political authorities, in close co-operation with the Russian Orthodox Church, succeeded within five years in formally liquidating the Uniate Church in Galicia and Trans-Carpathia, as well as in the Ukrainian-populated part of Czechoslovakia. The story of this modern 'conversion' is well known, and need not be related here in detail.[10]

After the death of Metropolitan Andrei Sheptytsky (1864–1944) and the succession to the Metropolitan See of Halych of Archbishop Josyf Slipyj, the latter attempted to accommodate his

Church to the new political reality. In December 1944 Metropolitan Slipyj sent a delegation to Moscow in the hope of getting the Soviet Government to recognise the legal status of the Uniate (Greek Catholic) Church in the U.S.S.R. The Soviet authorities did not commit themselves since the plan for the liquidation of the Uniate Church was evidently already conceived.

Just before World War II ended, all Uniate bishops on Soviet territory were arrested and transferred to a Kiev prison along with two others from Peremyshl (now in Polish territory). Soon after an Action Initiative Group was formed, headed by the priest Havryil Kostelnyk, with the aim of 'reuniting' the Greek Catholics with the Russian Orthodox Church. The Group received immediate recognition from the Government of the Ukrainian S.S.R. as the sole provisional church–administrative body over Uniate parishes.

With the help of Party and secret police officials, the Group collected signatures from priests adhering to its programme. These were extorted either under the threat of arrest or, simply, under the false pretence that they were only a declaration of loyalty to the regime. During 1945 alone, over 800 priests were arrested, temporarily held or deported. In response to the activities of the Action Group, and to the persecution of the Uniates, 300 priests sent a letter of protest to the Government in Moscow requesting freedom of religion for the Greek Catholic Church; a freedom guaranteed to all citizens by the Soviet constitution. Instead of answering this plea, the Government intensified the terror against the 'recalcitrants'. At the same time, Patriarch Alexii of Moscow addressed an appeal to the Uniates 'to break all the ties with the Vatican'.

In this climate of fear, the Action Group, with the help of the Orthodox Church hierarchy and Soviet authorities, prepared the final act of the drama. On 8–10 March 1946 a Synod of the Greek Catholic Church was held in Lviv attended by 214 priests and 19 laymen, plus participants from the Orthodox hierarchy and representatives of the Government. The Synod resolved to break the Union of Brest with Rome (1596) and to 'reunite' with the Russian Orthodox Church. The Patriarch of Moscow and the Soviet Government immediately sanctioned this decision. The Lviv Synod was strongly condemned by many Uniates in the U.S.S.R. and by Ukrainians, as well as Vatican spokesmen in the

West as being an 'uncanonical' political tool of an atheist regime, deserving the name of a 'pseudo-Synod'.[11]

None of the nine Ukrainian Uniate bishops attended the Lviv Synod because just before the Synod they had been secretly tried in Kiev. The members of the Uniate hierarchy were sentenced (for alleged collaboration with Nazi occupation authorities and for 'war crimes') to long years of imprisonment and hard labour. Most of the bishops died in prison or concentration camps.[12]

The Uniate Church in Trans-Carpathia (formerly a part of Czechoslovakia and incorporated into the U.S.S.R. in June 1945) was 'reunited' only in 1949 by an act of annulment of the Union of Uzhhorod (1646). Two years before, in November 1947, the local bishop, Theodore Romzha, had been murdered under mysterious circumstances.[13] The Uniate eparchy of Pryashiv (Prešov) in Czechoslovakia followed suit. In April 1950 a 'popular-ecclesiastic' convention terminated the Union with Rome, using the same methods of conversion that were practised in the Western Ukraine.[14] Thus ended, by a political fiat, the 350-year-old Union of the Eastern and Roman Churches in the Ukrainian lands.[15]

What was the role of the nationality factor in the incorporation of the Ukrainian Greek Catholics into the Russian Orthodox Church? In their propaganda, promoters of the 'reunion' have accused the Uniate Church of being Polish-inspired, and of not serving the interests of the Ukrainian people but only of the ruling nations – Poland, Austria, Hungary. Later it was argued that the Church was a tool of other foreign interests, particularly those of the Vatican, with its 'Anti-Communist crusade', and of Nazi Germany. The Uniate clergy and hierarchy, it was charged, had betrayed the cause of the Eastern Slavs and become the bulwark of Roman Catholic expansion against Russia, and also against Orthodox Ukrainians and Byelorussians.[16] In particular, the Uniate Church was accused of making common cause with the Ukrainian nationalists, who in the course of World War II found themselves on the German side fighting the re-establishment of Soviet power in the Ukraine.

On the other hand, noting the national character of the Church in the Ukraine, the authors of the 'reunion' decided to respect, at least temporarily, the ethnic characteristics of the Church in the Western Ukraine, and abstained from making substantive changes in the rituals and local customs. The Ukrainian version of the

Slavonic language was kept in the liturgy; typical Uniate ceremonies and rituals remained initially untouched; a Ukrainian-
language Orthodox monthly was published, etc. Only in 1950
did the Orthodox Archbishop of Lviv, Makary Oksiyuk, initiate
the process of 'orthodoxisation' (*opravoslavlennya*) of former
Uniates by issuing, with other West Ukrainian bishops, a pastoral
letter which listed 'sixteen points to be implemented by the converted priests. The points referred to certain liturgical practices
considered to be the result of Latin Rite influence. These were to
be eliminated from church usage.[17]

The clergy, particularly those of local origin, were kept in the
Western *oblasti* in order to maintain the appearance of continuity
and of the national character of the Orthodox Church in the
Ukraine. Two former Uniate priests, members of the Action
Group, Antoniy Pelvetsky and Mykhaylo Melnyk, were appointed
bishops of Stanyslaviv and Sambir-Drohobych eparchies respectively. The Lviv archeparchy obtained a native, West Ukrainian
hierarch only in 1960 in the person of Hryhorii Zakalyak, now
Archbishop of Uzhhorod. Such considerations did not apply to
the eparchies of the Eastern Ukraine where Russification had
already made strong inroads.

THE UNDERGROUND CHURCH

The Synod of Lviv did not solve the problem of the Uniates. The
'reunion with the Mother Church' was merely a formal act, enforced by the police apparatus, which did not succeed in totally
destroying the Ukrainian Uniate Church. The Church continues
to exist under the most strenuous conditions, as an illegal community, permanently exposed to persecutions and reprisals. Its
members are now dispersed all over the Soviet Union. They may
live in Siberia as forced settlers, after having spent many years
of exile in the labour camps; thousands of them live in the Eastern
Ukraine, outside the traditional Uniate territory.

Only in compact communities, and mainly in remote areas,
are they able to assert their commitment to the Catholic Church
according to traditional religious rites. Otherwise, there is the
family which, if not ethnically mixed and religiously indifferent,
does continue the traditions and practices of the suppressed
Church. The Uniate religion in such cases becomes somewhat
analogous to the Muslim religion, i.e. not an institutionalised

Church with formal hierarchy and status, but rather a psychological attitude and national–cultural identification, with a certain set of customs and practices zealously kept. Major religious feasts are observed within the family or among close friends (Easter, Christmas Eve, religious name-days, etc.). Baptism, religious nuptial rites, and funerals are frequently performed by a Christian priest, often secretly, and some times even by a Uniate priest.

The majority of Uniates maintain the attitude that the performance of certain church functions even by Orthodox priests does not infringe on their Uniate identity and consciousness. This is particularly true if the Orthodox priest is a former Uniate who only superficially adopted the administrative jurisdiction of the Orthodox Church. In general, this seems to be the present state of mind and faith among the majority of believers in the Western Ukraine. They attend services in the same church, often have a local priest, practise virtually the same religious rites and customs, and receive the same sacraments, as they did prior to 1946. For them very little has changed. The common people even make a distinction between the parishes and priests who continue to be 'our own', and those who are exponents of the new ecclesiastical policy and accept fully Russian Orthodoxy.[18] The latter are suspect and avoided by the Uniate faithful.

It is difficult to establish how many former Uniates have totally and sincerely converted to the Orthodox Church. No statistics are available, nor could public opinion be surveyed in this respect. From casual conversation with people from the Ukraine and from reports of tourists, one can estimate that the number of such people is minimal. The majority of the faithful, i.e. those more or less practising the religion, have apparently remained Uniates at heart, as have some 'converted' priests. A certain number of parishes and priests in the late 1950s openly repudiated Orthodoxy in expectation that the Khrushchevian 'thaw' would eventually result in the restoration of the Uniate Church[19]

Moreover, there is a category of Uniates who refuse to accept Orthodoxy and who steadfastly continue to assert their commitment to Catholicism. In a few cases, mainly in West Ukrainian cities where some Latin Rite churches and priests are still active, they are satisfying their religious needs by attending those churches. There were 132 Roman Catholic parishes in 1961 in the Ukraine.[20] Visitors to Lviv report that services in the Roman Catholic cathedral are attended by many Uniates. The genuine 'recalcitrants' depend on the services of 'true' Uniate priests, i.e. those who did not pass to Russian Orthodoxy. Such priests are active, although it is difficult to establish their number. A figure of 200 to 300 now residing in Western *oblasti* would be a conservative guess.[21]

The émigré press frequently publishes the obituaries of priests in the Ukraine, most of whom remained Catholics to the end. In 1955–56 many Uniate priests returned from exile, having survived ten to twelve years' imprisonment. Although some were physically broken, they continued religious services in private. There was also a certain number of priests, monks and nuns who did not sign the act of subjection to the Orthodox Church, and who formally declared themselves as having left the religious life. If not arrested, they continued to perform certain religious functions, such as baptism, confession, liturgical services, funerals, etc., and even offered religious instruction to minors.[22]

The Soviet press reported the existence of theological courses for those aspiring to the priesthood in the Uniate Church.[23] The religious communities, both male and female, also continue their precarious existence and maintain novitiates. Employed in various professions, nuns and monks live in small groups according to monastic rules. They conduct services in private homes, take care of their co-religionists, and are active in charitable work. All the pre-war religious orders and congregations are known to have members. These include the Basilians, Studites, Redemptorists, and, among the female communities, Basilian Sisters, Servants of Immaculate Mary, St Vincent's Sisters, Josephite Sisters, etc.[24]

In the countryside, the religious life of the Uniates is less suppressed. Local authorities occasionally tolerate services in abandoned churches and chapels, which do not have an Orthodox priest and have not been converted into storage quarters. In cases where a priest is not available on Sundays and holidays, the people gather in private homes or in the woods to celebrate matins or vespers, a practice which is permissible according to the church rules. The figure of the travelling Uniate priest going from one village to another is an integral part of the national landscape in the Western Ukraine. In addition, many people are participating in religious services by listening every Sunday to the Vatican

Radio broadcast of liturgy in the Ukrainian–Byzantine Rite, as well as to other religious programmes.

In 1968–69, during a campaign of reprisals against the active priests, at least two dozen names of 'recalcitrants' became known through the Soviet press and from Ukrainian or Russian *samizdat* publications. Their homes were searched, and religious books, vestments and money confiscated. Many were arrested, beaten and then released; others were tried and fined or jailed.[25]

In the autumn of 1968 authorities began a new campaign of closing and transforming certain churches which remained vacant (without priests) into storage places for corn. However, at night the peasants would throw out the stored goods and clean up for Sunday services. In one case, peasants in the village of Mylyatyn decided to protest by not going to work on the collective farm. The strike lasted three days and, finally, the church was saved, although the organisers were fined thirty to fifty roubles each, for 'participating in a religious strike and for opposition to authorities'. A more dramatic event took place in Tysmenytsya in the Ivano-Frankivsk *oblast*. The church was to be demolished, but the people saved it by locking themselves inside prior to the arrival of the demolition crew. They did not leave for several days. Again there were trials as a consequence of this act of religious resistance.[26]

The most revealing event in recent years was the arrest and trial of Bishop Vasyl Velychkovsky.[27] A former Redemptorist abbot, Velychkovsky was condemned to death in 1946, but his sentence then was commuted to ten years' imprisonment. He was released from a Vorkuta camp and has lived in Lviv since 1956. Velychkovsky was secretly consecrated bishop by the Metropolitan Josyf Slipyj, when the latter was still in the U.S.S.R. In the 1960s, there was some evidence that he was co-ordinating the activities of the underground Church. In January 1969 Bishop Velychkovsky was arrested and tried for alleged contacts with Uniate centres abroad, for listening to Vatican broadcasts and for anti-Soviet sermons. According to the Soviet press, he had written a religious book on the miraculous ikon of the Mother of God of Perpetual Help, which contained 'many slanders against the Soviet state'. 'He also attempted', the reports continue, 'to prove that Uniate priests are Ukrainian patriots . . .'.[28] After completing his three-year sentence in a prison in the Donetsk region, the Soviet authorities released Velychkovsky and ordered him to leave the country.[29]

Radical groups among the Uniates assert their opposition to the Soviet religious policy more openly. The Soviet press in the Ukraine occasionally reports on the Uniate group called *Pokutnyky* (Penitents), whose members resort to typical methods of secret sects. They assemble at night in private homes for prayer, religious singing and preaching. They defy the authorities by advocating a negative attitude towards public life and indifference to the economic programmes of the Government. According to their teaching, the Ukrainian people must repent their sins of the past in order to be delivered from their present yoke. The existence of the *Pokutnyky* movement and its fanatical attachment to certain cults (the pilgrimages to the place of 'apparition' of the Holy Virgin in Serednya, the insistence on strict preservation of all the feast days, fasting, etc.) have been pointed out in a recent Soviet publication on religious matters:

> The most strikingly anti-social and anti-Soviet form of intertwining religion and nationalism is the 'Neo-Uniate faith', the so-called *Pokutnyky* movement which found a certain number of followers in the Western *oblasti* of the Ukraine. On the one hand, the Neo-Uniates declare themselves as a purely religious group, a 'genuinely apostolic faith'; on the other hand, they are playing on national feelings by asserting that the Ukraine which 'has been oppressed in captivity and serfdom for long centuries' is being now 'resurrected by God'. Thus, they try to foment hatred of other peoples, primarily of the Russian nation which, allegedly, introduced atheism in the Ukraine. Although the *Pokutnyky* are not widely spread, this, none the less, means that, under particular conditions, there is a possibility of close interaction between religion and nationalism.[30]

Along similar lines, yet in another Uniate milieu, a trend towards a new ideological orientation of Ukrainian Catholicism has been observed. Its existence was confirmed by a Soviet author who, in a book on atheism, wrote about Uniate initiatives 'to establish a Church of Kievan-Christian tradition which would have Orthodox rituals and Catholic dogmas'.[31]

The Soviet press reported 'a marked intensification of the

activities of the former Uniate clergy in separate *oblasti* of the Ukraine in recent times' and their 'illegal agitation' for the re-establishment of the Uniate Church.[32] On a number of occasions, Uniate believers attempted to legalise their Church by petitioning the Soviet authorities to register Uniate parish congregations, according to existing regulations.[33] However, all their requests were refused without explanation.

A Soviet Russian author, in a book on the Catholic Church, also refers to such initiatives on the part of former Uniates in the Ukraine:

> The propaganda of ideas and decisions of Vatican II by the foreign press and radio which is, in one form or another, designed for the Soviet Union, has inspired certain Uniate churchmen. They are spreading among the people, and in particular among the former Uniate faithful who returned to the Orthodox Church, diverse rumours; they slander Soviet reality, inspire letters to various Soviet authorities with demands to restore the Greek Catholic Church in the Ukraine.[34]

The Russian dissidents also acknowledged intensification of religious resistance among Ukrainian Uniates. *The Chronicle of Current Events* reported in 1969 that 'the Eastern Rite Church has become more active in recent years, and the number of its priests detained and beaten up by the police has grown'.[35]

THE RUSSIAN ORTHODOX CHURCH VERSUS UKRAINIAN UNIATES

There can be no doubt that the leaders of the Russian Orthodox Church willingly collaborated with the Soviet Government in the continuous suppression of the Uniate Church. This collaboration was not affected by the fact that the Russian Church, too, became the target of Soviet anti-religious policy. The Uniates in the Western Ukraine, however, were found more dangerous from a political point of view than the Orthodox Church; hence the support given by the regime to the Orthodox leadership in 're-uniting' West Ukrainians.

The Russian Orthodox hierarchy never achieved the desired results in the 'Orthodoxisation' (*opravoslavlennya*) of the Western Ukraine. It had to satisfy itself, at least temporarily, with the formal recognition of the supremacy of the Moscow Patriarchate, as well as with the administrative banning of the Uniate church organisation. Marginal activities of a handful of Uniate priests could be tolerated. However, when such activities became a visible threat to the position of the Orthodox Church in the Ukraine, the Orthodox bishops and clergy began a new struggle against the 'remnants' of the Uniates. In 1968–69, the problem became more serious when news penetrated from neighbouring Czechoslovakia about the restoration of the Uniate Church under the impact of the 'Czech spring'.[36]

This coincided with attempts to legalise the Uniate Church in the U.S.S.R. The unwanted consequences of an eventual restoration of the Eastern Catholic Church were realised by both the Russian Church and the Soviet authorities, and they felt compelled to move vigorously against such attempts. The Government feared the national character of such a Church, and the Orthodox leadership recognised that a Catholic Church with Eastern rites might be attractive to some Orthodox elements disillusioned by the opportunist policy of the Moscow Patriarchate *vis-à-vis* the Communist State.

Consequently, new reprisals against the Uniates began in the autumn of 1968 after the invasion of Czechoslovakia. *Samizdat* sources attribute the initiative for this action to the Kiev Metropolitan Filaret (Denysenko). In 1968 a conference of the Orthodox deans and clergy from the Western Ukraine was held at the monastery of Pochaiv (Volhynia region). At this assembly complaints were raised by some Orthodox priests that the illegal Uniate activities constituted a serious obstacle in discharging their duties, and obstructed the consolidation of Orthodoxy in the Western Ukraine. The Metropolitan promised to request the Soviet Ukrainian authorities to intensify repressive measures against the Uniates. The underground source observes: 'On the basis of this request, instructions were issued by the Procuracy organs that the remnants of the Greek Catholic Church be liquidated before the centenary of Lenin's birth (1970), and thus the Russian Church may be freed from this competition.'[37]

To counteract the influence and popularity of the Uniate Church both at home and abroad, the Orthodox hierarchy intensified their anti-Uniate propaganda. The anniversaries of the liquidation of the Unions of Brest (25th) and of Uzhhorod (20th) were commemorated in the Ukraine with grand éclat. In May

1971 celebrations took place in the city of Lviv with seven Ukrainian bishops, headed by Filaret, the Exarch of the Ukraine, in attendance. The patriarchal *locum tenens,* Metropolitan Pimen, praised the 'reunion' in a special message. Filaret, in his speech, labelled the Uniate Church as 'anti-people and an alien factor' in Ukrainian life and history. 'Instead of church unity', said Filaret, 'it has brought us divisions, hostility and hatred. It suppressed the religious and national self-consciousness of our people . . .'. Moreover, the Union was denounced from the ecumenical point of view. The Kiev Metropolitan stated that the Union of Brest was 'a violation of Christian conscience and it did not serve the unity of faith, but the unity of external organisation and the power of the Roman Church'.[38] None the less, Filaret had to admit that the Lviv Synod of 1946 was made possible 'as a result of Soviet victory in World War II and the liberation of the Western Ukraine'.[39]

Similar arguments and ideological rationalisation for the liquidation of the Uniate Church were presented by Filaret at the Zagorsk *Sobor* two weeks later. Here the Exarch of the Ukraine also expressed the need for a cautious treatment of the 'reunited' Ukrainians, and characterised the religious situation in the Western Ukraine as follows:

> Much has been done by bishops and priests in overcoming the consequences of the Union and in strengthening the Orthodox consciousness. . . . Yet we should not forget that, in the course of 350 years, the Union has left a definite impact on the religious consciousness, as well as on the rituals. The hierarchy and the clergy ought to continue thoughtful efforts to overcome the consequences of the Union, attentively respecting the local church customs which do not contradict the Orthodox faith and teachings.[40]

Among its decisions, the Zagorsk *Sobor* adopted a resolution concerning the dissolved Union of the Ukrainian Church with Rome which read:

> The *Sobor* marks, as a notable event in the life of the Russian Orthodox Church, the return to Orthodoxy in 1946 and 1949 of Greek Catholics in Galicia and Transcarpathia, as well as the annulment of the Brest and Uzhhorod Unions, which in their times were imposed by force.[41]

Filaret's speeches and the *Sobor* resolution set the tone for other official statements by the spokesmen of the R.O.C. Recently the Archbishop of Lviv, Nikolai, gave an interview to a Ukrainian-language Communist weekly in New York. Nikolai's statement, a highly polemical document, was directed against the Ukrainian Catholic hierarchy abroad, headed by Archbishop Major Josyf Slipyj, which had marked the 375th anniversary of the Brest Union by issuing a joint pastoral letter in Rome in October 1971.[42]

Reaction to the continuing existence of the Ukrainian Catholic and Orthodox Churches outside of the Soviet sphere of control, and to the increased interest in them among the Soviet Ukrainian population, is not expressed only in polemics, invectives and reprisals.[43] Both the Moscow Patriarchate and the Soviet regime are trying to neutralise the influence of the Ukrainian churches abroad by granting certain concessions to the national sentiments of Ukrainian believers. In the West Ukrainian eparchies and parishes, the Ukrainian version of Church-Slavonic is still in liturgical use, and the sermons are mostly preached in Ukrainian. Former Uniates are allowed to maintain certain rituals, forms of ecclesiastic vestments and decors, local customs, religious songs and music, all displaying more local characteristics. The ecclesiastical authorities in Moscow and Kiev caution their subordinates against hasty 'Orthodoxisation'.[44]

In the last few years, other limited concessions have been granted to Ukrainians which, at least on the surface, play down the prevailing Russian character of the R.O.C. in the Ukraine. Those concessions, far from being a genuine Ukrainianisation and autonomisation, are manifested in the following measures.

1. The formal status of the Ukrainian Exarchate, the only one existing in the U.S.S.R., has been somewhat upgraded.[45] For the first time a native Ukrainian was named the Exarch in 1966, Filaret Denysenko.

2. The hierarchy in the Ukraine now consists predominantly of ethnic Ukrainians (14 out of 16 bishops). This was not the case in the 1940s and 1950s. A number of native Ukrainians serve as bishops in other parts of the U.S.S.R., and even abroad. In the ranks of the hierarchy in the Ukraine there are presently three former Uniates: Nikolai Yuryk of Lviv-Ternopil (promoted in 1971 to the rank

of Metropolitan), Yosyf Savrash of Ivano-Frankivsk, and
Hryhorii Zakalyak of Uzhhorod-Mukachiv.

3. Recently, a greater role was assigned to Kiev for activities
outside the U.S.S.R. In December 1969 a Ukrainian
branch of the Patriarchate's Department of External
Ecclesiastical Relations was established in Kiev.[46] A vicar
of the Kievan Metropolitan, Bishop Makariy Svystun,
was placed in charge of all patriarchal parishes in Canada
and the United States.

4. In 1968 the publication of the Ukrainian Orthodox
monthly *Pravoslavny visnyk* was resumed (having started
in Lviv in 1946,[47] but suspended in 1963). Initially intended only for Western Ukrainian eparchies, the
monthly was later made into the official publication of
the Ukrainian Exarchate with the editorial offices transferred to Kiev. For the first time since the 1920s, an
Orthodox prayer book was published in 1968 in
Ukrainian and the Ukrainian rendition of Church-
Slavonic. There is also a modest annual edition of the
Church Calendar in Ukrainian.

During the last few years the Soviet Government and Moscow
Patriarchate have followed closely and with some concern certain
activities in the Ukrainian churches abroad. These include efforts
by the Ukrainian Catholics to establish their own Patriarchate (of
Kiev-Halych) within the Catholic Church, and a parallel movement among the Ukrainian Orthodox to consolidate their several
jurisdictions into the single Ukrainian Orthodox Autocephalous
Church.[48] Not surprisingly, the Ukrainian problem has promi-
mently figured in Moscow's recent diplomatic and ecumenical
contacts with the Holy See, and in its relations with the Ecumenical
Patriarchate of Constantinople. For the improvement of Soviet-
Vatican relations, and expanded ecumenical dialogue, in which
the Roman Curia is strongly interested, Moscow presents a high
price: recognition of the *fait accompli* of the liquidation of the
Uniate Church in the Ukraine: less stress on the existence of the
Ukrainian Catholic Church in the West; and cessation of any
support for the Ukranian religious and national aspirations. There
are, apparently, influential circles in the Vatican which attentively
follow such suggestions and overtures.[49]

At the same time both the Moscow Patriarchate and the Soviet anti-religious press have been attacking the Ukrainian Autocephalous Orthodox Church – its past activities in the Ukraine and its continued existence abroad. One of the most recent attacks appeared in the well publicised message of March 1972, addressed by Patriarch Pimen of Moscow to the Ecumenical Patriarch, attempting to dissuade Constantinople from any contacts with this 'schismatic' and 'chauvinistic' Church.[50]

Despite a continuing propaganda barrage against the two Ukrainian national churches,[51] there have been many indications of a rising interest in the Ukrainian religious heritage among the Ukrainian intelligentsia and youth. In the face of intensified denationalisation pressures, the young creative intelligentsia, in particular, has shown an increasing awareness of the close, intimate links between traditional religion, native culture and nationality. Hence their revived interest in theology and liturgy, religious tradition and customs, and church music, art and architecture. It appears that the present Ukrainian generation is anxious to preserve these values as part of their national heritage. Consequently it is not surprising that the government-sponsored Society for the Protection of Historical Monuments has found a genuine response among many people, since, through it, they attempt to preserve some old churches, ikons and other religious artistic objects.[52]

Some young artists and literati in the contemporary Ukraine are religiously inspired in the most genuine way. The woodcuts of Borys Soroka revive Ukrainian pre-Christian mythology, as well as biblical themes. A young poet, Ihor Kalynets, pours directly from the foundation of religious imagery and resounds like a real Christian bard preaching evangelical virtues, sacrifice and piety.[53]

This national-religious awareness of the intelligentsia helps to explain the tremendous popularity of the officially published novel *Sobor* (The Cathedral) by a leading Ukrainian Soviet novelist, Oles Honchar. The novel – 100,000 copies were printed – was belatedly criticised, and as a result its second printing was confiscated and destroyed.[54] In this work, Honchar sings an ode to a Baroque Cossack cathedral standing for the Ukraine's national past and for her present national distinctiveness. It is a symbol of the permanence and survival of the Ukrainian nation. Honchar's novel castigates the bureaucrats and 'poachers' of national monuments, anxious to destroy the cathedral. 'Guard the cathedrals of your souls, friends. Yes, the cathedrals of your souls!', exclaims one of the characters of the novel to his contemporaries and to the future generations.

This close linkage between national culture and religious tradition was dramatised by a leading Ukrainian dissident intellectual, Valentyn Moroz, in his essay 'The Chronicle of Resistance'. Writing about the Uniate Church in the Western Ukraine, Moroz summed up the new awareness of the young Ukrainian intelligentsia:

> . . . the most convenient way of destroying foundations of a nation is to employ the pretext of fighting against the Church. The Church has grown into cultural life so deeply that it is impossible to touch it without damaging the spiritual structure of the nation. It is impossible to imagine traditional values without the Church. Finally, one must understand that the struggle against the Church means a struggle against the culture.[55]

NOTES

1. Ukrainian Catholics or Uniates were rarely referred to simply as Catholics; they were called Greek Catholics or, at the present time, Ukrainian Catholics, somewhat separate from other Catholics in their own mind, and in the popular opinion of their non-Ukrainian co-religionists.
2. Asked about their nationality, the people often identified themselves as being Orthodox or Uniates or, when asked about their religion, they would answer as being of the 'Ruthenian faith' (*Ruska vira*).
3. M. Hrushevsky, *Z istorii relihiynoi dumky na Ukraini* (From the History of Religious Thought in the Ukraine) (Lviv, 1925); V. Lypynsky, *Relihiya i Tserkva v istorii Ukrainy* (Religion and the Church in the History of the Ukraine) (Philadelphia, 1925).
4. This is recognised even by such critics of Ukrainian and Byelorussian Autocephaly as Harvey Fireside, *Icon and Swastika. The Russian Orthodox Church under Nazi and Soviet Control* (Cambridge, Mass., 1971).
5. For the historical treatment of the Union of Brest (1596) and of the Uniate Church, see *Ukraine: A Concise Encyclopaedia* (Toronto, 1971), Vol. II. This writer presented his critical assessment of the Union and its aftermath for Ukrainian religious and political developments in a recent article 'Beresteyska Uniya z suchasnoi perspektyvy' (The Union of Brest from a Contemporary Perspective), *Ukrainsky Samostiinyk* (Munich), Nos 10, 11, October, Nos 11, 12, November–December 1972.
6. 'Khronika oporu' of V. Moroz was published abroad in many Ukrainian periodicals, among others, *Ukrainsky Samostiinyk*, October 1970 (translation mine). English edition: *Chronicle of Resistance in Ukraine* (Baltimore, 1970).

7. According to Moroz: 'In the conditions of Eastern Europe, the Church was the only force independent of authorities. Let us take the Ukrainian renaissance in Galicia. What a miserable role the teacher played here in comparison to that of the priest! The teacher was a state employee; he trembled in order not to be dismissed from his work. A priest did not share this fear. The majority of the Ukrainian cultural leaders came from a priestly background. The priest was often and justly criticised, but it must not be forgotten that he was the one on whose shoulders the Ukrainian movement rested. It should be clearly stated that it was the Ukrainian Church which constituted the barrier against Polonization in Galicia' (*ibid.*).

8. The fullest, though not necessarily sympathetic Western treatment of Ukrainian Autocephaly, appears in F. Heyer, *Die Orthodoxe Kirche in der Ukraine von 1917 bis 1945* (Köln-Braunsfeld, 1953).

9. Until recently, the official name of this Church was the 'Greek Catholic Church' and this name is still used in the Ukraine. In the 1950s, the Uniates abroad began to use the name 'The Ukrainian Catholic Church', a practice to which the Vatican also adheres.

10. On the fate of the Uniate Church after 1945 see *First Victims of Communism* (Rome, 1953); I. Hrynioch, 'The Destruction of the Ukrainian Catholic Church in the Soviet Union', *Prologue* (New York), Vol. IV (1960), pp. 5–51; and B. Bociurkiw, 'The Uniate Church in the Soviet Ukraine: A Case Study in Soviet Church Policy', *Canadian Slavonic Papers*, Vol. VII (1965), pp. 89–113.

11. For the official Synod proceedings, see *Diyannia Soboru Hreko-Katolytskoi Tserkvy u Lvovi 8–10. III. 1946* (Lviv, 1946).

12. Metropolitan Josyf Slipyj (tried several times) spent 18 years in prison and labour camps, was liberated in 1963, and now lives in Rome; he is the only surviving member of the war-time Uniate hierarchy in the Ukraine; Bishop Hryhoriy Khomyshyn of Stanyslaviv (died in 1948 in prison); Bishop-auxiliary Ivan Lyatyshevsky of Stanyslaviv (spent 10 years in a concentration camp, died in 1957); Bishop Yosafat Kotsylovsky of Peremyshl (died in prison in 1947); Bishop-auxiliary Hryhoriy Lakota of Peremyshl (died in labour camp in 1950); Bishop-auxiliary Nykyta Budka of Lviv (died in labour camp in 1949); Bishop Mykola Charnetsky, Exarch of Volhynia (died after 10 years' imprisonment, in 1959); Monsignor Petro Werhun, Apostolic Administrator for Ukrainians in Germany (died in Siberia in 1957).

13. R. N. 'Holhota Unii v Karpatskii Ukraini' (Golgotha of the Union in the Carpatho-Ukraine), *Zhyttya i slovo* (Innsbruck), Vol. 3–4 (1948–49), pp. 327–46 (an eye-witness report).

14. Bishop Pavlo Goidych was arrested in 1950, condemned to life imprisonment, and died in prison in 1960. His Auxiliary, Vasyl Hopko, was arrested at the same time and held without trial in prison until 1967. He is now residing in Pryashiv (Prešov), pursuing his archpastoral duties but has not been entrusted by the Vatican with the administration of the rehabilitated Greek Catholic Church of Czechoslovakia. See J. Kubinyi, *The History of Prjašiv Eparchy* (Rome, 1970); *The Tragedy of the Greek-Catholic Church in Czechoslovakia* (New York, 1971).

15. The Uniate Church in Eastern Europe was preserved only in Yugoslavia (Ruthenian–Ukrainian and Croatian faithful, numbering 50,000), Hungary (mostly Hungarians and partly Magyarised Ruthenians, 200,000), and in Bulgaria (20,000 Uniate Bulgarians). In Poland the Uniate Church is tolerated, but is not recognised by the authorities and has no hierarchy of its own. There now are approximately 200–300,000 Ukrainian Uniates in Poland. This is due either to the fact that Soviet influence on the religious policies of these countries was not total, or that these religious minorities were politically

120   *Religion and Atheism in the U.S.S.R. and Eastern Europe*

insignificant. In Romania, however, the Uniate Church, numbering over 1,500,000 (among them some 20–25,000 Ukrainians) was forcefully 'reunited' in 1948 with the Romanian Orthodox Church.

16. Particularly attacked were the activities of the late Metropolitan Sheptytsky: his interest in the Slavic East prior to and during World War I, his creation of the Russian Catholic Exarchate, and his contacts with Byelorussians, as well as with the Ukrainian Orthodox leaders. See the pamphlet by V. Rosovych (Ya. Halan), *Ƶ khrestom chy nozhem* (With a Cross or a Knife?) (Lviv, 1946).

17. *Pravoslavny visnyk*, No. 8 (1968), a jubilee article by Archbishop Nikolai of Lviv, p. 17; see also B. R. Bociurkiw, 'The Orthodox Church and the Soviet Regime in the Ukraine, 1953–1971', *Canadian Slavonic Papers*, Vol. XIV, No. 2 (1972), pp. 191–211.

18. In a few West Ukrainian cities special 'Russian parishes' were open for believers who came there from Russia (Bociurkiw, *loc. cit.*, p. 198).

19. *Ibid.*, p. 199.

20. *Ukrainska Radyanska Entsyklopediya*, Vol. VI (Kiev, 1961), p. 253.

21. A. Montonati, 'Il Cristo Distrutto dei Cattolici Ucraini', *Famiglia Cristiana* (16 April 1972), gives the figure of 300 individuals who joined the priesthood and religious orders *after* 1946.

22. According to underground reports published abroad, a priest in the village of Yaremche was sentenced in 1968 to two years' prison for teaching children catechism. The *samizdat* journal, *Ukrainsky visnyk*, Vol. I–II (Paris, 1971) and Vol. III (Winnipeg, 1971) covers the resistance of Uniates and Soviet reprisals in the Ukraine. See also 'Die Ukrainische Kirche lebt. Ein Dokument aus der Verfolgung', *Der Fels* (Regensburg), No. 5 (1972), pp. 146–9.

23. *Lvovskaya pravda*, reporting on the trial of Bishop Velychkovsky in January 1969, mentioned that he helped set up such training in the city of Ternopil. Cf. *Tserkovny Kalendar* (Chicago, 1971), p. 151. Another priest, Fr Bakhtalovsky from Kolomyya, was tried in October 1969 for secretly giving lectures in theology to a group of people. Cf. *Der Fels, loc. cit.*

24. Information on the situation of religious orders is based on the reports of recent visitors to the Ukraine.

25. This happened in villages of the Horodok *rayon* to the Uniate priests Roman Choliy, Petro Horodetsky and Petro Pyrizhok. Cf. *Ukrainsky visnyk*, Vol. I–II, *loc. cit.* and *Der Fels, loc. cit.*

26. The village blacksmith Vasyl Vasylyk was sentenced to seven years in a labour camp, and another peasant Dzyurban to five years. The indictment cited Article 62 of the Penal Code of the Ukrainian S.S.R. (anti-Soviet agitation). Cf. *Ukrainsky visnyk* and *Der Fels, loc. cit.*

27. Velychkovsky is one of several secretly consecrated Uniate bishops in the Ukraine. Their names are publicised neither by the Soviet press, nor by Uniate sources. However, their existence can be proven by reports of priestly ordinations.

28. *Vilna Ukraina* (Lviv), 14 December 1969.

29 Velychkovsky was first sent to Yugoslavia, and since the end of February 1972 he has resided in Rome. Western news agencies and press took notice of his release, and in February 1972 reported more or less correctly on his life and activities. Official Vatican sources were silent on his identity as a bishop, and referred to him only as 'Father Velychkovsky'. He settled in Canada in July 1972 with the title of 'Bishop of Lutsk', and died on 30 June 1973.

30. V. L. Bodnar, 'Osobennosti razvitiya ateizma v protsesse kulturnoi revolyutsii v nationalnoi respublike (na materialakh zapadnykh oblastei USSR')' (The Specifics of the Development of Atheism in the Process of Cultural Revolu-

tion in a Union Republic [Based on the materials from the Western Oblasti of the Ukrainian S.S.R.]) in *Ateizm i sotsialisticheskaya kultura* (Atheism and Socialist Culture) (Moscow 1971), pp. 37–52. See also B. R. Bociurkiw, *loc. cit.*; *Ukrainsky visnyk*, Vol. III., *loc. cit.*, stresses the 'increasing influence of this group in the Western Ukraine', and attributes to it 'not only religious but also national opposition character'.

31. It is noteworthy that a similar ideological trend exists among Uniates abroad.
32. B. Bychatin and O. Suhak, 'Pered sudom istorii. Uniya-yakoyu vona ye' (Before the Court of History: Union as It Is), *Robitnycha hazeta* (Kiev), 15 March 1973.
33. In villages of Mokhany of Horodok *raion*, Khorosnytsya of Mostyska *rayon*, and others. Cf. *Der Fels*, *loc. cit.*
34. M. P. Mchedlov, *Katolitsizm* (Catholicism) (Moscow, 1970), p. 243. The author denounced the Pope's pronouncements, during his Fatima pilgrimage, on the 'Church of silence' which 'are nourishing the Uniates' activity'. He also attacks Cardinal Slipyj and the émigrés: 'It is not accidental that the attempts to artificially restore the Greek Uniate Church in the Ukraine and to consolidate its organisation, as well as to unite Ukrainian ecclesiastical entities, received support from both the Ukrainian counter-revolutionary clergy in exile, and from the lay bourgeois nationalists' (p. 245).
35. *U. S. News and World Reports*, 5 June 1972.
36. The Western press suggested that one of the Soviet motives for invading Czechoslovakia and cutting short the Prague experiment in democratic socialism was the fear of repercussions in the neighbouring Ukraine. On the religious front there was a rapid revival of the Eastern Rite Catholic Church in Slovakia, a tempting example for Uniates in the Ukraine. 204 out of the 240 'converted' Orthodox parishes opted in 1968–69 for Uniatism. Also, the Uniate hierarchy was re-established, and is tolerated even now, in what is one of the few vestiges of the 1968 liberalisation.
37. *Der Fels*, *loc. cit.* The same source mentions another measure taken by the Orthodox hierarchy: the dismissal of certain unreliable priests from among the former Uniates.
38. *Pravoslavny visnyk*, No. 7 (1971), p. 10.
39. *Ibid.*, p. 13.
40. *Zhurnal Moskovskoi Patriarkhii*, No. 8 (1971), pp. 7–14.
41. *Ibid.*, No. 6 (1971), p. 3.
42. *Ukrainski Visti* (New York), March 30, 1972. Nikolai characterised the Rome jubilee observances and the pastoral letter as 'a falsification of the situation of the Church and the people in the Ukraine'. 'Its authors', said the Orthodox prelate, 'aim to sow national animosity among brotherly nations of the Soviet Union, especially between the Ukrainian and Russian peoples'.
43. One of the critics, a Uniate priest, H. Budzynovsky (arrested in 1969), argues against the Russian character of the Orthodox Church in the Ukraine as follows: 'The Orthodox Church does not exist as a whole, but as separate Churches: Russian, Georgian, Armenian, Polish, Czechoslovak, etc. However, in fact, there is no Ukrainian Orthodox Church [in the Soviet sphere of influence. – V.M.]. In the Ukraine, the Russian Church is dominating with all the consequences following thereof. The Ukrainian language is prohibited [in the church] like in the times of the Romanovs . . . . Those were not true Orthodox people who forced others to accept Russian religion, but actually the protagonists of the godless sect of militant atheism. It is an undeniable fact that the Russian Church ceased to be an authentic Orthodox Church and turned into an atheistic-Orthodox one. . . .' See *Ukrainsky visnyk*, Vol.

I–II, *loc. cit.* Dissatisfaction with the Soviet religious policy also is felt by certain Orthodox quarters in the Ukraine. In January 1972 an Orthodox priest, Vasyl Romanyuk from Kosmach, was arrested. He wrote a letter in defence of dissident V. Moroz to the Supreme Soviet of the Ukrainian S.S.R.

44. *Pravoslavny visnyk*, No. 7 (1971), p. 12.

45. The status of the Ukrainian Exarchate (established in 1921) is not constitutionally defined as that of an autonomous Church. It is rather an honorific title due to traditional privileges of the Kiev Metropoly. Ukrainian eparchies are directly ruled by the Synod in Moscow. *Mutatis mutandis*, its status is reminiscent of the Soviet statehood of the Ukrainian S.S.R.

46. B. R. Bociurkiw, *loc. cit.*, pp. 209–10.

47. From January 1946 to January 1948 the publication was entitled *Eparkhiyalny visnyk*.

48. Filaret devoted considerable attention in his speech at the Zagorsk *Sobor* to both Ukrainian Churches. See *Zhurnal Moskovskoi Patriarkhii*, No. 8 (1971), pp. 7–14.

49. Both the Russian Church and the Vatican oppose, for their own reasons, the establishment of the Ukrainian Catholic Patriarchate, qualifying such aspirations as nationalist and politically inspired. Cardinal Willebrands as the head of the Roman Catholic delegation at the *Sobor* in 1971, did not object to the *Sobor*'s decision confirming the annulment of the Union of Brest which, for over twenty years, was considered by the Holy See to be an act of violence and injustice. Nikolai of Lviv labelled the idea of a Ukrainian Catholic Patriarchate as 'directed against the interest of Ukrainian people and detrimental to our beloved fatherland'. Cf. *Ukrainski visti* (New York), 30 March 1972.

50. See *Zhurnal Moskovskoi Patriarkhii*, No. 5 (1972), pp. 7–8.

51. Here is an incomplete list of titles (in English translation) of polemical books and pamphlets, published recently in the Ukraine, against the Uniate Church: *In the Shadow of St. George's Cathedral*, by V. Dobrych; *Celestial Manna*, by A. Hrabovskyi; *The Ideology of Treason and Corruption*, by A. Shysh; *Night Birds*, by V. Byelyaev; *Following the Path of Infamy and Treason*, by S. Danylenko; *The Cross and Treason*, by V. Symakovych; *When Dawns Crimsoned*, by S. Marchuk; *Indivisible Boundaries*, by M. Postnikov; *The Real Face of the Union*, by R. Dubovyk; *The Truth about the Union* (documents and materials); *An Alliance of Swastika and Trident*; *Coadjutor with the Right of Successor*. See also S. Danylenko, *Uniaty* (Moscow, 1972). A special 'documentary' film, *Since the Times History Remembers*, was produced to prove the anti-Soviet record of the Uniate Church.

52. The Society, although a public organisation, is not capable of seriously tackling its objectives; often Party considerations prevail over the historical and conservationist. Because of this, many patriotic individuals resort to personal initiatives: private collections of rare books, icons, organisation of little memorial museums, protection of the cemeteries of Ukrainian soldiers, etc.

53. Kalynets' poems which could not pass Soviet censorship were published abroad under the title *Poezii z Ukrainy* (Poetry from the Ukraine) (Brussels, 1970).

54. Three editions of *Sobor* were published abroad in Ukrainian; the novel is now also available in German and Polish translations.

55. V. Moroz, *Khronika oporu, loc. cit.*

7 Religious Behaviour and Socio-cultural Change in the Soviet Union

ETHEL DUNN AND STEPHEN P. DUNN

I. INTRODUCTION

The present paper has two major aims. First, we will undertake to state in general terms the model for the social interpretation of religious behaviour developed by Soviet sociologists of religion. Secondly, we will undertake to test this model against the facts adduced by these same scholars in order to evaluate its effectiveness.

Certain implications of the method proposed need to be emphasised. In particular the method implies that we accept (for the purposes of the argument) the philosophical interpretation of religion developed and adhered to by Soviet Marxist scholars. According to this interpretation, religion is a fantastic reflection of physical and social reality in the mind of man. In class society, a particular religious outlook serves as the ideology of a specific class or other social group – i.e. as a justification of its position in society. It follows that in a society without antagonistic classes such as Soviet scholars assume their own society to be, religion cannot exist, or at least can exist only as a 'survival'[1] – something preserved by a kind of social inertia and out of keeping with the present social order. From this it follows in turn that observed instances of religious behaviour in the Soviet context require specific explanation in each case.

It should be emphasised that in speaking of the survival or non-survival of religion in Soviet society, we and our Soviet colleagues are referring to religion *as a social phenomenon,* which has discernible effects on outward behaviour, and not as an abstract attitude of the individual alone in his study. This latter aspect is not in general amenable to sociological investigation.

The method chosen for this paper also precludes us from making any independent judgement as to the *facts* reported by Soviet sociologists of religion. This limitation is more apparent than real, since in any case we are not in a position to make independent observations. In short, our method obliges us to operate entirely within the empirical and conceptual framework established in our sources. We of course have our own point of view in regard to the interpretation of the facts and will set forth this point of view in the closing section.

II. RELIGIOUS BEHAVIOUR IN TSARIST RUSSIA AND THE SOVIET UNION AS VIEWED BY SOVIET SCHOLARS

In this section, we will state in general terms the model used by Soviet sociologists of religion to explain the changes which have taken place in religious behaviour among the Russians over the course of history and those currently taking place. In accordance with Marxist assumptions, this topic falls into two parts: religious behaviour before the Revolution – i.e. under the conditions of class society; and under the Soviet regime. Different forces are assumed to be at work during these two periods, even though the process itself is unified.

The ebb and flow of sectarian movements in Tsarist Russia and in the Soviet period has been brilliantly set forth by A. I. Klibanov,[2] who writes:

> Russian religious dissidence falls into that category of socio-historical movements which it is customary to term those of religious reformation. It possesses features differentiating it from the movements of religious reformation which had taken place in Western and Central Europe in the 15th–17th centuries. A reformational movement in Russia, in the form of anti-feudal heresies, developed at the same time as the Reformation in the West. But at that time, the Russian movements of reformation were, if not exclusively, then predominantly urban in character.

But in the 15th–17th centuries, the peasants did not respond, as they did in Germany, to urban movements for reformation, and

the spiritual dictatorship and economic oppression of the Orthodox Church were not broken by a battle of national dimensions.
In the 18th century, with increasing class stratification, 'religious
dissidence appeared as a kind of "second edition" of the reforma-
tional movements', with its principal support in the villages. This
time, however, support was lacking in the towns, and 'religious
dissidence offered no prospects of ever becoming a universal form
of peasant movement'. Klibanov further says that sectarian religious dissidence was

> a sharp protest against the church, the clergy and the entire
> organisation and system of Orthodoxy, which gave its blessing
> to the system of serfdom. Reverence for ikons, belief in
> miracle workers, reverence for the letter of the Holy Writ,
> and the luxurious church ceremonial and ritual were con-
> demned by the dissidents as worship of the 'God of the dead',
> as superficial, false faith for the purposes of display. Con-
> trasted to all this was a faith based on 'internal conviction'
> and service to God 'in spirit and in truth.' In contrast to the
> established, ruling church, there developed the formula: a
> man is his own church. This ideology of anti-feudal protest
> contained a positive ideological element.
>
> The . . . appeal to individual freedom, to a man's inner
> conviction, and [the] expressed confidence in man's intellec-
> tual and moral strength, enable [religious dissidents] to pro-
> claim man 'the living temple' – all represented the founding
> in the peasant environment of the ideology of bourgeois
> individualism, clothed in religious guise.

Apparently for Klibanov it is the condemnation of the established
Orthodox Church, which supported serfdom, that is positive.
Unconsciously, the peasant was

> striving for the bourgeois order of things, in which the
> peasants hoped to take their place as free commodity-pro-
> ducers. This is why the world view of the modern religious
> dissidents is a bourgeois ideological survival in the most
> exact sense of those words. The world view of religious dis-
> sidence thus differs from that of Orthodoxy which, while
> it pays tribute to bourgeois ideology, also bore and still
> bears an enormous burden of ideological carry-overs from

feudalism. It must not be forgotten that the Orthodox Church made its appearance in Russia many centuries before religious dissidence and unswervingly served the feudal lords and serf-owners throughout its history.

Religious dissidence in Tsarist Russia was a 'profoundly contra-dictory phenomenon', which was 'not adapted to active participa-tion in the social struggle', and which became reactionary by 1905 (with the first Russian Revolution). Klibanov quotes an in-teresting passage from Marx[3] in support of this thesis: 'Sects have their (historical) justification so long as the working class has not yet matured to [*sic*] independent historical movement. As soon as it attains this maturity, all sects become essentially reactionary.'[4]

Klibanov rejects the rational–mystical classification of sects and sees the fragmentation of religious groups into new sects as a manifestation of the class struggle. It is noteworthy that in his latest book Klibanov asserts that at the end of the 1920s sects of Western origin (Baptists, Adventists, Pentecostalists, Jehovah's Witnesses) experienced a decline, as had sects of Russian origin (Molokans, Dukhobors, Khlysty) earlier, 'with this difference: no new forms of sectarianism arose to replace them'.[5] He considers that the True Orthodox Christians (I.P.Kh.) and the True Orthodox Church (I.P.Ts.) are not sects, but Orthodox move-ments, outside the Church.

In the 20th century, 'parallel to a bourgeois-reactionary orien-tation, the principle of religious individualism has taken on a directly anti-social meaning. . . . The counterposing of the "inner man" to social man is what is distinctive in the "philosophy" of late religious dissidence. . . .' The sects became 'a historical anachronism' even though there was good reason for them to con-tinue to exist and even experience a renaissance in the Soviet period, 'as long as the millions of toiling folk of the countryside functioned in fragmented individual forms,' and as long as there were kulaks.[6] During World War II, and into the middle 1950s in Central Russia, and the late 1950s and early 1960s in Kazakh-stan, for example,[7] sectarian movements experienced some growth, but Klibanov asserts that the trend is downward, because sectarian movements have been abandoned by working people, becoming the province of the elderly, the female, and to some extent the alienated segments of Soviet society.[8] Klibanov suggests that the preoccupation with theological issues that characterised sectarian movements (primarily asserted in the idea that inner change preceded social change) in the period of revolution has today been greatly intensified: 'Central to this ideology is the concept of man entirely absorbed by his relationship to God and, on that basis, condemnatory of any active attitude toward society.' This is why religious dissidence is 'profoundly reactionary . . . a distorted survival of capitalist society.'[9]

Klibanov's precise statement of the Marxist model for explaining the behaviour of sectarian groups was first published in 1961 and prepared the way for numerous sociological studies, based on statistics and the attitudes of the believers themselves rather than on an ideologically dictated assumption that all sectarians are hostile to the Soviet regime and potentially dangerous.[10] The changes over the succeeding decade in the Soviet model for studying religious behaviour have been very slight, so slight as to be perhaps better classified as refinements. For instance, Klibanov now states that there can be a contradiction between 'the social practice of believers and their religious views,' as well as, by implication, between the believer's personal views and those of his religious community.[11]

In turn, L. N. Mitrokhin stresses the social nature of religious beliefs in a manner calculated to place sociology of religion within the broader framework of Soviet sociology:

> Religion is not simply an error of the mind, not some 'incorrect' conception of this or that law of nature and society. It is a world-view, reflecting and embodying a definite attitude of man towards society, a definite understanding of his place in it. Education (if, of course, we take it not from a formal point of view but as a means of assimilating sociocultural values) – is also one of the features of the given person's connection with society. Of course, religion and semi-literacy accompany one another. But the ease of action of religious ideas on a person is determined not by the fact that he is semi-literate, but by the fact that in this case we are dealing with a man who finds himself in a definite relationship to society, and semi-literacy itself appears as one of the signs of this relationship.[12]

As Soviet scholars turn their attention to the educational level of believers, especially as it relates to their skill-levels and job-qualifications, it is natural that they should begin an examination of the actual participation of believers, doubters and atheists in various forms of public and social activities. One young scholar found that convinced atheists are more than twice as active as those merely indifferent to religion [non-believers], more than seven times more active than doubters, and more than eighteen times more active than believers. He then goes on to say:

> Sometimes in our literature this fact is either underestimated or entirely ignored. There is a widely held view that in general people come to religion who have experienced personal misfortune (illness, handicap, the death of dear ones, etc.), or who are materially insecure, pensioners, those who have left their jobs, etc. Undoubtedly, such assertions have a large grain of truth, but one should not absolutise the given proposition. We know that by no means every believer has suffered personal misfortune, and that on the other hand not everyone who has suffered becomes a believer. Apparently we have to deal here with a whole complex of reasons, motives and various circumstances of an objective and subjective nature in which this or that man finds himself.[13]

The increased willingness of Soviet scholars to consider individual psychology as one of the factors involved in an assessment of religiosity has obliged them to deal with contemporary religious ideology.[14] Most studies of religious philosophy done by Soviet scholars place heavy emphasis on the mysticism and otherworldliness to be found there, but some sociologists no longer hesitate to say that Baptists in particular are able to claim moral superiority by default, because atheistic propaganda speaks of Communist morality in the abstract, without reference to individual concrete existential human problems.[15] On the whole, however, all the studies of religious behaviour we have seen confirm the model as outlined by Klibanov.

III. EVALUATION OF THE SOVIET MODEL

In this section we will attempt to test the Soviet model for the explanation of religious behaviour which has been summarised above against the empirical data gathered by Soviet sociologists of religion under current conditions. Before proceeding to the actual test, however, we must deal with a preliminary question of great methodological importance: what kind of data is available on current religious behaviour in the Soviet Union, and to what limitations are these data subject? In evaluating the character of Soviet data on the sociology of religion, it should be remembered that this field, like that of technical sociology itself (i.e. in the Western sense), is only slightly more than a decade old in the Soviet Union. This does not mean that no sociological information is available for earlier periods. Before the Revolution, a fairly extensive literature dealing with sectarian movements and with non-church groups in the Russian Orthodox tradition was produced by missionaries, government officials, journalists and writers; despite the polemical intent of much of this literature, it is useful if approached with the requisite caution. Likewise, after the Revolution, some work of empirical value was produced by Party functionaries and agitprop workers who went into the countryside to investigate centres of sectarian activity. Some of these workers – particularly F. M. Putintsev – were quite systematic in their methods, using questionnaires and other formal devices. The results of their studies, however, remain in the archives, for the most part.[16] The main thrust of these early works was towards evaluating the extent to which various sectarian groups might represent a threat to the Soviet regime or to its plans for social change. However, when the empirical sociology of religion was revived in the late 1950s, after a period of almost complete silence, both its emphasis and its methods were rather different. To begin with, Soviet sociologists of religion have begun a systematic search for statistical validity and reliability, which has always been missing from discussion of sectarian behaviour either in the pre-Revolutionary or Soviet periods.[17] By the same token, researchers are employing ethnographic techniques for intensive small-scale studies of religious behaviour in face-to-face local communities.[18]

In order to arrive at some estimate of the volume of material dealing with the sociology of religion published in the Soviet Union, we may cite on the one hand the totals of Klibanov's bibliographical survey and on the other hand the section 'Sociology of Religion' in the latest annual Soviet bibliography on religion available to us, relating to the year 1968. Klibanov states that a total of 380 works on sectarianism had appeared in the post-Revolutionary period, 199 of them since 1955. A little more than half of these works were essentially critical (polemical) in nature; 17 per cent dealt with Jehovah's Witnesses, 12 per cent with the Evangelical Christian Baptists, 9 per cent with the Pentecostalists, 7 per cent with the Adventists, and 3 per cent of the literature dealt with all the other sectarian groups.[19] Taking Klibanov's totals as one estimate, and possibly a rather inflated one, let us pass now to the other extreme. The section 'Sociology of Religion' in the bibliography compiled by Vorozhtsova for 1968 contains twenty-seven separate items. Other sections of the same bibliography, such as 'Socio-Moral Problems and Religion' and 'Contemporary Religion in the U.S.S.R. and the Socialist Countries' contain other material of sociological importance, including general surveys on particular religious bodies.[20] It is our impression that the body of work represented here compares favourably in quantity with what is now being done in the West, if one does not include in the latter category research and publications specifically sponsored by various church groups.

In evaluating the current Soviet research on problem of the sociology of religion, we are faced with a dilemma, in that we have no independent testimony concerning the social phenomena which the Soviet researchers describe, and no means of getting any. All we can say therefore is that Soviet research in sociology of religion seems to us serious, scientific and worthy of study. It is not unbiased – far from it, but at least its bias is clearly, not to say compulsively, stated, which is more than can be said for the work of many Western social scientists.

IV. THE TEST ITSELF

It is now time to embark on an actual test of the Soviet model for the explanation of religious behaviour in society. This will be done in the following manner. We will set up two contrasting hypotheses and measure the empirical data on the religious behaviour of the Soviet population against each of them in turn. These hypotheses are not intended to be mutually exclusive. However, in general, to the extent to which hypothesis *A* is confirmed, the Soviet model is to be considered generally adequate and to the extent to which hypothesis *B* is confirmed, the Soviet model is to be considered generally not adequate.

Hypothesis *A*: Religion is maintained in Soviet society by the force of tradition within individual face-to-face communities (including particularly the family) and is not promoted by any positive objective factors operating within the society. The religious tradition can therefore be expected to die out within a foreseeable period of time.

Hypothesis *B*: Religious behaviour in Soviet society is a response to actual social conditions on the part of persons who are or feel themselves to be excluded for structural reasons from the main stream of Soviet society. This does not mean that these people are themselves aware of the structural reasons for their exclusion; it merely means that this exclusion, real or apparent, can be accounted for in terms of policy priorities and social processes.

The test of hypothesis *B* will require us to answer a further question: is the structural condition presupposed in this hypothesis temporary or permanent? In other words, does the evidence presently available, and the trend of historical development, indicate that the structural factors contributing to the survival of religion will be eliminated by processes and policies now in operation, or that their elimination will require changes in these processes and policies?

1. *The Indices of Religiosity*

Soviet researchers spend a great deal of time collecting data on what might be called the clinical incidence of religiosity: how much religious behaviour is exhibited, what is its nature, who is involved, and what are the conditions? One of the most obvious symbols of religiosity is, according to most Soviet researchers, the presence or absence of ikons in the home. However, two things need to be said of this as a true index. In pre-Revolutionary Russia, ikons in the home were an obligatory symbol of political loyalty, inasmuch as a man could be exiled for discarding them. In the post-Revolutionary period, many Russians have ikons because they think them beautiful, because others have them, and old people in the home insist on going with the crowd, or because ikons are considered traditionally part of Russian culture.[21] Of course, the presence of ikons does say something about the owner's position in society, and it is worth quoting Arutyunyan on this point, since his attitude is that ikons suggest a lack of culture, and though he has little else to say on the subject of religion, he does indicate that a number of factors enter in:

> A certain difference exists in the distribution of ikons among the families of workers, white-collar people, and collective farmers. In families in which the heads work in government institutions, only 21 per cent of the families have ikons; in the families of workers and office-personnel, 30 per cent do; among collective farmers, the figure is 47 per cent. We are not speaking of pensioners and those not employed, among whom a majority (60 and 75 per cent, respectively) decorate . . . with ikons. Thus, the 'saturation' of collective farmers' homes with ikons is 50 to 100 per cent greater than that of workers and white-collar people. To some degree this has to do with the greater age of collective farmers. Thus the average of family heads working in enterprises and government institutions, respectively, are 40 and 42.8, while among collective farmers it is 46.2. The lower level of education of the collective farmers also makes itself felt. Although the difference among white-collar people, workers, and collective farmers in this regard is perceptible, it is much more significant, of course, among persons of different levels of qualification. In families whose heads are employed primarily in skilled mental work, only 7 per cent of the homes are 'decorated' with ikons, while the figure is 24 per cent among those doing mental work of low skill, 34 per cent among those doing skilled physical work, and 47 per cent among those doing unskilled physical work. Thus, the range between the extremes is almost seven to one, while between groups. it is two or three to one. . . . [D]ifferences within classes are manifested considerably more strongly than interclass differences. Just as the presence of books does not testify to a reading habit, ikons do not always signify religiosity. Therefore we supplemented the description of household inventory by a control question on the subject's attitude toward religion. It was found that the number of families possessing ikons but not religious was relatively small, as was, contrariwise, that of religious homes with no ikons. However, these families are distributed proportionately through the population groups and do thus not affect the general tendency.[22]

Belief in God, in an afterlife and in regular attendance at church are said to be other sound indices of religiosity, but statistical material gathered on this score suggest that the situation is in flux, and some Soviet sociologists are beginning to make careful distinctions among various levels of religiosity, and to subject these findings to statistical analysis. A. A. Lebedev[23] has one of the largest and most complex samples. He distinguishes seven types of religious behaviour, extending the concept into the negative range – from the convinced believer to the convinced atheist. The convinced believer (B_1) asserts belief in God and immortality of the soul, claims that man's goals are God-given, relates positively to religion and negatively to atheism, engages in religious practice and disseminates his views. The second-rank convinced believer (B_2) exhibits all these traits but the last. Waverers of the first rank (W_1) are those who do not maintain belief in God but do believe in something supernatural; they can give no definite answer as to their views on the immortality of the soul, or on the goals set for man, but they do not connect these goals with God; they react neither positively nor negatively either to religion or to atheism, but they do engage in religious practice for religious motives. Waverers of the second rank (W_2) neither confirm nor deny belief in God, do not believe in the immortality of the soul, have a materialistic outlook on human goals, no definite relationship to either religion or atheism, engage in religious practice, but not for religious reasons. The indifferent (I) are those who neither believe in God nor immortality, say that man's goals depend on him, have neither a positive nor a negative relation to religion or atheism, and may sometimes engage in religious practice for non-religious reasons. The atheist (A_1) denies God and the immortality of the soul, has a materialistic outlook on man's goals, relates positively to atheism and negatively to religion, and does not engage in religious practice. The convinced atheist (A_2) disseminates his views.

It is interesting to compare A. A. Lebedev's findings (Table 1)[24] with those of L. N. Ulyanov,[25] whose sample is a rural one, although Ulyanov's indices of religiosity are considerably less precise than Lebedev's. It is apparent from his data that the rural believer is experiencing considerable confusion about some of the most basic aspects of belief. Furthermore, believers tended on the

TABLE 1

Religious Behaviour Among Residents of
Oktyabrsky rayon, city of Penza

*Index**	*Groups according to outlook*						
	B_1	B_2	W_1	W_2	I	A_1	A_2
Go to church sometimes or regularly	85	71	57	38	14	10	12
Approve religious holidays	85	63	35	13	4	—	—
Regularly or sometimes meet religious people and talk to them	84	55	65	43	28	21	61
In house (apartment) are religious objects	77	64	48	38	17	8	10
Approve manifestations of religiosity among people	69	68	60	41	24	—	—
Believe in Providence and God's omnipotence	69	49	30	4	—	—	—
Belong to a definite faith	62	68	52	13	5	—	—
Pray daily before ikons	62	28	9	1	—	—	—
Consider religion harmful, both to society and to the individual	—	—	—	—	—	98	99
Consider atheistic work necessary	—	7	4	15	28	69	85
Consider that the believer must be helped out of his religious views	—	—	—	6	12	49	68
In the last year attended atheistic lectures and other atheistic undertakings	—	7	17	15	19	26	46
Regularly or occasionally read atheistic literature	—	3	13	7	18	23	68

* Answers given in percentage of numbers in each group.

whole to see greater lapses of faith in their relatives than in themselves, while waverers held the contrary view.[26] According to such theoreticians as D. M. Ugrinovich,[27] faith in God is basic to religiosity, and judged by this index alone there has been a marked decline in religiosity in every community studied by Soviet sociologists, no matter what the religious persuasion. E. Duluman *et al.* put the question to 299 believers in the Ukraine (Table 2),[28] with results which suggest that principles of dogma are not what hold people in religious communities.

TABLE 2

Idea of God

	Total number	Age			Education					Religious Affl.					Attend Prayer Meetings				Conduct Relig. Prop.	
		Under 30	30–50	50 plus	Illiterate	Primary	5–7 grades	8–10 grades	Higher	Baptists	Pentecostalists	Jehovah's Witnesses	Adventists	Russian Orthodox	Constantly	Periodically	Do not attend	Not determined	In the Family	Outside the Family
1. Concrete-perceptible	45	5	11	29	9	26	7	3	—	8	3	—	12	22	17	9*	7	2	14	7
2. Abstract	113	14	50	49	13	71	21	6	2	60	22	21	—	10	59	36	4	14	31	14
3. Mixed (indefinite)	96	4	33	59	15	57	20	4	—	37	7	7	9	36	32	42	14	8	17	4
4. No Answer	45	4	24	17	5	30	8	2	—	17	6	4	1	17	17	22	4	2	6	2
Totals	299	27	118	154	42	184	56	15	2	122	38	32	22	85	125	119	29	26	68	27

* We have reproduced the table as it appears in our source. It appears that '9' in this column should read '19'.

2. Public Opinion and the Family

Community pressure for conformity more than pressure within the family is a factor in the continuance of religion. Data collected by Ulyanov indicate that family insistence on a christening is not the chief reason young people participate. Forty-two per cent of those questioned on this point said that they were following tradition and did not wish to be different from those around them who also christened children.[29] When the sample is broken down by age groups, it seems clear that younger people are also motivated to conform, although the largest percentage falls in those over 50.[30]

Sometimes, however, it is difficult to say where community leaves off and family begins, particularly in a rural or suburban setting. A. I. Klibanov[31] studied Evangelical Christians Baptists and Adventists living in the Sokolniki *rayon* of Moscow in 1959 and found that 30–40 per cent of the people were members of some identifiable kin group, and that 60 per cent lived compactly, either in neighbouring houses or on neighbouring streets. Twenty per cent of the Adventists in Lipetsk *oblast* and 30 per cent of the Voronezh city Evangelical Christian Baptist community were related in some way. He cites the work of V. N. Lentin, who discovered that 30–60 per cent of urban Adventists were related, and that in rural localities the percentage rose as high as 90. In Moldavia, D. N. Tabakaru studied Evangelical Christian Baptist communities and reported, Klibanov says, that in the 1962–66 period, between 65·4 per cent and 75 per cent of the members were related. By way of comparison, in Kiev 23 per cent of the members of sectarian groups are related. The family is thus of considerable importance to maintenance of the religious group, and within this context, age, sex and occupational status are of interest (see Tables 3–4).[32]

TABLE 3

Composition of Adventist Communities (in %)

Adventist Communities

	Rural	Urban
Men	30–35	10–15
Women	65–70	85–90
Age group older than 60	30–35	over 50
Non-Working	35–40	60–80

TABLE 4

Regional Comparison of the Composition
of Adventist Communities (in %)

Adventist Communities	Number of Women	Age group older than 60	Illiterate and semi-literate	Non-Working
Gorky	89·7	62·0	74·9	83·1
Kiev	85·0	46·4	65·8	76·4
Moscow	87·5	58·8	54·8	73·8
Seven Moldavian Communities	68·8	25·6	63·5	10·5

TABLE 5

Composition of Religious Communities
In the Eastern Regions of the BSSR (in %)

	Brest Oblast	Mogilev	Gomel	Vitebsk
Men	33·6	13·0	25·0	23·0
Women	66·4	87·0	75·0	77·0
Not working	10·3	47·0	53·0	60·0
From 20 to 40 years of age	26·4	12·0	15·3	7·2
40 to 50 years	13·5	—	—	—
40 to 60 years	—	45·0	40·7	34·5
50 and older	60·1	—	—	—
60 and older	—	43·0	44·0	58·3
Illiterate and semi-literate	71·4*	65·0	55·0	35·3**

* Including illiterate of more than 30%.
** 35·3% are semi-literate and have low primary education, not in
Vitebsk *Oblast*, but in the city of Vitebsk, according to the data of a
sample study published in Moscow in 1965.

3. *Education*

Other socio-political factors, such as later incorporation into the
Soviet Union and previous religious history of individual religious
communities, are also important. Klibanov present tabular data
concerning Evangelical Christians Baptists in the Byelorussian
S.S.R. (Table 5).[33] Data collected by E. S. Prokoshina[34] among

Russian Orthodox and Catholics indicate that Evangelical Christians Baptists are on the whole a slightly younger group and are perhaps better educated, but, in general, Soviet researchers are only beginning to talk about the attractiveness of various forms of sectarianism for anyone with more than secondary education. In an urban context such data might correlate with the fact that women who are capable of working (from the standpoint of health and education) often do not, for a variety of reasons, including the unavailability of suitable employment. In a rural context, the often poor quality of non-religious entertainment is an additional factor.[35]

4. *Nationalism*

Nationalism is almost certainly a factor in religious adherence, though Klibanov is one of the few sociologists to suggest its importance for Russians. He says that 30 per cent of the Evangelical Christians Baptists in Voronezh *oblast* are Ukrainian (43 per cent in the city of Voronezh itself); by the 1959 census data, Ukrainians were 7·6 per cent of the population as a whole.[36]

Material appearing in the press indicates that Soviet educators are having some difficulty in separating religious from national motifs. This relates both to the status of churches and ikons as important works of folk art and to the status of certain religious figures as national heroes. On 12 December 1970, in the newspaper *Uchitelskaya gazeta,* a correspondent of the journal *Nauka i religiya* commented on two letters of inquiry from teachers (in Arkhangelsk and Omsk *oblasti*) concerning the propriety of conducting field trips to churches and having religious objects displayed in school museums. In the first case the teacher is advised to use books on church architecture and ikon painting.

> In any contemporary functioning church, there are ikons of the Trinity. What does such an ikon say to the unprepared excursionist, and what can the excursion leader say in conditions when around them there are flickering candles, and people are praying and the priest is reading a sermon? But in a study circle which is devoted to a book that has been read, schoolchildren can learn how the great painter Rublev, when he painted his famous Trinity in the beginning of the 15th century, when there was a process of unification of the

Russian lands, was able to express in this ikon the unity of
Russian lands.

As for what can go into a museum: '[any object] which allows
the visitor to see with his own eyes the life of Tsarist Russia which
has unalterably receded into the past.' The message seems clear:
religious influence is to be avoided, but the use of religious material
for nationalistic purposes is permissible and even salutary.

5. *Religious training*

Soviet researchers have devoted considerable attention to ways
in which religious education is continued within family groups.
A. A. Yeryshev[37] points out that sectarian groups are more
insistent on educating children in a 'religious spirit' than are
Russian Orthodox. Lensu and Prokoshina[38] present data suggesting
that while schismatic Baptists have led the fight, one reason may
be because they as a group have more children.[39] Religious
education for children is considered by many Soviet scholars --
including Klibanov[40] -- almost as an attempt to set up a counter-
culture, although no Soviet sociologist would use such a term. The
Soviet researcher prefers to see attempts by religious parents to
foster their views as a manifestation of ignorance, or as a sign
that religion has entered a period of crisis. The ageing of religious
congregations has been established beyond doubt, but under Soviet
conditions church buildings are not essential to the continuance
of religiosity; in fact, the majority of those who consider themselves
believers do not attend church regularly, even in religious bodies
historically known for an insistence on participatory church
attendance, such as Baptism (as opposed to passive or traditional
attendance as is common among Russian Orthodox).[41]

In our view, the attractiveness of religion for the younger
generation almost certainly depends on the extent to which young
people remain in the traditional family religious environment,[42]
or the strength of ties to the communities into which they were
born. A number of researchers, such as Klibanov, have indicated
that although the family is a significant reservoir for the continuance of religious congregations, in many localities and at
certain periods of time, religious communities have grown or
even remained stable because the number of newcomers attracted
more or less balances the number of those who die or leave the

community for other reasons.[43] Whether this situation can continue indefinitely obviously cannot be a matter of simple statistical projection.

6. *Social and Civic Participation*

Soviet researchers too would like to know whether policy changes on the part of the regime will be necessary before religion dies away completely. Current Soviet sociological studies therefore have begun to inquire whether the believer as worker differs significantly in his attitudes from the atheist as worker.

In this aspect of the research, the Soviet student will be guided by the pioneering works of Zdravomyslov[44] and Shubkin[45] and Zaslavskaya.[46] Since detailed comparisons would carry us beyond the scope of this paper, a few words attempting to characterise this work will have to suffice. Most of the sociology of labour revolves around a few simple questions, such as how does the worker feel about his job, his comrades and his superiors at work, and his chances for advancement? When he leaves his job (as in some areas of the country workers do with alarming frequency), what motivates him – the conditions under which he works, his wage or personal family reasons? Two questions are asked about education. Does the worker care about getting it, and is it possible that a worker can be over-educated? Since women are a significant proportion of the labour force in most branches, and a majority in some, the researcher wants to know if there are sexual differences in the responses, and hence two questions asked are: What does the worker want to be? If he wishes to be something other than he was or now is, and if he desires a specialty in which the State has an oversupply of workers, is this good or bad? Further, does the way in which the worker spends his leisure time have any bearing on any or all of these questions?

If the questions asked are simple, the answers received are not. It has been discovered that those engaged in monotonous work, or labour requiring low skill or none, have a low opinion of the social significance of their labour and frequently do not care about their comrades at work, or have few expressed opinions about superiors. Such people would like to continue their studies but frequently cannot (because of health, family responsibility or lack of opportunity); their desire for further education is less acute than among the younger generation, whose educational level is

higher. Women generally have less opportunity to continue education because of family responsibilities; they are also less active than
men in public affairs for the same reason. Women also tend to
spend their leisure time with family and neighbours. Young
people generally want to specialise in useful, glamourous or well-
paid occupations; in rural communities this means that a low
value is put on parental occupation (often by both child and
parent). The young person changes jobs more frequently and is
less often used to carry out social assignments; he also in some
contexts demonstrates a certain passivity in regard to using his
leisure in culturally useful pursuits, such as attending lectures or
even reading. This puts the young person in the same category
as women.[47] It is indeed possible to be both young and female,
and passivity can extend into every social group, but it remains
unclear precisely how the addition of religious belief modifies
these factors.

7. *The Sexual Differential*

It seems we must accept the Soviet assertion that religious groups
are overwhelmingly female, with the qualification that religiosity
in men can be high in youth, in a rural setting, and when the men
are most actively engaged in raising a family.[48] Interest in religion
does not seem as intense in men as in women, for the very good
reason that men have greater social mobility than women. Such a
finding does not contradict earlier ones demonstrating that the
leaders of religious communities are more frequently men than
women.[49] Masculine leadership in Christian churches in Russia
is traditional and, many sectarians assert, founded on the Bible.
However, as Saprykin notes, the thesis that pensioners automati-
cally turn towards religion needs refinement, since much depends
on what the pensioner did before retirement, and what his opportunities are to continue his interests.[50] Likewise, Baykov asserts
that in a secular atmosphere women seek self-expression not in
the church but in secular activities – a point he backs up with a
number of tables. Let us take two to serve as examples (Tables
6–7).[51]

What is surprising, considering reports on the religious situation
in the U.S.S.R. circulated by some church-oriented observers in
the West, is that believers participate in civic activity at all.[52]
Soviet researchers have consistently countered Western criticism

TABLE 6

Motives for taking up civic activity
(in % of those questioned who specified
attitude towards religion)

Motives for social work	Non-believers	Believers
Expand spiritual interests	8·5	6·6
Expand feeling of collectivism	19·9	10·0
Help to gain habit of directing social work	15·2	6·6
Receive moral satisfaction	11·1	3·3
Fulfill obligation without desire	8·3	3·3

TABLE 7

Participation in public affairs in past and
present in relation to attitude towards religion
(in absolute numbers)

| | Attitude towards social work in the past | | | | Attitude towards social work now | | | |
| | participated | | didn't | | participated | | didn't | |
	m	f	m	f	m	f	m	f
Non-believer	146	205	56	62	153	200	39	43
Believer	4	24	—	1	4	26	—	—

of treatment of believers in the U.S.S.R. by claiming that to deprive believers of the right to participate in educational benefits and the management of Soviet institutions (cultural, economic or political)[53] is a distortion of Soviet religious policy. V. A. Chernyak and others have recommended specifically that believers and other groups (the young and the less educated) be drawn into civic activities, since this is the best way of combating religious influence.[54] It is possible that a differential exists between the Russian Orthodox and sectarians in point of civic participation, either as a matter of official policy or as a byproduct of the world-views of these two groups. Account must be taken of the extent to which, if no external threat to the believer exists, he will be compelled to invent one, because of his world-view.[55] The most obvious threat to the believer today is not so much a particular political system to be viewed as the antichrist as an inexorable process taking place all over the world – secularisation. As we have suggested, churches in the U.S.S.R. are feeling the impact of secularisation and adjusting to it accordingly, with sermons and pronouncements of various sorts. A number of studies have been made which compare the frequency of church attendance with the frequency of attendance at Soviet-sponsored institutions, such as the local club. On the surface the religious leader appears to be in a better position to influence the believer. Pivovarov, for instance, discovered that 31 per cent of his sample were not reached by mass communication media.[56] We should note that this figure appears to correspond to the finding of sociologists concerned with the effectiveness of Soviet cultural measures on the population as a whole. Furthermore, it can no longer be suspected that believers are outside the perimeters of Soviet-directed efforts at culture change, because it has been shown that to some degree, in all his contacts with the outside world, the believer has at least to test his conclusions against the reality of his observations.[57]

The fact that the believer often does not reject the material benefits of Soviet society but exercises a stubborn selectivity in his acceptance[58] is one of the sociologists' major concerns because it suggests to them that a man can act on something without necessarily believing in it, or *vice versa,* if he believes without acting, his reliability comes into question. Baykov asserts that only a quarter of the believers in his sample thought about the social usefulness of labour, but Table 8 indicates some differences in attitude by sex as well as belief. The asserted utilitarian attitude (66·6 per cent of believers and 52·7 per cent of waverers) towards work[59] probably is not much more characteristic of believers than it is of people with few skills engaged in monotonous physical labour who are culturally speaking rather passive.

Soviet researchers are in fact frightened of ideological passivity, although their own data indicate that even Party members suffer from it to some extent.[60] That is why they spend so much time investigating the nature of religion, and why it sometimes seems that they do not trust their own data. A survey carried out by Baykov[61] seems to indicate that most Soviet people believe that religion will die out, but Soviet researchers do not appear to be taking any bets. One of the most important factors in the preservation of religion, as Manuilova[62] has pointed out, is the moral

TABLE 8

Motivation for work by sex, depending upon
attitude towards religion (in %)

| | Sex, and attitude towards religion | | | | | |
| | Non-believer | | Waverer | | Believer | |
Motives	male	female	male	female	male	female
That work is good in which you are the most useful and are necessary	10·9	14·5	2·7	11·1	0	10·0
You mustn't forget the wages, but the basic thing is the work and its social usefulness	9·4	11·1	0	30·5	0	6·6
The wages are the main thing, but you have to think of the meaning of the work	9·2	13·5	8·3	11·1	0	13·3
Any work is good if it is well paid	10·5	12·6	11·1	22·2	10·0	43·3

support which believers receive from the religious community in
facing problems of everyday life – such as those of an elderly
pensioner who needs wood for the winter, or of a semi-literate,
widowed, divorced or separated mother whose children question
her values.

V. CONCLUSION

We are now ready to make at least a tentative judgement as to
the degree to which our initial hypotheses have been confirmed.
We think that the verdict must be a qualified confirmation of
hypothesis *B*, namely that religious behaviour in the Soviet context is a response to objective conditions – to the actual or felt
exclusion of certain groups from the mainstream of Soviet society.
This judgement is based on three major differentials in amount
and kind of religious behaviour within the Soviet population –
differentials which are admitted and in fact emphasised by Soviet

researchers. The first is between men and women. The opinion
that religion is primarily 'women's business' (despite the ritual
primacy of men) and the empirical situation from which this
opinion derives are of course not specifically Soviet or even specifically Russian. Restricted social mobility and cultural opportunities for women have been and are almost universal. In this sense,
the situation in the Soviet Union can legitimately be described as
a survival from the past. However, the question posed in the
second clause of hypothesis *B* as to whether the structural factors
presupposed by it are temporary or permanent must be answered
in respect to the position of women with a verdict of 'insufficient
data'.

The second major differential in religious behaviour which is
admitted by Soviet researchers is that between the rural and urban
populations. It is our contention that the overall decline in religious behaviour for the entire Soviet population reflects not so
much the secularisation of the countryside as the drain of population into the cities, with the accompanying exposure of millions
of persons reared in a traditional way of life to a mass of new
stimuli and experiences. It follows from this that when the drain
of population into the cities slows and stops, as it eventually must;
the process of secularisation must also slow and stop, unless it can
be continued by other means. This is of course possible but it
would require a considerable reordering of priorities in the direction of more cultural opportunities and greater social mobility in
terms of prestige. This last is an extremely stubborn problem,
because it depends not primarily on objective factors which can
in principle be controlled by legislation and policy decisions, but
upon values. Once again, the verdict with respect to the second
clause of hypothesis *B* must be left open.

The third major differential in religious behaviour has to do
with education. In view of the valuable achievements of the Soviet
educational system, one would be justified in predicting that
within the foreseeable future, this differential would cease to exist.
This prediction, however, must be subject to an important qualification, which has to do with the differential availability of
education for various groups, and the differential availability of
work and living conditions commensurate with education
received.

One final reminder is due the reader: everything in this paper

has been based on the assumption – explicitly stated in our Soviet
sources, and adopted by us as a conscious methodological measure
– that religion is purely a social phenomenon and in particular an
expression of social pathology. As individuals, we would find such
a definition of religion unacceptable.

NOTES

1. The Marxist interpretation of primitive religion is a topic of great theoretical
   importance which cannot be gone into here. Certain Soviet theorists (see for
   example B. F. Porshnev, 'Attempts at Synthesis in the Field of the History of
   Religion', *Soviet Anthropology and Archeology* (1968–69), Vol. VII, No. 3, pp. 20–
   36), with impeccable Marxist logic but questionable good sense place the
   animistic beliefs found in societies at the stage of 'primitive Communism' in a
   category different from that of the more advanced religions of class societies.
   Others, such as S. A. Tokarev, are not prepared to go this far.
2. A. I. Klibanov, 'The Dissident Denominations in the Past and Today', *Soviet
   Sociology* (1965), Vol. III, No. 4, pp. 44–60. (Until otherwise stated, all quotations are from this work.)
3. Marx and Engels, *Sochineniya* (Works), Vol. XXVI, p. 174.
4. Klibanov, *op. cit.*, p. 47.
5. A. I. Klibanov, *Religioznoye sektantstvo i sovremennost (sotsiologichesk ye i istori-
   cheskiye ocherki)* (Religious Sectarianism and the Present [Sociol gical and
   Historical Essays]) (Moscow, 1969), p. 5. L. N. Mitrokhin considers that the
   problem of shifts among sectarian groups, most frequently in a more extreme
   direction, deserves further study, but if he thinks this is an example of class
   conflict, or even of deficiencies in the administration of socialism, he has never
   said so to our knowledge. (See L. N. Mitrokhin, 'Education in Atheism and
   Methodology of Studying the Survival of Religious Beliefs', *Soviet Sociology*
   [1962], Vol. I, No. 1, p. 31.)
6. Klibanov, 'The Dissident Denominations . . .', p. 52.
7. V. A. Chernyak, *O preodolenii religioznykh perezhitkov: opyt konkretno-sotsiologiches-
   kogo issledovaniya po materialam Alma-Atinskoi oblasti* (On the Overcoming of
   Religious Survivals; Experience of Concrete Sociological Research Based on
   the Data of the Alma-Ata *Oblast*) (Alma-Ata, 1965), and V. A. Chernyak,
   *Formirovaniye nauchno-materialisticheskogo ateisticheskogo mirovozzreniya (Sotsio-
   logicheskiye problemy)* (Formation of Scientific-Materialist Atheist World-view
   [Sociological Problems]) (Alma-Ata, 1969).
8. See A. I. Klibanov, 'Problems in the Psychology of Religious Sectarianism',
   Soviet Sociology (1971), Vol. IX, No. 4, pp. 505–66.
9. A. I. Klibanov, 'The Dissident Denominations . . .', pp. 57, 59.
10. Klibanov himself has warned against a too easy acceptance of either extreme,
    saying that if sectarians were not always reactionary, neither were they (in a
    political sense) revolutionary, and they should never be idealised. See Klib-
    anov, *Religioznoye sektantstvo . . .* , pp. 28–31. However, even such a sophisti-
    cated sociologist as Chernyak (*O preodolenii*, pp. 7–8) has based her entire
    approach on the theory that sectarian religious organisations are the only
    legally tolerated opposition to the Soviet regime and that therefore constant
    ideological vigilance is necessary.
11. A. I. Klibanov, 'Nauchno-organizatsionnyi i metodicheskii opyt konkretnykh
    issledovanii religioznosti (po materialam tsentralnykh oblastei R.S.F.S.R.)'

(Scientific-Organizational and Methodological Experience of Concrete Research on Religiosity [Based on the Data of Central *Oblasti* of the R.S.F.S.R.]) in *Konkretnye issledovaniya sovremennykh religioznykh verovanii* (Concrete Research on Contemporary Religious Beliefs), edited by A. I. Klibanov *et al.* (Moscow, 1967), p. 33.

12. L. N. Mitrokhin, 'O metodologii issledovanii sovremennoi religioznosti' (On the Methodology of Research on Contemporary Religiosity), in *Konkretyne . . .*, p. 49. Compare this with Yu. V. Arutyunyan's statement: 'Under our conditions, in which the decisive condition in determining a person's place in society is not property but skill level as evaluated by the state, education acquires particular social significance. It is difficult to overestimate the social importance of the process of dissemination of education among the rural population' ('A Preliminary Sociological Study of a Village [Part III]', *Soviet Sociology*, 1971–72, Vol. X, No. 3, pp. 289–90).

13. V. A. Saprykin, 'Rol subyektivnogo faktora v preodolenii religii v usloviyakh sotsializma', (The Role of Subjective Factor in the Overcoming of Religion in Conditions of Socialism) in *K obshchestvu, svobodnomu ot religii (Protsess sekulyarizatsii v usloviyakh sotsialisticheskogo obschshestva)* (Towards a Society Free of Religion [The Process of Secularisation in Conditions of Socialist Society]), edited by P. K. Kurochkin *et al.* (Moscow, 1970), p. 117.

14. Out of a growing literature, we cite by way of example E. G. Filimonov, *Baptizm i gumanizm* (Baptism and Humanism) (Moscow, 1968), and P. K. Kurochkin, *Evolyutsiya sovremennogo ¦russkogo pravoslaviya* (Evolution of Contemporary Russian Orthodoxy) (Moscow, 1971).

15. See V. A. Chernyak, *Formirovaniye . . .*, p. 352, and E. Duluman *et al.*, *Sovremennyi veruyushchii; sotsialno-psikhologicheskii ocherk* (Contemporary Believer: A Social-Psychological Essay) (Moscow), p. 78.

16. A. I. Klibanov, 'Fifty Years of Scientific Study of Religious Sectarianism', *Soviet Sociology* (1970), Vol. VIII, No. 3–4, p. 265. He also says that the number of studies published during the first period (1920–26) was small – no more than 30, even counting articles in *Bezbozhnik* (*ibid.*, p. 240).

17. V. I. Lebedev, 'Konkretnye sotsiologicheskiye issledovaniya religioznosti naseleniya Penzenskoi oblasti', (Concrete Sociological Research on the Religiosity of the Penza *Oblast* Population) in *K obshchestvu . . .*, pp. 48–50, quotes the local-lore expert V. Gorbunov as saying that official statistics listed no sectarians in a village he personally had studied and knew contained 36 such persons. This denial of the existence of sectarians and Muslims in the guberniya was typical of the tsarist-Orthodox official approach.

18. See, for example, K. I. Kozlova, 'Experience Gained in Studying the Molokans in Armenia', *Soviet Sociology* (1970), Vol. VIII, No. 3–4, pp. 318–28. This and other ethnographic studies are discussed in some detail in Ethel Dunn, 'The Importance of Religion in the Soviet Rural Community', in *The Soviet Rural Community*, ed. James R. Millar (Urbana, 1970), pp. 346–75.

19. Klibanov, 'Fifty Years . . .,' pp. 269–70. Some scholars have suggested that the emphasis on sectarian groups is a trifle heavy, and that more attention might better be paid to Russian Orthodoxy or to Islam.

20. L. A. Vorozhtsova, 'Kratkaya bibliografiya ateisticheskoi literatury, izdannoi v SSSR v 1968 g.' (Brief Bibliography of Atheist Literature Published in the U.S.S.R. in 1968), *Voprosy nauchnogo ateizma* (Questions of Scientific Atheism), No. 10 (Moscow, 1970), pp. 409–430.

21. See, for example, N. P. Andrianov, R. A. Lopatin, and V. V. Pavlyuk, *Osobennosti sovremennogo religioznogo soznaniya* (Peculiarities of Contemporary Religious Consciousness) (Moscow, 1966), p. 23.

22. Arutyunyan, *op. cit.*, pp. 306–7. He has a footnote at this point which says (p. 328) that the incidence of religion in this group in the Ukraine corresponds to that found in a survey of three kolkhozy in Orel *Oblast*, in which 36 per cent' of those surveyed declared themselves religious. The data can be found in *Kollektiv kolkhoznikov: sotsialno-psikhologicheskoye issledovaniye* (Collective of the Kolkhoz Farmers: Social-Psychological Examination), edited by V. N. Kolbanovsky (Moscow, 1970), pp. 227–52.

23. A. A. Lebedev, 'Sekulyarizatsiya naseleniya sotsialisticheskogo goroda (Secularisation of the Population of Socialist City), in *K obshchestvu* . . ., pp. 138–9.

24. *Ibid.*, p. 147. The sample includes 5,955 persons 18 years of age and older; 42·5 per cent are men and 57·5 per cent are women; 77 per cent were born after the Revolution; 33 per cent are under 30 years of age; 44·4 per cent have higher, incomplete higher, secondary specialised and unspecialised education; 93·6 per cent are Russian, and 4·8 per cent said they belonged to another nationality; 80 per cent of the adult population was employed, 46·3 per cent being workers and 33·7 per cent were engineering-technical and other white-collar workers; 72 per cent had come to Penza at various times and at various ages, two-thirds of them being formerly rural residents, and a large percentage settled in Penza 10–15 years ago. Only 2 per cent said they were Baptists, Muslims, Jews or Catholics (pp. 140–41).

25. L. N. Ulyanov, 'Izmeneniye kharaktera religioznosti' (Change in the Character of Religiosity), in *K obshchestvu* . . ., p. 171, 173–4.

26. Ulyanov, *ibid.*, p. 175.

27. Quoted *ibid.*, p. 162.

28. E. Duluman *et al.*, *op. cit.*, p. 126.

29 Ulyanov, *op. cit.*, p. 180.

30. *Ibid.*, p. 178.

31. Klibanov, *Religioznoye sektantstvo* . . ., p. 100.

32. *Ibid.*, pp. 100–101.

33. *Ibid.*, p. 82. Data on the village of Olshany, Brest *oblast*, are also interesting (pp. 84–5).

34. E. S. Prokoshina, 'Iz opyta issledovaniya religioznosti naseleniya v Byelorusskoi SSR' (From the Experience of Research on the Religiosity of the Population of the Byelorussian S.S.R.), in *Konkretnye* . . ., pp. 72–83.

35. For instance, Prokoshina, *ibid.*, p. 77, states that 2 per cent of her sample of about 10,000 adults and children had secondary and higher education. M. Ya. Lensu and E. S. Prokoshina, eds., *Baptizm i Baptisty* (Baptism and the Baptists) (Minsk, 1969), p. 41, report that the percentage of Baptists with incomplete-secondary and secondary education in urban communities is higher than in rural (73 per cent and 27 per cent), but Table 6 (p. 43) lists 7·2 per cent of Baptists with secondary and higher education. K. M. Bokarev divides his sample survey of the residents of Valdai into three groups who reached age 18 in 1928, 1958 and 1969. The results should be compared with our general knowledge of stages in the cultural revolution in the U.S.S.R. ('Vliyaniye dukhovnoi kultury na preodoleniye religii i razvitiye massovogo ateizma' [The Influence of Spiritual Culture on the Overcoming of Religion and Development of Mass Atheism], in M. P. Gapochka *et al.*, eds., *Ateizm i sotsialisticheskaya kultura* [Atheism and Socialist Culture] [Moscow, 1971], p. 26).

36. Klibanov, *Religioznoye sektantstvo* . . ., p. 77. A schismatic Baptist group is said to have arisen as early as 1957 in Voronezh, and, to complicate matters, one of the issues between the schismatic Baptists and the established Baptist Church was that the church hierarchy was controlled by those who in the past

had belonged to the Evangelical-Christian Church; this group was heavily Ukrainian in origin. (Klibanov, pp. 113–14; see also A. I. Klibanov and L. N. Mitrokhin, 'Raskol v sovremennom baptizme' [Split in Contemporary Baptism], *Voprosy nauchnogo ateizma*, No. 3 [1967], pp. 84–110.) Unfortunately, this point is not examined in detail.

37. A. A. Yeryshev, 'Opyt konkretno-sotsiologicheskikh issledovanii religioznosti naseleniya na Ukraine' (Experience of Concrete Sociological Research on Religiosity of the Population in the Ukraine), in *Konkretnye . . .*, pp. 138–44.

38. M. Ya. Lensu and E. S. Prokoshina (eds.), *op. cit.*, p. 49.

39. Recent Soviet materials in the field of public health present the beginnings of efforts to correlate social status and attitudes with the number of children. To our knowledge, Lensu and Prokoshina are the first to apply this factor to a concrete religious situation.

40. Klibanov, *Religioznoye sektantstvo . . .*, p. 110.

41. D. E. Manuilova, 'Religioznaya obshchina v usloviyakh sekulyarizatsii' (Religious Community in Conditions of Secularisation) in *K obshchestvu . . .*, pp. 202–3. She even goes so far as to assert that, because Soviet law prohibits militant proselytising, there has been a 'deformation' of traditional Baptist missionary activity: activists work on more passive members of the community.

42. *Ibid.*, p. 206.

43. Klibanov, *Religioznoye sektantstvo . . .*, pp. 78, 84–5.

44. *Man and His Work*, ed. A. G. Zdravomyslov *et al.*, translated by Stephen P. Dunn (White Plains, New York, 1970).

45. V. N. Shubkin, *Sotsiologicheskiye opyty (Metodologicheskiye voprosy sotsialnykh issledovanii)* (Sociological Experiences [Methodological Questions of Social Research]) (Moscow, 1970).

46. T. I. Zaslavskaya (ed.), *Migratsiya selskogo naseleniya* (Migration of Rural Population) (Moscow, 1970).

47. These questions have all been examined in remarkable detail by Chernyak, in *Formirovaniye. . . .*

48 See Chapter VIII in Kolbanovsky (ed.), *Kollektiv kolkhoznikov*, especially Charts 1 and 2 on pp. 230–31.

49. The possibility of masculine leadership for men, and moreover, for old men, in the churches may explain a curious finding by Lensu and Prokoshina (*Baptizm i Baptisty*, p. 263): of the few Baptists interested in atheistic literature (6 per cent), 80 per cent were male, and 62 per cent were over 50 years of age. Some researchers have pointed out that believers read atheistic literature in order to discover details of religious history and philosophy.

50. Saprykin, *op. cit.*, p. 130. Other researchers have found that participation in public affairs, based on the frequency of assignment of social tasks, markedly decreases with age.

51. E. M. Baykov, 'Izmeneniye tsennostnykh orientatsii lichnosti' (Change of the Value Orientation of Personality), in *K obshchestvu . . .*, pp. 228–30. Similar data are presented by V. G. Pivovarov, 'The Religious Group of Parishioners in the System of a Church Parish (a Preliminary Model)', *Soviet Sociology* (1970) Vol. VIII, No. 3–4, p. 306.

52. While we do not question the genuineness of the cases cited by Western observers, our interpretation does vary from theirs. People undoubtedly are imprisoned in the U.S.S.R. for infringements of laws which severely restrict the right of a believer to spread his views, these laws undoubtedly are more protective of non-believers and atheists. Nevertheless, men make up a very high percentage of those imprisoned – a much higher percentage than their

supposed numbers in religious communities. This fact should be subjected to rigorous sociological analysis, since, as E. Dunn has suggested (*op. cit.*), the tsarist and Soviet regimes have traditionally tried to curb sectarian movements by administrative measures, and have apparently always failed.

53. We use the word 'political' in the sense we think Lenin used it when he said that there is no such thing as an apolitical man.
54. V. A. Chernyak, *Formirovaniye* . . ., p. 273.
55. This point is cogently argued by Klibanov ('Problems in the Psychology of Religious Sectarianism'). Our own field work among Molokans in America tends to support Klibanov's view.
56. Pivovarov, *op. cit.*, p. 305.
57. Lensu and Prokoshina, *Baptizm i baptisty*, p. 165, Table 11.
58. Lensu and Prokoshina, *ibid.*, p. 170, say that 91·2 per cent of the Baptists surveyed expressed sympathy for the Soviet regime and indicated that they observed all Soviet holidays.
59. Baykov, *op. cit.*, p. 232, Table 49. Compare Chernyak, *Formirovaniye* . . ., p. 179.
60. Cheryak, *Formiirovaniye* . . ., p. 352, Table 35.
61. Baykov, *op. cit.*, p. 240.
62. Manuilova, *op. cit.*, p. 196.

8 Rearing the New Soviet Man

Anti-religious Propaganda and Political Socialisation in the U.S.S.R.

DAVID E. POWELL

The Soviet regime has, for more than half a century, sought to mould the perceptions, attitudes and behaviour of its citizens. Perhaps no other ruling élite in all of history has attempted so strenuously to implement Aristotle's dictum: 'The citizen should be moulded to suit the form of government under which he lives.'[1] The Communist Party of the Soviet Union has chosen to re-fashion in its own image the values of an entire people. It has made a systematic effort to suppress dissent, to reorient the educable, and to indoctrinate the younger generation with approved messages and symbols. It has sought to alter the views of adults and to inculcate into younger people – who have fewer and less firmly held preconceptions and attitudes – views which it deems 'correct'. To do this, the Party has employed a variety of measures – persuasion, coercion and the threat of coercion. According to official rhetoric, coercion and the threat of coercion have been directed only against anti-Soviet or other hostile forces within society. To gain the support and loyalty of the population, and to mobilise them to achieve the goals set for them, the Party has relied primarily on a highly self-conscious programme of political socialisation.

'Political socialisation' has been described as the process by which one generation passes on political standards and beliefs to succeeding generations.[2] It focuses on 'the process of induction into the political culture. Its end product is a set of attitudes – cognitions, value standards, and feelings – towards the political system, its various roles, and role incumbents.'[3] The term describes a continuous learning process, relevant both for children and adults, since everyone constantly encounters stimuli which may in some measure restructure his political orientations.

Political socialisation in the U.S.S.R. – or, as the Soviets term it, 'the Communist education [*kommunisticheskoye vospitaniye*] of the populace – has involved a deliberate effort to break down traditional belief-systems, replacing them with a set of beliefs which the regime considers more suitable for the present and the future. The Party has sought to fashion a new political culture and to rear a 'New Soviet Man', whose noble character traits and behaviour will be worthy of the ultimate Communist society. In place of individualism, bourgeois nationalism, chauvinism, indolence and 'religious prejudices' there will be intelligent, creative and humane citizens, imbued with feelings of collectivism, proletarian internationalism, socialist patriotism, love of labour and militant atheism. The objective of political socialisation in the Soviet Union, then, is to produce discontinuities and systemic change rather than to preserve the old order or to provide intergenerational continuity.

Since the late 1950s, the Party has expanded its indoctrination and socialisation programme. One of the most crucial dimensions of this effort has been the renewed drive to eradicate religious beliefs and practices from the U.S.S.R. This drive began in Lenin's day; it reached savage proportions during the 1930s, only to lose momentum during and after World War II. Today it has assumed considerable importance once again. Since Stalin's death, the anti-religious programme has been the subject of three Central Committee resolutions, thousands of articles and books and millions of lectures. Indeed, as the Communist Party claims to be drawing the Soviet people closer to Communism, society's defects have become the subject of greater concern and the target of more intense and energetic propaganda.[4]

Religion is seen as an embarrassing vestige of the nation's 'bourgeois' past and a disruptive factor in its current social, political and economic life. The anti-religious effort, then, is not conducted in a vacuum; it is not an end in itself. As two officials of the Central Committee's Propaganda Department have observed: 'The struggle against religion is not a campaign, not an isolated phenomenon, not a self-contained entity; it is an inseparable component part of the entire ideological activity of Party organisations, an essential link and necessary element in the complex of Communist education'.[5] The atheist effort, then, involves more than anti-religious propaganda; it has a positive side as well. The programme is aimed at eliminating unscientific notions and at inculcating into the citizenry the more 'scientific' messages of Marxism–Leninism. While the authorities are combating a religious morality which they regard as pernicious, they are substituting for it an allegedly loftier 'Communist morality'. They are seeking to mould the New Soviet Man.

To achieve their anti-religious objectives, Soviet officials employ a wide array of propaganda devices.[6] These range from such conventional media as the press, radio, television, theatre, lectures, clubs, films, museums and debates to the staging of scientific experiments (which 'unmask religious miracles') and the assigning of specially trained agitators to individual believers. Of all the measures employed by the Party, two seem particularly well suited to achieve success: (1) anti-religious training provided by the regular school system, and (2) the new network of secular holidays and ceremonies which affirm 'Socialist' or 'Communist' traits. Both types of measures reach a very large audience, and the audience for both would seem to be unusually well suited to internalise the propaganda messages. None the less the authorities have encountered considerable difficulty in achieving their objectives, and the success of both programmes appears to have been limited.

The school system is potentially the Party's most powerful weapon in the struggle against religion. By inculcating the appropriate views into the minds of impressionable young children, the regime can – at least in theory – utterly eradicate religion within the space of a few generations.[7] Resourceful teachers can weave attacks on religious beliefs and persons into virtually any kind of lesson. Physics, biology, chemistry, astronomy, mathematics, history, geography and literature can all serve as jumping-off points to instruct pupils on the evils or falsity of religion. For example, the laws of motion and the laws of the conservation of matter and energy are used to refute religious miracles and the notion that God created the world out of nothing. Science and history lessons can discredit biblical descriptions of the origin of man and criticise the persecutions by church authorities of such figures as Galileo or Giordano Bruno. Elementary-school reading lessons can be and frequently are transformed into attacks on religion. Teachers are urged to acquaint themselves with the children's attitude towards religion, e.g. by observing their eating habits to determine who observes Lent.[8] Pupils in the middle grades in Central Asian schools receive anti-religious propaganda in their Russian-language classes. In pursuing the apparently innocuous task of learning Russian grammar, they are taught such anti-religious proverbs as, 'There will be no friendship between the Caucasian bard and the mullah'. The children are instructed in the following catechism:

Q.   Who is the Caucasian bard?
A.   He is a troubadour – a singer of folk songs.
Q.   And what does the mullah do?
A.   Mullah reads the Koran and when someone dies he reads prayers.
Q.   What does he read about in the Koran?
A.   We do not know.
Q.   Does he himself understand what he reads?
A.   No.
Q.   Does he read the prayers for nothing?
A.   No, he gets money for this.
Q.   Why is there no friendship between the mullah and the Caucasian bard?
A.   Because the troubadour loves people, life, weddings, merriment, songs and holidays, but mullah loves prayers, fasting and funerals. There is no place for the mullah where the Caucasian bard is.[9]

Extra-curricular activities, sometimes involving parents as well as pupils, are also directed towards anti-religious objectives. Lectures and field trips are organised, and even physical education and sports can be utilised to combat religion by attracting to school students who usually stay home on religious holidays. The most elaborate extra-curricular activity is probably the 'young atheists' club', which a number of schools have set up. Their activities are a smaller-scale version of adult atheist propaganda; they include plays, puppet shows, films, lectures, excursions, anti-religious newspapers, photographs, posters, etc. Some clubs assign the children to individual believers (adult or child) in an effort to persuade them of the falsity of religious belief. The Club for Young

Atheists in one primary school in the city of Gorky has even put together its own anti-religious museum, which takes up an entire floor of the school building. Pupils conduct guided tours for visiting school-children, parents and other adults, and the museum's holdings of interest are loaned out to various factories in the city.[10]

Despite the elaborateness of these programmes and activities, their contribution to the atheist effort appears to be limited. Students often work diligently at mastering their school lessons – even in the natural, physical and social sciences – and still retain their religious beliefs. They have already been subjected, it is said, to parental censorship, and therefore cannot assimilate their school lessons.[11] One report in *Nauka i religiya,* the principal atheist journal, tells of a schoolteacher who explained to her class that Soviet cosmonauts had reached an altitude of 300 kilometers in their flights and had never encountered God. Therefore, she concluded, God does not exist. Upon asking one of her second graders (whom she knew to be religious) whether she found this logic convincing, the child responded: 'I do not know if 300 kilometers is very much, but I know very well that only those who are pure of heart perceive God.[12] It is an argument which is difficult to rebut.

Moreover, few teachers share the enthusiasm of professional atheists. 'Why are the school and teachers so timid, at times even clumsy,' one atheist asks, 'in gaining entry into the lives, the home life of those families in which children are stupefied and maimed?' Alluding to teachers' reluctance to mix atheism and formal school lessons, she asks, 'Are we not committing an unpardonable error by sometimes keeping the sword of atheism in its scabbard during school lessons in physics, botany, zoology, history and literature?'[13] Some teachers conduct anti-religious discussions only during the period before Christmas and Easter, while others make no effort whatsover to undermine religion or inculcate an attitude of militant atheism. Teachers and principals sometimes refuse to act against pupil's religious beliefs as long as the children perform adequately in class. Some consider the subject irrelevant; others lack the requisite knowledge or simply prefer not to explore such an awkward and personal matter; still others themselves harbour religious beliefs and thus refuse to attack religion. Few teachers have the necessary training for atheist work: until recently the subject of scientific atheism was not taught in universities and pedagogical institutes. Thus only a handful of teachers and school administrators actively attack religion, while most spend their time on more familiar academic pusuits.[14]

The available textbooks provide only marginal assistance to the schoolteacher who is willing to combat religion in his or her classroom. Until the mid-1960s, ministries of education devoted little or no attention to the atheist training of school-children. As late as 1963 the list of works recommended for class use in the lower grades did not include any devoted entirely to religion and atheism. The study programme for outside reading for pupils in the lower grades showed a similar lack of concern with these problems, listing few books on anti-religious themes. The various teachers' manuals and workbooks either made no mention of religion or gave teachers vague and unsubstantial cues on how to introduce atheist materials.[15] The situation since that time has changed only slightly.

Conditions in institutions of higher learning are not appreciably different, although there has been some intensification of anti-religious propaganda in the past decade. Until 1959 Soviet higher academic institutions provided small doses of anti-religious material in courses in dialectical and historical materialism and the history of the C.P.S.U.[16] In 1959 a new elective course, entitled 'Fundamentals of Scientific Atheism', was introduced in higher academic institutions. Few students registered for it, and of those who did, most did not attend lectures. Indeed in some institutions the course was not given because no students enrolled in it.[17] At present the course calls for twenty-four hours of instruction (twelve lectures in a single semester), and the new syllabus devotes particular attention to the organisation, forms and methods of anti-religious propaganda. In 1964 the Central Committee made it a requirement for all university students and for those enrolled in medical, agricultural and pedagogical institutes.[18]

The purpose of the course is not simply to provide students with knowledge of anti-religious theory. Classroom instruction is accompanied by 'practical work'. Students take part in various anti-religious activities under the guidance of the Komsomol or the scientific atheism faculty. For example, the Komsomol assigns students to deliver anti-religious lectures to the general public and sometimes arranges 'agitation tours' to nearby collective farms. In addition, the Komsomol organisations in some institutions of higher learning have set up atheism clubs or 'schools for atheist propagandists.' Young scientists and students in the upper levels of technical schools and institutes are given intensive training by experienced anti-religious specialists. Each student is responsible for delivering lectures and arranging discussions on atheist themes on Sundays or during vacation periods.[19] Thus, while the basic purpose of atheist training in both schools and institutions of higher learning is to ensure that Soviet youth reject religious notions, the training serves a second purpose as well. Many young people serve as anti-religious propagandists while still at school, and some go on to become atheist specialists in later life. Those who are being socialised are at the same time called upon to socialise others.

Anti-religious work in Soviet universities suffers from many of the same problems visible in primary and secondary schools. Some faculty members choose not to interfere with the personal religious beliefs of students, while others are insufficiently well trained in scientific atheism. The faculty at most schools is more interested in the conventional academic disciplines than in conducting a propaganda war against religion.[20] The lack of interest of teacher and student alike is expressed in another way as well. Very few persons register for graduate work in scientific atheism in the Institutes of the U.S.S.R. Academy of Sciences or in the faculties of higher educational institutions. In the period 1957–63, only three doctoral dissertations and some sixty candidate's theses dealing with scientific atheism were defended.[21] There has been some increase in academic attention to atheism in recent years, but not much. For example, at present, only slightly more than ten per cent of all dissertations in philosophy deal with some aspect of religion and atheism.[22] The lack of scholarly research and interest, combined with faculty and student indifference to atheist themes in their regular classwork, suggest that the effectiveness of university-based anti-religious programmes is likely to be quite limited.

During the 1960s, while academic specialists devoted more attention to anti-religious matters, the Communist Party attempted to introduce a series of new secular holidays and ceremonies throughout the U.S.S.R. While the new rites are designed primarily to supplant religious holy days and ceremonies, they also contribute to far-reaching (though rather vague) goals, i.e. 'the ideological, ethical and aesthetic upbringing of the builders of Communism,' the 'rearing of . . . citizens . . . devoted to the ideas of the Party'.[23] While the new rituals help to satisfy basic human needs for beauty and entertainment, they also serve the political and ideological purposes of the Party by combating religion and contributing to the political socialisation of the Soviet people.

The new celebrations, devoid of religious content and infused with 'positive' secular symbols, are of two types: (1) public holidays and festivals, which the entire nation or entire population of some locality celebrates annually, and (2) rites which mark significant events in the lives of individual persons.

At present there are six state holidays: (1) New Year's Day (1 January); (2) International Women's Day (8 March); (3) International Labour Day (1 and 2 May); (4) Victory Day (9 May); (5) the Anniversary of the October Revolution (7 and 8 November); and (6) Constitution Day (5 December). Each of these provides an occasion for celebrating the regime's achievements; all are marked by a profusion of propaganda, public speeches, demonstrations and ceremonial meetings. None the less, the number of holidays is still deemed insufficient to meet the needs of the Party. Therefore, special 'labour holidays' and festivals, connected with the beginning or end of some phase of the production cycle, have been devised to meet these needs. Celebrated primarily (but by no means exclusively) in the countryside, these events are aimed at drawing people's attention away from religious holy days and to the success of the Soviet regime. The principal Christian holy days – Christmas, Easter and various patron saints' days – are the primary focus of these efforts.

An elaborate spring holiday, known by various names in different regions of the Soviet Union, is now celebrated at Eastertime. It is held in late March, at the conclusion of the spring field work – or, in the Christian calendar, at Eastertime. Individual days usually are set aside during the festival period to coincide with, and draw attention away from, the various holy days of the Easter period. In the Baltic States, for example, Spring Holiday is held for the entire week before Easter Sunday; a 'week of purity' is proclaimed – a direct parallel to the familiar Passion Week. The climax of the holiday is a series of processions, concerts, dances and games, and a rather pagan ceremony honouring spring. A pretty girl, adorned with flowers and ribbons, is chosen to represent 'Spring'. 'Spring' will then greet 'Winter' (usually an exemplarary worker, perhaps a member of a local Brigade of Communist Labour), offering thanks for the abundant snowfalls and promising to provide a rich harvest.[24]

A winter holiday, similar to the spring festival in both form and function, is designed to help undermine the celebration of Christmas. Known as Russian Winter or the New Year Holiday, it closely resembles the anti-Easter celebration.[25] In addition, other pre-Christian holidays have been revived and are celebrated in various regions of the U.S.S.R. Each is designed not simply to replace religious holy days, but also to emphasise the values and strengths of the Communist system and to stimulate future economic successes.[26] The new holidays honour labour, collectivism and the Soviet system in general. At the same time they honour those workers who distinguish themselves by their high productivity. Thus the Latvian holiday of Ligo, which is celebrated in the countryside at the conclusion of spring field work and in industrial areas at the end of the second economic quarter, is a 'holiday of summing up the results of socialist competition'. It is used 'to propagandise the best labour traditions, achievements in the socialist economy, to honour the best people in the city and the countryside . . .'. The best workers and peasants are given bonuses and other prizes, are awarded ribbons and banners, and are chosen to represent their work groups in the various ceremonies which take place during a holiday. Those whose work is disappointing, who have not met their socialist obligations, are exposed to criticism during the festival proceedings.[27] By rewarding some and criticising others, and by underscoring those traits which characterise the New Soviet Man, the system of secular holidays not only fulfils an anti-religious function, but performs a crucial socialising role as well.

In addition to these public holidays and festivals, various ceremonies and rites marking significant events in people's personal lives have been introduced. These celebrations are designed to serve as a substitute for the traditional religious consecration given to such events, and simultaneously to help mould the New Soviet Man. The Soviet conception of what constitutes personal or family joy or grief is substantially different from the Western notion. In the U.S.S.R., a celebration ought not to be merely personal or spontaneous; it must be organised by and for the entire community. 'In our country,' one Soviet writer has pointed out, 'people's personal lives are not only their private affair, but also a profoundly public matter. The collective must be far from indifferent as to what sorts of morals one or another comrade adheres to.'[28] This notion of collectivism, repeatedly underscored by Soviet authorities, is a central feature of all new Soviet ceremonies.

In the first decade after the Revolution, special Bolshevik ceremonies were created to compete with the religious sacraments, i.e. the *oktyabriny* or 'Octobrist' ceremony for births, 'red weddings', and 'red funerals'. They met with only limited success and gradually were abandoned. The *oktyabriny* ceremony suggests why this happened. The parents of several new-born children would promise to bring up their children 'not as slaves for the bourgeoisie, but as fighters against it'. Individual mothers would declare: 'The child belongs to me only physically. For his spiritual upbringing, I entrust him to society.'[29] Such ceremonies could hardly have been expected to satisfy the needs of people other than Party activists, and it is clear that they did not.

The ceremonies which have been developed over the past decade, while somewhat more sophisticated than their predecessors, have not met with an enthusiastic response. All are directed towards developing the qualities of the New Soviet Man – collectivism, patriotism, proletarian internationalism and love of labour. Emphasising the partnership between the individual and the State, they identify the personal joys and sorrows of citizens with the Party's purposes. At the same time they provide numerous opportunities to propagandise the achievements of the regime, thereby stimulating and reinforcing the political values, symbols and notions which the Party advocates. But it has proved difficult to devise rituals which provide both political propaganda and an aesthetically pleasing experience. Moreover, efforts to nurture collectivism have clashed with the objective of satisfying people's needs for personal or family celebrations. The task of uprooting traditions which have endured for centuries has sometimes generated frustration and impatience among officials. This in turn has led to excesses and errors which have harmed the entire programme of political socialisation.

The new ceremony celebrating the birth of a child, for example, has two objectives: to provide politically relevant messages to parents, and at the same time to introduce the child to the official belief system. It has proved difficult to achieve both aims. 'Children are not born atheists or believers,' a Soviet scholar has observed. 'They become one or the other under the influence of their environment or upbringing.'[30] A child who is kept from religious influences, and is instead confronted with those symbols of which the regime approves, is unlikely to become a believer and, it is hoped, will become an enthusiastic supporter of the political system.

The ceremony itself is usually rather elaborate. Celebrated for a single child or for a group of new-borns, it usually is staged as a 'Day of Family Happiness'. The infants are given memorial medals, certificates or gift packages which emphasise political themes and symbols. These vary from Little Octobrist pins, Pioneer neckerchiefs and Komsomol badges to ornate medallions heavily laden with political symbols. Medals given to children in Leningrad and Kiev, for example, are adorned with pictures of a Russian birch tree, a tractor, a freshly ploughed field, a high voltage line, an electric power station, and a picture of Lenin. It is said that these medals 'help engender feelings of love towards the Soviet Fatherland [and] the Soviet people', that they 'fill a person's heart with patriotism.'[31] At the very least they acquaint children at an early age with those values and symbols that the Party supports.

At the same time the ceremony accompanying the registration of babies links parents, relatives and close friends to the official value system. The official presiding at such a ceremony instructs them in their responsibilities to the child and to the country. In Moscow, for example, he declares to the parents: 'Raise your children to be honest, courageous, joyous, true patriots who love the Fatherland and labour . . .'[32] Relatives or close friends promise to help raise the child to be 'an honest and fair citizen . . . a devoted patriot who loves labour and is a cheerful builder of Communism'.[33] The ritual thus connects the personal joy parents feel in celebrating the birth of a child with appreciation for the Party's magnanimity and concern, and with the officially approved values of collectivism and patriotism.[34]

The second special event in an individual's life which has become the occasion for non-religious, ceremonial celebration is the attainment of maturity. New rites, designed in part to supplant the Christian practice of confirmation (especially prevalent in the Baltic States) and the Jewish *bar mitzvah* ceremony, have been devised. There are two basic patterns, one focusing on the receipt of a passport, the other organised around graduation from secondary school.

The issuance of passports, formerly a rather pedestrian event in the life of Soviet citizens who reached the age of sixteen, is now the basis for a special coming-of-age ceremony. The passport is used as a symbol of adulthood, and its acceptance is made to imply the simultaneous acceptance of the obligations and duties of an adult. The ceremony itself is designed to stimulate patriotism and love of labour. A Komsomol official urges the young people to emulate advanced workers, to 'do nothing which might disgrace the revolutionary and labour traditions' of the Soviet people. 'You must value your Soviet passport,' he says. 'This passport was earned by our fathers with their toil and blood. . . . Love your Fatherland and be its heroes!'[35]

In some areas of the country, officials arrange a coming-of-age ceremony for eighteen-year-olds.[36] It is at this age that most young people finish their schooling and become workers. Therefore the symbol of transition to adulthood is graduation from secondary school. In Latvia, for example, a day-long Coming-of-Age Holiday (*Prazdnik sovershennoletiya*) is held for groups of young people shortly after their graduation from secondary school. The boys and girls are assembled in a local club or ceremonial hall where they 'solemnly promise to devote themselves to the Fatherland, to labour, and to the construction of Communism'. Representatives of the previous year's celebrants, who have since become 'front ranking workers', entrust 'the most deserving' eighteen-year-olds with a special banner symbolising the link between school and productive labour. A similar, though somewhat more elaborate, holiday is held in Estonia.[37]

A third major event that is now celebrated with an elaborate secular ceremony is marriage. This is an event which people, including many whose religious convictions are by no means firm, have long celebrated in solemn surroundings in a place of worship. The occasion is generally regarded as demanding dignified and elaborate celebration, and the church traditionally has been the only institution to provide an appropriate setting and ritual. Because of intense criticism of the civil registrar's offices, where all

Soviet weddings formerly took place, the new rite is arranged in special 'wedding palaces'. These are buildings which have been set aside in all large cities, and in some provincial centres as well, to provide attractive surroundings for the new secular marriage ceremony.[38]

The ceremony itself is similar in form to Western weddings, though some of its features are quite distinctive. The bride is dressed in white, Mendelssohn's Wedding March is played, and there are flowers, gifts, champagne and an elaborate dinner. Certain elements, however, are uniquely Soviet. In a typical ceremony in the Krasnodar Territory, for example, young couples are urged 'to work faithfully for the sake of our beloved Fatherland'. They are told to rear children who will be 'ardent patriots of the Soviet Fatherland, diligent builders of Communism'.[39] The conspicuous use of political slogans and inevitable references to the State help to emphasise the profoundly public nature of the personal events they celebrate.

Soviet authorities have experienced a good deal of difficulty in devising a satisfactory funeral rite, primarily because of the delicate nature of the task. The ceremony which has been adopted, like the other ceremonies, is similar to a religious service. Speakers, as might be expected, focus on the contributions which their late comrade made to his factory or farm and to the national economic effort. The medals, orders and other awards which he may have received often are displayed and carried on red pillows as part of the funeral procession.[40] As the deceased is honoured and memorialised, so too is the idea of productive labour; the life and death of the deceased are given meaning in the context of official values and symbols. Thus, while obviously it is too late to socialise the deceased, a considerable effort is made to socialise the survivors.

Annual memorial ceremonies for the dead, which were introduced a decade ago, are perceptibly different from traditional church services.[41] They seem more festive than mournful. Flags and banners are raised, and 'popular and revolutionary songs' are sung. Old Communists, production leaders and schoolchildren deliver speeches. The ceremony is specifically designed to honour 'the fighters who have perished and the toilers who have died', those who have 'fallen in the Revolution', the martyrs of the Komsomol and the Party who died protecting the Revolution.

The ceremony and speeches are addressed only secondarily to those who have died or to their families; their essential purpose is to inspire the living and to glorify and magnify the purposes of the Party.[42]

Other festivals, holidays and ceremonies, apart from those described above, are arranged in the U.S.S.R., and suggestions have been made to introduce still more. Among the events considered deserving of public recognition and celebration are: departing for military service, receiving one's first pay for a job, and retirement from work. A solemn ritual has been devised to mark each of these events, but the number of communities which arrange such ceremonies is still relatively small. Many other proposals for new celebrations have been rejected outright as too elaborate, expensive or inappropriate.

It is difficult to assess how effectively these new holidays and ceremonies contribute to the political socialisation of the Soviet citizenry or help combat religion.[43] The authorities appear to be anxious to introduce them throughout the U.S.S.R. The available statistics indicate that the Party has made greater and greater use of the new ceremonies, particularly the new marriage ritual. Unfortunately the published data deal only with individual communities and districts – see Tables 1, 2 and 3 – and there is no way of knowing if the figures are representative of national trends. Nor is there any way of measuring the extent to which people have shifted voluntarily to the new rites, i.e. whether they have in fact been socialised. Nevertheless it should be emphasised that the new rituals are widely practised, even if they are not very popular.[44]

Certainly the new rites suffer from major shortcomings in planning, design and execution. Even their most enthusiastic supporters have criticised them for often being unattractive and colourless. Many holidays and ceremonies are said to be characterised by 'banality' and 'monotony'.[45] It has proved particularly difficult to strike the appropriate balance between the political and artistic sides of the new ceremonies. 'A genuine rite,' a leading Soviet analyst has suggested, '. . . while entertaining, is at the same time instructive, gradually [and] unobtrusively inspiring certain kinds of thoughts, views [and] moral norms.'[46] In practice, however, one or the other element has taken precedence. Some rituals are simply theatrical spectacles incapable of performing the political function assigned to them, while others are so filled with propaganda messages that they become didactic and wearisome.[47] The very impersonal character of the new rituals is another impediment to their success. Large numbers of persons are invited to take part in or view a given ceremony. If an essentially intimate and personal experience is celebrated with and for strangers in a large public place, its impact is not likely to be great, and it may even be transformed into an offensive charade.[48]

A discussion of Soviet efforts to combat religion and spread atheism suggests some interesting comparisons with the process of political socialisation in other nations. All political systems provide socialising experiences. What distinguishes the Soviet system is the vast and overt character of the programme, as well

TABLE 1

Percentage of Births, Weddings and
Funerals Marked by Religious Ceremonies

	Ryazan (1960)	Penza (1962)	Tallin (1963)	Tartu (1963)	Odessa (1964)	Komi ASSR (1964)	Yekabpilsky District (Latvia) (1964)
Births	60	48·5	14·3	n.a.	55·2	22	25·7
Weddings	15	6·4	3·2	4	14·5	0·2	7
Funerals	30	20·9	28·4	51	35·7	n.a.	19·4

Sources: *Voprosy istorii religii i ateizma* (Problems in the History of Religion and Atheism), XI (Moscow, 1963), pp. 67, 73, 80–82, as cited in Bohdan R. Bociurkiw, 'Religion and Soviet Society', *Survey* (July 1966), p. 70; M. D. Shevchenko, 'Rol semeinykh traditsii v nasledovanii religioznykh perezhitkov detmi i podrostkami', *Vestnik Moskovskogo Universiteta*, Seriya VIII (Filosofiya), No. 2 (1966), p. 33; V. Pomerantsev, 'Eksperiment', *Nauka i religiya*, No. 1 (1965), p. 4; Ts. A. Stepanyan *et al.* (eds.), *Stroitelstvo kommunizma i dukhovnyi mir cheloveka* (The Construction of Communism and Man's Spiritual World) (Moscow, 1966), pp. 225–6; L. N. Terentyeva, 'Rasprostraneniye ateisticheskogo mirovozzreniya i bezreligioznykh form byta sredi kolkhoznikov latyshei', in N. P. Krasnikov (ed.), *Voprosy preodoleniya religioznykh perezhitkov v SSSR* (Problems in Overcoming Religious Vestiges in the USSR) (Moscow, 1966), p. 65.

TABLE 2

Percentage of Births, Marriages and Funerals
Marked by Religious Ceremonies: Estonia, 1957–1965

	Baptisms	*Church Weddings*	*Religious Funerals*
1957	55·8	29·8	64·5
1958	49·3	28·0	65·9
1959	42·5	25·6	65·1
1960	34·5	18·0	62·8
1961	28·7	13·6	60·9
1962	22·3	9·1	55·4
1963	20·0	6·7	52·6
1965	15·1	3·4	n.a.

Sources: V. Pomerantsev, 'Eksperiment', *Nauka i religiya*, No. 1 (1965), p. 4; P. P. Kampars and N. N. Zakovich, *Sovetskaya grazhdanskaya obryadnost* (Soviet Civil Ceremonies) (Moscow, 1967), p. 220.

TABLE 3

Secular and Religious Coming of Age
Ceremonies: Estonia, 1957–1968

	Number of Summer Days of Youth Celebrants	*Number of Church Confirmations*
1957	36	10,000
1958	2,200	8,100
1959	6,300	6,400
1960	6,950	3,950
1961	7,000	2,730
1968	6,000	n.a.

Sources: L. Alekseyeva, *Sovremennye prazdniki i obryady v derevne* (Contemporary Holidays and Ceremonies in the Countryside) (Moscow, 1968), p. 20; G. Gerodnik, 'Grazhdanskiye i bytovye obryady' (Civil and Everyday Rites), *Nauka i religiya*, No. 7 (1962), p. 49; I. G. Kebin, *Sovetskaya Estoniya*, 11 April 1969, p. 2.

as the extent to which the Soviets systematically, directly and repeatedly communicate their political messages. The Party encourages a constant flow of explicitly political experiences, relying heavily on manifest, rather than latent, political socialisation.[49] The approach is simple and direct: its principal theoretical underpinning is expressed in a favourite saying of Nikita Khrushchev, *'povtorenie mat' ucheniya* [repetition is the mother of learning].'[50] Moreover, Soviet efforts involve constant repetition and reinforcement of lessons encountered as early as the pre-school years.[51] Soviet ideologists probably would agree with Herbert Hyman's contention that, to promote political stability, people 'must learn their political behaviour early and well and persist in it'.[52] Whether the lessons, symbols and values presented by the regime are in fact internalised by the masses is another matter.

We have already noted the deficiencies of anti-religious training in schools and through the network of new holidays and ceremonies. Other propaganda measures suffer from similar weaknesses. Perhaps most important, religious families and individuals have resisted the intrusion of the *antireligiozniki* into their private lives. While atheist propaganda aimed at young children is potentially a powerful force, its impact is severely limited when the child has been given religious instruction by his family.[53] Moreover, Soviet adults, like their counterparts elsewhere, tend to screen out hostile propaganda messages. The mechanisms of selective exposure, selective perception, selective interpretation and selective retention, which have been observed in other countries, are present in the U.S.S.R. as well.[54] Such responses are particularly likely when official propaganda directly challenges people's religious beliefs or behaviour. Soviet believers, both children and adults, conscientiously avoid atheists and the messages they offer. To a considerable extent, they have been 'inoculated' against antireligious propaganda and thus resist communications or experiences incompatible with their value system. Their recalcitrance, nourished by tradition and supported by the activities of church organisations, has seriously impeded the socalisation effort. It is not surprising, therefore, that the Party has decided to supplement its socialisation programmes with greater use of the criminal law and intensified pressure on religious believers. Soviet citizens may be unresponsive to atheist propaganda, but they cannot avoid the law.

NOTES

1. Aristotle, *Politics* (New York: Random House, 1943), Book VIII, Chapter 1, p. 320.
2. Richard E. Dawson and Kenneth Prewitt, *Political Socialization* (Boston: Little, Brown and Co., 1969), p. 6.
3. Gabriel A. Almond, 'Introduction: A Functional Approach to Comparative Politics', in Gabriel A. Almond and James S. Coleman (eds.), *The Politics of the Developing Areas* (Princeton: Princeton University Press, 1960), pp. 27–28
4. See, e.g., the editorial in *Kommunist Tadzhikistana*, 19 January 1971, p. 1.
5. *Pravda*, 12 January 1967, p. 2.
6. 'It is necessary', Lenin wrote in 1922, 'to present the masses with the most diverse materials on atheist propaganda, to acquaint them with facts from the most varied spheres of life, to approach them this way and that, in order to interest them, to rouse them from their religious dream, to shake them from the most varied sides, with the most varied means, etc.' V. I. Lenin, *Sochineniya*, 4th ed. (Moscow, 1951), Vol. 33, p. 204.
7. 'It is easier to educate a person than to re-educate him,' one academic figure has argued. 'The atheist must, without fail, be moulded within the walls of the school.' See *Izvestiya*, 27 November 1965, p. 3. Schools are asked to 'immunise' students against religion. See *Nauka i religiya*, No. 4 (1964), p. 77.
8. See, e.g., *Fizika v shkole*, No. 1 (1961); 'Teaching Methods Used to Form Atheistic Convictions in Soviet Students', *Sredneye spetsialnoye obrazovaniye*, No. 1 (1966), in *Joint Publications Research Service* (henceforth JPRS), No. 36,058, p. 10; N. I. Boldyrev *et al. Pedagogika* (Pedagogics) (Moscow, 1968), pp. 276–278. See also the two anti-religious stories written especially for children in *Nauka i religiya*, No. 9 (1968), pp. 70–79.
9. *Russkii yazyk v nerusskoi shkole*, No. 1 (1966), in JPRS No. 34,804, pp. 7–8.
10. *Nauka i religiya*, No. 9 (1964), pp. 46–9; No. 9 (1966), pp. 67–8, 72; No. 2 (1967), pp. 77–8.
11. *Pravda*, 12 July 1964, p. 3.
12. *Nauka i religiya*, No. 3 (1967), p. 64.
13. *Uchitelskaya gazeta*, 23 August 1966, p. 4.
14. *Nauka i religiya*, No. 9 (1961), p. 56; No. 12 (1961), pp. 79–80; *Pravda*, 6 March 1964, p. 2.
15. *Nachalnaya shkola*, No. 2 (1962), in JPRS No. 20,515, p. 28; *Pravda*, 6 March 1964, p. 2; *Nauka i religiya*, No. 10 (1966), p. 2; S. D. Skazkin *et al.*, *Nastolnaya kniga ateista* (Atheist's Handbook) (Moscow, 1968), p. 502.
16. Thus, the required course 'Dialectical and Historical Materialism' devoted approximately six hours of lectures and seminars (out of 140) to questions of religion and atheism. See *Administration of Teaching in Social Sciences in the USSR* (Ann Arbor: University of Michigan Press, 1960) for the programme of this course. An outline of the material on religion and atheism can be found on pp. 23–4.
17. *Sovetskaya Rossiya*, 6 July 1966, in *CDSP*, Vol. XVIII, No. 35, p. 7; *Nauka i religiya*, No. 2 (1962), p. 15.
18. *Komsomolskaya pravda*, 21 August 1962, p. 3; *Partiinaya zhizn*, No. 2 (1964), p. 23.
19. *Nauka i religiya*, No. 2 (1962), pp. 17–18; *Agitator*, No. 8 (1968), p. 48; *Sputnik komsomolskogo aktivista* (Companion of the Komsomol Activist) (Moscow, 1962), pp. 192–7; *Molodoi Kommunist*, No. 1 (1971), p. 98.
20. *Sovetskaya Litva*, 21 January 1960, in *CDSP*, Vol. XII, No. 10, p. 34; *Sovetskaya Rossiya*, *op. cit.*, p. 3; *Nauka i religiya*, No. 10 (1966), p. 2.

21. *Nauka i religiya*, No. 1 (1964), p. 33; *Voprosy filosofii*, No. 1 (1967), pp. 150–51 No. 11 (1967), p. 132.

22. *Voprosy filosofii*, No. 1 (1969), pp. 147, 149; No. 12 (1969), pp. 140–42.

23. A. Filatov, *O novykh i starykh obryadakh* (About the New and Old Rites) (Moscow, 1967), pp. 42, 20. See also P. P. Kampars and N. M. Zakovich, *Sovetskaya grazhdanskaya obryadnost* (Soviet Civil Ceremonies) (Moscow, 1967), pp. 8, 163.

24. I. P. Tsameryan, *Osnovy nauchnogo ateizma* (Foudations of Scientific Atheism), 2nd rev. ed. (Moscow, 1962), p. 391; *Politicheskoye samoobrazovaniye*, No. 7 (1962), p. 98; *Agitator*, No. 22 (1964), p. 48.

25. See L. Alekseyeva, *Sovremennye prazdniki i obryady v derevne* (Contemporary Holidays and Ceremonies in the Countryside) (Moscow, 1968), pp. 49–51.

26. 'The social and educational significance of these holidays and new ceremonies is great,' a high Ukrainian official (P. Tronko) has remarked; 'they inspire, they call people to labour feats'. *Izvestiya*, 2 June 1964, p. 6. See also Kampars, and Zakovich, *op. cit.*, p. 48.

27. Kampars and Zakovich, *op. cit.*, pp. 101–2. See also Filatov, *op. cit.*, pp. 88, 97, 100; Alekseyeva, *op. cit.*, p. 52; A. Orekhanov, 'Prazdnik posle vesennego seva' (Holiday after the Spring Sowing), in *Torzhestvenno, krasivo, pamyatno!* (Solemnly, Beautifully, Memorably!) (Moscow, 1967) (hereafter *Torzhestvenno*), p. 123.

28. *Partiinaya zhizn*, No. 6 (1963), p. 50.

29. Filatov, *op. cit.*, pp. 44, 45.

30. *Voprosy filosofii*, No. 4 (1964), p. 150.

31. N. Arkhangelsky, in *Torzhestvenno*, p. 39. See also *Partiinaya zhizn*, No. 6 (1963), p. 53; Alekseeva, *op. cit.*, p. 18.

32. A. Yefremova, in *Torzhestvenno*, pp. 16–17.

33. Filatov, *op. cit.*, pp. 49–50.

34. Because the children are too young to participate, the ceremony cannot be instructive for them. In some areas, therefore, birth celebrations are deferred until the child is several years old. However, this type of ceremony is not an adequate substitute for baptism, since parents who wish to baptise their children do so when the children are still infants. See *Nauka i religiya*, No. 7 (1962), p. 43.

35. T. Sivokhina, in *Torzhestvenno*, p. 93.

36. The Lutheran practice of arranging confirmation for young people at the age of eighteen influenced the Party, especially in the Baltic region where the Lutheran Church has a large following. Kampars and Zakovich, *op. cit.*, p. 204.

37. *Partiinaya zhizn*, No. 6 (1963), pp. 53–4; *Nauka i religiya*, No. 7 (1962), pp. 48, 49; Kampas and Zakovich, *op. cit.*, p. 207.

38. An *Izvestiya* reporter described the civil registrar's offices as 'official and sterile . . . irritating to everyone . . . soulless . . .' *Izvestiya*, 5 December 1959, p. 2. See also *Nauka i religiya*, No. 2 (1969), p. 37.

39. N. Kobovsky, in *Torzhestvenno*, p. 61; Alekseyeva, *op. cit.*, p. 23; *Agitator*, No. 21 (1963), p. 55.

40. Filatov, *op. cit.*, p. 63; Alekseyeva, *op. cit.*, p. 57; Kampars and Zakovich, *op. cit.*, pp. 210–11.

41. According to the official view, people traditionally visited cemetaries merely to listen to 'priestly ravings'. They were 'swindled out of money, a prayer was read, and that was it. Then a drinking bout began.' *Kommunist*, No. 11 (1960), p. 63; *Partiinaya zhizn*, No. 6 (1963), p. 52.

42. *Kommunist*, No. 11 (1960), p. 63; *Partiinaya zhizn*, No. 6 (1963), p. 52; Kampars and Zakovich, *op. cit.*, pp. 210–15.

170 *Religion and Atheism in the U.S.S.R. and Eastern Europe*

43. For an evaluation of the overall effort to combat religion, see David Powell, 'The Effectiveness of Soviet Anti-religious Propaganda,' *The Public Opinion Quarterly*, Vol. XXXI, No. 3 (1967), pp. 366–80.
44. See Nikita Struve, 'Pseudo-Religious Rites Introduced by the Party Authorities', in William C. Fletcher and Anthony J. Strover (eds.), *Religion and the Search for New Ideals in the USSR* (New York: Frederick A. Praeger, 1967), pp. 44–8.
45. *Politicheskoye samoobrazovaniye*, No. 4 (1963), p. 91; *Nauka i religiya*, No. 6 (1966), p. 51; Kampars and Zakovich, *op. cit.*, pp. 6, 201; Alekseyeva, *op. cit.*, p. 51.
46. Filatov, *op. cit.*, p. 20.
47. *Nauka i religiya*, No. 7 (1962), p. 43.
48. *Izvestiya*, 19 August 1961, p. 6; Filatov, *op. cit.*, p. 41; Rampars and Zakovich, *op. cit.*, pp. 202–3; N. Semakin and E. Bugrov, in *Torzhestvenno*, p. 44.
49. Manifest political socialisation 'involves the explicit communication of information, values or feelings toward political objects'. Latent socialisation is 'the transmission of nonpolitical attitudes which affect attitudes toward analogous roles and objects in the political system'. Gabriel A. Almond and G. Bingham Powell, Jr., *Comparative Politics: A Developmental Approach* (Boston: Little, Brown and Co., 1966), pp. 65–6. See also Almond, *op. cit.*, p. 28.
50. *Agitator*, No. 16 (1960), p. 37.
51. See Henry Chauncey (ed.), *Soviet Preschool Education* (New York: Holt, Rinehart and Winston, Inc., 1969), pp. 72–3.
52. Herbert Hyman, *Political Socialization* (Glencoe, Ill.: The Free Press, 1959), p. 17.
53. Joseph T. Klapper, *The Effects of Mass Communication* (Glencoe, Ill.: The Free Press, 1960), p. 61. There is also evidence which suggests that children place greater credence in the views of adults who are near to them than in the lessons of school books. See Gabriel A. Almond and Sidney Verba (eds.) *The Civic Culture* (Princeton: Princeton University Press, 1963), pp. 325–326, note 6.
54. See Aryeh L. Unger, 'Politinformator or Agitator: A Decision Blocked,' *Problems of Communism*, Vol. XIX, No. 5 (September–October 1970), p. 42 and the sources cited therein.

9 Religion and Soviet Foreign Policy:

A Functional Survey

WILLIAM C. FLETCHER

Religious organisations in the U.S.S.R. have been much involved in international affairs since World War II. Particularly since the death of Stalin, the Churches of the Soviet Union and Eastern Europe have conducted increasingly vigorous foreign relations, interacting with ecclesiastical leaders and religious groups throughout the world. These activities in the religious field have relevance for the secular interests of Soviet foreign policy, adding to the latter a dimension which has not as yet received sufficient attention in Western analysis of the international relations of the U.S.S.R. This chapter will attempt to survey the role of religion in terms of Soviet foreign policy, attempting to assess the significance of various aspects of the subject from the point of view of Soviet, rather than Western – and still less Western Christian – observers. Without denying the purely ecclesiastical side of the international affairs of Russian religious organisations, an attempt will be made to summarise and illustrate the ways in which these activities have made a contribution to the implementation of the national interests of the U.S.S.R. in the international arena.

The foreign policy of any major power (in this case the U.S.S.R.) may be summarised under three broad categories. First is normal, inter-state diplomacy, broadly defined to include not only the traditional ambassadorial and consular relations, but also trade, foreign aid, cultural and other transactions, and, in certain circumstances, the use or threat of military force. Second is the less conspicuous, and often extra-legal, channel of direct relations with foreign individuals and groups, which would include espionage and subversion, relations with foreign Communist Parties, or para-military relations with dissident or insurgent groups. The third major category of modern foreign policy is in the field of public opinion – the attempt to appeal directly to the people of a foreign state over the head of its Government.

Religion's major function is to contribute to the third field of foreign endeavour – the attempt to influence foreign public opinion. Although there have been examples of a religious dimension in nearly every aspect of Soviet foreign policy, it is in the arena of public opinion that the Churches have exercised their greatest impact. And even here it should be noted that religion's role has by no means been a commanding one; religion's place, while important, has been ancillary and sometimes quite peripheral.

The rationale behind co-operation between the Soviet State and the Church in international affairs is to be found in the nature of Church–State relations in the U.S.S.R. Since World War II a bargaining situation has prevailed.[1] The Church, in order to ensure its survival as an institution in Soviet society, has offered to the State its unequivocal support in political matters in return for concessions allowing it a restricted opportunity to minister to the people domestically. For its part, the State has accepted a temporary postponement of its commitment to the final eradication of religion from society in return for the political services of the Church. It is primarily in the field of foreign affairs that the Church has fulfilled its part of the bargain.

Immediately after World War II, the Russian Orthodox Church was able to play a direct role in Soviet foreign policy, engaging in vigorous activities to help secure Soviet hegemony in Eastern Europe, and seeking subsidiary bases of influence in countries not destined to enter the Soviet orbit. By 1948, however, with the stabilisation of Soviet influence in Eastern Europe and the rise of the Cold War elsewhere in the world, these activities lost much of their initial significance, and the Church's role in Soviet foreign policy shifted to a more defensive position, consonant with the stance adopted by the Soviet State, until the imbalance in atomic weapons and delivery capabilities could be overcome. The chief contribution which the Church could make in these conditions was in the field of propaganda for peace; Russian churchmen entered enthusiastically into the activities of the World Peace Council and other bodies. These early activities of the Church in foreign affairs have already been surveyed,[2] so they will not receive detailed treatment here.

After the death of Stalin, foreign relations of the Russian Churches came to embrace a vastly increased range of activities. With the successful construction of nuclear and strategic weapons systems the Soviet Union was no longer confined to a defensive approach in international activities, but could begin innovations in foreign policy. To be sure, the achievement of near parity in weapons of mass destruction resulted in a geopolitical situation which was frozen in its major parameters, with the world polarised between the U.S. and the U.S.S.R. and with little prospect for altering this situation. But the newly independent nations of the Third World represented an area with much potential, and Khrushchev revised the Stalinist ideological division of the world into the camps of Socialism and Capitalism by postulating a third category – a 'zone of peace' where nations, if not yet in the Socialist camp, were seeking to disengage themselves from Capitalism allowing the U.S.S.R. to enter vigorously into the competition for influence in the Third World. With the development of air and sea power and a flexible response capability during the sixties, Soviet foreign policy was able to abandon the continental approach of the Stalin period, which sought contiguous expansion only and displayed little interest in opportunities elsewhere in the world,[3] in favour of global approach, able to challenge its major adversary anywhere in the world. In conformity with this transformation in Soviet foreign policy, the religious institutions of the U.S.S.R. and Eastern Europe also expanded their activities, seeking active relations with religious (and, on occasion, non-religious) bodies throughout the world.

Given the geopolitical situation of a world polarised between two major powers, competition with the United States has been a major determinant of Soviet foreign policy. It is primarily the confrontation with the West which limits the parameters of Soviet foreign relations. The Churches have made a vigorous contribution to this confrontation, engaging in an almost limitless range of relationships with Western individuals, Churches, denominations, and national and international religious groups. While it would be beyond the scope of this paper to enumerate these relations, certain major functions can be discerned throughout the activities of the Churches of the U.S.S.R. in the East-West confrontation.

The most fundamental and successful of the services rendered to Soviet foreign policy by the Churches has been a contribution to the image building process. The excesses of the Stalin years had resulted in a critical deterioration in the U.S.S.R.'s image in the West, and at least until the mid-sixties much effort was devoted to overcoming this handicap. The Churches contributed enthusiastically, seeking out contact with religious individuals in the West, particularly those of influence, and making every effort to elicit a favourable public reaction to the U.S.S.R. Similarly, the long habit of isolation was broken by participation of Russian churchmen in international religious organisations, such as the World Council of Churches and the Baptist World Alliance. Much of their initial effort in these organisations was devoted to painting a glowing picture of the new society emerging in the U.S.S.R. Russian churchmen buttressed the Soviet Government's claim of full religious freedom with unrestrained statements about the excellent conditions their churches enjoyed at home, even when the rising anti-religious campaign of the 1960s was radically increasing the tensions and restrictions within the U.S.S.R. Inflated numbers of active churches were claimed (the number of Russian Orthodox churches was exaggerated by approximately 45 per cent)[4] and as the anti-religious campaign took its toll these unrevised figures receded further and further from actuality. To a man, the Russian churchmen were insistent in their support of the desired image of the U.S.S.R. as a land of complete religious freedom.

The results were impressive. If the hostile attitude of the West towards the U.S.S.R. during the Cold War has given way to a more open, more friendly attitude, the Churches of the U.S.S.R. and Eastern Europe must be given a share of the credit for the transformation.

A related function of the Church in Soviet foreign policy is to insulate the U.S.S.R. from criticism, delaying and, when possible, preventing the rise of a hostile reaction abroad to internal policies of the State. The Russian Churches have enjoyed almost unbroken success in this endeavour. Concurrently with the expansion of the international activities of the Church, the Soviet regime initiated an intense anti-religious campaign at home in the late 1950s, which by 1964 had reduced the number of open churches in the U.S.S.R. to approximately half their number of the preceding decade,[5] and which subjected religious citizens to an enormous range of pressures and restrictions.[6] Churchmen active in international affairs assumed the task of preventing any repetition of the pre-war experience, when restrictions against religions in the U.S.S.R. resulted in outspoken criticism and protest abroad. By their willingness and readiness to paint a reassuring picture of the domestic situation regardless of the actual events transpiring within the U.S.S.R. these churchmen enjoyed all but absolute success in shielding the Soviet State from adverse criticism in the West. A decade after the commencement of the anti-religious campaign, there was still almost complete ignorance in the Western Churches concerning the difficulties of Churches and religious people in the U.S.S.R., and the services of the Russian churchmen to Soviet foreign policy must be given credit for averting the possibility of a repetition of pre-war protests in the West.

Numerous instances of this form of service are available. In 1964 a meeting was held in Paris under the nominal leadership of the eminent François Mauriac in order to protest against religious injustices in the U.S.S.R., and particularly the regime's planned closure of the Pochaev Monastery.[7] At the time, France was in process of reconsidering its international alignment in such a manner as eventually to result in the withdrawal of French military support from N.A.T.O., and for any considerable French protest to develop would have been most inconvenient for the plans of Soviet foreign policy. Metropolitan Nikodim, the chief spokesman for the Russian Orthodox Church in the 1960s, was quick to deny the veracity of the charges made in Paris,[8] and the danger of a widespread protest developing in France was successfully averted. (In fact, the Soviet regime revised its plans for the Pochaev Monastery, allowing it to continue a truncated existence and taking care to arrange for selected foreign churchmen to visit Pochaev in subsequent years.)

The increasing restrictions of the anti-religious campaign resulted in a protest movement within the Russian Baptist Church which reached serious proportions by the middle 1960s.[9] This movement, known as the *initsiativniki*, began in 1962 to issue a series of appeals to the West against religious injustices in the

U.S.S.R., and, largely due to the efforts of Russian churchmen (see below), no major Western response resulted. In the latter 1960s, however, a British student of religion in the U.S.S.R., Michael Bourdeaux, began a serious study of the *initsiativniki* affair, occasioning sufficient apprehension in Moscow to result in Michael Zhidkov, one of the Russian Baptist Church's chief representatives in international affairs, making a special trip to London and elsewhere prior to the publication of the Bourdeaux study in 1968 to ensure that serious consequences in the Western Churches would not develop.[10]

Similarly, when a cognate protest movement developed in the Orthodox Church late in 1965,[11] the Moscow Patriarchate took pains to avert untoward reaction in the West. Although it took no official notice of this movement prior to the publication of the protest documents in the West in mid-1966, immediately thereafter Metropolitan Nikodim devoted considerable energy to presenting the Patriarchate's views of the events to Western church leaders.[12]

These are but illustrations of the endeavour to shield the Soviet State from unfavourable publicity, and, indeed, the effort formed a constant part of nearly all the international activities of the Russian Churches, evident not so much in specific events and operations, but carried on with steady and unremitting effort underlying the other, more pointed actions in the international religious sphere. The immense success of this endeavour can be gauged from the almost complete absence of public notice of the deteriorating religious situation in the U.S.S.R. in the major Western denominations.

The effectiveness of this effort can be seen in the converse international reaction to Soviet anti-Semitism. Unlike certain of the other religious denominations, the Jewish community in the U.S.S.R. is denied the right of institutional existence on a national scale, and as a result, with a very few exceptions, has had neither the capability nor the opportunity for actions of an international nature. Consequently, it has been difficult to divert Western attention from the regime's policies and actions against Jews within the U.S.S.R. The Jewish community in the West has initiated a massive campaign of publicity and protest against Soviet anti-Semitism, which has caused the Soviet State considerable international embarrassment. Heads of State, parliaments, organisations and individuals (such as the late Bertrand Russell) otherwise sympathetic to the U.S.S.R., and even Western Communist Parties have joined in denunciation of Soviet anti-Semitism. Much of the concern for their fellow believers in the U.S.S.R. is doubtless due to the great cohesiveness of the Jewish community, which learned a bitter lesson about the results of lack of concern during the Nazi period. But it remains true that the Jewish community has not enjoyed the extensive contact with Soviet counterparts in international affairs which has developed in the Christian Churches; that no similar protests have developed in the latter must be attributed, at least in some measure, to the services rendered by Russian churchmen to Soviet foreign policy.

Among the more specific goals of the Russian Church in international affairs is to influence individual Western churchmen, seeking to encourage those amicably disposed to the endeavours of the Soviet State and to minimise, and where possible to change, the reaction of those who are not. The chief instrumentality for achieving this goal during the 1960s was the Prague Christian Peace Conference (C.P.C.),[13] an organisation which allowed close co-operation between Churches of Eastern Europe and the U.S.S.R. in pursuing common international objectives.

Arising from an initiative taken by Czechoslovak churchmen in 1958, the C.P.C. quickly grew into a major attempt to influence public opinion in the international Christian community. Although the Russian Churches played a vigorous role in the C.P.C., the initiative remained with the Czech Churches, and much of the movement's success was attributable to the efforts and international stature of its founder and President, the Czech theologian J. L. Hromádka. Under his leadership, the C.P.C. held large All-Christian Peace Assemblies in 1961, 1964 and 1968, and there were frequent and highly publicised meetings by an array of subsidiary units of the C.P.C. in the intervening periods. Although according to the Statute of the C.P.C. the periodic Assemblies were the ultimate source of authority within the organisation, actual control was exercised by the Working Committee (with 16 members prior to 1964 and 25 thereafter), and, when it was not in session, by the even smaller International Secretariat.[14] The C.P.C. was generously funded,[15] and was able to exercise an impressive influence in the Churches, with increasing impact in the West and even more effect among churchmen from the Third World.

The C.P.C. was one of the most successful of the redesigned and expanded facilities for international propaganda developed during the Khrushchev period. By the middle 1950s the Soviet inspired peace movement, with its intransigent insistence on complete conformity among all its participants, had reached an impasse. With the termination of the Korean War and the consequent diminution of apprehension about the possibility of a third world war, the earlier peace movement entered into the doldrums, and its practical effectiveness had approached the vanishing point. Under Khrushchev's tutelage, intensive efforts were made to refurbish the peace movement and equip it for effective action.

One of the key techniques utilised in Soviet foreign policy under Khrushchev was a limited achievement approach, somewhat analogous to the 'small profit margin' concept in industry. Whereas former participants in a Soviet foreign policy operation were required to adhere in all points to a prescribed formula, under Khrushchev those who attended Soviet sponsored gathering were allowed, and even encouraged, to express themselves on a broad range of subjects having little or nothing to do with the international interests of the U.S.S.R., provided only that they co-operated on a small number of specifics which were of interest. Meetings and events were designed to achieve a limited number of highly focused results, and provided the specific resolutions desired were passed (e.g. on Vietnam, German rearmament, revolution, etc.) participants were free to take whatever other positions they might desire, including on occasion positions less than completely friendly to other aspects of Soviet activities. The result was that in the C.P.C. a broad range of theological and ecclesiastical topics could be discussed, and the passage of the desired resolution demanded only a portion of the participants' energies. Hence Western churchmen were increasingly well disposed towards the C.P.C. and considered co-operation on a small number of highly pointed topics, on which they might not otherwise have yielded, a small price to pay for the ecumenical interchange achieved.

It is doubtful that the C.P.C. could have enjoyed more than a fraction of its success without the intellectual contribution of Hromádka.[16] A creative theologian in his own right, Hromádka was able to provide a theological rationale for the C.P.C's activities which freed it from the burdensome necessity of utilising – or even considering – the ideological framework employed by Soviet foreign policy. Hromádka's theology, oriented almost exclusively to the social dimension of the Christian faith, took the achievement of social justice as its primary concern. Pointing to the many and obvious instances of social injustice in capitalist society with little attention to possible balancing virtues in the system, and taking the humanitarian goals of Communism at face value with little attention to possible injustices which might vitiate these goals in practice, Hromádka's theology, in effect, equated good and evil with Communism and Capitalism, respectively. The value of human life, an obvious prerequisite from a secular point of view for the achievement of any values whatsoever, was elevated to an almost absolute plane, such as practically to prohibit the taking of life in any circumstances whatsoever. This attribution of supreme value to human life, together with the doctrine of collective guilt, whereby the Christian, as a member of the interconnected global society, is enjoined to blame himself rather than any other person or agency for any evil in the world, effectively precluded the doctrine of the just war. The only exception allowed was wars of national liberation: so pressing was the need for eradication of the injustices suffered by economically deprived and oppressed people that revolution, including violent revolution, was not only allowable, but was demanded in many circumstances as a Christian virtue.

Khrushchev's emphasis on the doctrine of 'peaceful coexistence' was immensely useful to the C.P.C. Never concretely defined in the Soviet lexicon, 'peaceful coexistence' could be used in a number of ways. By no means implying a categorical denial of war, the term generally meant only an avoidance of major war between the two dominant forces in the world, or else avoidance of major war involving weapons of mass destruction, or even, perhaps, avoidance of major war initiated by the West. Wars of national liberation were permissible, and the U.S.S.R. was able to attempt major revision of the nuclear balance of power, as during the Cuban Crisis of 1962, without violating the concept of 'peaceful coexistence' (although it should be noted that opposing reaction by the West did constitute violations). Patient and persistent utilisation of the term was ultimately successful in narrowing the alternative to war to the single concept of 'peaceful coexistence,' thereby allowing pacifist sentiments among many Western churchmen to be channelled into a form more directly applicable to Soviet foreign policy.

The C.P.C. focused its primary attention on the problem of Vietnam. Long before such formulae became fashionable in the West, the C.P.C. was treating the fighting in Vietnam as outside aggression by the United States, unjustly supporting a corrupt regime in South Vietnam against the wishes of the Vietnamese people. The C.P.C. devoted great energy to the propagation of this position, examining and elucidating it from a wide variety of standpoints. As apprehension in the Western Churches began to deepen and the conviction grew that something must be done to halt the carnage, the C.P.C. was able to supply the Churches with an interpretive framework with detailed analyses from theological, scriptural, social, and other points of view. The result was that more and more, the formulae originally worked out in the deliberations of the C.P.C. began to be reflected in pulpits in the West. Doubtless the Churches would have risen in opposition to the war in Vietnam with or without the C.P.C's analyses, and even had they not, the cruelties, the uncertainties and the ambiguities of the war would have engendered a wave of repulsion. But as dissatisfaction with the war developed, the Churches, particularly in the U.S., did in fact play a role in its growth, and the C.P.C's ability to make a vital contribution to the process was a welcome adjunct to Soviet foreign policy.

After the invasion of Czechoslovakia in 1968 the period of effective usefulness of the C.P.C. came to an end. The technique of entrusting leadership of a foreign policy activity to an allied State apparently was not viable when the national interests of allied leaders began to conflict with Soviet foreign policy. The C.P.C. leadership proved unwilling to acquiesce without protest to the invasion. The increasingly stern approach of post-Khrushchevian policies soon effected the virtual destruction of the C.P.C. as an effective means of influencing foreign churchmen. J. Ondra, the General Secretary, was forced out of his position of leadership in 1969, and Hromádka resigned in protest.[17] When Hromádka died shortly thereafter, the C.P.C. was bereft of major assets for attracting Western Christians, and in view of the increasingly stringent limits imposed on its actions, it seemed doubtful that the organisation could continue to serve Soviet foreign policy interests effectively.

One of the most effective of the efforts of the Russian Churches in international affairs was the attempt to influence major international religious bodies. After the death of Stalin, the Churches of the U.S.S.R. undertook a policy of joining, rather than combating, such bodies. These efforts resulted in a considerable diminution of anti-Soviet sentiments within them, and a growth of tolerance and friendliness towards the Soviet Union.

Prior to the death of Stalin, the Baptist World Alliance had displayed considerable concern for the difficulties of the Russian Baptists. In 1950, for example, one of the B.W.A. leaders stated:

> There is a certain amount of toleration but no real freedom. At present the Russian State seeks to use the churches for its own purpose. Many ministers of religion have been 'liquidated'. When ministers of religion are imprisoned or banished, the Soviet Government never admits this is because they are preachers. Some trumped-up charge is made against them. . . .[18]

After the entry of the Russian Baptists into the B.W.A. in the mid-1950s, however, such sentiments tended to disappear from the official reports of the B.W.A., and instead a measure of sympathy and deference began to appear. To be sure, the Russian Baptists did not enjoy complete success in the B.W.A.: when thirty-two Christians from Siberia were denied asylum by the U.S. Embassy in Moscow in 1963, the B.W.A. lodged a protest with the U.S. Secretary of State.[19] However, the matter did not become a *cause célèbre* in the B.W.A. Similarly, the B.W.A. was most circumspect with regard to the *initsiativniki* affair, taking no official notice of it until well after the schism had been made public, and always thereafter taking into consideration the attitudes and opinions of the officially sanctioned Russian Baptist leadership in its comments on the schism.[20] Thus the interaction of Russian Baptists with the B.W.A. may have been instrumental in diverting B.W.A. opinion from a course of potential embarrassment to Soviet foreign policy.

The most important international activity of the Russian Churches during the 1960s was their participation in the World Council of Churches. A vast international body whose ecumenical activities may affect as many as 170,000,000 Christians in its member Churches, the W.C.C. had an immense desire to bring

Orthodoxy into the W.C.C., and the Russian Church was able to play an important role immediately on joining the body in 1961. In addition, its inflated claim of 22,000 active churches, which was accepted without question by the W.C.C., made it the largest single member Church, and hence there were excellent prospects for exerting an important influence within the W.C.C.

Benefits for Soviet foreign policy were forthcoming almost immediately.[21] In the Cuban Missile Crisis of 1962, officers of the W.C.C. issued the following statement:

> Taking their stand on statements made by the World Council of Churches' Assemblies, the Committees and Officers of the World Council of Churches have on several occasions expressed their concern and regret when governments have taken unilateral military action against other governments. The Officers of the World Council of Churches consider it, therefore, their duty to express grave concern and regret concerning the action which the U.S.A. government has felt it necessary to take with regard to Cuba and fervently hope that every government concerned will exercise the greatest possible restraint in order to avoid a worsening of international tension.[22]

One thousand delegates of the Lutheran Church in America then in conference voted to repudiate the statement because of its alleged one-sidedness;[23] however, Nikodim immediately issued a statement approving it, commending the W.C.C. officers, and encouraging them to further actions in the same vein.[24]

Similarly the Russian participants were not displeased with the choice of Eugene Carson Blake as the new General Secretary of the W.C.C. in 1966. Although an American, Blake had achieved international recognition for his progressive approach to ecclesiastical affairs, and had visited the U.S.S.R. on numerous occasions during the preceding decade. The problem of choosing a candidate had occasioned the W.C.C. considerable trauma, and great care was taken to avoid alienating the Russian members (or any other members, for that matter) in the selection; Blake's choice was apparently acceptable, for the Moscow Patriarchate responded with warm enthusiasm to the new appointment.[25]

The Russian participants in the W.C.C. did not enjoy complete success with regard to Vietnam, for the W.C.C. did not acquiesce to the formulae being promulgated by the C.P.C. While it did not minimise the role of the U.S. in the conflict, the W.C.C. was careful to temper its statements by a recognition of the involvement of other participants in the dispute, and did not give unequivocal support to the Soviet position. Later in the 1960s, the W.C.C. did make an oblique contribution to one of the subsidiary desires of the Soviet State, that the morale and effectiveness of opposing military forces be eroded, by creating a special fund to give assistance to American military deserters and evaders of the draft.[26]

The Soviet State enjoyed rather good – and perhaps unexpected – success with regard to the W.C.C.'s attitude towards the *initsiativniki* dissenters. In response to the escalation of the challenge of the *initsiativniki,* in 1966 amendments were made to the Russian penal code specifying certain offences which they had been guilty of perpetrating, increasing the penalties drastically for recidivists, and ameliorating the penalties for certain other offences.[27] Apprehension developed in the West, and the W.C.C. responded by issuing a statement, which was repeated in *Izvestiya* on 30 August 1966:

> A study of the text, which in fact contains three decrees, demonstrated that these decrees basically confirm, define and in some instances introduce greater flexibility into the laws which already exist. In contradiction to what was published in the newspapers, not one of these decrees prohibits free collections designed to meet the needs of the churches, nor is it recognised that discrimination against people in connection with their religious adherence can be legal.
>
> In order to illustrate the easing of conditions which previously existed, it may be noted that some violations of the law which were previously punished by imprisonment now merely carry a fine of up to 50 rubles. . . .

This article signalled the initiation of a vigorous wave of arrests and imprisonment of *initsiativniki*. In November of the following year the *initsiativniki* sent an appeal to the General Secretary of the W.C.C. giving particulars on over 200 Baptists then in prison. He stated that 'the World Council of Churches is studying the document closely',[28] but no further action was made public.

Nor was the issue raised in the report of the next meeting of the W.C.C. Executive Committee (February 1968), although the meeting did endorse protests in behalf of political prisoners in Greece and South Africa, and authorised the General Secretary to make a special visit to Greece to appeal for the release of prisoners held by the military Government.[29]

With regard to the Israeli-Arab conflict, the position taken by the W.C.C. was harmonious with that advocated by the U.S.S.R., although in this case it is doubtful that efforts of the Russian members were more than marginally instrumental in securing this happy result. The W.C.C. includes in its membership Churches enduring a precarious existence in Arab countries, and ill-considered action by the W.C.C. would almost surely have repercussions on them. The W.C.C. reacted to the Six-Day War in 1967 by expressing support for the efforts of the U.N. Security Council to effect a cease-fire,[30] and a fortnight later took an official position: 'We do not believe that the Israeli-Arab conflict is a political issue on which moral duty clearly requires us to take an absolute stand for or against either side.'[31] The W.C.C. sent aid to the refugees of both sides, for which the United Arab Republic expressed thanks[32] (there were not many Israeli refugees after the brief war). Subsequently the W.C.C. took a position rejecting decisions made by armed force and advocating the return of all occupied territories.[33] Thus even though the W.C.C. position may have been motivated by other considerations, it proved to be harmonious with that of the U.S.S.R.

Eastern participants in the W.C.C. secured at least a partial success with regard to the invasion of Czechoslovakia in 1968. A week after the invasion the W.C.C. issued a statement denouncing the action taken by the Warsaw Pact,[34] but during the critical week of the invasion itself, the W.C.C. refrained from adding its immensely powerful voice to the denunciations issuing from the Vatican, Canterbury, the National Council of Churches in the U.S., and a large number of other ecclesiastical, secular, governmental and even Western Communist organisations. Instead, on 22 August the General Secretary sent the following cable to member Churches in the invading countries: 'Please advise promptly attitude or position of your church on recent events in Czechoslovakia. C.C.I.A. [Commission of the Churches on International Affairs] sending to its commissioners and national commissions quotations from past statements issued by churches together relevant to present situation. Until things become clearer I am not proposing any new statement.'[35] Although in retrospect the chance of Western intervention seems remote, such precipitate action against the most Westernised of the Eastern European States, which has a common border with Western Europe, must have raised the possibility of a reaction from the West in Soviet minds, and for a significant element in Western public opinion to remain silent represented a desirable windfall. As has been noted, the W.C.C. did react strongly to the invasion one week later, but by then the danger had diminished by several orders of magnitude.

The position of the W.C.C. towards the Third World, and particularly towards the problem of revolution, was a spectacular windfall for Soviet foreign policy. Always attentive to the underdeveloped countries because of member Churches from the Third World, and with a long history of concern about racial discrimination, the W.C.C. was inclined towards a search for progressive, or even radical, solutions to these problems. In the late 1960s its position evolved rapidly towards that of Soviet foreign policy. At the W.C.C.'s 'Church and Society' conference in 1966, there seemed to be a developing tendency towards radical solutions to Third World problems. At the General Assembly in Uppsala, Sweden, in 1968 the W.C.C. took a position advocating revolution, not excluding violence in certain cases. In 1970 the W.C.C. Executive Committee allocated $200,000 to nineteen anti-racist organisations, fourteen of them in southern Africa.[36] A storm of controversy ensued, for not only were a number of the recipients committed to violence in their revolutionary efforts, but the grants, although intended for charitable and humanitarian purposes, were made without controls and without any guarantees that they would not be put to other uses. On 25 June 1970 *Izvestiya* had devoted an article to revolutionary movements in southern Africa, singling out three for special attention, F.R.E.L.I.M.O., M.P.L.A. and P.A.I.G.C. (operating in Mozambique, Angola and Guinea-Bissao respectively), which were receiving Soviet arms. All three were included in the list of recipients of the W.C.C. grants.[37]

This represented a significant benefit to Soviet foreign policy. The U.S.S.R. considered it advantageous to its international interests to support these revolutionary organisations; for them to receive additional funds from a non-Soviet source would augment the possibility of achieving results, and the fact that Russian churchmen were participants in the donor organisation would support an assumption by practitioners of Soviet foreign policy that churchmen can render useful services in the international arena.

The Russian Church also supported Soviet foreign policy by sending messages directly to foreign governments. Thus, for example, in 1962 Patriarch Alexii admonished President Kennedy for the decision to resume testing of atomic weapons: 'You are aware of how inhuman is the policy of intimidation which leads to the frightening nuclear armaments tests, and you know also how contrary this is to the commands of Christ, our Saviour.'[38] However, inasmuch as he made no comment about the prior resumption of testing by the U.S.S.R. it would not seem that there was any serious expectation of influencing U.S. policy by this protest, but instead it was made in order to generate a modicum of publicity unfavourable to the U.S. Later in 1962 when Russian religious leaders issued a public protest against the U.S. blockade of Cuba,[39] it would not seem that there was any serious effort to influence U.S. governmental leaders. Similarly, when Nikodim protested to the President of Israel in 1968 concerning incidents endangering Russian Orthodox properties it would seem that the desire to generate publicity was the major motive, for in response to the answering denial that such incidents had taken place, Nikodim, sending copies to W.C.C. leaders, itemised events which had taken place in 1964 and 1966.[40] It would appear that the primary reason for sending such messages directly to foreign governments is seldom an expectation of influencing the state in question, but rather a desire to generate publicity consonant with the interests of Soviet foreign policy.

A corollary of this public relations function in which the Russian Churches serve in foreign affairs is the rendering of support to the Soviet Government in time of crisis. The Church's reaction to the Cuban crisis has already been mentioned. Even more pointed was the reaction of the Moscow Patriarchate to the invasion of Prague in 1968. On a number of occasions the Patriarchate was instant in protesting against reactions to the invasion (e.g. by C.P.C.[41] and, later, W.C.C. leaders[42]). It gave absolute support to the Soviet justification of the invasion as necessary to defend true Czech Socialism threatened by outside interference. The Church also praised the invasion for having averted major war. Thus it would appear that in time of crisis the Soviet Government can rely on the Church rendering what little aid it can in supporting actions taken by the State.

This survey by no means exhausts the contribution of religious individuals and institutions to Soviet foreign policy. The international activities of the Russian and Eastern European Churches represent no small allocation of human and financial resources, and the logistics of planning, administration and control, and direct and indirect support services are complex. Even though matters of the spiritual and intellectual world are scarcely open to quantitative analysis, foreign relations of the Churches in the U.S.S.R. represent a serious and important aspect of the U.S.S.R.'s international operations.

It should not be imagined, however, that religion represents a leading entry on the agenda of Soviet foreign policy. As has been noted, religion renders an ancillary service at best, representing but one of a number of activities orchestrated in support of the State's international affairs. Large though the resources allocated to religious activities may be, they still represent only a miniscule, if not infinitesimal, fraction of the Soviet investment in foreign policy. Beneficial results have accrued from the endeavours of the Churches; but these results have seldom been of critical importance to an operation's success or failure.

Indeed the question has been raised in Western academia on at least one occasion as to whether the game is worth the candle after all.[43] Leaving aside any strictly ecclesiastical and ecumenical benefits of international religious activity, are the results achieved by the Churches' contribution to Soviet foreign policy commensurate with the deleterious effects, from the Communist point of view, of the continued existence of religion domestically? Even a brief survey, however, of the concrete services rendered by the Churches to Soviet foreign policy would suggest that the question is not well taken. Obviously such achievements are considered worthwhile by the practitioners of Soviet foreign policy; were the religious dimension of Soviet international activities allowed to lapse, the endeavours of the U.S.S.R. would be deprived of a useful, even though ancillary, adjunct. For so long as religious individuals and organisations continue to render concrete advantages to the international activities of the U.S.S.R., it seems safe to presume that religion will continue to play a significant role in Soviet foreign policy.

NOTES

1. For detailed analysis, see William C. Fletcher, *A Study in Survival: The Church in Russia, 1927–1943* (New York: Macmillan, 1965).
2. Wassilij Alexeev. *The Foreign Policy of the Moscow Patriarchate, 1939–1953* (in Russian; New York: Research Programme on the U.S.S.R., 1954); Matthew Spinka, *The Church in Soviet Russia* (New York: Oxford University Press, 1956); William B. Stroyen, *Communist Russia and the Russian Orthodox Church, 1943–1962* (Washington, D.C.: Catholic University of America Press, 1967); William C. Fletcher, *Nikolai: Portrait of a Dilemma* (New York: Macmillan, 1968).
3. E.g., in the case of the Huk uprising in the Philippines, where geographic impediments intervened, or the post-war turmoil in Burma, where geographic and political obstacles prevented easy access.
4. In applying for membership in the World Council of Churches in 1961 the Russian Orthodox Church claimed to have 22,000 active churches (*Time*, 5 May 1961, p. 57), whereas according to Soviet sources at no time since World War II have there been as many as 16,000 churches in the U.S.S.R. (A. Veshchikov, 'Milestones of a great journey,' *Nauka i religiya* [hereafter cited as *NiR*], No. 11 [November 1962], translated in *Religion in Communist Dominated Areas* [hereafter cited as *RCDA*], 24 December 1962, p. 2).
5. *Spravochnik propagandista i agitatora* (Reference Book of Propaganda its and Agitator) (Moscow, 1966), translated in *Research Materials*, October 1969, p. 1; cf. *RCDA*, 15/31 May 1966, p. 76.
6. Donald A. Lowrie and William C. Fletcher, 'Khrushchev's Religious Policy, 1959–1964', in Richard H. Marshall, Jr. (ed.), *Aspects of Religion in the USSR, 1917–1967* (Chicago: University of Chicago Press, 1971), pp. 131–55.
7. Comité d'Information sur la Situation des Chrétiens en Union Soviétique, *Situation des Chrétiens en Union Soviétique* (Paris, 1964).
8. *L'Humanité*, 14 March 1964.
9. See Michael Bourdeaux, *Religious Ferment in Russia* (London: Macmillan, 1968).
10. *Ecumenical Press Service* (hereafter cited as *EPS*), 25 January 1968, p. 5.
11. Michael Bourdeaux, *Patriarch and Prophets* (London: Macmillan, 1970).
12. *RCDA*, 15/31 August 1966, pp. 126–8.
13. For data on the C.P.C., see *Christian Peace Conference* (bi-monthly); *Information Bulletin of the Christian Peace Conference* (mimeographed, irregular); and various conference programmes, speeches, working papers and booklets issued in Prague by the C.P.C., such as *Task and Witness* (1958), *My Covenant is Life and Peace* (1964), and *Seek Peace and Pursue It* (1968).
14. 'Statute of the Christian Peace Conference', in *My Covenant is Life and Peace*, pp. 20–22.
15. In 1961 the C.P.C. annual budget was estimated to be $130,000, and in 1962 it was announced that the budget was to be doubled for 1963; thereafter budgetary data were not released by the C.P.C. The three ACPAs cost an estimated $1,000,000 each. In 1965 the nine meetings for which particulars

concerning attendance were given entailed approximately $55,000 in air fare alone, in addition to other meetings for which there were inadequate data for computation of costs, and continuing expenses (administration, overhead, publishing, etc.).

16. Detailed treatment of aspects of Hromádka's theology may be found in Charles C. West, *Communism and the Theologians: Study of an Encounter* (London: S.C.M. Press, 1958), and in Charles C. West, 'Josef Hromádka', in Thomas E. Bird, ed., *Modern Theologians: Christian and Jewish* (Notre Dame, Indiana: University of Notre Dame Press, 1966).

17. *Information Bulletin of the CPC*, December 1969.

18. Arnold T. Ohrn (ed.), *The Eighth Baptist World Congress*(Philadelphia, Pennsylvania: Judson Press, 1950), pp. 109–10.

19. *EPS*, 12 January 1963, p. 3.

20. Cf. B.W.A. News release (mimeographed) dated 12 January 1968.

21. It should be noted that the concrete chain of causation, if any, is irrelevant from the point of view of practitioners of Soviet foreign policy. The fact that after the entry of Russian participants into the work of the W.C.C. favourable decisions were forthcoming is evident to the Soviet State; conflicting reports concerning whether the decisions were taken as a result of, without reference to, or even in spite of the wishes of Russian participants would be of far less interest than the concrete fact that favourable actions were indeed taken by the W.C.C.

22. *EPS*, 26 October 1962, p. 2.

23. *Ibid.*, 2 November 1962, p. 2.

24. *Zhurnal Moskovskoi Patriarkhii* (hereafter cited as *ZMP*), No. 11 (November 1962), p. 7.

25. *Ibid.*, No. 5 (May 1967), pp. 8–9.

26. Cf. *EPS*, October 1970, p. 3.

27. *Vedomosti Verkhovnogo Soveta RSFSR*, No. 12 (1966), pp. 219–20.

28. *EPS*, 9 November 1967, p. 7.

29. *Ibid.*, 22 February 1968, p. 2.

30. *Ibid.*, 8 June 1967, p. 2.

31. *Ibid.*, 22 June 1967, p. 2.

32. *Ibid.*, 17 August 1967, p. 11.

33. Cf. *ZMP*, No. 11 (November 1967), p. 70.

34. *EPS*, 29 August, 1968, pp. 2–3.

35. *Ibid.*, 22 August 1968, p. 12.

36. For a summary of these events see *ibid.*, October 1970, pp. 3–5.

37. There is no indication that *Izvestiya*'s publication of Soviet arms aid for these movements played any role in the decision of W.C.C. leaders, many of whom may, indeed, have been ignorant of the newspaper's statement, or might have ignored it as irrelevant in any case. The fact that Soviet military support of the movements had been made public, however, would enter into the assessment of Soviet observers of the W.C.C. action.

38. *Ibid.*, 4 May 1962, p. 10.

39. *Izvestiya*, 25 October 1962, reprinted in *ZMP*, No. 11 (November 1962), p. 5.

40. *Ibid.*, No. 4 (April 1968), p. 4, and No. 5 (May 1968), pp. 6–7.

41. *Ibid.*, No. 10 (October 1968), pp. 2–3.

42. *Ibid.*, pp. 1–2.

43. Michael Klimenko, in 'Book Reviews', *Russian Review*, April 1969, p. 249.

10 The Catholic Church and the Communist State in the Soviet Union and Eastern Europe

GERHARD SIMON

The following survey of Communist policy towards the Catholic Church is an attempt to compare the liberty of and restriction on the Church in various Communist ruled countries. The difference in the degree of liberty the Churches enjoy in various countries of Eastern Europe are very significant. Although all the ruling Communist parties adhere to militant atheism as an integral part of their ideology and outlook, the extent to which they were able to implement such a policy differs greatly. In terms of their treatment of Churches, countries such as Albania and the Soviet Union today form the one extreme wing, where public activities of the Churches have been reduced to a minimum – Albania, incidentally, claims to be the 'first atheistic state in the world'.[1] At the opposite wing are countries such as Poland and the German Democratic Republic (G.D.R.), where the Churches still enjoy a considerable amount of rights and privileges and are relatively independent and able to speak with their own voice.

The third group of countries includes Hungary, Czechoslovakia, Romania and Bulgaria, in which severe repressions of the Stalin era have left behind ineradicable traces; nevertheless, overt ecclesiastical life in these countries has not been reduced to the extent equal to that in the Soviet Union and Albania. Yugoslavia represents a special case: there, after World War II, institutional religion – above all the Catholic Church – was subjected to terrorist reprisals, but, since the end of the 1950s, the Yugoslav religious policy has become markedly relaxed and liberal to the extent that the Catholic Church in Croatia and Slovenia is now subject to least state interference in entire Eastern Europe.

For this reason a comparative approach to Church–State relations in Communist ruled countries seems to be feasible and necessary. It not only will help to clarify and evaluate the discrepancies in different countries, where the Communist take-over occurred around the same time, but a comparison also will contribute to a better understanding of religious conditions in any one particular country of Eastern Europe. To be sure, 'liberty' and 'restriction' are in no way absolute terms; in each case they have to be determined and filled with concrete substance. A comparison, for example, shows that restricted religious instruction – as in Czechoslovakia and Hungary – has to be regarded as a privilege in comparison with the Soviet Union, where even private religious instruction of the youth is considered a crime, punishable by criminal law.

To my knowledge, relatively little scholarly work has been done so far to compare religious legislation, persecution and liberty in the different countries of Eastern Europe and the Soviet Union. Scholarly effort has been devoted largely to the study of Church–State relations in single countries with little consideration for the neighbouring Communists dominated state. Those works dealing with the religious situation of several or all East European states resort by and large to cumulative methods; the countries are treated separately and individually, and little or no attention has been given to a comparative approach.[2] Moreover, most of these highly informative books have been written during or shortly after the Cold War period; they are preoccupied with persecution and massive terror against the Churches in Stalinist Eastern Europe and hardly recognise the existing considerable differences between, for example, Poland and Czechoslovakia, let alone the Soviet Union. Other studies of Christian–Communist encounter do not dwell on single countries at all. They are interested only in establishing an overall pattern of Communist challenge and Christian response, and do not employ comparative method.[3]

The Catholic Church seems to be specially appropriate for an attempt to discuss Communist religious policy by stressing the common features on the one hand and the differences in various countries on the other, because the Roman Catholic Church exists in all countries under consideration, although in very different proportions. Whereas in Poland about 30 million people, or more than 90 per cent of the population, owe nominal allegiance to the Catholic Church, in Bulgaria it constitutes a negligible minority of about 60,000 believers or less than 1 per cent of the population. But the Catholic Church has a similar structure and self-image in all countries, and its ecclesiastical centre, the Vatican, is beyond Communist control. This is one reason why the clash between a party and a state, claiming to possess the whole and the only truth, on the one hand, and a Church, maintaining to constitute a *societas perfecta,* on the other, has been especially severe.

Communist states in principle do not differentiate in their policies towards Churches of different denominations. In reality the conflict with the Catholic Church has been particularly acute in almost all countries. The Orthodox and Protestant denominations often found it easier to reconcile themselves to the restricted sphere of activity, which a Communist-dominated society is willing to leave to the communion of the faithful. The Catholic Church depends more heavily on its institutional structure and thus offers a particular point of attack to a party and a state determined to minimise any effective competition on different world-views and to implement its own outlook not only by persuasion and education but also by administrative measures and terror. The Catholic Church is not only conditioned by its internal structure as divinely ordained, it is also bound as a *societas publica* to activity on a political and social level, be it in the area of education or charitable work. In this Roman Catholicism differs a great deal from Orthodox tradition which is much more inclined to transcendental contemplation and which views man and his environment more from the viewpoint of eternity than in temporal terms. All these factors intensified the inevitable conflict between the Communist State and the Catholic Church, a Church dependent on an ecclesiastical centre in the West, which during the Cold War period was, according to Communist terminology, the 'heart of imperialism' and 'chief agent of the U.S. espionage'.

The following discussion of relations between the state and the Catholic Church in Eastern Europe and the Soviet Union will proceed along three steps. First, I will deal with common features and objectives of Communist church policy. Second, we will try to relate church policy to the general political development in Eastern Europe after World War II. The third part will be devoted to differences and discrepancies in the religious situation in various Communist-ruled countries. In general, I have to limit myself to a juridical and political examination of the Church as a social institution. The theological and sociological aspects will largely be left out, important though they are.

I. THE AIMS AND METHODS OF COMMUNIST CHURCH POLICY

The ideological foundations of Communist church policy were laid down by Lenin and have hardly been developed any further since.[4] Lenin's attitude towards religion was twofold. On the one hand he stressed the point that 'under no circumstances can we consider religion to be a private matter with regard to our own party',[5] and he accordingly urged the revolutionary *élite* to change the consciousness of the working masses and to instil an atheist, scientific world-view into their minds. On the other hand, Lenin held that the struggle against religion and the Churches has to be subordinated to the general political objectives of the Party. The proletariat must not be divided by overemphasising the anti-religious struggle, which still remained an unconditional, integral part of the Party programme, contrary to the West European Social Democratic parties. The overcoming of 'religious prejudices' and the liquidation of 'religious relics' remained among the long-range aims of the Russian Communist Party[6] and of all its daughter-parties in Eastern Europe. Lenin and his contemporaries were convinced that with the elimination of the exploiting classes religion will lose all basis as an instrument of exploitation and oppression of the masses and would fade away. For this reason, and in view of opportunistic considerations, Lenin did not exclude under certain circumstances the compatibility of Party membership and allegiance to a creed.

When the expectation of the self-dissolution of Churches and the end of religious consciousness proved false, the Communist Party under Stalin relied all the more on militant atheism, carried out by administrative measures and terror. The Leninist double principle – the necessity to fight religion and the conviction that it will die out by itself – incompatible as it seems, proved to be excellent justification for a pragmatic, shifting policy towards the Churches. The conviction that religion will disintegrate anyway permitted one to grant it certain 'bourgeois' rights and privileges; the necessity to fight a bitter rival made heavy restrictions obligatory. The first end was achieved through provisions of the constitutions of the People's Republics; the second purpose is pursued by special religious laws and administrative decrees. This is the present situation, in which atheistic scholars and functionaries do not expect the final dissolution of the Churches very soon. On the contrary, they stress that there are 'objective reasons' for the perpetuation of religiousness in a socialist society. The formerly expected extinction of religion has been delayed *ad calendas graecas* not only by reality but also by contemporary theoreticians.[7]

The constitutional provisions of the Communist states pertaining to religious matters clearly show common features and are more or less derivations from the Soviet constitution. All constitutions guarantee freedom of conscience and of worship. Only the basic law of the Soviet Union and of Romania prohibit that the Churches found and operate schools for general education, although in all Communist-ruled countries the Churches have no, or only very limited, possibilities to run schools not destined for the training of priests. Generally, the constitutions of the People's Republics provide that no privilege can be granted or rights taken away from citizens because of their religious adherence. This seems to be an appropriate protection against any kind of discrimination; but reality shows quite a different picture, as will be discussed later.

It is not without interest to note that the separation of Church and State announced already by Lenin's decree of 23 January (5 February) 1918, and allegedly representing a basic principle of Communist church policy – has not been embedded in the constitutions of Czechoslovakia, Romania and the G.D.R.[8] In reality the separation of Church and State does not exist in several other states either, especially in the Soviet Union, and in Poland it has been realised in a somewhat restricted sense. But Czechoslovakia, Romania and the G.D.R. renounced even the juridical principle of the separation of Church and State. Czechoslovakia did this because local politicians were convinced that an efficient control of church activities could be effected most easily not by separation but by as close as possible a Church–State co-operation, that is, by a complete dependence of the Church on the State, mainly on State funds. Different reasons prevailed in the G.D.R. where the Communist State in 1949 – when the first constitution was adopted – was not in the position to enforce a complete separation of Church and State, which would have resulted in a breakdown of the institutionalised church which at that time was entirely dependent financially on state contributions.

The Soviet constitution of 1936 presents a peculiarity by combining 'freedom of religious worship' with 'freedom of anti-religious propaganda' (Article 124). Characteristically enough, freedom of religious propaganda is not mentioned; that is, it is prohibited. Although constitutional articles tend to be remote from reality, this stipulation reflects the fact that the Soviet Union belongs to those Communist countries which most strictly reduced the Churches' activities.

The main provisions concerning state–church relations were not stipulated by the constitutions, but by one or several decrees and laws fixing the legal status of the Churches. The general model for Eastern European governments was offered by Lenin's separation decree of 1918 and the Soviet law on religious associations of 8 April 1929, which strengthened state control over church activities and provided all necessary administrative instruments to hamper church life. Similar regulations, either as decrees or accords with the Catholic episcopate, have been adopted in Eastern Europe between 1948 (Romania) and 1953 (Yugoslavia, partly Poland). As will be noted, in no Communist country was it possible to conclude a concordat with the Vatican, the normal way to regulate relations between the Catholic Church and state authority. The only country never to have adopted any general church law remains the G.D.R. – to the advantage of the Churches in that country.

The decrees on Church–State relations were issued at the climax of the Stalinist period in Eastern Europe, as the law of the R.S.F.S.R. in 1929 had coincided with the consolidation of Stalin's rule in the Soviet Union. It belongs to the characteristics of Communist church policy that all these laws, with minor exception, have not been repealed to this very day, although in practice a considerable détente of Church–State relations was brought about since the end of the 1950s, except in the Soviet Union. But the Stalinist laws are still in force. Thus, at any time the State could revert to the old tough regulations and enforce them in full scope – as happened during Khrushchev's persecution of the Churches in the Soviet Union (1959–64).

The church laws of the Eastern European states pursued three major objectives: to limit the influence of the Church in the society, to control its activities, and to compel the leading church-men to loyalty *vis-à-vis* the Communist authorities.

As an example of a Communist church law we will briefly discuss the Romanian 'General Regime of Religion' of 4 August 1948.[9] The provisions of this law are neither particularly severe as those of the related Czechoslovak decrees of 14 October 1949 nor relatively liberal, as the corresponding Yugoslav law of 22 May 1953. The Romanian stipulations require all religions to be recognised by the Presidium of the Grand National Assembly. 'Recognition may be withdrawn . . . for good and sufficient reasons' (Art. 13). Each religion has to forward its statute 'for examination and approval' to the state authorities (Art. 14). Like-wise all local religious communities, parishes, groups, foundations, lay associations, etc., have to be registered with the appropriate authorities (Art. 17, 18). Gatherings other than for worship, such as lectures, local or nation-wide meetings and congresses, may be convened only with the approval of the authorities (Art. 24). The law further states that 'pastoral letters and circulars of general interest' have to be submitted to the censor in advance (Art. 25). This quite outspoken and rigid provision is complemented by another one subjecting all church budgets to government control (Art. 30). In view of the complete control of all financial matters, the only consolation remain the subsidies granted by the State to the recognised Churches (Art. 32).

Financial support in most Communist states has been used to regulate church life. Only the Soviet Union, Poland and Albania do not give any regular financial assistance to the Churches in their territories. The Soviet Union and Albania do so in order to strangle church life; the Catholic Church in Poland – on the other hand – is strong enough to refuse government aid which would make it dependent upon the authorities. This is but one example of the possibility of reaching the same end by opposite means: church life may be hampered by withdrawal of subsidies or by granting of financial aid.

Of special importance to the Catholic Church is a provision

of the Romanian church law which permits contacts with religious bodies abroad, that is with the Vatican, only through the Ministry of Foreign Affairs. Corresponding regulations in one form or another have been adopted in all Communist countries in order to reduce and control contacts with the Holy See, after rigorous attempts to completely separate the national Churches from Rome had failed. The church laws in Eastern Europe generally have been enforced against the bitter protests of the church leaders. They regarded these laws as substantial infringements of the Church's autonomy and as obvious violations of the constitutions.[10]

The implementation of the church laws and continuous supervision of ecclesiastical activities have been delegated to special agencies on religious affairs founded again after the Soviet model in Russian-dominated Eastern Europe. Departments of religious affairs were established in Romania in August 1948, in the Č.S.S.R. in October 1949, in Hungary in May 1951, in the G.D.R. in October 1951. The corresponding Soviet councils had been founded during the War in 1943 and 1944. Whereas the exact functions and competences of the Soviet councils have never been published, the respective Czechoslovak decree of 25 October 1949 circumscribing the jurisdiction of the office for church affairs is very outspoken. The jurisdiction of the office embraces the 'issuance of general rules and direction and supervision in all matters of Church and religion'. The office regulates 'personnel matters and emoluments of clergymen, teachers and employers of the theological schools', and likewise all matters connected with religious instruction of the youth. This meant that no appointment, election, transfer, etc., of any clergyman or teacher was valid without the previous approval of the office for church affairs. It was also entrusted with the censoring of church publications and even obliged to publish an official gazette for clergymen.[11]

Close control over church affairs established by the aforementioned laws and government bureau was complemented by efforts to ensure the loyalty of the clergy. Either by a general church law, or by special decree connected with this law, all clergymen became obliged to take an oath to the People's Republic. In some countries, as in Czechoslovakia and Poland, the Catholic episcopate could only be forced under heavy pressure and terror to pledge irrevocable loyalty to a militantly atheistic government. But at the high point of Stalinism, as for example in Poland in 1953, the only alternative remained prison, which went even further to deprive a clergyman of his effectiveness than if he would have taken a loyalty oath.[12]

So far we have dwelt upon Communist church legislation. We will now turn to the execution of the laws, in order to bring out more clearly the main common objective of church policy in all Communist-ruled countries: to restrict church life to cult and ritual. A variety of legal acts, administrative measures and police terror has been employed and is still in use to exclude the Church from society.

After World War II one of the first acts of the newly installed, not yet entirely Communist, governments was to announce comprehensive land-reform and to take over private and church schools. Education was declared a government prerogative. The Catholic Church in Hungary was hit particularly hard by the land-reform of March 1945, since it owned vast tracts of land which enabled it to carry on an extensive educational and charitable work. Almost 90 per cent of church land was nationalised in 1945, and further expropriation followed in 1951. As to social influence and activity, it proved even a harder blow when on 14 June 1948 all denominational schools were nationalised. By this act the latent conflict between Church and State in Hungary became evident; the resistance of the Church and the faithful caused bloody clashes and unrest. As a sign of protest, Cardinal Mindszenty had the church bells rung all over the country; on 3 July the militant Cardinal excommunicated the ministers who had drafted the nationalisation bill. Nevertheless the Catholic Church in Hungary lost all of its 1,216 elementary schools (six grades), 1,669 general schools (eight grades), eighty-six high schools, forty-nine gymnasiums, thirty-two teacher training schools, etc. By the accord between the Catholic bishops and the Government of 29 August 1950 only eight gymnasiums were returned to the Church. Administration of these gymnasiums remains the only permitted function of the Catholic orders in Hungary up to the present time.[13]

Similar steps to expropriate the landed property of the Church and to nationalise the educational system were taken in all East European countries. Only a handful of general schools remained at the disposal of the Church. These measures and others, such as civil marriage and registration of births, marriages and deaths not by church but by state authorities, were introduced mostly before the establishing of a one-party system. They were, in fact, not only Communist but liberal demands and were supported by the respective liberal parties. In reality, the separation of Church and State is by no means a Communist but a liberal principle. In other words, in several Eastern European countries as in Hungary, Poland, Yugoslavia, the Catholic Church resisted not only Communism, but also liberalism. By fighting against, for example, civil marriage it thus perhaps unnecessarily intensified the Communist–Christian encounter through a *Kulturkampf* lost already in Bismarck's Germany. The trouble with the Communist advocacy of the 'bourgeois' principle of separation of Church and State is that for Communists it served as a mere pretext for the suppression of the Church as a social force. It is characteristic that in those countries where the liberal principle not only was proclaimed but to a certain extent realised – as in Poland, the G.D.R. and Yugoslavia – the Church today possesses relative liberty.

Another liberal demand for the abolition of compulsory religious instruction in public schools was accomplished mostly between the end of the war and the Communist take-over. The Hungarian developments show how the Communists took advantage of the situation. By decree of 3 September 1949 religious instruction in schools became optional. But the tricky and complicated administrative regulations of September 1950, combined with heavy pressure brought to bear upon the parents, reduced the number of children attending religious instruction to only 11 per cent in 1952.[14]

With regard to religious instruction, three groups of Communist states could be distinguished. Some permit and control religious instructions in schoolrooms, but outside the curriculum: Czechoslovakia, Hungary, the G.D.R. In other countries catechism is taught only on church premises and special catechism centres: Poland, Romania, Yugoslavia – this is perhaps the most favourable solution for the Church, though private and unregistered religious instruction is prohibited and punished. The Soviet Union, Albania and Bulgaria do not allow any religious instruction of youth under eighteen years of age. The number of girls and boys attending catechism classes declined in all countries, due to secularisation and general political pressure. Before the Polish October in 1956, religious instruction had been eliminated almost completely from public schools; yet a year later probably 90 per cent of all children again attended religious instruction at schools; only in 1961 did the Polish Government finally ban religion from school premises, permitting the Church to set up special catechism centres.[15]

No inference about the parents' religious motives can be made from the sudden 90 per cent increase of children registered for religious instruction, just as no inference as to the number of Christians can be made from the small number of children who attended religious instruction during the years of intensified repression. Actually, in times of relative freedom in Eastern Europe participation in church life has been an expression of protest against the regime.

While the Church is not allowed to run public schools it has limited opportunities to train priests. But most seminaries and academies were closed at the end of the forties and during the early fifties and the remaining have to adhere to a strict *numerus clausus*. From thirteen seminaries and nine theological academies of the orders in Hungary there were only six seminaries left in 1965, the number of students declining from 1,079 in 1948 to 303 in 1965.[16] The situation is very similar in Czechoslovakia, where Catholic seminaries were reduced from seven to two and connected with the theological faculties in Litoměřice and Bratislava in 1950. Both countries suffer a severe shortage of priests as does the Catholic Church in the Soviet Union, where only one priest per diocese may be ordained each year.[17]

Of particular importance for the elimination of the social influence of the Church and its restriction to religious services was the limitation or prohibition of the church press and the Catholic lay associations. Sweeping measures in this respect were taken in all countries under consideration. Already in 1946 violent attacks against Catholic associations were launched in the Communist press in Hungary; they were charged with conspiracy against the new 'democratic order' and the Red Army. In July 1946 the Communist Minister for Internal Affairs was authorised by the Government to disband any association at his discretion. Consequently about 4,000 Catholic associations were dissolved and the entire lay movement was destroyed. Similar steps followed in other countries. In Poland in 1949 all Catholic associations, foundations, corporations, etc., were made subject to governmental registration; because the bishops refused to comply with what they regarded as an infringement of the Church's autonomy, most Catholic organisations, except the Caritas, were dissolved.[18]

The church press suffered equally heavy losses. In Czechoslovakia all Catholic publishing houses and libraries were confiscated in 1949. Already by January of that year fifty-three Catholic newspapers and journals had been suppressed. Particularly severe measures were taken by the Tito government immediately after the Nazi retreat in 1945; in Croatia and Slovenia all publishing houses and printing offices were nationalised; in 1953 only five Catholic publications remained out of more than 100 in 1944.[19] Similar developments took place in all Eastern European countries. Today the situation has somewhat eased compared to the early fifties. In most countries the Catholic Church is able to publish a few journals in a limited number of copies, bibles, liturgical books and some theological works. Only in the Soviet Union the Catholic Church, embracing more than three million faithful, is not able to publish any periodical and is lacking the most elementary liturgical books, although a Lithuanian missal was printed in 1968.

In order to confine the Church to mass and cult, it was of primary importance to limit or suppress all Catholic welfare activities, since charitable work has a considerable missionary significance in a secularised society. The Communist parties and states proceeded differently to reach this common aim. In Yugoslavia and Romania all Catholic welfare institutions, such as hospitals, orphanages, homes for old people, etc., had been dissolved or nationalised by the early 1950s. In Poland and Czechoslovakia the Caritas society which managed all Catholic welfare activities was not disbanded but, under protest from the bishops, put under government control in 1950. Since that time the Caritas has been more or less withdrawn from the influence of the hierarchy, curtailed in its activity and operated by 'progressive' priests and laymen.[20] In the Soviet Union any charitable work has been forbidden since 1929. In 1939–40 this prohibition was extended to the newly acquired territories with a considerable Catholic population. In contrast, in the G.D.R. there still are functioning hospitals operated by Catholic orders. The Soviet Union and the G.D.R. differ widely regarding the juridical rights of religious denominations.

Another common feature of Communist church policies has

been their hostility towards monasteries and convents. The Catholic orders in Czechoslovakia, Romania and Hungary suffered special hardships when in 1949 and 1950 all monasteries and convents were closed down, and some, in Czechoslovakia and Romania, were in fact turned into concentration camps. In Hungary alone more than 10,000 monks and nuns were forced to return to laity. Č.T.K., the official Czechoslovak news agency, announced the destruction of the orders on 18 April 1950, saying that they had become 'the tools of the foreign foes of the Republic . . . being used to shelter hostile agents, spies and even murderers . . . and many monasteries served as bases for espionage and disruptive activities'.[21] A better example for Stalinist language and policy will hardly be found. But it is also worth noting that no comparable campaign was launched in Poland because of the extremely strong position of the Catholic Church in that country.

A major development in Communist church policy in Eastern Europe was the forcible dissolution of the Uniate Churches and their 'reunion' with respective national Orthodox Churches. In these actions, which had put Catholic–Orthodox relations under great strain, the Communist State and the national Orthodox Church collaborated in integrating considerable sections of the population, which since the late 16th century and the 17th had been ecclesiastically united with Rome. By administrative fiat a great number of faithful were declared Orthodox Christians: by March 1946 almost four million faithful in the Ukraine, by February 1949 some 460,000 in the Carpatho–Ukraine, by December approximately 1·57 million Uniates in Romania and by April/May 1950 some 320,000 Catholics of Byzantine–Slavonic rite in Eastern Slovakia. As a result the Uniate Church, which at one time in Poland/Lithuania and in the Hapsburg Empire had been thought of as a step towards the unification of the entire Eastern Church with Rome, ceased to exist as a significant phenomenon in the ecclesiastical life of Eastern Europe. Today only small groups of Uniates exist in Poland, Yugoslavia, Hungary and Bulgaria.

After the decreed dissolution of the Union some of the faithful turned completely away from the Church, others became inwardly Orthodox Christians. But for a considerable number of faithful the consciousness of belonging to Rome remained alive. This was shown especially in 1968 in Slovakia where during the Prague

Spring the authorities again recognised the Uniate Church. The majority of the former Uniates joined their Church again. At this point some violent clashes developed between the Orthodox and Uniates. The Uniate Church is also alive in the Western Ukraine as an underground Church.

After World War II the newly won political unity of the Ukraine had to be complemented by an ecclesiastical one which would guarantee as smooth as possible and total an integration into the Soviet State. In Romania as well the motive of national unity rather than ecclesiastical–theological reasons stood in the foreground. However, the unconditional political loyalty of the Orthodox Church to the Government was surely another reason for the Communist State to integrate the restless element of the Uniate Church into the Orthodox Church. The Communist State was quite right in believing that an enlarged Orthodox Church was easier to direct and control than a branch of the Catholic Church with its own concepts of shaping political and social reality. For, ultimately, the decisive reasons for the struggle against the Uniate Church was to push back Vatican and Western influences in Eastern Europe – a viewpoint which played an outstanding role in the entire Communist church policy during the Cold War. Furthermore, the integration of large parts of the Catholic Church into the respective national Orthodox Church was in harmony with the Soviet principle of centralism. Finally, there may have been the expectation that a forced 'reunion' of the Uniate Church with the Orthodox Church would favour secularisation. This proved to be true since many parishes ceased to exist after the 'reunion' – naturally, a result which could only be welcomed by the Communist State.[22]

Another common feature of Communist church policy has been the discrimination against the faithful within the society. This phenomenon may be less obvious from the outside, but it still determines the everyday life of the Church to a large extent. Time and again the Communist governments issued provisions forbidding any discrimination against the faithful, from the Polish decree on the protection of freedom of conscience and religion of 5 August 1949 to the regulations of the Supreme Soviet of the R.S.F.S.R. of 18 March 1966 prohibiting discharge from a job or exclusion from an institution of higher learning because of religious allegiance. And yet, as a rule, no active and practising

Christian in a Communist-ruled country is able to occupy any responsible positions in society except within the Church itself. Only in Yugoslavia since the middle of the 1960s has this kind of discrimination been limited to positions within the party and state apparatus. In the G.D.R. for example, in 1958 all school-teachers were forbidden to work for the Church, and all teachers who were members of the S.E.D. had to secede from the Church. In the Soviet Union discrimination goes even further, children holding religious views are made fun of by teachers and class-mates. Many cases were known where students have been fired from institutions of higher learning because of their religious con-victions and activities.[23] Other kinds of discrimination include the prohibition to use any technical equipment within the Church or during religious instructions, such as movies, slides, or loud-speakers. In times of tension various administrative measures have been applied to hamper church life, such as heavy income taxes for priests; taxes also have been imposed upon the Polish Catholic Church for using former German church property in the Western Territories. But only in Poland was the Catholic Church strong enough simply to refuse the payment of discrimi-natory taxes.

All State–Church conflicts reviewed so far arose from Com-munist attempts to control church life from outside. There have also been Communist efforts to disintegrate the Catholic Church from within by patronising those priests and laymen willing to co-operate with the state and party authorities in spite of the resistance of the hierarchy. The so-called progressive priests and laymen often have been criticised and condemned in the West as oppor-tunists or even subversive instruments to destroy the Church from inside. It seems that a reappraisal of Christian–Communist col-laboration is imperative, since our judgements have often been short-sighted and rather pharisaical. In judging the progressive movement within the Eastern European Churches one has to take into account the extraordinarily difficult dilemma of the Church – legality versus an underground existence. One also has to keep in mind that the collaborating Christians frequently were able to ease tensions between Church and State though, obviously, a good deal of their political statements were sheer propaganda.

Immediately after the war the communists tried to sever the Catholic Church in the respective countries from Rome. But they succeeded only in Albania. There in 1951 a general assembly of the Catholic clergy discounted all relations with the Vatican and declared itself an independent national Church.[24] Similar efforts in Poland in 1946 met with only negligible success.

When the attempts to separate the local Catholic Churches completely from their ecclesiastical centre in the West proved a failure, Communist tactics resorted to building up groups of loyal priests willing to seek a compromise with the regime. In Poland, Bolesław Piasecki already in November 1945 founded a movement of progressive Catholics with the publishing house 'Pax' as its centre. The Pax Society became the most extreme and indiscriminating wing of collaborators in Poland. Piasecki, like the socialist movement within the Church in general, holds that the socio-economic objectives of Communism are perfectly compatible with the demands of Christian conscience. Starting from this assumption, most sections of the progressive Christian movement have without any criticism supported Communist domestic and particularly foreign policy throughout more than two decades.

Besides the Pax Society, a group of 'patriotic priests' was founded in Poland and, in 1949, was attached as a 'Commission of Priests' to the 'Union of Fighters for Freedom and Democracy'. The Commission was later affiliated with the National Front. Its members were given special privileges and financial support from the Government. Against the will of the bishops, patriotic priests were entrusted with responsible positions within the Church; stubborn hierarchs were replaced by co-operative progressive priests. Their influence in Poland reached its culmination point during the years 1953 to 1956.[25]

Between 1949 and 1951, similar organisations of progressive priests were founded in all other countries of Eastern Europe, except in the Soviet Union,[26] in connection with the launching of an international peace campaign of the Communist bloc. Although these groups embraced only a small percentage of the clergy and were declared illegal by the hierarchy and attacked by the Vatican, with most of their leaders excommunicated, these groups exerted a considerable influence within the Church. They helped to bring about the view currently prevalent in most Churches that some sort of *modus vivendi* with the Communist State has to be attained since the Church cannot sustain a confrontation for decades.

II.   CHURCH POLICY AND INTERNAL POLITICAL
      DEVELOPMENTS IN EASTERN EUROPE

Church policy of Communist states unfolded in accord with the two main periods of political development in Eastern Europe: (1) Stalinism, and (2) a certain *détente* since about 1956. Nevertheless this scheme needs some modifications. During the first post-war years the Church in Eastern Europe – outside the U.S.S.R. – was left relatively undisturbed up to 1948-49. Serious conflict and confrontation arose only by 1949, usually in connection with the Communist take-over of power. Only in Croatia and Slovakia did the persecution of the Catholic Church start immediately after the War, since in those countries the Catholic Church was to a certain extent compromised by its collaboration with the former Nazi–dependent governments. Another modification of our scheme concerns the G.D.R., where a Stalinist persecution of the Church in the proper sense never did take place.

Soviet policy towards the Roman Catholic Church also followed a somewhat different pattern. Organised Catholicism in the Soviet Union had been destroyed by the mid-thirties. In the newly acquired territories in the West in 1939–40, and later after the victorious end of the war, a rigorous persecution of the Catholic Church took place. It was at the same time directed against the non-Russian nationalities. When in 1945 in Lithuania, Latvia and Byelorussia Catholic priests were sentenced and deported, churches closed down and religious instruction banned, in Russia proper a relatively liberal phase of religious policy had come about as a consequence of the war. At the same time that the Russian Orthodox Church was able to rebuild its organisation, and was even enlarged by the administrative 'reunion' of the Uniate Church in the Western Ukraine with the Moscow Patriarchate, the Catholic Church suffered severe losses. The end result of this discriminatory policy was a more or less equalised situation of the Churches in the whole country, at a common, low standard. Therefore the model for the repressive religious policy in Eastern Europe was not Soviet behaviour towards the Churches in the U.S.S.R. during the 1940s in general, but merely the persecution of the Catholic Church in the newly annexed territories. During the post-Stalin era, ecclesiastical policy in the Soviet Union contrasted with the general 'thaw' marked by the twentieth Congress of the C.P.S.U. in 1956. From 1958 to 1964, during the peak years of Khrushchev's power, a renewed, vigorous attack on the Churches took place in the Soviet Union. It was without parallel in any Eastern European country. Only Khrushchev's fall arrested this anti-religious campaign, without restoring the *status quo ante*. A similar campaign against the Churches was launched in Albania in 1966–67, resulting in a complete suppression of institutional religion.

To all these modifications of the two-phase scheme of communist church policies after 1945, one must add that the differences and discrepancies among individual Communist countries grew considerably since the late 1950s. The different characteristics of Church–State relations in Poland, Yugoslavia and the Soviet Union became much more apparent during the last decade than in Stalin's lifetime when the Eastern European states were considered Moscow's satellites.

What then was the extent of Moscow's influence upon the communist church policy within the bloc? There is no doubt that the Soviet Union served as a model in terms of the final objectives of religious policy and the many instruments employed to reach those aims. But, on the other hand, Soviet politicians left considerable responsibility to their Eastern European junior partners of executing religious policies in predominantly Catholic or Protestant countries. It is also likely that many striking parallels and common features of their policies are not the result of a dictate from the Kremlin, but rather a product of co-operation and consultation between the makers of religious policy in various countries. There did not exist in 1945 an overall plan for destroying the influence of the Church in Communist-dominated areas; it developed gradually, relying on the Soviet experience during past decades and being modified either by the resistance and the inner strength of the Church – as, for example, in Poland – or by limited communist power in the face of the Church's strong ties with the West – as, for example, in the G.D.R. Most instruments employed to hamper church life were products of the Stalin era. The period from 1949 to 1956 was characterised by a mass terror against the Catholic clergy. In Czechoslovakia alone up to 1955, thirteen bishops had been removed from their sees, five had been sentenced and the others kept in confinement. In several Communist countries during the fifties show trials were staged against bishops, leading monastic clergy and Catholic laymen. They ended with self-accusations and all other forms of Stalinist humiliation, invented during the great purges in the Soviet Union in the 1930s. Officially, of course, no ecclesiastics were brought to trial because of their creed or allegiance to the Catholic Church, but because of espionage for the Vatican or the C.I.A., high treason, collaboration with the Nazis, etc. Early in 1951 more than 2,000 Czechoslovak priests were arrested. During the amnesty in 1960 about 800 priests were released, but only very few were restored to ministry.[27]

In a memorandum to Tito in September 1952 the Yugoslav Catholic episcopate stated that there were still more than 200 priests in prison and that during the previous eight years more than half of the clergy had been imprisoned for a certain period of time. Already on 11 October 1946 the Yugoslav Primate Archbishop Stepinac had been sentenced to sixteen years' imprisonment, of which he served five years.[28] A similar fate awaited other Eastern European primates: Cardinal Mindszenty of Hungary was sentenced to life imprisonment in February 1949; Archbishop Beran of Prague was ousted from his post in March 1951; and Cardinal Wyszyński of Poland was kept in secret confinement from 1953 to October 1956. It has been estimated that by 1955 about 5,000 priests and 10,000 nuns had been sent to prison or forced labour camps in Eastern Europe.[29]

In contrast to the Stalin period, the Communist authorities avoided creating martyrs during the 1960s. The problem of vacant sees proved soluble when Pope John XXIII in 1960 appointed eight Yugoslav bishops, and five Hungarian bishops were consecrated in 1964 in conjunction with the accord between the Vatican and the Hungarian Government.[30] Even in Lithuania between 1965 and 1970 four new Catholic bishops could enter office. An agreement with Czechoslovakia was reached in early 1973.

Unlike during the Stalin period, the present restrictions and assaults are not primarily directed against church leadership. Leading bishops are to a certain extent publicly accepted and honoured. They are allowed to travel abroad and participate in international meetings; they normally receive their visa to visit the Vatican. Attacks are directed against the bases of the Church, against ordinary priests, local congregations, religious instruction or a seminary. In addition, restrictions on church activities have often been imposed by the church leadership itself under pressure and by order of the state authorities. This came out very clearly during Khrushchev's persecution wave in the Soviet Union, which was in part implemented by circulars and directives of the church leadership addressed to the clergy and the flock. The natural consequence, perhaps intended by the regime, was a loss of authority of the bishops in the eyes of the faithful.

In spite of continuing restrictions the period after 1956 brought substantial relief for the Catholic Church in Eastern Europe. Even though the process of contraction of the institutional Church has not at all come to a standstill, physical terror was discontinued and, within limits, church life became again relatively normalised. But just as the irresistible process of secularisation made itself felt, atheistic education and more sophisticated discrimination against the Church in society were not without results.

The Church, on the other hand, had actively contributed towards finding a *modus vivendi* with the State. There could be no longer a question of confronting the established Communist power and calling the faithful to martyrdom. The Church was faced with the necessity of finding a new form of loyalty or at least neutrality, so that Church and State could coexist to a certain degree. There was no other alternative for the Church than to recognise and work within a new social and political environment which it could no longer change fundamentally. The years of terror had proved that massive confrontation would endanger the continuation of the Church. Another alternative would have been for the Catholic Church to go underground, but for this it was neither theologically nor organisationally suitably prepared. Hence there existed no other alternative to the *modus vivendi,* that is to the restricted and constantly precarious legality which demanded a certain preparedness for non-resistance from the Church. Bishops' inclination towards compromise made it, moreover, possible to decrease internal tensions within the Church, for a limited compromise with the Communist State reduced the strength of the priests' peace movement.

The waves of unrest and liberalisation which swept over some East European countries in the post-Stalin era have had a moderating and liberalising influence on church policies. Cardinals Mindszenty and Wyszyński returned in October 1956 as heroes to their respective capitals. With them hundreds of priests and monks were released from prison. In Poland a *modus vivendi* was reached by an accord of 8 December 1956, signed by representatives of the episcopate and the Government, reinstituting many rights taken away from the Church during previous years by administrative measures.[31] It perfectly fits the pattern that the new Gierek/Jaroszewicz leadership, installed after strike waves in December 1970, turned to the Catholic Church for moral support, promising a 'complete normalisation' of State–Church relations. As the first step, the Government announced a transfer to the Catholic Church of the property rights to the former German church property in the Western Territories. On 3 March 1971 the Polish Premier received Cardinal Wyszyński for the first time in eleven years.

But in the same way that popular uprisings and the overthrow of conservative governments affected State–Church relations positively, the subsequent reaction and 'freeze' in domestic politics resulted in renewed restrictions on the liberty of the Church. This happens today in Czechoslovakia, where the liberal chairman of the Secretariat for Religious Affairs, Erika Kadlecova, who had only assumed this position in March 1968, had to resign in July 1969. Characteristically, her predecessor and successor in this post was the same man – Karel Hruza. A year before she wrote in *Rudé právo* that 'our society cannot be infringed upon by a consistent observance of religious liberty, but rather by its restriction'.[32] In 1970 the concessions to religious instruction were recalled, the *numerus clausus* for theological seminaries was re-established, and the Slovak authorities ordered a complete halt to the building of new churches; since 1968 in East Slovakia alone 87 churches and 48 parish priests' houses were under construction.[33]

The discussion of the fate of the Catholic Church in Communist societies has so far hardly mentioned the role of the Vatican and its impact on Christian–Communist encounter. This seems to a certain extent justifiable, since the Vatican did not exercise decisive influence upon the attitude of the Eastern European Catholic Church towards the Communist system. Catholicism in Eastern Europe was to a large extent dependent on itself. During the Cold War period, Rome was active in sharpening the conflict between the Church and the Communist states; since the late 1950s, however, it has exercised a moderating influence upon the Eastern

European episcopate. In other words, the Vatican followed the line of general political development, pursuing the way from anathema to dialogue (Garaudy). Thereby the rapprochement between the Vatican, on the one hand, and the Soviet Government and the Russian Orthodox Church, on the other, represents the most striking evolution.

The significance of the *aggiornamento* becomes obvious only against the background of the decree of the Holy Office of 1 July 1949 forbidding Catholics any kind of co-operation with Communists and excommunicating those Catholics who belonged to the Party or were willing fellow-travellers. The decree was closely connected with the beginning of the open struggle against the Catholic Church in Poland, since the Government called this decree an act of aggression against the Polish state and blocked its implementation. Other Communist governments proceeded in a similar way. Likewise, the excommunication of leading progressive priests by the Vatican in the following years was of little avail to the Churches in Eastern Europe, since the Czech or Hungarian episcopate were not able to enforce ecclesiastical penalties against collaborators supported by the regime. Obviously, Pope Pius XII overestimated his power.

During the mid-1950s the *Osservatore Romano* still fought against any tendencies in Catholicism towards co-existence and stressed the impossibility of a dialogue. The first *modus vivendi* between the Catholic Church and the Government in Poland in 1950 was accomplished without sanction from Rome, although it was perhaps the most favourable accord ever reached by the Church after the Communist take-over in Eastern Europe. The second agreement in 1956 had express approval from Rome, although Pius XII made the reservation that the Polish model was not applicable to other countries.

This reservation was done away with during the pontificate of John XXIII, whose associates Bea, Willebrands and Casaroli worked for a new Eastern policy of the Holy See. It was of decisive significance that by the late 1950s Vatican diplomacy was convinced that Communism no longer could be regarded as a 'temporary evil' and that, secondly, the Church was not able to sustain a confrontation indefinitely. No doubt the thaw since 1956 contributed considerably to this turn of Vatican diplomacy. It found its most obvious expression in agreements concluded with the Hungarian Government on 15 September 1964 and with the Yugoslav Government on 25 June 1966. By these accords the Communist governments recognised the canonical jurisdiction of the Pope over the Catholic Church in their territories, while the Vatican on its part acknowledged and endorsed the principle of loyalty towards a Communist state.[34] To be sure, diplomatic arrangements do not resolve the urgent everyday problems of the Church in Eastern Europe, but they may open certain prospects for the future.

III.   HISTORY AND THE PRESENT. FROM THE U.S.S.R. TO
       THE G.D.R.

So far we have discussed instruments and objectives of Communist church policy and their relation to the general political development. But the picture would be incomplete and misleading without a cursory survey of the concrete situation in some countries, showing – in spite of many common features – considerable discrepancies and variations which have to be explained by differences in history, national culture, time and place.

   The Soviet Union belongs to those countries where church life has been restricted most sharply. This, of course, has to be attributed to the fact that the Communist regime has been established there some thirty years earlier than in Eastern Europe; it also proved easier to reduce the Orthodox Church, rather than Catholicism, to a cult church. The Soviet authorities for their part were eager to apply the framework to which they had restricted the Orthodox Church to all other denominations. Moreover, the conflict with the Catholic Church in the Soviet Union was intensified by its connection with Polish, Lithuanian and Ukrainian (in the case of the Uniates) national consciousness, offering an additional target for Soviet attacks. The absence of identification with the Great Russians made it easier to mobilise Soviet patriotism against the Catholic Church. Already in 1950 prelates from Lithuania and Latvia publicly declared their pro-Soviet political attitude, actively participating in the peace-campaign launched at that time. At the time most Eastern European bishops still avoided any statements supporting Soviet political strategy.

   Catholic church organisation in the Soviet Union was completely destroyed during the 1930s, and Catholicism was – in contrast to most other denominations in the Soviet Union – not allowed to re-establish a central apparatus after World War II. Today a national conference of bishops is not tolerated, and only Lithuania and Latvia are divided into regular dioceses which are now mostly headed by apostolic administrators. Within the six Lithuanian bishoprics the number of faithful was estimated at about two million, cared for by 834 priests in 1969. The two Latvian dioceses embraced about half a million faithful and 143 priests in 1965.[35] There is not a single Catholic monastery or convent, welfare institution or Catholic school in the U.S.S.R. Only two small theological seminaries are operated in Kaunas and Riga; in 1969 the Kaunas seminary was attended by only twenty-five students and in Riga only correspondence courses seem to be offered. Although two bishops were consecrated early in 1970, there are still three Catholic bishops in Lithuania and Latvia confined to far-away parishes, not allowed to resume office, but not sentenced by a regular court.

The Catholic Church was severely affected by the persecution wave under Khrushchev, when in Byelorussia alone about ten churches were closed down and the number of priests and churches reduced from eighty in 1945 to twenty-five in 1965. By the early 1960s the figure of the candidates for the priesthood at the Kaunas seminary was limited to less than half. Again arrests and trials occurred as during the immediate post-war years. In Vilnius, in January 1962, two priests were sentenced to eight and six years' imprisonment respectively because they had managed to build a new church in Klaipeda.[36] Although the campaign of systematic closing of churches came to an end in 1965, we know from *samizdat* that subsequently attempts have been made to close Catholic churches in the district of Grodno by administrative measures.[37] Atheistic activities seem to be particularly well organised in Lithuania.[38] The heavy restrictions imposed upon the Church in the early 1960s resulted in considerable signs of unrest among the Catholic clergy and laity, parallel to the opposition movement within other denominations.

Under Khrushchev, just as during the 1930s, Soviet church policy reached far beyond the aim of reducing the Church to a cult Church. Many faithful were even denied the opportunity of worshipping in clear violation of the Constitution. In other Eastern European countries within the Soviet sphere of influence such a systematic campaign of closing churches has never taken place.

For the Catholics in the Soviet Union it remains a disappointment that the rapprochement between the Vatican and Moscow has so far not resulted in a more conciliatory attitude of the Soviet authorities towards the Catholics in their territory.

It seems that in the latter half of the 1960s the Eastern policy of the Vatican was excessively guided by a quest for spectacular 'successes', manifested by diplomatic travels and visits, without energetically representing the interests of the Catholic Church in Eastern Europe. Obviously, the extraordinarily difficult but nevertheless burning question of the Uniate Catholics in the Ukraine is completely ignored by Rome. On the other hand, there remains the question whether the Kremlin or the Moscow Patriarchate would accept at all the question of the Uniate Church as an object of negotiation, and whether any insistence on this topic would not disrupt the connections that have been established. Clearly, this lies neither in the interest of the Catholics in Eastern Europe nor of the ecumenical movement.

Regarding the situation of the Catholic Church – as in many other respects too – the Soviet-Polish border is the most distinct in all of Eastern Europe. The gap is widened by the unique position occupied by the Catholic Church in Poland. Although the situation in Czechoslovakia, Hungary, Romania and Bulgaria is not as severely restricted as in the U.S.S.R., it is still more similar to the Soviet Union than to Poland. The traditional and undejected adherence of the Polish population to the Catholic Church has often been compared to conditions in Spain or Italy. Fifteen per cent of the Catholic population in Rome and Paris are reported to attend Sunday mass, 25 per cent in Madrid, and almost 50 per cent in Warsaw.[39] A Polish newspaper in 1970 wrote that a sociological inquiry at some provincial high schools showed 62 per cent of the students as adherents of the Catholic Church. The newspaper stated that the atmosphere in most small and middle-sized cities was such as to demand a considerable amount of courage from the youth to break with the Church. And it seems even more strange when the Polish episcopate in a pastoral letter of 3 September 1959 called on the flock for tolerance towards non-believers.[40]

The Catholic Church in Poland is the only one in Eastern Europe showing a considerable increase in the number of priests, parishes, monks and nuns; it disposes today of a much larger organisational structure than in pre-war years. This phenomenon can only be explained partly by the growth of the population and the taking-over of all churches in the former German provinces. The Polish Church in 1969 had 13,290 places of worship, compared to 7,251 in 1937. The hierarchy consisted of over 60 bishops and 18,109 priests (including 4,592 regular clergy), whereas in 1937 it comprised only 11,348 priests. The corresponding figures for the parishes are 6,361 and 5,170. Training for the priesthood today is given in 70 seminaries, attended by more than 4,000 students. All figures showed a slow but steady increase during the 1960s.[41]

There are a number of reasons for the extraordinary strength of Polish Catholicism, which poses a serious challenge to the Party; their relationship has represented an uninterrupted chain of conflicts and clashes during the past twenty-five years. There is no other country in Eastern Europe where practically only one denomination counts; never before in modern Polish history has the Polish state embraced less non-Polish, non-Catholic citizens than since 1945. Moreover, spokesmen for Polish Catholicism seem to be fully convinced that it represents the only true heritage of national culture and national history. This came out very clearly in the famous letter of the Polish episcopate to the German bishops of 18 November 1965: 'In Poland the symbiosis of Christendom, Church and State existed from the very outset and was properly speaking never dissolved'. 'Polish means at the same time Catholic'.[42] In other words, the Polish bishops simply ignored the present rulers of the country, one of the reasons that infuriated Gomulka about the letter.

After 1945 the Church identified itself with the number one national problem: from the outset the Catholic Church regarded the newly obtained German provinces as its justified heritage. 'The hour has struck to balance the centuries-old bills,' wrote Primate Cardinal Hlond in a pastoral letter of 24 May 1948. In September 1965, on the occasion of the twentieth anniversary of the establishment of the new church organisations in the Western and Northern territories, Cardinal Wyszyński preached in Wrocław and claimed that the stones of Wrocław are speaking Polish.[43]

Also in other respects the Church took the occasion to speak up for the interest of the people. Already several times before and lately in connection with the December 1970 strikes, the bishops formulated their social demands, requiring higher wages, more apartments and a higher standard of living, while at the same time urging the workers to show patience and calm. The strength of Polish Catholicism rests to a large extent on the traditional adherence to the Church and piety of the population. This offers two dangers: complacency from inside and secularisation from outside. The secularisation is obvious in industrial centres among skilled workers, technical specialists and with the intelligentsia in general. Conservatism and self-isolation of Polish Catholicism is no longer unchallenged in the country itself. But Cardinal Wyszyński still seems to articulate the attitude of the majority when he declares that the present unrest in the *ecclesia catholica* was only liable to bewilder the Polish people and to disturb church life, resting with a staunch faith and an undisturbed relation towards authority.[44] The conservatism of Polish Catholicism was particularly evidenced during Vatican II when the Polish bishops opposed the introduction of the vernacular into the liturgy and in 1964 came out with a far-reaching proposal concerning Mariolatry which was supported only by the Spanish, Mexican and Sicilian bishops.

We won't get a true picture of Polish Catholicism without keeping in mind the severe losses it suffered during the past two decades, in spite of its relative present strength. The Church is discriminated against also in Poland in that a professional career or occupation in any responsible position is incompatible with active participation in church life. There is an influential progressive priest movement opposed to the hierarchy, which continues to generate conflict within the church. The progressive clergy control a part of the Catholic press and the Caritas society. Finally, the Church is not only exposed to a Party determined to restrict the Church whenever possible, but also to a growing tendency among the younger generation to turn its back on the endless struggle between Church and State – a tendency to indifferentism. So it may very well be that a serious crisis for Polish Catholicism is ahead.

Perhaps the most unexpected and perplexing impression is derived from a look at the Catholic Church in the German Democratic Republic. Although this country is in many respects governed most rigidly by Communist hard-liners, the Churches enjoy perhaps the most extensive juridical rights in all of Eastern Europe.

This is in the first respect due to the very close connections the Churches were able to maintain with their counterparts in the Federal Republic of Germany; only in 1969 the G.D.R. managed to completely split the Evangelical Church in Germany. The Catholic Church is primarily a diaspora-Church, relying in many parishes on co-operation with the Protestant *Landeskirche*. The Catholic Church embraces about 1·4 million faithful, or 8 per cent of the population. Its close connection with the West becomes evident if one keeps in mind that four of its seven ecclesiastical districts are parts of West German dioceses. Moreover, the bishop-ric of Berlin is composed of three parts: East Berlin, West Berlin and some G.D.R. territory. Up to 1952 priests could be transferred from the West to the East and vice versa, and up to 1958 West German bishops were able to visit their respective parishes in the G.D.R. Only since the construction of the Berlin wall in 1961 are the Eastern bishops no longer permitted to participate in the conference of German bishops in the Federal Republic of Germany. Since no institution for the training of priests existed on the territory of the G.D.R., the Catholic Church was permitted to establish a seminary in 1952 in Erfurt. With substantial support from West Germany, the Catholic Church in the G.D.R. managed since the war to reconstruct 25 churches and build 325 churches and chapels, as well as to renovate thoroughly 302 churches. However, during the 1960s construction almost came to a stand-still. During the Stalinist period of heavy suppression, the Churches in the G.D.R. were thus left relatively unhindered. Today they are limited in their activities, although charitable work is still possible on a relatively large scale. A large percentage of the youth has been driven away from the Church by atheistic indoc-trination in schools and social institutions, as well as by secularisa-tion, which has advanced much further in the G.D.R. than, for example, in Poland. The Catholic Church, for many years strongly and in principle, opposed to the Ulbricht regime, is now turning to a more conciliatory attitude towards a state in which it will have to exist not only temporarily as was thought during the 1950s. The S.E.D. refrains from noisy campaigns against the Churches and resorts to close control and support of secularisation and indifference.[45]

A fourth case of a peculiar relationship between Church and State we find in Yugoslavia. The strength and vulnerability of

Catholicism in this country are based on its close connection with Croatian and Slovenian nationalities. In the struggle against the Catholic Church in post-war Yugoslavia, Tito's mostly Serbian partisans were determined to take revenge for the persecution of the Serbs in Ante Pavelic's Independent Croat State. Attempts to suppress the Church as a social institution in Yugoslavia did not only start earlier than in other Communist-ruled countries, but were in some respects even more rigid and ruthless, intensified by national hate, popular resentment against the hierarchy and spontaneous pogroms. Not only were some Catholic priests shot without trial in 1945, but as late as 1952–53 there were still cases of bishops and priests being beaten and ill-treated by mobs, as the police stood by without interfering. Bishops were even drafted into the army in 1953. This happened despite Tito's break with the Cominform in 1948 which had brought about a short-lived *détente* in Church–State relations.

A lasting relaxation of tensions between the Catholic Church and the Yugoslav State came only by the late 1950s and culminated in an agreement with the Vatican on 25 June 1966. Restricted diplomatic relations were re-established, with Yugoslavia becoming the only Communist State accepting a Vatican diplomatic representative. Since the time of the Vatican Council a remarkable revival of Catholicism in Croatia and Slovenia has introduced a new phase. Catholic journalism achieved a high standard and is able to argue against any atheistic attack – a unique situation in a Communist country. The Church also enjoys independence in such matters as training for the priesthood and personnel questions. There is no shortage of candidates for clergy. It is characteristic that a relaxed climate of Church–State relations brought into the foreground the internal problems and unrest within the Church, connected with the end of the traditional Church. A similar phenomenon could be observed in Czechoslovakia in 1968. In spite of the liberalisation in Yugoslavia the fact remains that the Catholic Church is still only partly able to fulfil its social functions; as before, it has no right to engage in organisational work among youth or maintain public schools and charitable organisations.[46]

What are the results of Communist church policy? It has, no doubt, to a certain extent been successful in driving away the

Church from the public and from the public consciousness. In most countries of Eastern Europe the Church is no longer a first-rate social force; it is not independent and strong enough to determine current social development. But the Church remains a lasting challenge to the Communist Party, because it offers an alternative philosophy of life – in most countries the only permitted opposition concerning one's *Weltanschauung*. Communist measures to restrict the Church to ritual resulted in a considerable decrease of social activities and influence. The consequence of the discriminatory attitude towards practising Christians has been to reduce increasingly the active members of the Church to a lower social strata. This may be one of the reasons for a general conservatism and reluctance towards reform movements within the Church. But the main cause for the tenacity of tradition and established patterns in custom and dogma doubtlessly remains the permanent stress and pressure under which the Church is forced to live. The necessity to concentrate on defence and apology did not allow the Church to turn its attention to internal reforms. It is worth noting that even the so-called progressive priests tend to advocate a conservative theology, except for social ethics.

Did atheistic propaganda and indoctrination attain its aim of speeding up the process of secularisation and doing away with 'religious relics'? Hardly; it may very well be that the number of the faithful, for example, in East and West Germany does not differ considerably, although in their outward appearance the institutionalised Churches differ greatly from each other. On the other hand, the ignorance about Christianity among the youth in some Eastern European countries is striking, though it does not necessarily signify a commitment to atheism.

The Church in a militantly atheistic society is forced to face the unavoidable dilemma between martydom and collaboration. This has very often led Western observers to divide Eastern Christians into martyrs and collaborators, Reality is much more complicated, and the Church has to find its way somewhere in between the two extremes; either would lead to disaster.

NOTES

1. *Frankfurter Allgemeine Zeitung*, 22 April 1969.
2. For example, V. Gsovski (ed.), *Church and State Behind the Iron Curtain* (New York, 1955); A. Galter, *Rotbuch der verfolgten Kirche* (Recklinghausen, 1957; in English: *The Red Book of the Persecuted Church*, Westminster, Md., 1957, 2nd ed.); K. Hutten, *Christen hinter dem eisernen Vorhang*, 2 vols., (Stuttgart, 1962–63; in English: *Iron Curtain Christians: The Church in Communist Countries Today*, Minneapolis, 1967).
3. For example, R. Tobias, *Communist-Christian Encounter in East Europe, 1917–1951*, (Indianapolis, 1956).
4. B. R. Bociurkiw, 'Lenin and Religion', in L. Schapiro and P. Reddaway (eds.), *Lenin: The Man, the Theorist, the Leader. A Reappraisal* (London, 1967), pp. 107–34.
5. Cited from Bociurkiw, *loc cit.*, p. 116.
6. 1961 Programme of the C.P.S.U. (B. Meissner, *Das Parteiprogramm der KPdSU, 1903–1961*, Cologne, 1962, p. 229).
7. L. N. Mitrokhin, 'Chelovek v baptistskoi obshchine' (Man in Baptist Congregation), *Voprosy filosofii*, No. 8 (1968), pp. 42–52; L. N. Velikovich, 'Adzhornamento i antikommunizm' (Aggiornamento and Anti-Communism), *Voprosy filosofii*, No. 11 (1970), p. 156.
8. Jan F. Triska (ed.), *Constitutions of the Communist Party-States* (Hong Kong, 1968).
9. English translation appears in Tobias, *op. cit.*, pp. 340–47.
10. Cf. the petition of the Czechoslovak episcopate to the Government of 21 October 1949 (Gsovski, *op. cit.*, pp. 35–7) and the memorandum of Cardinal Wyszyński, Primate of Poland, of 8 May 1953 (Galter, *Rotbuch der verfolgten Kirche*, [Recklinghausen 1957], p. 150).
11. English translation of the decree of 25 October 1949 appears in Gsovski, *op. cit.*, pp. 41–2.
12. For the wording of the oath, cf. Tobias, *op. cit.*, p. 342 (Romania), p. 479 (Hungary); Gsovski, *op. cit.*, p. 49 (Czechoslovakia).
13. Hutten, *op. cit.*, Vol. I, pp. 187, 200–1; Gsovski, *op. cit.*, pp. 90–91.
14. Galter, *op. cit.*, pp. 342–3.
15. S. Staron, 'State-Church Relations in Poland', *World Politics*, Vol. XXI, No. 4 (1969), p. 591; F. Dinka, 'Sources of Conflict Between Church and State in Poland', *Review of Politics*, Vo.. XXVIII, No. 3 (1966), p. 337.
16. E. András and J. Morel, *Bilanz des ungarischen Katholizismus* (Munich, 1969), p. 119.
17. G. Simon, *Die Kirchen in Russland. Berichte-Dokumente* (Munich, 1970), p. 123.
18. Galter, *op. cit.*, pp. 315–18; Hutten, *op. cit.*, Vol. I, p. 101.
19. Galter, *op. cit.*, pp. 172–4, 382.
20. Hutten, *op. cit.*, Vol. I, pp. 101–2, 151.
21. Gsovski, *op. cit.*, p. 38; Galter, *op. cit.*, pp. 203–05, 351–2; Hutten, *op. cit.*, Vol. I, p. 159.
22. For a detailed study of the liquidation of the Union, see B. R. Bociurkiw, 'The Uniate Church in the Soviet Ukraine: A Case Study in Soviet Church Policy', *Canadian Slavonic Papers*, Vol. VII (1965), pp. 89–113; cf. P. Mailleux, 'Catholics in the Soviet Union' in R. H. Marshall, Jr. (ed.), *Aspects of Religion in the Soviet Union, 1917–1967* (Chicago, 1971), pp. 369–76.
23. Hutten, *op. cit.*, Vol. II, pp. 175–6; *Religion in Communist Dominated Areas*, Vol. IX, No. 5–8 (1970), pp. 34–6.

24. Hutten, *op. cit.*, Vol. II, p. 488.
25. B. Stasiewski in *Polen. Osteuropa-Handbuch*, ed. by W. Markert (Cologne-Graz, 1959), pp. 357, 361–2; Staron, *loc. cit.*, pp. 580–4; H. Stehle, *The Independent Satellite. Society and Politics in Poland since 1945* (London, 1965), pp. 104–9.
26. There is no organisation of progressive priests in the Soviet Union, although prior to World War II a similar type of movement had existed in the U.S.S.R. It was known as the *Renovationists*.
27. A. Bucko, 'Kreuzweg der katholischen Kirche in der Slowakei,' *Südost-Stimmen*, Vol. IV, No. 6 (October 1954 [third Catholic special issue]), p. 21; Hutten, *op. cit.*, Vol. I, pp. 155–7, 162–4.
28. E. Bauer, 'Die katholische Kirche im kommunistischen Jugoslawien', *Südost-Stimmen*, Vol. IV, No. 2, March 1954 [second Catholic special issue], p. 20; Galter, *op. cit.*, pp. 394–7.
29. B. Stasiewski, 'Die Sowjetisierung Ostmitteleuropas. Die religiösen Gemein-schaften,' unpublished manuscript, pp. 36–7.
30. *Kirche in Not*, Vol. XIV (1967), pp. 106–7.
31. Stehle, *op. cit.*, pp. 309–10.
32. *Rudé právo*, 18 May, 1968.
33. *Ökumenischer Pressedienst*, November 1970, p. 14; *Herder-Korrespondez* Vol. XXIV, No. 11 (1970), pp. 569–73; Vol. XXV, No. 2 (1971), pp. 113–14.
34. H. Stehle, 'Vatican Policy Towards Eastern Europe', *Survey*, No. 66 (January 1968), pp. 108–16; W. Daim, *Der Vatikan und der Osten* (Vienna, 1967), pp. 58, 60, 89, 99, 439–42; *Kirche in Not*, Vol. XIV (1967), pp. 54, 116–19.
35. *Kirche in Not*, Vol. XIV (1967), p. 99; V. Mačulin, 'Das religiöse und kirch-liche Leben in Litauen,' *Acta Baltica*, Vol. VIII (1968), p. 31.
36. *Kirche im Osten*, Vol. X (1963), p. 134.
37. *Khronika tekushchikh sobytii*, No. 15 (August 1970); No. 16 (October 1970), *Posev, Shestoi Spetsialnyi Vypusk* (February 1971).
38. R. Conquest (ed.), *Religion in the USSR* [Contemporary Soviet Studies Series] (London, 1968), pp. 96–7; *Religion und Atheismus in der UdSSR*, November–December 1970, p. 2.
39. H. Stehle, 'Im Jahr nach dem Millennium. Polens Kirche zwischen Kampf und Koexistenz mit dem Kommunismus,' *Wort und Wahrheit*, Vol. XXII, No. 3 (1967), p. 263.
40. *Glos Wybrzeża*, 7 and 8 February 1970, cited in *Osteuropa*, Vol. XX, No. 12 (1970), p. A 889; Stehle, *Independent Sattelite*, p. 86.
41. *Rocznik statystyczny 1970* (Warszawa, 1970), p. 19; Staron, *loc. cit.*, p. 588.
42. Daim, *op. cit.*, p. 278.
43. *Ibid.*, pp. 250, 257.
44. *Katholische-Nachrichten-Agentur* (KNA), 24 April 1969, p. 11.
45. *Kirche in Not*, Vol. XI (1964), p. 121; Vol. XVIII (1971), pp. 106–23; *Die katholische Kirche in Berlin und Mitteldeutschland* (Berlin, 1962, 3rd ed.); Hutten, *op. cit.*, Vol.II, pp. 9–420.
46. *Kirche in Not*, Vol. XI (1964), pp. 105–7; Vol. X (1963), pp. 90–4; Vol. XVIII (1971), pp. 101, 104.

11 The Fate of Judaism in the Communist World

JOSHUA ROTHENBERG

The term 'Judaism' has, as is well known, several meanings. In the narrower sense the term denotes only the Jewish religion. In the broader sense it comprises the religion, Jewish secular culture, Jewish languages (Hebrew, Yiddish, Ladino, etc.), Jewish history, Jewish ethnicity and the concept of nationality. The intertwining of 'national' and 'religious' components in an ethnic group's consciousness is characteristic not only for the Jewish group but also for Armenians, Muslims, Ukrainians, Lithuanians and even for the majority nation in the Soviet Union – the Russians. In 1963 one of the rare sociological studies made in the Soviet Union endeavoured to find the causes of the vitality of baptism by investigating the inhabitants of the Vyborg *rayon* of Leningrad. The survey found that 25 per cent of the total number of children in the area were baptised, and one of the principal reasons given by the parents for the observance of this rite was 'because it is a *Russian* custom'.[1]

If this intertwining and overlapping of the 'national' and 'religious' is a complicating factor in separating the two domains in the case of, for example, the Armenians whose Church is not very different from other Christian Churches, or for the Russians whose Church is the same as that of several other nationalities, then how much more complicated becomes the isolation of the religious component in Judaism. The Jewish religion stands very much apart from all other religions. For centuries it has been in violent conflict with most of them, and it is practised by only one ethnic group. In the Soviet Union it is practised, with few exceptions, by only one officially recognised nationality, and in that country the distinction between a Jew by religion (a

Judaist) and a Jew by nationality or ethnicity cannot be reliably ascertained.

Most Jewish philosophers, particularly in modern times, have put to scrutiny the various components of Judaism and have come up with divergent views. The State of Israel has wrestled with the problem 'Who is a Jew?' and until now has not been able to formulate a satisfactory answer. In this chapter we cannot hope to do better than the philosophers and the Israeli State, but we want simply to take note of the difficulty inherent in the definition of 'Judaism' before proceeding to a discussion of the fate of Judaism in the Communist world.

In any general discussion of the Communist world the Soviet Union occupies a central place, and when Jews in the Communist world are discussed most of the discussion is focused on Soviet Jewry. With an estimated population of three million, the Soviet Jews now constitute around 23 per cent of the Jewish people in the world. Soviet Jews thus make up the second largest (after the United States) Jewish community in the world; one which still has an estimated half million more Jews than Israel. The number of Jews in the rest of the Communist world is much less significant, totalling an estimated 220,000 persons, or less than 2 per cent of the world's Jewish population. It must, however, be added that although the absolute number of Jews in some of these countries is small, their *proportion* to the total population is not that much lower than in the Soviet Union. In the Soviet Union, Jews constituted, according to the 1970 census, about 0.9 per cent of the total population, while in Hungary they constitute 0.8 per cent (only one-tenth less than in the Soviet Union) and in Romania 0.5 per cent.

It may be natural that scholars and statesmen are more preoccupied with the fate of three million than of 220,000 people. However, if one is to investigate the variations and possibilities of existence of Judaism in a Socialist or Communist system, the organisational frameworks in which these, sometimes very small, Jewish communities operate become basic subjects for a comparative study. They may constitute prototypes. One should, therefore, attempt to categorise in types of 'models'; the organisational structures, modes of operations and activities of the Jewish groups in the various Communist countries.[2] Four general types can be distinguished:

Type 1

The Jewish religious associations are isolated and are identical with particular houses of prayer; they have exclusively religious prerogatives. There are no organised Jewish communities (*kehilahs*), no central organisations, agencies or religious publications. Heavy pressure is exercised by the Government and local authorities to curtail religious activities.

The only country in the Communist world belonging to this type is the Soviet Union. The Soviet Union has about sixty functioning synagogues, most of them in the Caucasus and Central Asia, and an estimated ten to fifteen rabbis. No kosher restaurants exist. In the secular Jewish area, an average of two–three Yiddish books are published annually and several small Yiddish theatrical groups perform. Two periodicals appear, of which one is a literary magazine.

Type 2

Organised Jewish communities (*kehilahs*), some of them embracing several synagogues, exist and are united in a central union. The prerogatives of the *kehilahs* and of the union are principally, but not exclusively, religious. Social welfare activities are permitted. Pressures exist but not to a degree which would substantially impede religious observance.

To this category belong Romania, Hungary, Czechoslovakia and, in another part of the world, the miniscule Jewish community in Cuba.

In *Romania*, with an estimated 100,000 Jews, the following Jewish establishments exist: seventy-five organised Jewish communities (*kehilahs*), 180 institutions, including congregations, nine kosher restaurants, a trilingual (Hebrew, Yiddish, Romanian) bi-weekly and a yearbook. Extensive welfare activities are conducted. In the secular area, there exists a Yiddish state theatre.

In *Hungary*: The Jewish population numbers 80,000. There are seventy organised Jewish communities (thirty synagogues in Budapest) with thirty rabbis. The Hungarian-Jewish community publishes one periodical, has several schools, a museum and the *only* Jewish theological seminary in the Communist world. Yearbooks and several scholarly works are published. Kosher meat shops, an orphanage and a home for the aged are operating.

In *Czechoslovakia*: The present Jewish population numbers around 10,000. The one central union was recently divided into two unions, Czech and Slovak. An estimated six to seven Jewish communities still exist, with no rabbis left. Two periodicals and an impressive Jewish state museum which has published scholarly works still function. The number of Jews has decreased and their position has significantly deteriorated since the Soviet bloc intervention in 1968, but religious life has been allowed to continue with little change.

In *Cuba*, there are some 1,800 Jews with a congregation and a kosher restaurant in Havana, and one part-time clergyman. Welfare and cultural activities are allowed.

East Germany has a Jewish population of about 1,000. One small congregation exists in East Berlin. There are practically no Jews in *Albania*.

Type 3

The organisational framework includes two separate central bodies – one religious and the other secular-cultural.

To this category belong *Poland* and, until recently, *Bulgaria*. The number of Jews in Poland has decreased dramatically since 1968 from an estimated 25,000 to about 8,000. Anti-Jewish policies forced most of the Jews to leave the country. In both Poland and Bulgaria Jewish activities were mostly of a secular character. Until 1967 Poland had extensive Yiddish cultural activities: two Yiddish periodicals and some 400 Yiddish books were published from 1946 to 1967 – an average of twenty books annually. Several Yiddish schools, a state theatre and an Historical Institute existed. At the time of writing the theatre, the Institute and one periodical still exist. The religious associations are presently inactive.

In *Bulgaria* the Religious Union has been dissolved and Jewish activities are presently conducted by the Cultural and Educational Society.

Type 4

Jewish communities are organised in *one* central body of which the *main* functions are not religious but secular-cultural. To this category belong *Yugoslavia* and presently *Bulgaria*, each with an estimated Jewish population of around 7,000. In both countries Jewish periodicals are published and various cultural activities are conducted. The Jewish community in Yugoslavia is the more active of the two.

Thus there is one category of Communist countries where there is no central Jewish organisation and no organised local Jewish communities (*kehilahs*); another category where there is one central organisation of a predominantly religious character and organised *kehilahs*; a third category where two central organisations exist: a religious and a cultural-ethnic; and a final category with one central organisation of a predominantly cultural-ethnic character.

The Communist regimes which came into existence after World War II have not followed the policy of the Soviet Union regarding the Jewish minority, either in organisational structure or in the scope of religious freedom granted to their citizens. Not one of these regimes embarked on a decisive policy of liquidation of the Jewish religious establishment and Jewish religious observance as did the Soviet Union. With some differences, it may be mentioned that a similar divergence of policies exists in regard to non-Judaic religious cults.

There are, of course, several plausible explanations for this divergence: differences in historical background, the manner in which the respective regimes came into power and have established their power, the measure of popular support and the ethnic composition of the multi-national Soviet Union as compared to the more homogeneous populations of Eastern Europe. But all of these possible factors and even the fact that the Soviet Union, as the first country to establish a Communist-led regime, overacted in various ways cannot fully explain why the Soviet leadership considered the eradication of religious beliefs so acute a problem not only in 1928 but again in the 1950s and 1960s.

The relatively extreme Soviet policies may have been motivated less by objective factors than by anger at facts which refused to adjust to theory. Since the Soviet Union claimed to be the country farthest on the road to Communism, the sources begetting religious belief should already have largely disappeared. As Bohdan R.

Bociurkiw remarked in his essay, 'Religion and Atheism in Soviet Society', if religious beliefs are still very much alive it must, in Soviet thinking, be due to extraneous sources, 'to ideological, external capitalist influence . . . the inadequacy of anti-religious propaganda . . . and illegal activities of churchmen.'[3] The Soviet leadership can understand such obstacles, especially the imperfection of anti-religious propaganda and 'the illegal activities of churchmen'; it can confront them and take action. In fact, it must act, under the penalty of admitting that a socialist order does not eliminate the sources of religion. One should also not underestimate the all too human frustration of seeing still alive a dragon supposedly slain long ago. (The leaders of the other Communist countries have never claimed to have killed or even mortally wounded the dragon.)

The differential status and treatment accorded the Jewish religion in the Soviet Union compared to the other countries in the Communist world is obvious. Where this divergence corresponds with an overall divergence in the treatment of all religious cults, further discussion is not necessary in the context of this paper. But the reasons for the differential treatment in the Soviet Union of the Jewish religion and the Jewish people in comparison with most other religious and ethnic groups needs some elaboration.

The answer lies partly in the peculiar situation into which the Jewish nationality has been thrust in the Soviet Union, and partly in the gravity of the nationality problem in the Soviet Union. In no other Communist country, excepting perhaps Yugoslavia, is the nationality problem so potentially dangerous, and in no other country, including Yugoslavia, is the impact of religion on so great a number of minority nationalities so persuasive. The problem of the Jewish religion is not only intertwined with the problem of the Jewish nationality in the Soviet Union, it is to a large degree subordinated to it. 'Jewish separateness', is the main adversary and 'the fewer synagogues the fewer the opportunities to congregate and to keep Jewish separateness', as one Soviet official has said to a visiting journalist.[4]

To properly understand both the present attitudes of a large part of the Jewish population in the Soviet Union and the Soviet regime's present position, one must trace back Soviet history, and the role of the Jews in it, since the beginning of the Soviet State.

.   .   .   .   .   .

Because the Jews were a minority severely oppressed by the Tsarist regime, with each of the two generations preceding the Revolution subjected to a wave of bloody pogroms, they enthusiastically welcomed the 'bourgeois' February Revolution. The October Revolution was much less enthusiastically received by the overwhelming majority of the Jewish population, although active opposition to the regime or active obstruction of its policies was rare. Contrary to widely held opinion, both the number of Jewish Bolsheviks and the role the Bolshevik Party played among the Jewish population were insignificant. Only in the highest echelons of leadership was there a large proportion of Jews, and those were highly assimilated persons with no ties to the Jewish community. In 1918 when Yiddish was spoken by at least 90 per cent of the Jewish population the new regime could not find even half-a-dozen prominent members of the Bolshevik Party with a knowledge of Yiddish to take over the leadership of the *Yevsektsiia*. Only later did the number of Jewish party members grow, when many of the leaders and members of the dissolved Jewish socialist parties, the Bund, Poale Zion and other groups went over to the Communist Party. Jewish participation and acceptance of the new order increased considerably during the civil war when the opponents of the Soviet rule resorted to anti-Jewish acts and pogroms. It grew again in the late 1920s, particularly among the young Jewish generation for whom new economic, political and social avenues, never accessible to Jews in Russia, were for the first time opened. Jews paid a heavy price, often in blood, for their support of the new regime, not only in Soviet Russia during the civil war but also in the neighbouring countries where Jews, as a group, were often accused of supporting Communism. In Poland bad treatment of Jews was often justified by the allegation of their being *Żydo-Komuna* (Judo-Communist). There, Trotsky, not Lenin, and certainly not the ethnic Pole Dzerzhinsky, who headed the Red Terror and Cheka, symbolised the Soviet regime even long after Trotsky had been expelled from the Soviet Union.

Although anti-Jewish sentiments were encouraged by Stalin, at the time of his conflict with Trotsky, and although restrictions against Yiddish culture were ordained in the middle 1930s, a differential treatment of Jews in the area of their civil rights and status became apparent rather suddenly and dramatically in the 'anti-cosmopolitan' campaign and during the 'Doctor's Plot' in the years 1948–53. The Jews called this period the 'Black Years'.

Solzhenitsyn describes in his novel *The First Circle* the shock experienced by both a Russian Communist Party hack and a Jewish colonel in the secret police when they first became aware of the sudden change in the status of the Jews. 'That beautiful, proud word *cosmopolite* that united all worlds of the universe . . .,' says Solzhenitsyn, 'had been distorted . . . and came to mean "kike" (*zhid*).' The Russian Party official reflects: 'Could his memory be playing him false? During the revolution and for a long time afterward the word "Jew" had had a greater reliability than the word "Russian". A Russian had to be checked on more than a Jew.'[5] As a group, the Jews were indeed the stoutest supporters of the Soviet regime and the least inclined to opposition or sabotage either before or during the German–Soviet war.

The period of the 'Black Years' was a turning point in the history of the Jews in the Soviet Union and in the relationship between the Soviet regime and Soviet Jews. Nothing that happened later or is happening now in Soviet–Jewish relations can be properly understood without a deep comprehension of the effects of the experience on Soviet Jews and non-Jews alike. It demonstrated for the first time the never anticipated possibility of the existence of an anti-Semitism condoned and fostered by socialist authorities. It ushered in a deep-seated and long-lasting emotional conflict and antagonism between the Jews of the Soviet Union and the Soviet leadership, an antagonism which by its inner logic almost inescapably led to the present-day violent confrontation and open revolt of many young Jews and Jewish intellectuals who want to leave for Israel. It brought out attitudes which were a breeding ground for later Soviet policies – the continued prohibition of a meaningful Jewish culture, the 'economic trials' of Jews in the 1960s, the writings by Kichko and the like, and the character – not the fact but the peculiar quality – of the anti-Israel barrages. The gnawing suspicion grew among Jews, and was steadily reinforced, that the anti-Jewish attitudes were not just a temporary aberration of a Stalin, a Beria or another clique, but had become an integral part of the Jewish condition in the Soviet Union.

The unexpected notion that Jewish citizens might be considered 'security risks' in certain positions could not but bring forth Jewish antagonism to the initiators and perpetrators of such a policy. This antagonism would in turn reinforce suspicions that Jews cannot indeed be fully trusted. The stage was set for a vicious circle of antagonism and distrust. Anti-Jewish policies create a desire in some Jews to leave the country, which is in turn taken as proof by the authorities that the Jews never had an attachment to the country.

The distrust of the Jews by Soviet leadership was deepened by the evolving attitudes of many Russian intellectuals of Jewish descent who in the beginning either fought for or fully accepted the Revolution. The initial terror and brutal methods of the Revolution were acceptable for them the way a surgical knife is acceptable, i.e. when it is used for the swift removal of the source of sickness and pain. However, when the surgical operation, and the pain, became open-ended these intellectuals changed their attitudes. The Stalin years of indiscriminate arrests, shootings and trampling of human dignity were the source of tragic disappointment for a whole generation of Russian writers and intellectuals of Jewish descent. Not only Babel, Pasternak and Mandelshtam but a multitude of lesser known intellectuals belonged to that category. This phenomenon of disappointment was not specifically Jewish, but the proportion of intellectuals of Jewish descent disillusioned by the conduct of the Revolution seems to have been very high, and added another dimension to the antagonism between the Soviet regime and the Jews.

In later years the violent, totally unobjective attacks on Israel (an author of an article in *Delo*, a periodical published in Yugoslavia, a country which does not maintain diplomatic relations with Israel, calls them 'furious, exceeding all reasonable proportion')[6] and the equally intemperate attacks on the Jewish religion could not but reinforce or bring forth anti-Semitic feelings among the bureaucracy and at least part of the population. Nadezhda Mandelshtam, in her recently published memoirs, explains that she personally has not encountered anti-Semitism among ordinary Russian people, but rather an abundance of it among the bureaucracy and in the universities. She noted: 'it is always among the semi-educated that fascism, chauvinism, and hatred for the intelligentsia most easily take root' (p. 342). The age-old animosities and the opposition of the Christian Church to the Jewish religion probably reinforced these feelings, at least on a subconscious level, even among declared non-believers. For example, Judas is not infrequently mentioned in anti-Judaic propaganda. It was the Polish poet of Jewish descent, Julian Tuwim, who has said that he knows atheists who do not believe that Jesus existed but who believe that the Jews killed him.

The long-range aim of the Soviet leadership is the fusion of all nationalities, and it is the contention of many that the Jewish group was selected to be the first group to begin this assimilation process, both as a nationality and as a religion. Since the one feeds the other, both must be eradicated.

On the surface, and by objective yardsticks, the Jewish minority can be considered the ideal national group to be the forerunner in the long-range Soviet objective of the fusion of all national groups into one Russianised conglomerate. The Jewish minority is territorially dispersed, urbanised, linguistically assimilated, largely non-observant. It has been deprived of all outlets for national expression since 1948, and if the war years are included, for more than three decades.

The results of this attempted fusion have, however, been totally disappointing, partially because of the peculiarities of the Jewish minority group, which, as historically proved, is not so easily given to being dissolved, and partially because the methods the Soviet leadership used to achieve that goal were self-defeating and counter-productive.

During a recent visit to Moscow, Rabbi Richard G. Hirsch met a young man who wore a skullcap and a beard in the orthodox Jewish fashion. He told Rabbi Hirsch that he is an atheist but he wears a beard and skullcap because these are symbols of Jewishness and he wants to demonstrate these symbols to the outside world.[7] Soviet anti-religious education, after having achieved its goal of producing atheists, sees these atheists milling around synagogues on Jewish holidays and adopting religious symbols in a blend of nationalism and religion of a past era. In the pre-revolutionary period, nationalities, deprived of the free expression of their ethnic and cultural ethos, turned to the Church for support. After combating Jewish religion and Jewish nationalism in separate ways for so many years, and trying to use secular

Judaism against religious Judaism, the Soviet leaders are now confronted with the phenomenon of the mingling of the two among a sizeable and important part of the upcoming Soviet Jewish generation.

By a strange ironic twist of history the weakened and decimated Jewish religious establishment, the two or three dozen synagogues in the European part of the country, and the handful of still-officiating rabbis, get sustenance from the non-religious, often atheist part of the Jewish population. The curtailment of a meaningful Jewish *secular* culture has endowed the religious establishment with a central place in Soviet Jewish life. In Moscow, Leningrad, Kiev, Odessa and other towns where synagogues are open, the synagogue is the only 'Jewish address' for Soviet Jews and foreign Jewish visitors. The only other place in the country which can make a claim to being a Jewish institution is the office of the Yiddish periodical *Sovetish Heimland* in Moscow. Some Jewish tourists do visit the editorial offices of the periodical but young Soviet Jews never congregate there.

The steady dilution of the concept of internationalism and the parallel rise of nationalism, even chauvinism, have strengthened the concept of a dominant nation, of a *host nation,* and weakened the position of all ethnic minorities, but particularly that of the non-territorially concentrated minorities, such as the Jews. This notion of the indigenous 'host nation' which explicitly or implicitly considers other groups, and especially territorially dispersed groups, as guests – welcome or unwelcome – is very well reflected in the lines from Joseph Kerler's poem, *The Score.*[8]

Many Soviet Jews feel just as Kerler did, that they are no longer co-owners of the land where they were born and for which they fought so hard, but merely individuals who must constantly proclaim and prove their allegiance and love for the country. They have heard all too frequently: 'You are eating *our* bread and should not grumble.'

It should be emphasised that even small inequities and minor restrictions which most Jews accept without much complaint in many countries, such as not being able to hold high office or being excluded from certain types of desirable occupations, are not willingly accepted in a state which proclaims itself to be socialist, and in a regime for whose upbuilding Jews have suffered so much.

This explains, in large part, the violent reaction to inequities of many Jews in the Soviet Union at the present time.

It will not be an overstatement to say that for those Soviet Jews who are now defiantly declaring their estrangement from the Soviet State the more painful grievance is not economic or political discrimination but the injury to their dignity, both as members of the ethnic group to which they belong and as individuals. The religion, the State, and the largest political movement of their people are described as the condensation of evil and depravity. The history of their people is deleted and their culture is silenced, while the creations and achievements of other nationalities, and above all of the Russian people, are extravagantly extolled. 'I could not be a proud Jew in the Soviet Union,' declared the 21-year-old emigrée Alla Rusinek in her television appearance on 21 March 1971.

The fate of Judaism in the other Communist countries has evolved differently and varies from country to country. The position of Judaism, and of the Jews, was intensely affected by the internal problems each particular Communist government faced, by these governments' relationship with and the pressures exerted on them by the Soviet Government, and by the vicissitudes of the international scene.

In both Czechoslovakia and Poland the Soviet Union either instigated or supported the tactics of using the Jews both to divert the population's attention from grievances actually due to serious economic and political difficulties, and to divert their animosity towards the Russian mentor to another target. The idea was developed of a world-wide Zionist (i.e. Jewish) conspiracy for world control, and for the conquest of the Communist world which must put up a united front to this international menace. Zionism became the 'objective enemy'. Hannah Arendt has pointed out the significance of the notion 'objective enemy' for the functioning of totalitarian regimes: 'He is never an individual whose dangerous thought must be provoked or whose past justifies suspicion, but "a carrier of tendencies" like the carrier of disease.'[9]

Anti-Jewish policies in the smaller socialist countries were not initiated, basically, out of hatred for the Jews. As neo-Marxian Polish philosopher Leszek Kołakowski noted:

The struggle against the Jews is seldom an objective in itself. . . . Anti-Semitism has the function of creating a universal symbol of evil which is then desired to associate in people's minds with those phenomena in politics, culture, science which have to be combated. Jewishness has to be made into an insult, used to condemn everything that is to be annihilated.[10]

To this one must add that Jewishness made into an insult, under the camouflage of various terms, is used to condemn not only *everything* that is to be destroyed but, most importantly, also *everybody* who is to be destroyed.

In Czechoslovakia both the Slansky trials and the liquidation of the Dubček liberalisation period were accompanied by portrayals of prominent Jewish officials as guilty of causing the serious difficulties in the country. The code name 'cosmopolitan' or 'Zionist' was used to denote the Jewish bureaucrat and Jewish intellectual as an anti-patriotic trouble-maker at best, and as a foreign paid agent at worst. There is now sufficient evidence to conclude that during the period of the Slansky trials and on later occasions the Soviet leadership supported the whipping up of anti-Jewish sentiments in all countries under its influence in order to suppress opposition to the domestic Communist regime and to its Soviet patrons.

In Poland, when anti-Soviet sentiments have periodically come to the fore, most recently during and after the 1967 Six-Day War, they were stifled by a fierce counteraction which characterised them as 'Zionist' inspired. The expelling of most Polish Jews was a stop-gap in a deteriorating political and economic situation. Paul Lendvai has prophetically remarked in his book *Anti-Semitism Without Jews*, which appeared before the 1971 political crisis in Poland: 'The Jews have left or are leaving Poland, and when the profound social contradictions spark off the next crisis, there may be no one to serve as scapegoat.'[11] This indeed happened.

'Zionism' in Poland and Czechoslovakia as well as in the Soviet Union has now replaced Trotskyism which had denoted the embodiment of evil for three decades. Trotskyites, and now 'Zionists', are depicted and used by official Communism much the same way in which the Devil served Christianity or was depicted in non-Christian lore. There is, for instance, no need to ask the Devil what his position is, or whether he has perchance recently changed his opinion on any specific issue: the only problem is to find him, to unmask him. Extermination, in benign cases expulsion, becomes the logical consequence of this Manichean philosophy.

The official policy towards the Jews might now be considered one fairly good yardstick to measure a country's internal strife or its independence from the Soviet Union. The friendly attitude to Jews of the liberal Dubček regime, for example, has given way to their present inimical position. Yugoslavia and Romania, the two states least subservient to Soviet influence, have given their Jewish populations their greatest amount of religious and cultural freedom among the countries in the Communist world. So-called 'popular anti-Semitism' should not be seen as the source or the stimulus for a given anti-Jewish policy; it merely provides convenient support when a pertinent policy decision has already been made at the highest levels of power – as can be seen from the example of Romania, a country with a long history of anti-Semitism, both popular and official. Romania's independent policy in regard to the State of Israel has not of course been adopted because the regime has discovered greater understanding of the historical rights of the Jewish people to the land of Israel, but rather because this policy is one expression of Romania's general independent policy in foreign affairs.

In Poland and Czechoslovakia, where the organisational structure and permissible areas of religious and secular Jewish activities had once allowed Jews to lead a tolerable existence, intermittent internal difficulties and the regime's precarious relationship with the Soviet Union in the end endangered the continued existence not only of Judaism but of the Jews in each of the two countries.

Whether seen from the perspective of the regime or of the Jewish people, conflicts between the Communist State and Judaism (and perhaps other religions as well) appear to be more political than ideological. It should be noted that certain Soviet and non-Soviet Jewish religious leaders, as well as many religious believers, did not consider the existence of a society where the means of production would be socialised as being inherently in contradiction to religion. Several Jewish religious figures, foremost among them Rabbi Alexandrow, painfully groped to find a common ground for religion and Socialism.[12] If most, although not all, Soviet-Yiddish writers tended in their works to treat religious believers who tried to reconcile religion and Communism as hypocritical or weak-minded, the Jewish Russian writer Isaac Babel looked at it differently. Old Gedali, in a story of the same name, would accept the idea of Socialism and international brotherhood, but only if not forced to renounce his religiosity. 'The Resolution – we will say 'yes' to it, but are we to say 'no' to the Sabbath?' Gedali cannot assent to the cruelty of the new leaders. 'Bring good people to our town and we will hand over all phonographs to them,' he says, 'I want an International of good people.'[13] In another of Babel's stories, the rabbi's son, a Red Army soldier who died on the floor of the army train, left in his scattered belongings 'portraits of Lenin and Maimonides and communist leaflets with crooked lines of ancient Hebrew verse'.[14]

The Communist leadership and Jewish Communist officialdom, however, regarded the coexistence of Lenin and Maimonides as a sham. They also considered their own short-lived creation, the 'Living synagogue,' established in opposition to the old synagogue, a sham, as indeed it was. Although Jewish religious believers always approvingly acknowledged some of the new regime's good deeds, such as the abolishment of the tsarist restrictions on Jews in employment, residence, education and civil rights, the moral degradation and inhumanity of the Stalin era put an end to searches for an ideological common denominator between them and the Soviet regime.

One can hardly be optimistic about the fate of Judaism – in the broader sense of the word – in the Communist world. Even in countries which grant more cultural and religious freedom to the Jewish minority than does the Soviet Union, the feeling is that these rights are still 'granted' by the host nation and can be revocable. Jews whose religious or cultural ties to Jewishness remain strong may not be acceptable or welcome in certain positions. Most committed Jews do not presently consider it possible to perpetuate the Jewish culture and Jewish heritage in socialist countries.

Organised Jewish life under Communism is today the most active and free in Romania. However, many Romanian Jews feel that this situation will not prevail indefinitely. They are all too aware of the fact that Jews and Judaism were subjected to attacks, arrests and intimidation for a number of years prior to the present liberalisation. As the policy has changed swiftly from suppression to relative freedom, so it can change, they feel, in the other direction as well. This residual uncertainty combined with the fact that several hundred thousand Romanian Jews have emigrated to Israel while most of those few Jews remaining in Romania have close relatives in Israel are factors which will contribute to a gradual diminution of the Jewish community in Romania.

Hungary's official attitude towards the Jews and Judaism is similar to Romania's. In Hungary the majority of the Jews are linguistically and culturally assimilated. Judaism in Hungary faces the difficult problem of survival in a majority culture, a problem not unlike that which Judaism faces in many a non-socialist society.

The prospects for a continued presence of a meaningful Jewish community in Poland are very slim. Among those Jews who left the country in 1968 were most of the leaders of Jewish activities, heads of the Central Cultural Union, Yiddish writers and actors, and younger people. The majority of the Jewish population still in the country are elderly or ailing. Even if the official attitudes of the Government were to change, it is very doubtful whether many Jews would return to Poland. The shock of rejection and ejection has left too strong a mark on those who left and on those who remained. Several institutions, the Yiddish theatre and the Historical Society may nevertheless remain open because of their symbolic and propagandistic value.

In Czechoslovakia the situation is essentially similar to that in Poland except that here the religious associations have played a much greater role than in Poland and may be expected to remain alive for some time. The representative institutions of internationally recognised tourist attraction – the historic synagogues and the Jewish museum in Prague – will certainly remain open regardless of what happens to the Czech Jewish community.

In Bulgaria the process of assimilation, coupled with a high rate of intermarriage, leaves little expectation for a continued existence of the Jewish religion or culture.

In Yugoslavia the Jewish population is small and is politically, socially and culturally fully integrated into the life of the country. It has no strong attachment to religious Judaism, and has not developed a Jewish vernacular, such as Yiddish in Poland. Nevertheless, and contrary to logical expectations, the Yugoslav Jewish community displays a very lively Jewish cultural activity which has not diminished during recent years.

The Jewish population in the other socialist countries (East Germany, Cuba and Albania) is so small that one cannot realistically speak of Judaism having an existence or future there.

In the Soviet Union the situation is much more complicated because of numbers. When difficulties with a community of 15,000 or even 100,000 become too unyielding they can be solved by emigration. The problem becomes qualitatively different when the number is three million. The importance of Soviet Jews in the sciences and in the economy of the country adds to the difficulty. On the one hand, the Soviet Government may be tempted to get rid of the irritant, but, on the other hand, a regime which is in competition with the capitalist world may also be apprehensive about eliminating an important segment of its cadres, not to speak of other considerations involved in mass emigration.

Short of the total and absolute abolition of all restrictions and quotas with regard to the Jewish group in the Soviet Union, no solution seems possible. The process of treating the Jewish people separately, which began in the 1930s and culminated in the 'campaign' of 1948–53, lasted too long and went too far to be fully reversed. Half measures – a few concessions in the religious field, opening a Yiddish theatre, partially reviving the idea of an autonomous Jewish region in Birobidzhan (a suggestion which is now in the news more than it has been for twenty-five years) – will not make an appreciable difference.

The only real alternative to the total restoration of equality to Soviet Jews in all fields seems to be mass emigration. *Fakty upryamaya veshch* ('Facts are a stubborn thing') the Soviet leaders are fond of saying, and the facts concerning the Jewish minority in the Soviet Union are stubborn and becoming quite clear. They cannot be brushed under the carpet, they cannot be brushed aside with paragraphs of the constitution and a few slogans..

Post-war developments have demonstrated to the surprise of many that the establishment of a socialist order in a given country has not solved the so-called 'Jewish problem'. It has not brought about either of the two alternatives: a complete integration and dissolution of the Jewish group in the surrounding population, or conditions for a free and continued existence of Jewish religious and cultural life, with a simultaneous safeguarding of full equality for the individual Jew. An analysis of the situation in all socialist countries seems to indicate that the perpetuation of Judaism in a socialist political system is theoretically possible, given suitable conditions. It can be built around one or a combination of several types of Jewish organisational frameworks which were discussed at the beginning of this chapter. But conditions for a perpetuation of Jewish life in a socialist political system are very difficult to achieve. The basic precondition would have to be the rejection of the tenet of an 'indigenous population' and a 'host nation'.

NOTES

1. D. M. Aptekman, 'Causes of the Ceremony of Baptism under Modern Conditions, on the Basis of the Results of a Concrete Sociological Investigation', *Soviet Sociology* (Fall 1965), Vol. 4, No. 2, pp. 10–16. Translated from *Voprosy Filosofii*, No. 3 (1965). In the more rural Ryazan oblast 60 per cent of all children born in 1960 were baptised in church. See Bohdan R. Bociurkiw, 'Religion and Atheism in Soviet Society', in R. H. Marshall, Jr. (ed.), *Aspects of Religion in the Soviet Union 1917–1967* (Chicago University Press, 1971), p. 58.

2. Data about religious and non-religious organisations and institutions in the Communist countries were culled from various sources: Jewish publications and periodicals in the respective countries, *American Jewish Year Book* (New York, 1967, 1968, 1969, 1970), *The Jews in Soviet Russia since 1917* (Oxford: Oxford University Press, 1970). In addition, for Romania: L. Kuperstein, 'Yivrit mi-Mamaakim' (Hebrew from the Depths.), an interview with Chief Rabbi Dr D. M. Rosen in *Am ve-Sefer*, No. 41/42 (1970), pp. 33–6. Note in *Jewish Journal of Sociology* (June 1970), p. 120. The volume *The Jews in the Soviet Satellites*, by Peter Meyer *et al.* (Syracuse: Syracuse University Press, 1953), was consulted as a source for the post-war history of the Jewish communities in the respective countries.

3. Bociurkiw, *loc. cit.*, p. 46.

4. Joseph B. Schechtman, *Star in Eclipse: Russian Jewry Revisited* (New York: Thomas Yoseloff, 1961), p. 146.

5. Alexander Solzhenitsyn, *The First Circle* (New York, 1968), p. 489.

6. Andrei Novak, 'A Lesson to Soviet Jews', *Delo* (30 December 1930), as quoted in *Religion in Communist Dominated Areas* (January 1971), p. 2.

7. Richard G. Hirsch, 'A Trip to Russia', *Jewish Frontier* (November 1971), p. 2.

8. Kerler, a Soviet–Yiddish poet who was wounded in the war, has been denied publication in his country after applying for an exit visa to Israel four years ago. This poem was sent abroad and published in the Israel magazine *Goldene Keit*: At every turn / you don't stop demanding 'lest I forget: / I breathe your air / I eat your bread / : . . . We are *even* now / for everything /, I've paid for everything / and not exactly with 'Jewish gold' / . . . If you'd like to know – your power is founded on my sweat and marrow / and my blood too.' 'And now,' the poet says, 'the score is even, let me go.' Kerler and his family finally arrived in Israel in March 1971.

9. Hannah Arendt, *The Origins of Totalitarianism*, 2nd ed. (New York, 1962), p. 31.
10. *Poprostu*, No. 27, v. 56, as quoted in *Bulletin on Soviet and East European Jewish Affairs*, No. 6 (1970), p. 29.
11. Paul Lendvai, *Anti-Semitism Without Jews* (New York, 1962), p. 239.
12. Zvi Gitelman, 'The Communist Party and Soviet Jewry', in Marshall, *op. cit.*, p. 334.
13. Isaac Babel, *The Collected Stories* (New York, 1955), p. 71.
14. *Ibid.*, p. 193.

12 Polish Catholicism and Social Change

VINCENT C. CHRYPINSKI

In recent years there has emerged in Poland an impressive number
of writings on Polish Catholicism, with the books and articles on
the subject produced not only by the Catholics but by the Communists as well. As might be expected, their views – even on the
Catholic side – were highly diversified and the perception of
Polish Catholicism emanating from the debate was far from
uniform.

On the one hand, Polish Catholicism was glorified. The
admirers praised its millenial tradition, close associations with
Polish nationalism, deep emotional attachment of the masses to
the Church and, last but not least, the dynamic manner in which
the Catholic Church has carried on its apostolic mission in a
Communist-ruled country. On the other hand, the story was
totally different. The critics emphasised negative features such as
the backwardness of the Polish Church, apologetic attitudes towards the past, the shallow intellectual content of religious
beliefs, sentimentality, and stress on the external, ritualistic aspect
of worship unrelated to a moral and eucharistic life.[1]

In spite of all the differences, both groups were in agreement
on one point, namely, that Polish Catholicism was undergoing
a highly significant transition. The dynamics of change was determined by the interaction of the past and of the present. The
past was, above all, represented by the traditional religiosity of the
masses and the close bonds between Catholicism and Polish
nationalism. The present is expressed not only in the Marxist socio-
economic order, industrialisation and urbanisation, but also in
the conciliar renewal of the Church attempting to revitalise and
modernise traditional religiosity.

Although official Polish sources do not give quantative data on the religious affiliation of the Polish people, it is generally assumed that well over 90 per cent of all Poles are Roman Catholics. This is true in the sense that this many people were baptised in the Catholic rite and have not formally left the Church. Naturally, all Polish Catholics cannot be treated as a monolithic unit. Differences in age, education, occupation – to name a few factors – create a variety of internal distinctions indicating a possible range of diversity in attitudes and in behaviour.

The purpose of this paper is to examine the changes that have taken place in Polish Catholicism after World War II, with the major focus on the attitudes of social groups, especially peasants and workers, towards prevailing religious practices. The primary source of data is material published in Poland. Unfortunately, empirical studies in the sociology of religion are rather scarce in Poland and usually they are limited to single communities. In addition there exists a problem of reliability since the authors are sometimes motivated by obviously partisan considerations. Hence there exists a need for supplementing quantitative data with less exact descriptive analysis, based on a variety of sources, including personal observations of this author. It is hoped that the combination of these approaches will provide a satisfactory synthesis.

Polish Catholicism has probably been most significantly influenced by the religiosity of the rural dwellers who still amount to about 50 per cent of the total population of Poland. Despite intensive atheistic propaganda, faith among the peasants remains very deep. Almost all profess belief in Catholic dogmas and a great majority (83 per cent) recognise the Catholic Church as an intrinsic part of their lives.[2] Farmers' sons form the bulk of the clergy (up to 90 per cent in rural dioceses), and provide the Church with the greatest number of vocations (up to 60 per cent even in industrialised areas).[3] Traditional religiosity, cohesion and resistance to secularising external influences, as well as the high prestige and elevated social standing of the priests among the villagers, make the peasantry the basis of the Church's strength.

The Polish countryside is undergoing a rapid transition. It is caused – among other reasons – by the process of urbanisation which means not only the numerical decline of the rural population from 72·6 per cent in 1931 to 48·5 per cent at the end of 1969, but also urbanisation of the villages themselves. It brought

changes in their socio-economic structure, deterioration of traditional social and cultural patterns, departure from agricultural
occupations and acceptance of urban styles of life. Without question, these changes have affected the religious life of the Polish
peasantry.

The transformation follows two main trends, each characterised
by a search for selective values.[4] The first, rather mechanistic trend,
involves the decline of certain religious beliefs and practices which
the peasants today find superfluous. The increase of knowledge
about nature and scientific methods of controlling it, especially
in matters related to agriculture, cause the people to focus all their
attention on the pursuit of success by their own efforts, without
the assistance of religion. It results in the abandonment of various
rituals which were employed in the past to protect man and his
farm against the unknown. Thus, spring processions to the fields
have disappeared almost completely and the practice of feeding
sick livestock with blessed herbs has also significantly decreased.

Similar consequences follow the growing acceptance of urban
styles of life by the rural population. For instance, the customary
greeting of Polish peasants. 'Blessed by Jesus Christ', is giving way
more and more to a secular 'Good day' after the manner of the
townspeople.

The second trend is much deeper and more consequential. Its
essence lies in the questioning by rural Catholics of certain aspects
of the Church's teaching in the fields of dogmas and morals. Thus,
while the presence of God and the divinity of Christ are not
challenged, doubts are expressed in matters relating to scriptural
explanations of the creation of the world and of man, of the existence of heaven and hell, and even of the reality of immortal soul.
More and more people violate ecclesiastical interdictions against
abortions, use of contraceptives and pre-marital sexual relations.

As might be expected, this trend is mainly noticeable among the
younger generation, especially men who attend high schools and
universities, and those who belong to a novel sub-group of the
so-called 'peasant-workers' living in villages and commuting to
work in urban centres. The extent of the drift escapes statistical
estimates mainly due to the phenomenon of 'sham religiosity'.
Quite often, under the influence of long-established tradition, as
well as pressure from parents and brides, even agnostics, whose
number is not yet large, but growing, conclude church marriages,

baptise their children and participate in religious practices in a purely formal and conventional way.

Declining rural religiosity is particularly accentuated in the areas with numerous state farms whose employees are especially weak religiously. Although sociological research into religious practices of this group have not yet supplied sufficient statistics for diagnosis, it may be said already that there exists a definite correlation between the number of state farm workers and the level of religious practices in a parish.[5] The phenomenon is usually explained by the abnormally high mobility of this group as a whole and subsequent social uprooting.

The crisis of faith and a decay of certain rituals leads naturally to the loosening of traditional bonds between parishioners and their pastors. In addition, while in the past almost all social activities of a rural community were parish centred, today there are many attractive secular magnets (movies, dances, TV, etc.) pulling the people away from the Church. This proliferation leads to a decline in the functional authority of priests, who are left only with cultic affairs, adversely affects their influence over the parishioners and results in the lowering of obedience to the Church's commands and proscriptions, especially in matters which are not religious *sensu stricto*.

Secularisation is much clearer among city dwellers, but its extent and its expressions are still not fully known since studies on urban religiousness in Poland are only in their inception.[6] In general it manifests itself in religious indifferentism, departure from traditional standards of Catholic morality and in a decrease of devotional activities. Sometimes it reveals itself in openly antireligious attitudes.

A scholarly study made recently of a provincial capital in the Western Territories[7] reveals interesting changes of religiosity which might be taken – with proper concessions for local conditions – as an indication of the transformation taking place in the country as a whole. The population growth of the city in question (from 38,500 in 1950 to 77,500 in 1968)[8] was partly due to the influx of newcomers, mostly from villages, who ultimately amounted to 40 per cent of the total community. Thus the findings provide an interesting, case study of the impact of the process of urbanisation on popular religiosity.

The research, conducted over a three-year period (1964–66) by a Polish Catholic priest, centred on the observation of religious conduct. It shows that the vast majority of urban Catholics strongly adhere to 'single-time' practices, i.e. to rituals which take place once in a lifetime. Thus virtually all parents – even non-believers – baptise their children, regardless of whether they were born in a Church-sanctioned union (80 per cent), civil marriage (10–12 per cent), or out of wedlock. However, there is a growing lapse of time between birth and baptism, usually ranging from one to three months. The study did not elicit responses to tell us whether the negligence is due to religious indifference or to other considerations. The practice of first holy communion is almost equally common. Most of the children (92–95 per cent) receive the sacrament after undergoing proper catechetical preparation.

The situation is different in regard to marriages. Although the majority of urban dwellers (73 per cent in 1964, 78·8 per cent in 1965, and 66 per cent in 1966) still contract sacramental nuptials – usually immediately after the required civil ceremony – the number of those marrying outside the Church seems to be growing. While the statistics are clear, the reasons behind them are more complex. Some persons seek church sanction outside the city where they are well known and perhaps occupy politically sensitive posts. Some postpone the religious ceremony for practical reasons, such as desire to expose their union to a trial period. Some, whose number is constantly expanding, cannot receive religious blessings due to canon law impediments – usually a previous Catholic marriage. Others, however, are motivated by religious indifference.

The pattern of burials reverts to that of baptism and communions. During the period under survey, between 90 per cent and 92 per cent of those whose death was recorded at the registry office were buried with Catholic rites. Among the remaining percentage an undisclosed number were refused religious funerals due to canonical interdictions, such as – for example – suicide or ecclesiastically illegal marriages.

Single-time practices, being 'once-in-a-life' affairs, are quite often treated as part of well-established custom and tradition, an occasion for family celebrations in which the religious essence of the sacrament is obscured by external ritual and lay paraphernalia (receptions, gifts, etc.). To learn more about religiousness, one must look to other kinds of religious conduct as well. Attendance at Sunday masses, reception of holy communion and other optional practices are a necessary subject for investigation.

Only about 50 per cent of the people of the city concerned attend Sunday masses; among them there is a slightly higher percentage of women (55·1 per cent) than of men (44·6 per cent). Among those missing from mass are 33 per cent of high-school students who receive catechetical instructions, but occasionally fail to meet their Sunday obligation. Easter communion counts have not been made, but on the basis of other studies,[9] it may be safely assumed that the figure is probably higher than that for Sunday mass attendance since many 'holiday Catholics' receive communion in a purely customary fashion. Contrary to this, however, the number of hosts dispensed at a Sunday mass is rather low with only 6·7 – 8·4 per cent of the attendants receiving holy communion. Among them, women definitely prevail (71·4 per cent) over men (28·6 per cent). The total sum of hosts during the year in one of the eight city parishes gives the very low index of 6·4 per statistical Catholic. It needs to be stressed, however, that this small figure, pitiful by West European or American standards, does not manifest a new phenomenon, but rather a continuation of strong Jansenistic[10] traditions in Polish Catholicism.

Not unexpectedly, participation in optional practices is very small. Week day masses are attended only by 3–5 per cent of city Catholics, with some increase (10–15 per cent) on first Fridays and non-obligatory feast days. Attendance at Sunday vespers is not any greater and amounts to a mere 2·6 per cent of all believers. Most of the worshippers are women, who usually form over two-thirds of the congregation.

A very important practice is catechetical instruction of children and youth which, since 1960, is conducted outside of schools, often in difficult material and moral circumstances. In spite of the difficulties, the percentage of participants is quite strong (70–75 per cent) with the highest proportion (95 per cent) before first communion and the lowest among high-school seniors (45–50 per cent). The decline is to a large degree due to the lack of appreciation of religious education by both the parents, who very rarely (14 per cent) raise religious themes with their children, and the pupils, of whom less than 15 per cent attend classes for spiritual reasons.

Summing up the study, the author presents a typology of the city under inquiry. Thus – following the classification used by J. Fichter[11] – he puts 5 per cent–10 per cent of the Catholics in the 'elite' category of those whose faith is intense and whose religious life consistently conforms to both obligatory and non-obligatory practices. Some 55–60 per cent are tabulated as 'habitual Catholics' who attend Sunday masses, fulfil the obligation of Easter confession, and send their children, especially at elementary school age, to catechism classes. Between 15 per cent and 20 per cent are allotted to the growing group of 'fringe Catholics' who turn up at a church on the occasion of major feasts (Christmas and Easter) or religious family events (baptism, first holy communion or burial). They show declining desire to conclude church sanctioned marriages or to provide religious education for their children. And finally, 10 per cent are recorded as 'dormant Catholics' who are outside religious life. Some of them still baptise their children, send them to first holy communion and will request a Christian burial for someone close to them, but they do so mostly as a concession to tradition or to the urgings of relatives.

On the whole the study is a significant document testifying to the process of change taking place in the religiousness of the Polish urban populace and to the progressive differentation in respect of religion. Although the findings warrant some general conclusions, one must be aware not only of local specifics,[12] but also of the fact that the research was limited in scope, covered a short period of time, and did not take into consideration such important factors as education and occupation which divide the city dwellers into two basic groups: the workers and the intelligentsia.

In 1891 Pope Leo XIII lamented the loss of the working masses to Catholicism. But the situation in Poland does not justify his pessimism. The reasons are complex, but two seem to be of the greatest importance. While in Western Europe the workers considered the Church to be an ally of their class enemy, the bourgeoisie, and consequently wanted to weaken its ranks by leaving, the specific socio-economic situation in post-war Poland made this motive for desertion completely immaterial. Also the process of urbanisation, which in the long run brings with it the danger of secularisation, has thus far in Poland resulted in an increase of religiosity among the workers – even if only in a statistical sense – due to the influx of pious peasants.[13] The impact is, of course, not one-sided, but reciprocal and – whatever the final outcome – it is certain that the process of urbanisation will lead to a new form of religious life among the urban proletariat.

Thus, at present, there is no basic difference in religiousness between the peasants and the workers with 75 per cent of skilled and 82·2 per cent of unskilled labourers declaring themselves as 'believers'.[14] There are some exceptions, however. Big cities like Warsaw and Łódź, as well as some new industrial centres like Nowa Huta, show a lower than average index in the volume as well as in the quality of religious practices.[15] Also there seems to exist a reverse correlation between the size of urban centres and positive attitudes of their population towards religion.[16]

The picture of the religiousness of the Polish intelligentsia is very complex. Much of the problem comes from never-ending debates as to the genealogy, structure and role of this social stratum.[17] It is impossible to offer here even a perfunctory listing of arguments advanced in the controversy. Whatever variations there are, however, two relevant points emerge for our discussion. One is the importance of the intelligentsia in the fabric of Polish society; the other, the significant transformation that this group is undergoing. The change involves not only a rapid numerical expansion of the group by the influx of newcomers of non-intelligentsia origin, but also an evolution of traditional value systems and of well-established patterns of behaviour.

The Polish intelligentsia is very fragmented[18] with the lines of division not only running along the traditional social and economic cleavages between sub-groups, but related to divisive ideological issues. In regard to religion, the intelligentsia seems to be divided into the following segments.[19]

There is a naturally declining group of older Catholics whose faith is not built on foundations of Christian philosophy, but rather on the religio-patriotic traditions of Polish Catholicism. They are loyal to the Church, admire its cultural heritage, and respect its moral and disciplinary influence. In doctrinal matters they are on the orthodox side, although their knowledge of theological and social teachings of the Church is rather superficial.

Former members of pre-World War II Catholic organisations, such as 'Odrodzenie', 'Iuventus Christiana' or 'Marian Sodality', make up the backbone of a second group of Catholic intelligentsia. Their relationship with the Church is dynamic, since they do not limit themselves only to the faithful exercise of religious practices. They are willing to learn more about the Christian Gospel and to practice fully its spiritual and social message. They are vitally interested in the life of the Church and do not hesitate to express their criticism of certain practices and institutions. As a result of their missionary zeal, as well as of their conscious involvement, the group is constantly expanding and forms a Catholic intellectual elite whose appearance has not passed unnoticed by Marxist sociologists.[20]

Its influence is especially noticeable among the Catholic intelligentsia of the same, or younger, age who are mostly traditionalists, bound more with the Church as an institution than with its Christian essence. Gradual comprehension of the true meaning of religion deepens their faith and turns them into more active members of their communities. The young technical intelligentsia does not fit into this category, however, and their future development is at present a matter for speculation.

At the other end of the spectrum, there exists several segments of the intelligentsia with an adverse relationship to the Church and to religion. Among the older generation, a small cluster of 'humanists-positivists' treat religion as a purely social phenomenon. Though not hostile to the Church, they are completely disinterested in its affairs and in its welfare. Much larger (10 – 20 per cent) is that group of Catholics who, because of their social position, the incompatibility of their personal conduct with ecclesiastical laws, or their spiritual laziness, remain outside the Church. Finally, one finds members of the intelligentsia who are declared atheists and thus, for philosophical or socio-political reasons, are decidedly opposed to the Church.

This analysis of the Polish Catholic intelligentsia would be incomplete without mentioning the attitudes of its members towards Marxism and the new socio-economic order being constructed in Poland by the Communists. Broadly speaking, they may be divided into two generic groups: 'progressive' and 'orthodox'.

The 'progressivists' are split into several clusters, of which the most important is 'Pax' led by Bolesław Piasecki.[21] In spite of various differences, mostly tactical, all those sub-groups are united by a common desire to build – with or without the approval of the Church– a bridge between Marxists and Catholic world-views and to co-operate with the Communist regime in the realisation of its socio-economic goals.[22] The exact numerical strength of the 'progressivists' is not known, but it is generally believed not to be very great.

On the 'orthodox' side the situation is no less intricate, and at least three main sub-groups should be mentioned in its description.[23] The extreme right considers Communism as a mortal enemy and rejects any form of collaboration with its adherents. This 'integrist' position is basically defensive, promoting a *sui generis* form of escapism from reality into the past. Its proponents treat the Church not only as a community of believers seeking salvation, but as an alternative to the State – a substitute for the entire society and for the totality of its goals. As a by-product of this attitude, the group evidences clericalism and intolerance. Not unexpectedly, this form of Catholicism exists almost exclusively among the older generation, especially in small urban centres.

The 'centrists', of whom the group 'Znak' is most representative,[24] form probably the largest segment numerically. They exhibit a restrained opposition to Communist rule, but avoid getting involved in a life or death struggle with Communism. Unlike the 'progressivists', they do not believe in the possibility of reconciling Catholic and Marxist doctrines. However, inspired primarily by patriotic motivation, they joined in the reconstruction of the ruined country in the 1940s and even supported certain policies – agricultural reform and nationalisation of industry – that established new long-term patterns for Poland's post-war development. In the area of State-Church relations they advocated the conclusion of mutually advantageous agreement.[25]

The 'leftists', whose views are reflected in the Warsaw-based monthly *Więź*, are attempting to establish a *modus vivendi* between the Catholic Church and the Communist State by inducing the revision of ecclesiastical attitudes. In particular, they propagate the abandonment of the traditional concept visualising Poland as a 'bulwark of Christianity' against the pagan East, substantial reform of religious practices and of pastoral activities, as well as the final recognition of the new socio-economic reality.

Having concentrated on the religious attitudes and practices of different Polish social groups, we want to conclude by at least sketching the institutional and personnel aspects of the Church's organisation. On the whole, both seem to be equal to the post-war challenges.

The organisational structure of the Church, especially in the countryside, is broad and strong. The number of churches and chapels totals over 13,200 and the number of established parishes 6,558. Approximately 17,000 centres provide religious instruction to primary and high-school pupils. After tremendous war losses (close to 30 per cent), the number of clergy now reaches a new height of almost 18,000, thus restoring pre-war proportions of one priest for every 2,300 of the faithful.[26] The number of new ordinations is 30 for each 100,000 Catholics, and the number of vocations is even higher than before the Communist take-over (one for every 9,400 of the faithful in 1962, as compared to one for every 10,828 in 1939).[27] While in 1937 diocesan seminaries had an enrolment of 2,078 clerics, in 1970 there were 4,070 seminarians.[28]

The work of diocesan priests is assisted by monks and nuns, who not only greatly enlarged their number after World War II (from about 22,000 in 1939 to 36,500 in 1960), but also show remarkable vitality in organisational development (there were 2,022 monasteries and convents in 1937; 2,512 in 1950, and 2,977 in 1958) and in pastoral work.[29] It is highly characteristic that the most dynamic growth is shown not by contemplative orders like the Benedictines or the Dominicans, but by the newer orders, such as the Pallottines, or those whose orientation is towards special pastoral work among particular social or professional groups (e.g. the Salesian order which specialises in labour among the workers) and towards missionary work among the masses.

The whole of church activities is directed by the episcopate, doubly numerous in comparison to its pre-war size, headed by the very strong, single-minded Primate of Poland, Cardinal Stefan Wyszyński. Due to political circumstances, and especially due to the absence of a Vatican nuncio in Warsaw, the Primate received from Rome special powers which seem to have elevated him from the traditional position of *primus inter pares* to one of distinct superiority over other hierarchs.[30] Clearly enough, this circumstance created very favourable conditions for a unity of action and greatly facilitated operations of the entire clerical apparatus.

To what conclusion does this summary lead? Presumably to the simple one that Polish Catholicism is a complex phenomenon, one which is certainly not in a petrified state, but rather in a process of transition resulting mainly from the abrupt advancement of the new 'industrial civilisation'. Its arrival was accompanied by the process of laicisation, normally associated with drastic social and cultural upheavals, whose impact was especially strong on young people, in particular on those who were removed from their social environment. The situation was further aggravated by the actions of the Communist regime which deliberately promoted the atheisation of Polish society and created serious difficulties in the pastoral functioning of the Church.

As a result of this combined assault Polish Catholicism sustained losses – hard to assess with accuracy, but not disastrous – which manifested themselves in a numerical regression, in a weakening of spiritual ties of the Catholic community and in a decline in the traditional religiosity of the masses. Some Polish sociologists claim that these currents provide the proof of growing secularisation and even predict an early success of this process.

Their views are questionable, however. In spite of many difficulties the traditional Catholic formation in Poland proved to be extremely durable and the apparent recession may rather indicate a search for new forms of religious life than a total de-Christianisation. This quest may very well give a renewed depth to the faith of Polish Catholics and create a more profound awareness of their ties with the Church. In the last decade there have already appeared definite signs of religious renewal, especially among the Polish intelligentsia. This trend was initially élitist and introspective, but it is now becoming more dynamic and its adherents assume greater responsibility for the Church as a whole. The fact that half of the Polish intelligentsia is of peasant and worker origin[31] greatly extends the social range of their potential influence.

The future of Polish Catholicism will depend on the outcome of the struggle between the forces of laicisation and those of religious renewal. Particularly important in this contest is the attitude of the post-war generation, its aptness to relate the religious faith to contemporary conditions and its ability to pass the new religiosity on to their children.

One should not assume that these tasks will be easy. On the contrary, there are many and major obstacles in the path of Polish Catholics. Most of them have a common source – Communist domination of the country.

There is no need, I suppose, to explain why the Communist government is interested in an intensification of secularising tendencies and why it is unwilling to assist the Church in the complex endeavour of readjusting to modern times. But it is mandatory to mention, at least, that the Communist rulers of Poland quite frequently resorted to administrative means in order to hasten the process of de-Christianisation. Quite naturally, the Church did not remain passive and consequently their relations approached the boiling point. More recently direct confrontation occurred during the 1966 celebrations in observance of Poland's Christianity and nationhood.

The present Communist leadership under Mr Gierek seems to be more sensitive to the needs of the Church. As a result the delicate State-Church balance was restored and a new spirit of co-operation seems to establish itself in mutual relations. Hopefully, it will last longer than the time needed for the Communists to overcome the crisis generated by the workers' riots of December 1970.

NOTES

1. For example, a 1959 study conducted among Polish youth by the Research Centre of Public Opinion of the Polish Radio revealed a striking inconsistency of views among the persons declaring themselves as Catholics (78 per cent of the total interviewed). Thus, for instance, 70·9 per cent of this group did not condemn abortion, 14·5 per cent had no intention of concluding a Church-blessed marriage, and 9·3 per cent expressed no desire to educate their children in a religious spirit. Quoted after Tadeusz M. Jaroszewski, 'Dynamika praktyk religijnych . . .' (The Dynamics of Religious Practices . . .), *Kultura i Społeczeństwo* (Warsaw), Vol. X, No. 1 (January–March 1966), p. 135.
2. Adam Pajert, 'Praktyki i przekonania katolików' (Practices and Convictions of Catholics), *Hejnał Mariacki* (Warsaw), No. 8 (August 1969), pp. 2–3. NOTE: *Hejnał Mariacki* is a popular Catholic magazine, but the figure given is supported by an official study of 1961 which showed 83·8 per cent of the rural and 75·6 per cent of the urban population to be in the 'believers' category. Figures quoted in Stanisław Markiewicz, *Sprzeczności we współczesnym katolicyzmie* (Contradictions in Contemporary Catholicism) (Warsaw: KiW, 1964), p. 129.
3. Józef Majka, 'Socjografia powołań kapłańskich' (Sociography of Priestly Vocations), *Ateneum Kapłańskie* (Włocławek), No. 1–2 (1967), pp. 48–57. The only exception is the maritime diocese of Gorzów, where the countryside

provides only an insignificant fraction of vocations. *Catholic Life in Poland* (Warsaw), No. 7/55 (1970), p. 21.

4. The following is based primarily on Kazimierz Dobrowolski, 'Przeobrażenia świadomości społecznej ludności chłopskiej ...' (Transformations of Social Consciousness of Peasants ...) in Adam Sarapata, *Przemiany społeczne w Polsce Ludowej* (Social Changes in People's Poland) (Warsaw: PWN, 1965), pp. 429–33.

5. For example, the study of Rev. Władysław Piwowarski, *Praktyki religijne w diecezji warmińskiej* (Religious Practices in the Varmia Diocese) (Warsaw: Academy of Catholic Theology, 1969), as reported in *Catholic Life in Poland* (Warsaw), No. 7/55 (1970), p. 29.

6. One of a few general analyses is Rev. W. Piwowarski, 'Religijność miejska w XX-leciu powojennym w Polsce' (Urban Religiosity During the Twenty Post-war Years in Poland), *Znak* (Cracow), No. 141 (March 1966), pp. 297–315.

7. Rev. Aleksy Nowak, 'Praktyki religijne w mieście' (Religious Practices in a City), *Znak* (Cracow), No. 191 (May 1970), pp. 655–63.

8. At this time there were in Poland 25 cities in the same statistical category (50,000–100,000 inhabitants) with a joint population of 5·2 million, i.e. 10·4 per cent of the total figure of urban dwellers. *Rocznik Statystyczny, 1966* (Statistical Yearbook, 1966), Table 5, pp. 23–4.

9. E.g. Piwowarski, see note 5 above.

10. The teaching of Cornelius Jansen (1585–1638), characterized by an unusual harshness and moral rigorism.

11. J. Fichter, *Southern Parish* (Chicago: University of Chicago Press, 1951).

12. For example, studies conducted in Warsaw showed – depending on the Catholic or Communist source – the average attendance at Sunday masses to be 53 per cent or 20·5 per cent respectively. Józef Majka, 'Jaki jest katolicyzm polski?' (What is Polish Catholicism?), *Znak* (Cracow), No. 141 (March 1966), p. 278.

13. Jan Guranowski, 'Istota i metody laicyzacji życia społecznego' (The Essence and Methods of Laicization of Social Life) in *Religia i laicyzacja* (Religion and Laicization) (Warsaw: KiW, 1961), p. 237.

14. Jaroszewski, *op. cit.*, p. 138.

15. *Ibid.*

16. *Ibid.*, p. 135.

17. For an example see the monthly *Życie i Myśl* (Warsaw), No. 1 (January. 1967).

18. Jerzy J. Wiatr, 'Inteligencja w Polsce Ludowej' (Intelligentsia in People's Poland) in *Przemiany społeczne w Polsce Ludowej* (Social Changes in People's Poland) (Warsaw: PWN, 1965), p. 451.

19. The following based mainly on Józef Majka, 'Jaki jest katolicyzm polski?', *loc. cit.*, pp. 289–90.

20. For instance, Jaroszewski, *op. cit.*, p. 133.

21. Lucjan Blit, *Eastern Pretender* (London: Hutchinson, 1965).

22. Most representative for this school of thought is Bolesław Piasecki, *Zagadnienia istotne* (Fundamental Issues) (Warsaw: Pax, 1954).

23. For an interesting discussion see 'Głosy o współczesnych postawach religijnych w Polsce' (Voices Regarding Contemporary Religious Attitudes in Poland), *Znak* (Cracow), No. 90 (1961), pp. 1611–77.

24. Adam Bromke, 'The Znak Group in Poland', *East Europe*, Vol. 11, Nos. 1 and 2 (1962).

25. For an analysis of the problem see Stanislaw Staron, 'State-Church Relations in Poland', *World Politics*, Vol. XXI, No. 4 (July, 1969), pp. 575–601.

26. Although in the cities it reaches up to several thousand more.
27. Józef Majka, 'Socjografia powołań kapłańskich', *loc. cit.*, pp. 48–57.
28. *Catholic Life in Poland* (Warsaw), No. 5/54 (1970), p. 64.
29. Czesław Stryjewski, *Zakony* (Orders) (Warsaw: KiW, 1961), p. 149.
30. Wiesław Mysłek, *Kościoł Współczesny* (Contemporary Church) (Warsaw: KiW, 1963), p. 41.
31. Wiatr, *op. cit.*, p. 469.

13 The Status of Religion in the German Democratic Republic

George H. Brand

This is a case-study in national delimitation and integration under authoritarian auspices. It deals with a crucial issue in political science: how and to what extent religious institutions may be deliberately used by an authoritarian state in building a new political community. Specifically, it deals with Communist attempts to manipulate two dimensions of Chuch–State relations in the German Democratic Republic: (a) the role of Church and State respectively, in the political socialisation of East German youth; and (b) the role of the Church (in this case the Evangelical Church) in furthering East German nation building – what might in effect be viewed as protective state building and integration – under the sponsorship of the Socialist Unity Party (S.E.D.)[1] of the G.D.R. In other words one is dealing here with a paradoxical situation, wherein a Communist leadership is engaged, at one and the same time, in a concerted attempt to *minimise* the role of religious institutions in the upbringing of youth and to *maximise* the usefulness of these institutions in constructing a clearly delimited sovereign East German state with a separate identity.

It would seem helpful to analyse this process in the context of several distinct phases in the interaction between Communist and religious institutions in the G.D.R. These phases, while to some extent anchored in specific time periods, are not intended to represent precise chronological units. Periodisation can only be, as in most other cases, but a rough approximation of actual historical stages; in fact, a number of official actions as well as responses of the Church tended to overlap in this case. Under the circumstances attempts to pinpoint specific phases in the process are concerned primarily with delineating in a schematic way the crucial characteristics of each stage in the evolving relationship between Church and State in the G.D.R. By the same token they are concerned with the main issues at stake rather than with chronologically precise, historical accounts.

The highest policy objective of the S.E.D. regime has been the attempt to gain formal recognition of the German Democratic Republic by the German Federal Republic. The economic, social, political and religious policies of the S.E.D. leadership have been directed to aid the process of East German 'nation-building'. Although it is difficult to determine the degree of loyalty that East German citizens feel towards their government, it can be said that the citizens of the G.D.R. take pride in the industrial achievement of their political system, and especially since the creation of the Wall accept their separate status from their West German neighbours.

However, to accept a difference in status does not mean to lose the sense of a common German nationality. In a recent poll of workers the Party discovered that '71 per cent considered Germany rather than G.D.R. as their fatherland'.[2] Such a statistic is undoubtedly highly disquieting to the Party for it indicates at the deepest level the still inadequate formation of a national consciousness. Since its inception, the G.D.R. has waged an internal and external struggle to emerge as a nation-state among the European community of nations. The S.E.D. leadership has given highest priority to this political objective.

It is within this framework that the question of religion and the Church in the G.D.R. takes on particular significance. Policies towards the Church in the G.D.R. have been consistently motivated by both fears and objectives on the part of the state leadership that must be interpreted in the light of the particular political conditions in which a divided nation seeking indentity and a national consciousness finds itself. The fundamental instability which is a consequence of this division may explain the particular strategies employed by the Ulbricht regime in its attacks against the Church. Viewed from this vantage point, anti-religious policies will be seen to be motivated by considerations that are far more consequential than a mere desire to maintain ideological purity with regard to the Marxist doctrine of 'religion as the opiate of the people'. As Peter Ludz has pointed out, one of the overriding concerns of the S.E.D. leadership has been to 'free itself from the shadow of its powerful, politically recognised sibling to the West'.[3] S.E.D. policies towards the Church may be viewed as one such attempt to establish a social order with a distinct identity, thereby leading to a further consolidation of G.D.R. sovereignty.

To attain this objective, Party policy towards the Church was pursued on three levels. First, a direct assault was made on all aspects of religious education with intent of causing the steady erosion of a once powerful influence in society and thereby enhancing the ability of the regime to consolidate its own power and manipulate the socio-political attitudes of the young. Second, there was a concentrated effort to destroy the existing unity of the Evangelical Church of Germany (E.K.D.)[4] and to isolate those elements in the Church that were critical of the G.D.R. and sought reunification on terms other than those suggested by the S.E.D. Third, considerable energy was expended on developing a core of 'progressive' clergy who would view Christianity and Socialism as striving for similar societal goals, thereby acting in a supportive manner to state initiatives with regard to the socialist transformation of society.

THE FIRST PHASE: ALL OUT ASSAULT AGAINST THE CHURCH

In January of 1949 the S.E.D. established itself as the party of Marxism-Leninism. Following the model of the Communist Party of the Soviet Union, the S.E.D. initiated the ideological struggle to mobilise the population for the purpose of effectuating a transformation of society based on the Party's interpretation of the principles of Marxism-Leninism. From the outset the state leadership had to face a severe political dilemma. The S.E.D. was in control of only part of a nation, and the part it did not control claimed to be the only legitimate German state.

In the years immediately following the war, many Western observers viewed the G.D.R. as a territory held together only by the presence of Soviet troops, and considered it an anomaly of temporary duration. This political estimate of East Germany led to the expectation of eventual reunification on terms favourable to the German Federal Republic. Leading churchmen in both parts of the divided nation held to the notion that the G.D.R. was a 'Marxist aberration on hallowed German soil'.[5] Churchmen and laymen alike who could not accept the idea of a divided Germany pointed to the E.K.D. as an example of the continued existence of German unity. The E.K.D. was a confederation which included the Lutheran, Reformed and United Churches in Germany. Of particular political significance was the fact that after the formal division of Germany, the E.K.D. did not undergo a similar division. All the Evangelical churches in the twenty regional bishoprics in the West as well as the Evangelical churches in the eight regional bishoprics in the East were members of the E.K.D. In addition to strengthening the sense of spiritual communion among its member churches, the E.K.D. served to reinforce the already prevailing attitude that the German Democratic Republic was a passing phenomenon. The Church was seen as the remaining indestructible tie between East and West. From the viewpoint of the state leadership in the Democratic Republic, however, the unity of the E.K.D. was seen as a dangerous political factor disguised in religious terminology.

Under these circumstances, the S.E.D. was confronted with the monumental task of developing indigenous social and political forms that would create a national consciousness and destroy the traditional ties of the G.D.R. citizen towards West Germany. If the Party was to establish its stated goal of being the conscious vanguard of a new order, existing institutions would have to be permeated with a new ideological content that would serve to reorient traditional social and political values along the new directives prescribed by the S.E.D. In support of this objective the process of 'socialist education' took high priority as the young members of society were the anticipated carriers of these new political values and general philosophical orientations.

Emphasis was placed on fully integrating the youth into the new social and political system at the earliest possible age. The young had to be educated in the spirit of Marxism–Leninism in order to develop in them a socialist class consciousness. Ulbricht outlined the essential role youth must play in the creation of the new social order:

> What is at stake is not only an improvement in the means of production. It is essential that accompanying the improvements in production there exist a step by step transformation of German society.

Today, German youth possesses not only the right, but
actually has the obligation to ask: What are we working for
now? What purpose does our work serve? What guarantees
must be provided so that this time our labour creates a better
future for the people?[6]

Ulbricht skilfully utilised the tragic events of the recent German
past in a strategic manoeuvre to mobilise the idealism of youth. Not
only could there not be any commitment to a past that had produced the unspeakable horrors of the Hitler regime, it was absolutely necessary to eradicate every last remnant in society that
could be associated with the period of National Socialism. Only
the creation of a new democratic order would make possible the
total elimination of Nazi ideology and guarantee the growth of
progressive forces. Ulbricht welcomed the young to develop a
spirit of national unity and devote their talents and energy to the
construction of this new society.

Party officials were admonished to impress upon the young
that it was their duty to become members of the organisation
known as Free German Youth (F.D.J.).[7] Like the Komsomol in
the Soviet Union, the Free German Youth had to recognise the
leading role of the Party. Ulbricht spoke of the F.D.J. as a broad
mass organisation that encompassed all freedom-loving and demo-
cratically-minded German youth. Leaving the propagandistic
statements aside, the political function of the Free German Youth
was to serve as an active instrument of the S.E.D. in the socialisation of society. Uncompromising and unqualified loyalty to Party
ideology was demanded of all the young adherents. As an essential
ingredient of this ideology was a materialistic world-view and an
atheistic explanation of man and the social order, the controversy
over the philosophical orientation of the young developed into
one of the first and one of the most bitter conflicts between the
Church and the State.

Under a section designated 'Content and Limits of State Power',
the 1949 G.D.R. constitution contained a special heading called
'Religion and Religious Societies'. Articles 41–48 were the fundamental declarations on the relation between Church and State.
The constitution formally guaranteed freedom of conscience and
freedom of religious belief to all citizens of the G.D.R. It also
stipulated that the practice of religion is protected by the State

and that there would not be a single official State Church. Also guaranteed was the freedom to unite in religious congregations, with each congregation organising and administering its own affairs in accordance with the common law.

Concerning the important issue of religious education, the Church was guaranteed the right to give religious instruction on school premises and select the teachers of religion from its own ranks. In addition, parents were given the right to determine whether their children should participate in the programme of religious instruction until they reached the age of fourteen.

Of particular political significance was the clause dealing with public functions of the Church. The right of the Church to express its views concerning vital social issues was recognised. But there was also a clause which stated that religious institutions and teachings cannot be used for unconstitutional political purposes. The constitution clearly implied that the Church can express its opinions on vital social issues, but these opinions could not deviate from the policies expressed by the vanguard of the people – the Party.

It seems possible to interpret the State's willingness to have the Church make 'constitutional' pronouncements on vital issues affecting society as an early indication of an attempt which was intensified in subsequent years to encourage the Church to act in a supportive manner with regard to the domestic and foreign policies of the S.E.D. This was especially the case in the repeated attempts to identify the Bonn Government with a neo-Nazi revanchist ideology which was utilising the Church in the West to legitimate its policies of aggrandisement. The two-fold objective of such a tactic was to drive a wedge between the Church in the G.D.R. and the Church in the German Federal Republic, and to enhance the position of the G.D.R. in the eyes of the East European states as a necessary buffer against a resurgent neo-Nazi mentality. In an area where the painful memories of the war were still very much on the surface such a tactic was not without effect.

Traditionally, the Evangelical Church had occupied a privileged position in German society. To adjust its life-style to the realities of a new political climate which seriously curtailed its previous status, was to become a long and at times painful task of self-examination. But as the durability of the G.D.R. was by no

means clear in the early years following the war, the Church reacted vehemently to any attempt on the part of the State to
inculcate the young with an ideology that was, from the Church's
viewpoint, in diametric opposition to the Christian faith. The
State, by contrast, would not tolerate the efforts of any organisation to impede the process of the socialist transformation of society.
The constitution notwithstanding, the S.E.D. viewed the Church
as propagating a counter ideology which threatened the development of socialist consciousness and the unity of Communist rule.
Various forms of pressure were therefore exerted which were
designed to frustrate the effectiveness of the Church to educate
youth in the Christian faith.

In July of 1950, less than a year after the promulgation of the
G.D.R. constitution, the Third Party Congress of the S.E.D. met
in Berlin and launched a vituperative attack against what it called
reactionary church leaders. The indictment read in part:

> Certain church leaders are undertaking a reactionary move-
> ment that runs contrary to those who are fighting for freedom
> and runs contrary to the democratic order of the German
> Democratic Republic. These are the same church leaders in
> high offices who consistently defended the power of the
> Monopolists and the Junkers, who approved Nazi terror, and
> who blessed the weapons of Hitler's aggressive war. Today,
> these church leaders are again assuming the role of warmon-
> gers and reactionaries, and are fulfilling the instructions of the
> Anglo-American imperialists and their German henchmen.[8]

As the above quote indicates, the hysterical tone of the charges
levelled against the clergy reveals the fears of a regime still unsure
of its own status. The year 1950 was significant on the international political scene as June of that year witnessed the outbreak
of the Korean War, and with that event the accompanying American insistence that West German rearmament was necessary for
the defence of Europe. If one considers these factors in conjuction
with the widespread attitude among leading churchmen in both
parts of Germany that the G.D.R. regime was unstable and illegitimate, it becomes easier to understand why the S.E.D. chose the
summer of 1950 as the moment to launch a vigorous campaign
against what it considered to be reactionary elements in the
church. It should also be noted that at this same Party Congress

the S.E.D. went out of its way to praise those few clergy who aligned themselves with the National Front and supported state policies.

During the early 1950s policies towards the Church that were initiated by the S.E.D. may be seen as a determined effort to build group loyalty and group cohesion among the citizenry in response to a defined set of social and political values intending to consolidate the position of the G.D.R. as an independent state. Central to this process of re-education was the position of the young. The mobilisation of youth became one of the most essential factors in promoting the socialist transformation of society. Addressing himself to the central council of the Free German Youth in December of 1952, Ulbricht stated:

> The F.D.J. organisations must involve themselves more thoroughly with political and ideological questions, for only then will the struggle yield more favourable results. It is necessary to expose and isolate the reactionary powers that serve the church administration in West Berlin and Bonn.[9]

The immediate task was to develop a process of education that would incorporate the young into Marxist–Leninist orientation. To assist this venture, the S.E.D. was desirous of establishing a tight bond between parents, schools and what were called democratic mass organisations.[10] The mass organisations referred to the Communist youth groups, the Pioneers for the younger children, and the F.D.J. for the older ones. Recognising the necessity of parental co-operation the S.E.D. consistently pointed to the advantages that would come to those young people who were members of these groups. At the same time various measures were devised by the S.E.D. which were designed to seriously hamper the Church in advancing its programme of Christian education.

On any number of pretexts, school rooms were frequently not made available for religious instruction. When the rooms were made available, unfavourable hours for religious instruction were assigned which made it difficult for the children to attend. In addition, those teachers who agreed to participate in the programme of religious instruction found themselves in disfavour with school officials. Whenever the Church planned youth programmes and church-sponsored youth festivals, the Communist youth groups would have their major events scheduled at the same time. Also, special career opportunities and the opportunity for advanced schooling was offered to those young people who were members of the Communist youth organisations. The lesson of the 'single alternative' was not lost on the young: either you move with the Party, or you stand isolated.

The S.E.D. singled out the church organisation for evangelical youth (*Junge Gemeinde*)[11] for particular opprobrium. Not their religious beliefs, but their alleged political activities became the focus of Party persecution. The General Secretary of the C.D.U.[12] (East), Gerald Götting, assailed the leadership of the evangelical youth for inciting the young and using their organisation for the express purpose of building pockets of resistance against the new democratic order. The evangelical youth could not be permitted, Götting asserted, to become the centre of anti-State activities. S.E.D. propaganda made it appear as if the evangelical youth were members of a prohibited organisation of conspirators, and the official newspaper of the S.E.D. labelled the evangelical youth as 'American agents', and accused their organisation of being 'centres for espionage'.[13] The real target of this attack was the entire programme of church-sponsored religious education which was instilling in the young church members a social orientation that was considered to be in direct opposition to the stated objectives of the Party.

This struggle was intensified by the creation of especially designed mobilising tools on the part of the State to compete with religious institutions and traditions. One such effort was the programme of Youth Dedication (*Jugendweihe*), which was designed to serve as a secular substitute for church confirmation. As confirmation prepares one for membership in the Church, the year of study culminating in the ceremony of Youth Dedication had the express purpose of preparing the children to become active members of the new social order. The children were given a scientific and materialistic explanation of the origin of the world and the development of the process of history. It was impressed upon them that the victory of a socialist structure of society was inevitable.

In presenting the children with an integral world-view, the Marxist notion that religion is false consciousness was emphasised in conjuction with the belief in the autonomy of reason. Reason was seen as the sole instrument capable of establishing and disposing of the criteria of all truth. From the Church's viewpoint, this total reliance on reason was the source of the initial separation of man from God.

Attempting to deter the youth from participating in the programme of Youth Dedication, the Church decided to exclude transgressors from the sacrament of holy communion and from eventual marriage rites within the Church. Given the strong tradition of the Evangelical Church in the life of the community, the church leadership assumed that these measures would be sufficient to maintain a firm hold on the young.

The State, however, possessed measures at its disposal that proved to be of greater persuasion. Through the schools, Pioneer and F.D.J. organisations massive pressure was exerted on children and parents alike. Confronted with the threat that participation in Youth Dedication was a necessary condition for advanced schooling and entrance into the professions, the attempt of the Church to force parents to decide between Youth Dedication and confirmation did not succeed. The Churches finally had to agree to confirm their young members one year after the ceremony of Youth Dedication and grant to them all the rights of church membership.

The result of these policies was a systematic reduction in the influence of religious faith. Scientific knowledge could rationally explain all existing phenomena between heaven and earth, and the world as well as the process of history itself was devoid of mystery. A young generation was growing up with the awareness that to place oneself into the guiding hand of the Party, was to become an active and creative participant of the inevitable future.

THE SECOND PHASE: THE QUEST FOR LIMITED
ACCOMMODATION

In spite of the draconic crackdown that the Church experienced during the first phase of its relations with the State, in the late 1950s there were some definite indications of an alternative approach. All these indications came to fruition in what might well be regarded as a distinct second phase in the relationship between Church and State in the G.D.R.

While in the first phase the treatment of the Church was almost totally negative, there is evidence to suggest that the G.D.R. regime came to view the East German religious establishment as a potentially important ally in gaining some newly crystallising objectives. Accordingly, one is dealing here with a phase wherein the regime sought to involve the local religious establishment in the performance of positive, politically helpful functions.

Ironically, it was an act of the E.K.D. itself that initiated this second phase and in the process unwittingly facilitated Ulbricht's duel objective of unifying the 'progressive' churchmen within the G.D.R. while at the same time enabling him to intensify the attack against the unity of the E.K.D. In the spring of 1957 the E.K.D. concluded with the Bonn Government a military chaplaincy agreement which enabled ministers to perform pastoral duties for members of the armed services.. Binding itself legally and organisationally to the State at least in one aspect of its activities, the Church offered Ulbricht the necessary ideological weapon to launch a major offensive against the so-called 'revanchist' nature of the E.K.D. The military chaplaincy agreement was interpreted by Ulbricht as an overt approval on the part of the E.K.D. of N.A.T.O. policies, West German rearmament and the use of atomic warfare. The E.K.D. was accused of permitting itself to be used as a legitimating agent for policies of aggression directed against the G.D.R. Ulbricht characterised the chaplaincy agreement as being anti-humanist, and compared the leading churchmen of the E.K.D. in West Germany with the group known as German Christians who, during the period of National Socialism, supported the Hitler regime.[14]

To emphasise the non-hostile nature of the agreement, the E.K.D. offered to conclude a similar chaplaincy agreement with the G.D.R. which would serve the armed forces in the East. In fact, the E.K.D. leadership naïvely assumed that such an offer to the G.D.R. would substantiate its non-political character. The offer was flatly rejected. Writing to the chairman of the council of the Evangelical Church in Germany, Bishop Dibelius, the G.D.R. Minister of Defence, Stoph, said in part: 'In the German Democratic Republic there are no armed forces. The National People's Army, both in its character and in its duties stands in diametric opposition to the previous armed forces of Hitler, and to the N.A.T.O. army of Bonn.'[15]

The fact that E.K.D. had bound itself legally to the Bonn Government through the military chaplaincy agreement was used

by Ulbricht as the pretext for juxtaposing two separate and funda-
mentally irreconcilable expressions of Christianity as practised
by the Church. The militaristic N.A.T.O. Church of West
Germany was not to be compared with the humanistically oriented
Church of the G.D.R. This was to become a persistent theme in
Ulbricht's efforts to split the E.K.D.

The heated controversy over the military chaplaincy agreement
appeared to Ulbricht as an opportune moment to emphasise
policies towards the Church which would serve to maximise the
usefulness of these religious institutions in creating a sovereign
state with a separate identity. To attain this objective the vehement
anti-church measures of the early 1950s were suspended, and
emphasis was now placed on the common nature of Christianity
and the humanist aims of Socialism.

The period between 1960 and 1964 witnessed a number of statements on the part of Ulbricht which were intended to demonstrate
the possibilities for co-operation between Church and State in the
G.D.R. The substance of these statements constitute what may be
viewed as the Ulbricht version of a Marxist-Christian dialogue.
Its political objective was to systematically discredit the E.K.D.
and exert pressure on the Churches in the G.D.R. to withdraw
from that organisation.

Addressing the *Volkskammer* on 4 October 1960, Ulbricht took
the initiative and expanded the principle of Church-State accommodation in a major policy statement. He stated that as a consequence of the supportive propaganda of leading West German
churchmen on behalf of Bonn's militaristic policies,[16] the previous
co-operation between the Government of the G.D.R. and 'a West
German so-called German Church Administration' was no longer
possible. The 'so-called German Church Administration' was an
obvious reference to the E.K.D. Ulbricht had let it be known that
the organisational unity of the E.K.D. could no longer be tolerated.
Pointing to the increasing number of influential churchmen in
the G.D.R. who were beginning to understand the attitude of the
State towards 'West German N.A.T.O. politicians in clerical dress'
and the institutions in which they were represented, Ulbricht
concluded:

> We regard this as a sign that the Evangelical Church in the
> G.D.R. has a growing understanding of the aims and tasks

of our socialist community. There is no contradiction between Christianity and the humanist aims of socialism. Christianity which was once the religion of the poor, the religion of peace, has for hundreds of years been misused by the ruling classes. Today it is misused by the forces of militarism to support a policy of atomic armament. The old longing, expressed in the text: 'On earth peace, good will towards men' can only find fulfilment if the high ideals of humanism and socialism are achieved.[17]

A further development of this theme occurred on 9 February 1961, when Ulbricht, eager to find allies within the Church, received a delegation of church officials and theologians including Professor of Theology Emil Fuchs of the University of Leipzig. In the ensuing conversations Ulbricht asserted:

I am coming more and more to the conclusion in the course of our practical and friendly co-operation, that socialists, communists, and Christians – regardless of their different ideologies – belong together and simply must work together to shape life and society, and to secure peace on this earth. A Christian who takes his humanist and social ideals seriously, who has freed himself of prejudices and the burden of a dead past, should in fact not be able to do otherwise than unite with socialism. And I believe we should always welcome Christians on all state and social levels and treat them with respect and friendship.[18]

This appeasement of the Church within the G.D.R. coincided with intensified efforts to split the E.K.D. As of 13 August 1961 it was no longer possible for church agencies of the E.K.D. to hold meetings. Synodical conferences as well as the council of the E.K.D. were forced to meet separately in East and West Germany. The S.E.D. regime was thereby pursuing one of its primary objectives – the creation of an independent state with an independent Evangelical Church.

Ulbricht's policy of accommodation with the Church culminated in a meeting with Bishop Moritz Mitzenheim of Thuringia on 18 August 1964. Emphasising once again the importance of co-operation between Church and State in the G.D.R., Ulbricht declared:

In the immediate post-war years, when the aftermath of the war still made itself terribly felt, we have had arguments. This was quite natural, for we came together with totally different world views. But in the course of solving the great problem of creating a peaceful German society we have come closer and closer together. We now work in mutual understanding.[19]

Actually, the 'mutual understanding' referred only to a small group of ministers and theology professors who aligned themselves with Ulbricht's 'new course'. This small number of 'progressive Christians' notwithstanding, Ulbricht's doctrine of Christian humanism became an important ideological weapon in preparing the campaign for the final organisational division of the E.K.D.

THE THIRD PHASE: STATE BOUNDARIES ARE CHURCH BOUNDARIES

The unyielding efforts of the S.E.D. leadership to establish a Church in the G.D.R. that would have no organisational ties to the Church in West Germany came to fruition in what might be called the third phase in Church–State relations. The argument was pressed with growing intensity that two fundamentally differing expressions of Christianity existed in Germany. One variety was devoted to the principles of humanism, whereas the other served the interests of military revanchism.

On 9 February 1967 the First Secretary of the C.D.U. (East), Gerald Götting, gave a clear indication of forthcoming S.E.D. pressure when he stated:

The free and independent churches of the G.D.R. cannot be spoken of in the same breath with the Evangelical Church in West Germany which is bound and obligated to N.A.T.O. through the military chaplaincy agreement. Between these two extremes there can be no institutional unity.[20]

Two months later at the Seventh Party Congress of the S.E.D., Ulbricht intensified his objective of 'nation-building' as he announced that there now existed two completely separate German states that were differentiated not only by their social order, but also by the fundamental principles of their domestic and foreign policies.

At almost the same time as the Seventh Party Congress of the S.E.D. in April 1967, the Eastern regional synod of the E.K.D. met at Fürstenwalde. From this gathering came a unanimous declaration of the unity of the Church. Responding to Gotting's charge that 'the Churches of the G.D.R. cannot be spoken of in the same breath with the Church in West Germany, 'Bishop Krummacher replied:

> When Christians, who are united in One Lord and who belong together as members of one church, can no longer be spoken of in the same breath, then the concern is no longer about an institutional question, but rather about the communion of faith in one Lord. . . . In faithful obedience to our One Lord we hold fast in every breath to our communion with Christians of other races, colour, and socio-political origin.[21]

Despite the eloquent Fürstenwalde declaration on church unity, political events made the subsequent division of the E.K.D. inevitable. In February of 1968, Bishop Mitzenheim of Thuringia, who for many years had co-operated with the S.E.D. leadership, declared that 'state boundaries must be considered as church boundaries'. This concept was incorporated into the new G.D.R. constitution of 9 April 1968, and confronted the Church with a set of political realities that required a reassessment of its position.

Article 39 of the new constitution which dealt with the question of religion in the G.D.R. stated:

1. Every citizen of the German Democratic Republic has the right to profess a creed and carry out religious activities.
2. The churches and other religious communities are to arrange and carry on their affairs and their activities in conformity with the constitution and the legal regulations of the German Democratic Republic. Details can be arranged through agreements.[22]

The last sentence carried particularly ominous overtones since it created the possibility that the State might negotiate independently with the regional Churches in the G.D.R., thereby preventing the expression of any unified church position. In response to this situation, representatives of the eight regional Churches founded the Synod of the Federation of Evangelical Churches in the G.D.R. on 10 June 1969. On that date, the formal organisational unity of the E.K.D. was dissolved. With this division of the E.K.D., one of the long range objectives of 13 August 1961 had been fulfilled – all segments of East German society were within the wall.

In answer to the question whether the new constitution was the basic reason for the creation of the Federation of Churches, the administrator of the Bishop's office in East Berlin, Albert Schönherr, pointed out that it was necessary to make a distinction between the 'cause' and the 'occasion'. The cause, said Schönherr, is the will of the Church to better express its interests. The Church faced fundamental problems that could only be resolved through unity. The occasion that required immediate action, he continued, was the new constitution of 1968.[23] Schönherr also stated that: 'Church agencies must serve the witness of the church. When they can no longer do this, they must be changed. The witness of the church takes priority over its form of organisation'.[24] Schonherr was suggesting that the withdrawal from the E.K.D. and the creation of the Federation pointed to an awareness on the part of churchmen in the G.D.R. of existing political realities. The Church had to meet its responsibilities under a government whose stability was no longer in question. It had to perform its religious functions with a defined geographic boundary, and had to view itself not as the Evangelical Church of Germany, but as the Evangelical Church of the German Democratic Republic.

In retrospect it may be said that the division of the E.K.D. was a far greater blow to the Church in West Germany than to the Church in the G.D.R. The Eastern Churches had grown accustomed to survival in a hostile environment, whereas many churchmen in the West still harboured the myth of eventual German reunification. The division of the E.K.D. seemingly extinguished that myth.

As for the Church in the G.D.R., the Federation may be a step towards greater union. The eight regional Churches are comprised of five Union (combined Reformed and Lutheran) and three Lutheran Churches, which in the past have experienced differences over the interpretation of church doctrine. At present a dialogue is under way attempting to bridge the differences and form a single Church in the G.D.R.

272   *Religion and Atheism in the U.S.S.R. and Eastern Europe*

In the current setting the 'N.A.T.O.' argument can no longer be used to browbeat the Church, and neither can churchmen be accused of representing 'foreign' interests. Future debates will take place in an environment where both Church and State accept the reality of the other's continued existence.

NOTES

1. Sozialistische Einheitspartei Deutschlands.
2. Robert Gerald Livingston, 'East Germany Between Moscow and Bonn', *Foreign Affairs* (January 1972), p. 304.
3. Peter Christian Ludz, *The German Democratic Republic From the Sixties to the Seventies* (Center for International Affairs, Harvard University), 1970, p. 61.
4. Evangelische Kirche Deutschlands.
5. This notion is analysed by Jean Edward Smith in 'The Red Prussianism of the GDR', *Political Science Quarterly* (September 1967), pp. 368–85.
6. Walter Ulbricht, 'Mit uns zieht ein neuer Geist', *An die Jugend* (Berlin: Verlag Neues Leben, 1968), p. 28.
7. Freie Deutsche Jugend.
8. Quoted in Hans-Gerhard Koch, *Neue Erde ohne Himmel* (Stuttgart: Quell–Verlag, 1963), p. 59.
9. Walter Ulbricht, *op. cit.*, 'Die nächsten Aufgaben der FDJ bei der Schaffung der Grundlagen des Sozialismus in der DDR', p. 117.
10. Documents dealing with the educational policies of the S.E.D. may be found in *Dokumente zur Bildungspolitik in der Sowjetischen Besatzungszone* (Berlin: Bundesministerium fur Gesamtdeutsche Fragen, 1966).
11. Literally, Young Congregations.
12. Christian Democratic Union.
13. *Neues Deutschland*, 24 April 1953.
14. Walter Ulbricht, 'Militarseelsorgevertrag ist anti-humanistisch und gegen die Kirche gerichtet', *Marxisten und Christen wirken gemeinsam für Frieden und Humanismus* (Berlin: Der Staatsrat der Deutschen Demokratischen Republik, No. 5, 1964), p. 57.
15. *Kirchliches Jahrbuch* (Gutersloh: Verlaghaus Gerd Mohn, 1957), p. 48.
16. The reference is to the Military Chaplaincy Agreement of 1957.
17. Reinhard Henkys, *Bund der Evangelischen Kirchen in der DDR* (Witten–Frankfurt–Berlin: Eckart-Verlag, 1970), Document No. 11: 'Das Christentum und die humanistischen Ziele des Sozialismus sind keine Gegensätze', p. 52.
18. *Ibid.*, Document No. 14: 'Sozialisten und Christen verbinden gemeinsame Ideale und Ziele', p. 60.
19. *Ibid.*, Document No. 19: 'Unsere Gemeinsamkeit in der Wahrnehmung humanistischer Verantwortung ist von grosser nationaler Bedeutung', p. 77.
20. *Ibid.*, Document No. 28: 'Aus einem Referat Göttings auf einer Kirchenpolitischen Tagung der CDU (Ost)', p. 90.
21. The entire declaration is contained in a pamphlet entitled: Die Einheit der Evangelischen Kirche in Deutschland, Erklarungen der 4. Synode der EKD in Furstenwalde und Berlin–Spandau, vom 1. bis 7. April, 1967 (Berlin: 1967).
22. Verfassung der Deutschen Demokratischen Republik (Berlin: Nationalrat der Nationalen Front des demokratischen Deutschland, 1968).
23. *Der Tagesspiegel*, 21 January 1969.
24. *Ibid.*

14 Church–State Schism in Czechoslovakia

PETER A. TOMA AND MILAN J. REBAN

As is evident throughout this book, the interaction between religion and politics in the U.S.S.R. and Eastern Europe is very close despite the constitutional provisions in several countries separating the affairs of Church and State. The developmental relationship of both institutions may follow a symmetrical or an asymmetrical pattern. Religion may socialise individuals into the existing system, thus performing an integrative function, or it may be utilised by the political authorities as an ancillary instrument of coercion. In either case, religion serves the interests of the ruling *élite* and hence performs an auxiliary role in the political system. However, an asymmetrical relationship develops when religion and the political system are in conflict – the religious solutions that are proffered and the practices that are followed frequently show no regard for political boundaries and clash with the interests of the ruling *élite*.[1] In Czechoslovakia, this latter pattern of behaviour has characterised the relationship between religion and politics for the past twenty-five years, although the ruling *élite* has sought from time to time to utilise certain persisting aspects of religion to make its own position more secure.

While it is true that in February 1948, when the Communist leaders of Czechoslovakia seized the monopoly of power, the ruling *élite* was equipped with the teachings of Marxism–Leninism–Stalinism, it is also true that this ideology was not effective in dealing with functional differentiation and societal complexities. Thus, shortly after taking power, the Party leadership, in its pursuit of legitimacy, resorted to such dysfunctional controls as the use of terror. Coercion coupled with 'persuasion' was given priority over rewards, and the religious organisations felt the impact of this quest.

After this incubation period, no dramatic changes were made in the diverse patterns of behaviour that emerged until the Dubček era when it was discovered that the participatory thrust of the various interests in Czechoslovakia – including the religious interests – produced the far-reaching pressures for reforms. Since April 1969 the severely shaken political leadership once again has been preoccupied with the problem of legitimacy, and has again reverted to the instruments of coercion and 'persuasion' in an attempt to resolve the problem of religious-political interaction.

The issue is now further compounded by the commitment on the part of the leadership to the creation of a new political culture: the Czechoslovak population must be resocialised and its personality restructured. Yet the Communists are forced to engage in competitive behaviour with the religious organisations – both, after all, influence the behaviour of the citizens; both elicit symbolic responses; and more importantly, the recruitment and socialisation of the people into the system are greatly influenced by religious activity. Furthermore, the interaction between politics and religion in Czechoslovakia is exacerbated by the international dimensions of the problem: the Roman Catholic Church has its international linkages and the Vatican, the Greek Catholics of Slovakia have their religious brethren in the Ukrainian S.S.R. and there are the world dimensions to the Jewish population, to mention but three examples.

It is within the preceding context that we propose to examine the 1948 events, the reforms of 1968 and the period of consolidation since April 1969.

THE POLITICAL–RELIGIOUS CONFLICT OF 1948

According to the last census on religious affiliation, in 1930, the breakdown of the 14,729,536 population of Czechoslovakia for the most important religious denominations was as follows:[2]

Roman Catholic	73·5 %
Greek Catholic and Armenian Catholic	3·97%
All Protestants (including the Evangelical Church of Czech Brethren 2·2% and the Lutheran 3·99%)	7·67%

Orthodox Church	0·99%
Czechoslovak Church	5·39%
Jews	2·42%
No affiliation	5·80%

There are no reliable figures available for the various religious groupings in Czechoslovakia after 1930. Nevertheless, in February 1948, when the Communists took power in Czechoslovakia, the Roman Catholic Church had claimed 75 per cent of the 12,339,000 inhabitants. There were approximately 8·5 per cent Protestants and about 7·5 per cent were members of the Czechoslovak Church. The remaining 9 per cent of the population made up a complex mosaic of several smaller denominations.

Between 1930 and 1948 there occurred significant shifts in religious affiliation, mostly because of World War II. Some 600,000 ethnic Germans emigrated from Czechoslovakia during the war and nearly two and one half million were expelled immediately after. Czechoslovakia also lost most of its Jewish population during the war. The annexation of Subcarpathian Ruthenia into the Ukrainian S.S.R. in late 1944, with the loss of nearly one million persons and some shifting of population between Hungary and Slovakia, makes the pre-war Czechoslovakia statistics on religious affiliation inaccurate.

With the expulsion of the German ethnic group, which was predominately Roman Catholic, the ranks of the clergy in Czechoslovakia were decimated. In the Litoměřice diocese, for example, the clergy declined by 78·82 per cent.[3] Similar reductions occurred in other Czechoslovak cities with large German populations. In all, some 1,400 to 1,500 priests were expelled.

In Slovakia the war left its scars. The rise of Slovak nationalism culminated not only in the truncated Slovak independence but in the creation of a Nazi satellite. Following the Munich agreement Czechoslovakia was dissolved into the Slovak Republic and the Protectorate of Bohemia and Moravia. Although the Slovak state was a German–Nazi vassal, its Slovak nationalism was closely linked to the Roman Catholic Church. Hence, after the war, punitive measures against those affiliated with the quisling Slovak state were meted out to several prominent Catholic leaders—politicians, including the ex-president, Monsignor Joseph Tiso. Although many Slovaks objected to these measures, Tiso was tried for treason and ultimately executed. This unnecessary act of revenge against a doubtful martyr only added to the hatred of the Czechs by many Slovaks and created a new division between the two nations which was very skilfully exploited by the Communists in the post-1945 Provisional Czechoslovak Government. For these reasons, the various demands for Slovak autonomy, agreed upon during the twilight of World War II, and formulated into the Košice Programme, were not implemented until 1968 under Alexander Dubček.

After the Communist victory in February 1948, the overall pattern of politico-religious relations was relatively simple. The new ruling *élite* chose to curb rather than quash the influence of its arch-enemy, the Roman Catholic Church, and thus gain as much legitimacy as possible. Therefore when the Communist monopoly of power was established, the Church was requested to give its approval to the new regime. The Czechoslovak bishops considered this request, but replied that no special proclamation was called for because the Roman Catholic Church did not tie itself to any particular political expression – a position which marked the opening of a long struggle. The new regime then sought the formal endorsement of several of its candidate-priests who were running in the May 1948 elections. Instead of receiving their approval, the Catholic bishops threatened to suspend the priests whose names appeared on the Government ballot sheet as political **candidates.⁴**

Shortly after the February coup of 1948, the regime created, under the auspices of the Czechoslovak National Committee, a commission for religious affairs which upon the insistence of the Roman Catholic Church was divided into Catholic and non-Catholic sections. The first meeting of the Catholic section was held on 10 May 1948. Bishop Trochta led the church delegation while Dr Alexei Čepička headed the Government group. A broad agenda, ranging from education to press coverage and compensation for nationalised properties, was discussed; but no agreement was reached on any of the issues. Nor did the episcopate grant its unqualified endorsement to the new ruling *élite*. While the Gottwald regime was negotiating with the church leaders, the number of priests listed on the ballot sheet was reduced to three – all three were later suspended by the Church.

The church leaders harboured few illusions at this time. In

fact, as early as 1945 Bishop Trochta raised the question with Mgr Montini at the Vatican, what would happen if they had to live under Communism? It is purported that Mgr Montini replied that the Church must be prepared for all exigencies.[5] In this spirit, the bishops in 1948 sought to prepare the population as much as possible for events yet to come, by encouraging stronger religious convictions; using less formalised methods of religious instruction; encouraging families to do the same, and so forth. On the other hand, the Communist Party of Czechoslovakia (C.P.C.) acted on the assumption that the Roman Catholic Church could be transformed into a 'national Church' – divorced from the Vatican – without turning the Catholic population against the regime.[6] The Communist plans to subvert the Church through peaceful means were augmented when the Yugoslav–Soviet split imposed a new set of strategy and tactics on the people's democracies. The Cominform called for an intensification of class warfare aimed at a variety of forces in Czechoslovakia, especially at the senior clergy who were identified as a major source of reactionary influences. This struggle served a useful function for the new regime as it distracted attention from varied internal difficulties, including economic dislocations. The self-fulfilling battle against the so-called internal enemies only verified their existence, and the increased vigilance only served to reveal extensive religious activity and hastened the formulation of the major laws of October 1948 on Church–State relations which prohibited religious authorities from attacking the new political order.

Before the end of 1948, the regime stepped up its war against the Roman Catholic Church. The episcopate, without any warning, was given an ultimatum to sign the proclamation of loyalty. Consequently a formal meeting of the episcopate was called for on 22 March 1949, in Nový Smokovec, but it was soon adjourned when listening devices were discovered in the room.[7] The bishops declared that they were prepared to sign the loyalty oath if the State promised to uphold the Church's right *not* to compromise its God-given rights. After this stand off, a period of ostracism followed. Religious questions were now handled by the regime without the participation of the Roman Catholic Church. The new strategy was characterised by the C.P.C. leader, Klement Gottwald, when he told members of the Central Committee: 'We don't wish to lead a formal battle to a breaking point, a kind of

'February' of the church, that we don't want as yet, but we must create the conditions for it.'[8] The immediate response to Gott-wald's order was the launching of an intensive campaign to pro-mote cleavages within the Church, primarily by supporting the more 'progressive' Catholics. This tactic proved to be successful only because some of the non-Catholic Churches gave the new regime at least partial support.[9]

What could not be accomplished by the fellow-travellers from within the Church was later achieved by the regime through co-ercive laws. Measures were implemented to secure the legal control of the Church as well as to deprive the clergy of their influence by isolating them from their flock. But the most crucial develop-ment in this period was the creation of the administrative organs for church and religious affairs within the system of the national committees which were given the authority to deal with both substantive and procedural matters of religious activities in the country. As a consequence, limitations were imposed upon religious instruction, and the various parochial youth organisations were merged into state-sponsored youth organisations. By April 1949 all press activity of the Church, including mimeographing and communications within the church hierarchy, were disrupted. Most of these measures against the Church were taken quietly at different times in scattered parts of the country, with the aim of avoiding an open conflict with the organised Church.

While the regime kept constant pressure on the Church through its local administrative organs, the C.P.C. was exploiting those priests who for various reasons were willing to co-operate with the new regime. The first formal session with the activist priests was held on 28 April 1949. The intention of this meeting was, first, to revive and stress the cult of Cyril and Methodius as a Slavic-oriented Catholic manifestation; secondly, to demand the use of Czech and Slovak languages in church services and to stress the reactionary role of the Vatican; and thirdly, to organise a so-called Catholic Action movement which would oppose the old church hierarchy. In spite of the great effort and publicity in support of this movement, the Catholic Action failed to achieve its goal. Only 16 per cent of the clergy approved the resolution requesting the above changes in the Church; 11·2 per cent opposed it and about 16·2 per cent of the clergy were willing to give their oral approval. Some of the clergy who signed the document added qualifying remarks, such as that their approval was pending on official approval by the episcopate. The episcopate, of course, rejected the resolution and issued a statement forbidding the reading of the document in the churches. A reading was scheduled for 19 June 1949, and the following day the bishops' consistories were placed under direct supervision of the Ministry of Education. An Austrian law of 1874 was cited as a precedent for guiding State–Church relations and the support of churchmen from public funds. Thereafter, the supervisor had to approve every communication emanating from the consistory which, of course, prevented future church-imposed penalties against the priests actively cooperating with the regime.

In the meantime the efforts of the Communist authorities to create a viable counter-organisation met with disappointment; recruitment of priests lagged behind expectations. When the regime applied more coercive measures against the dissident clergy, spontaneous clashes developed between the faithful and the police. In Slovakia, for instance, open conflicts were reported in the Košice region, Orava and Spiš. These coercive measures proved to be counter-productive and hence the Catholic Action was brought to an abrupt end.

In attempting to cope with political pressures, the Roman Catholic Church found itself in further isolation when the new law of 15 July 1949, which dealt with the financing of church activity and payment of salaries for the clergy, was approved by all other religious groups. While this law was hailed by the representatives of the Catholic Action, it was criticised by the hierarchy of the Roman Catholic Church. Out of some 4,540 clergy, there were letters of protest from 132 Czech and Moravian vicariates and 1,628 priests. In the end, however, the law was implemented without the consent of the Roman Catholic Church. As a result, the regime laid the foundation for relations legitimising an extensive involvement of the State in Church affairs. When on 14 October 1949 the Czechoslovak National Assembly created a Government Bureau for Church Affairs, the will of the Church was broken and its influence subdued.[10]

Subsequent governmental measures were aimed at the episcopate itself, and for the next two years the struggle took on inhuman proportions. The C.P.C. leadership began to replace the bishops with the activists. The dissident bishops were restricted to their

residences, with the exception of Bishop Tomášek who for a
short time only was permitted to perform his episcopal duties.
Before moving decisively against the bishops, monasteries and convents were attacked, and many of their spiritual leaders arrested.
In a military-like action on the night of 13 April 1950 the residents
of the monasteries and cloisters were interned.

At the same time the regime moved swiftly and decisively
against the Greek Catholic (Uniate) Church in eastern Slovakia.
When the Communists came into power in 1948, the ruling *élite*
made several attempts to sever the union of the Greek Catholic
Church with Rome just as it tried to break the ties between Rome
and the Roman Catholic Church. In 1950 the Greek–Catholic
priests were finally forced to give up their parishes and their flock
was compelled to join Orthodoxy.[11] This ruthless move on the
part of the regime coincided with the Soviet precedent to outlaw
the Greek Catholic Church in the Ukraine and with the Stalinist
purges in satellite Europe. Most Greek–Catholic priests, including the Bishop of Prešov, Pavel Gojdič, were imprisoned, died
in prison or were displaced throughout the country. For the next
eighteen years the Church ceased to function normally, but there
is ample evidence to suggest that secretly the Greek Catholic
Church continued to operate because its people refused to submit
to either the C.P.C. dictates or to Eastern Orthodoxy.

The coercive party policies of the late 1940s and early 1950s
set the stage for C.P.C. control and subjugation of all aspects of
religious life in Czechoslovakia. The issue of religion in Slovakia
was treated in the same manner as in other parts of Czechoslovakia. Since de-Stalinisation in Czechoslovakia took place as late
as 1965, there were no drastic changes in policy towards the
organised Church until 1968. Prior to 1968, aside from some
modest adjustments, the religious-political interaction remained
largely similar to the framework set in the early years of the
socialist system. What were some of the significant results of these
policies? At the top, only a few dioceses were run by bishops. The
remaining dioceses were led by vicars–capitular and others from
the rank and file of the Church whose selection was manipulated
by the State. The diminishing ranks of clergy were severely handi-
capped in the exercise of their activities by limitations on transfers,
travel, and the like. All of these had to gain approval from Secretariats for Religious Affairs which had been, in more recent years,

subordinated to the Ministries of Culture, with secretariats in Prague for the Czech lands and in Bratislava for Slovakia.

One study shows the toll of this overall policy. In the Diocese of Litoměřice, in 1967, for the 443 parishes there were only 169 clergy available and only 146 of the total number had their own pastors.[12] In Prague Diocese, for the 835 parishes there were only 333 active priests. On the other hand, Slovakia had a relatively ample supply of priests. Yet the overall picture was bleak. In 1948 there were 5,779 secular priests in Czechoslovakia with an additional 1,163 priests of various religious orders. It is estimated that by 1967 the overall total had fallen to 3,107. The age distribution was flagrantly affected by the limitation on recruitment. In Bohemia, as of early 1968, there were only 927 priests who had been ordained after 1930; thus more than one half of the priests in Bohemia were over 60 years of age. Only one-sixth of these were younger than 40 and only 9 per cent were less than thirty.[13] All seminaries were closed during this period except one in Litoměřice for the Czech lands and another in Bratislava for Slovakia. Approximately 70 students applied annually for entry into the seminaries but only about 20 were accepted by the authorities and only about 12 completed their course of study.[14]

Although the most dramatic liberalisation occurred in 1968, there were a few modest political changes prior to the Dubček era, which somewhat eased the burdens of the Roman Catholic Church. With the introduction of the policy of peaceful coexistence by N. S. Khrushchev, international tension had been substantially reduced not only between the two major powers but also between the smaller powers subjected to this ideological division. In Czechoslovakia the thaw was symbolised by the release of some high-ranking clergy from prisons and a modest increase in closely supervised contacts with the Vatican. In 1963, for example, Archbishop Beran was formally released and in 1965 permitted to go into exile in the Vatican. Despite such gestures, however, the so-called patriotic priests, organised in the National Peace Council of the Catholic Church in Czechoslovakia, continued their campaign against the Vatican. As late as August 1967 the Novotny regime interrupted ongoing negotiations pertaining to the methods of administration of eight of the twenty diocese because the Vatican refused to accede to the Czechoslovak demands that at least some of the vacant posts be filled by the loyal priests.[15]

THE PRAGUE SPRING OF 1968

After an initial period of system-building, the Communist authorities had been compelled to cope with the more complex demands of system management. To do so effectively, the ruling *élite* had to come to grips with several urgent problems. One was the issue of participation, another the state of the economy, and a third the question of two nations (the Czechs and the Slovaks) in one state. These issues were the key stimuli for pluralistic and participatory ferment in 1968. Since the leadership chose to play the role of interest aggregator, it had to respond to pressures from below rather than by imposing pressure on society from above. Under these circumstances the religious groups became the modest beneficiaries of the vast upheaval of 1968 and its antecedents. It is doubtful that the religious questions were considered particularly significant at a time when the priorities were the economy, nationhood and the role of the C.P.C. in a socialist state with a human face. Evidence for this can be found in the blueprint for the Reform of 1968, the far-reaching Action Programme of April 1968 which did not address itself specifically to the issue of churches and religion. Still, there were some discernible developments that came with the 1968 reforms.

Since Czechoslovakia was experimenting in 'socialist humanism', under which believers and non-believers were accorded an equal role towards the betterment of man, a considerable measure of religious freedom was realised shortly after Dubček came into power. Socialism with a human face, as it was called, sought to free man from within, to give him a new look, a new identity. The same philosophy was expressed for the Protestants by Professor Joseph Hromádka, and the Roman Catholics through the themes expressed by Pope John XXIII, especially in his *Pacem in Terris* encyclical.

Several significant steps were undertaken towards the renewal and rehabilitation of the Greek Catholic Church. On 13 June 1968 the Prague Government discussed the problem and in a decree stated that the unresolved questions would be handled democratically and humanely during the following six months. As a result the Uniates received moral as well as financial support and by

8 September 1969 some 248 Greek Catholic parishes had been brought to life again. Yet the Church encountered all sorts of obstacles. It was a religious organisation without leadership – for eighteen years the Church had functioned underground without a bishop or ordained priests. So, for example, when one of the local priests returned from a forced labour camp to his village, he had to perform thirty-six weddings at his first Sunday service. Although the Uniates lost some of their freedom and privileges after the occupation of August 1968, nevertheless strong religious conviction continued to live on.

For those who sought more rapid reforms, measures such as those pertaining to the Greek Catholic Church were wholly inadequate. Many felt that the Dubček regime was procrastinating. For example, the last release of a clergyman from prison and the reopening of some old seminaries did not take place until seven months after Dubček came to power. Nevertheless religious reforms were considerable. Charity homes, which had been under direct political supervision since the 1950s, were, in April 1968, permitted to manage themselves without supervision. Scores of priests were once again assigned to previously abandoned parishes. Religious processions celebrating the festival of Corpus Christi were held once again in such traditionally Catholic towns as Levoča and Staré Hory. In eastern Slovakia 83 churches and 47 parish houses were built in 1968. *Katolícke noviny* (The Catholic Gazette) again became a popular newspaper with a circulation of over 80,000 and the Society of St Albert printed over one million calendars that year. Several new churches were started and the Catholic Action movement was dissolved and replaced by a new organisation, 'Dielo koncolovej obdoby' (The Work of Council Renewal), which also sought to play a political role in the country, but far different from its predecessor. According to the new organisation's leader, Chaplain Rudolf Baláž, the preceding twenty years marked the period of a feudal oppression and, therefore, the new movement aimed at restoring normal Church–State relations. Many of its members were young priests who became activists during 1968.[16]

Other religious groups, too, sought remedies for past injustices. When the 16th Synod of the Evangelical Church of Bohemian Brethren convened on 19–22 February 1969 in Prague, it lodged several complaints against the political system. Specifically, the

Synod charged that the admission of only three students annually to the Comenius Divinity College was not enough; that press coverage and the handling of religious education were demeaning and inadequate; that consultation on the selection of new church dignitaries be conducted with the political authorities *after*, not before, the voting; and finally, that retiring evangelicals be entitled to their own homes. Some at the Synod went as far as to seek the abrogation of the fundamental laws of 1949, but subsequently a more cautious stand was agreed upon which addressed itself to the questions of supervision and economic matters, such as the plea for higher remuneration for the clergy. The Synod also called for the abolition of the death penalty, the ratification of the U.N. Universal Declaration of Human Rights, and expressed openly its reservations about some of the contemporary manifestations of anti-Semitism.[17]

THE C.P.C. AND RELIGION AFTER DUBČEK

The primary aim of the ruling *élite* since April 1969 has been to make the C.P.C. again the undisputed power in the State. The post-Dubček regime was willing to employ any means at any cost towards that objective. One of the immediate tasks facing the new leadership was to achieve an effective method of socialisation which would eliminate any alien influences exerted upon the Czech and Slovak people during the Dubček era, including influence by the Church. At the same time, however, the regime moved swiftly to consolidate the clergy in a manner that would make them responsive to Party directives.

After several sharp clashes of opinion on the question of ideology and religion, the C.P.C. took the conservative position that there is no difference between religion as a form of protest and religion as an opiate. Thus the views of such Communists as Erika Kadlecová, a prominent sociologist, who headed the Government's secretariat for religious affairs under Dubček, were condemned as misguided humanist views. Since religious ideologies – which are passed on to the younger generations primarily through their parents – were considered responsible for the retardation of the thinking of man, it had become the function of political socialisation to prevent such deterioration in the society in the future. The guidelines for this policy were atheistic upbringing, re-education of the people in a scientific world outlook, and Communist morality. Consequently schools were now charged with additional responsibilities, especially in Slovakia where 70 per cent of the population showed strong religious convictions, to explain to the pupils that religion contributes much to the psychosis of fear and inferiority.[18] The party now also insisted that religious education in Czechoslovakia in fact never ceased, although the enrolment levels in religious classes continued downward through the early 1960s.[19]

The first decisive steps towards consolidation of religious education were taken on 1 June 1970. On that day a set of directives was issued with the aim of strengthening the scientific *Weltanschauung* and to cut down on the number of pupils receiving religious instruction. Surveys conducted that year showed that religious instruction at different schools was most often requested by the children of physicians, members of the police and the army. The publication of these survey findings evidently led these and other parents to withdraw their children from religious classes in 1971. Other means were employed by the authorities to lower the enrolment in religious instruction, including the discouragement by school directors of the parents seeking religious instruction for their childen, as well as the reporting of parents to the political authorities if their children showed great trust in the Church.

Recently the Ministry of Education recommended to school administrators that they concentrate their attention on children between the first and sixth grades. While educators are admonished not to eliminate religious instruction altogether, they are also told not to have too many pupils enrolled in classes on religion. Teachers are warned that if their own children seek religious instruction, this will be *prima facie* evidence of their parents' weak adherence to Marxism–Leninism. The Ministry inspectors shall take note of such instances and appropriate action – no doubt dismissal – will follow.[20]

In order to clear up some of the shortcomings of the previous directives, more stringent ones were issued in August 1971 for all basic one-year schools. These new directives were designed to make it still more difficult for children to acquire religious instruction. Declaring that religious instruction is not a legitimate subject-matter in the school curriculum, the directives stated that it may be conducted in schools by any state-approved religious group.

Children between the second and seventh grades are eligible to apply; but their application form must be signed by *both* parents – a requirement which is likely to be a deterrent in those homes where the career of one signatory may be impaired or where religious differences exist. Instruction is to be conducted only by approved personnel, certified by the regional national committees. In cases where there is a lack of adequate personnel, lay persons offering religious instruction may seek the approval of the national committee's cultural section. In all cases, however, the Secretariat for Religious Affairs of the Ministry of Culture has the final word. The clergy shall teach without pay, whereas the non-clergy are to be paid from the funds of the religious organisations. Strict hours of instruction were imposed, again in order to limit the enrolment. Thus in classes with more than sixteen pupils, two hours weekly are permitted; if, however, less than sixteen pupils are in a class, then only one hour per month is allowed.[21] The provision whereby instruction in religion can begin only after all other requirements have been met – which is at least one month after the start of the school year – has tended to limit enrolment in religious classes.

It is evident from the new directives that the surge of religious interest and activity during the Dubček era caused considerable alarm among the ruling *élite*. In order to inculcate atheism in the society more fully, a widely co-ordinated attack on religion was launched through the media of broadcasting, television, print, film and the theatre; the schools, however, were given the main role to play in this campaign.

Another significant development of the post-1969 era was the renewed effort to harass the clergy of the Roman Catholic Church so that they would become fully responsive to political commands. The anti-Catholic campaign began in early 1970 with a Radio Prague dispatch which claimed that some sixty progressive clergy – no names were mentioned – publicly disassociated themselves from the policies of the Dubček period. Then a new political screening was announced, according to which all clergy interested in the continuation of their services had to present a certificate showing a 'clean' police record. In addition other restrictions, freedom, communication and travel, were imposed on the priests. As for the retired priests and those engaged in manual labour, they were forbidden to say mass, even in private, without prior permission from the state authorities. Most novices inducted during the liberalisation period were dismissed and the nuns were once again restricted to nursing.[22] Measures were also taken to limit the training of religious personnel, whose numbers had almost doubled during the Dubček period. In 1970 the total enrolment in all Czechoslovak religious schools was 815 students, 71 of whom were female.[23] In Slovakia, in the autumn of 1971, 120 men sought admission to seminaries but only 12 were admitted.

While the Roman Catholic Church suffered the most, other religious groups had their share of troubles after 1969. The status of the Greek Catholic Church today appears precarious, and a gradual reversal of the 1968 rapprochement may be contemplated. Many articles published in Czechoslovakia have expressed reservations about the revival of the Uniate Church following the 13 June 1968 liberalisation. Several authors noted that within Christianity as a whole attempts have been made to reconcile the differences separating the Eastern and Western Churches. The meeting of Paul VI and Patriarch Athenagoras on 5 January 1964 was recalled so as to suggest the reconciliation between Orthodoxy and Rome will make the Uniate Church irrelevant in the long run.[24]

The Jews of Czechoslovakia have also apparently experienced restrictions in the post-Dubček era. The year 1969 marked the millennium of Jewry in what is today Czechoslovakia, but at the April 1969 session of the representatives of various Jewish communities, a terse announcement revealed the postponement of the millennial celebrations. Instead the community activities were channelled into some cultural undertakings and the improvement of the appearance of the Terezín ghetto. Still, the brief mention of the postponement evoked a lively discussion in the Jewish communities in Czechoslovakia and abroad.[25]

Other religious groups felt pressures from the Government, too. For example, the paper *Kostnické jiskry* of 5 January 1972 apologised to its readers for its irregular publication schedule during the preceding year and announced the suspension of its publication due 'to the exhaustion of the allocated quantity of paper,' terminating the volume with only thirty-three instead of the customary fifty-two issues.

One of the most successful, government endorsed, religious movements today is *Pacem in Terris*. It emphasises secular activities in the country and views the institution of the State as 'God's instrument for leadership towards well-being'.[26] However, not all of the Catholic clergy consider the movement a positive instrument of the Roman Catholic Church. As long as it helps the regime more than it does the Church, the critics are reluctant to promote *Pacem in Terris*.

CONCLUSIONS

In Czechoslovakia since 1969 the ruling *élite* has once again chosen to emphasise coercive measures against religion, and their rationale in support of such measures has often been rather simplistic. Only during the 1968 liberalisation did it seem possible to alter the assymmetrical pattern of Church–State conflict which has been the role in Communist Czechoslovakia. The writings of Erika Kadlecová exemplify an alternative – religion and Marxism could coexist and compete for the same goals of man. While committed to the ultimate desirability of atheism, Kadlecová seems to have grasped that the atheistic stance is in itself complex – unlike those who tend to see it as a religious experience in reverse – and that its achievement must somehow be an enriching experience for man, and that the campaign to reach that goal must not be divisive but carried out in a spirit of confidence without alienation.[27] Kadlecová wished to explain the particular manifestations of religion in Czechoslovakia along with its differentiated manifestations within the different strata of the population and its evolution during recent history. Although the social order had changed, she estimated that religiosity in various forms existed in some 40 per cent of the population and suggested that to diminish this figure posed a challenge of inordinate complexity. 'These citizens are in a certain sense immune to the old methods of atheistic propaganda and the ideological struggle for their consciousness and attitude will be more complex, more difficult and prolonged.'[28] This observation by a first-rate scholar and member of the C.P.C. is completely ignored by the present policy makers on religious affairs. To view religiosity as a carryover from the past is too weak an explanation for its existence, yet this appears to be the basic premise behind the steps taken to cut down on religious education in Czechoslovakia today. In fact, to view religion as some sort of a vestigial remain is seen by many critics as an attempt to revive pre-Marxist or even pre-Feuerbachian atheism which looked upon religion in the context of dupes and swindlers.

According to the Czechoslovak critics of religion, the reasons for the continued appeal of religion to the individual are several. Among these are the normative aspects of religion, the importance accorded the ordinary man in various religious observances, the continued appeal to women on account of their still largely private and isolated existence, and the like. In short, religion still constitutes a response to various forms of alienation, including the alienation by the system. In this respect, then, it is significant to note that higher levels of education do not necessarily eliminate religiosity; in fact, a higher number of educated people in Czechoslovakia as elsewhere are churchgoers. Several studies undertaken in the late 1960s confirm these findings. A recent study for Slovakia, reported in the quarterly of the Sociological Institute of the Slovak Academy of Sciences, points towards a gradual decline in the intensity of religiosity, but atheism does not show a commensurate gain. According to this study, 70·7 per cent of the population in Slovakia are still believers.[29]

For the time being, however, the implications of these studies for policy making go unheeded. But, just as in 1968, when the problems that gave rise to that fateful year multiplied and the policy makers were forced to cope with them constructively, so it may be in the future when the atmosphere for reconciliation is more favourable that the ruling *élite* will once again be forced to return to resolve the problems of Church–State relations.

NOTES

1. For a discussion of this problem, see J. Milton Yinger, *The Scientific Study of Religion* (New York: Macmillan, 1970), especially Chapter 18.
2. See Vratislav Bušek and Nicolas Spulber (eds.), *Czechoslovakia* (New York: Frederick A. Praeger, 1957), p. 141. At the present time there are 18 recognised religious organisations in Č.S.S.R.: the Roman Catholic Church; Orthodox Catholic Church; Czechoslovak Hussite Church; Jewish committees; Czechoslovak Evangelical Brethren; Union of Brethren; Church of the Brethren; Silesian Evangelical Church; Slovak Evangelical Church of Augsburg Confession; Reformed Christian Church of Slovakia; Evangelical Methodist Church; Union of Baptist Brethren; Unitarians; Seventh Day Adventists; Old Catholic Church; Christian Gatherings; and the Greek Catholic Church. See Dr Jaroslav Hájek, 'Socialistický stát, cirkve a náboženské společnosti' (Socialist State, Churches and Religious Societies), *Nová Mysl*, special ed., No. 1 (February 1972), p. 116.

3. 'Die Situation der Kirche in der Č.S.S.R.' (mimeo.) released by Studiengesellschaft für Fragen mittel- und osteuropäischer Partnerschaft (Bonn, 1971), p. 4.

4. See Jaroslava Radouchová, 'Československý stát a katolická cirkev po únoru 1948' (The Czechoslovak State and the Catholic Church after February, 1948) *Revue dejin socialismu*, No. 1 (March 1969), pp. 37–62 and Ludvík Němec, 'The Communist Ecclesiology During the Church–State Relationship in Czechoslovakia, 1945–1967', *Proceedings of the American Philosophical Society*, Vol. 112 (15 August 1968), pp. 245–76.

5. Mgr Montini is now Pope Paul VI. Reference in J. Radouchová, *op. cit.*, p. 42.

6. *Ibid.*, p. 43.

7. In reply to Archbishop Beran's complaint, Interior Minister Václav Nosek claimed that they were placed there either by the foreign press or some secret control organ of the Church. This reply alone suggests the configuration of forces at this time. See Radouchová, *op. cit.*, p. 44.

8. Quoted in *ibid.*, p. 45.

9. See, for example, Bohdan Chudoba, 'Czech Protestants and Communism', *America* (12 November 1949), pp. 149–51.

10. Němec, *Proceedings of the American Philosophical Society*, pp. 258–9.

11. When Czechoslovakia was created in 1918 there were approximately 555,000 Greek Catholics of whom some 180,000 belonged to the Prešov eparchy. Although the Greek Catholic Church in Subcarpathian Ruthenia was abolished in 1949, about one fifth of the parishes that traditionally belonged to the Mukačevo–Užhorod eparchy remained active in south-eastern Slovakia. In 1948 there were about 300,000 Uniates in all of Czechoslovakia; approximately 235,000 of those belonged to the Prešov eparchy; the rest belonged to the eparchy of Užhorod; and some fell under the apostolic administration of Szatmár in Hungary. See Ivan Marianov, 'Greckokatolícka cirkev v Č.S,S.R.' (The Greek Catholic Church in the Č.S.S.R.) *Obroda*, No. 3, (29 January 1969), p. 15.

12. 'Die Situation der Kirche in der Č.S.S.R.', p. 4.

13. See Johannes Hoffner, *Kirche in der Č.S.S.R.* (Munich: Sozialwerk der Ackermann-Gemeinde, 1970), pp. 39–40.

14. See James F. Drane, 'The Church', *America* (30 November 1968), p. 548.

15. *The New York Times*, 18 October 1967.

16. See, for example, Ján Hadvičák, '"Svätí" križiaci v boji proti komunizmu' (The 'Holy' Crusaders in the Struggle against Communism), *Pravda* (Bratislava), 30 July 1971, p. 4.

17. Zdeněk Salaquarda, 'Evangelíci v politickem životě' (The Evangelicals in Political Life), *Zemědelské noviny*, 25 February 1969, p. 3.

18. See B. Kuchár, 'Náboženstvo podporuje deformácije vo vývine emocii' (Religion Aids Deformation of Emotional Development), *Pravda*, 2 February 1972, p. 3, as well as *Pravda* articles of 1 and 3 February.

19. According to one report, the number of school children registered for religious instruction in Czechoslovakia was only 4 per cent in 1964, but because of the gradual thaw after that year, in Slovakia it rose to 38 per cent and the Czech lands to 13 per cent by 1967. (Radio Bratislava, 19 September 1969, reported in *RFE Czechoslovak Situation Report*, No. 39, 27 October 1971, p. 7.) In 1970, however, religious instruction rose from 14 to 22 per cent in Bohemia and Moravia, and from 38 to 52 per cent in Slovakia. (Hájek, *op. cit.*, p. 117.)

20. For this remarkably forthright statement, see Jozef Melichár and Bohumil Bičan, 'MŠ SSR o prihlasovania na náboženstvo' (Ministry of Education of Slovakia about the Application for Religious Instruction) *Učitelské noviny*, No. 25 (17 June 1971), p. 4.

21. See 'Směrnice ministerstva kultúry' (Directives of the Ministry of Culture), *Věstník Ministerstva školství a Ministerstva kultúry Č.S.S.R.*, 16 (332) (9 August 1971), p. 146.
22. 'Peace Priests Surface Again', *America*, 30 May 1970.
23. *Kostnické jiskry*, 7 April 1971, p. 3.
24. Dr Alexander Horák, 'Spája nás jeden krst Pánov ...' (We are Joined by One Christening of the Lord), *Katolícke noviny*, 24 January 1971, p. 3.
25. See *Věstník židovských náboženských obcí v Č.S.S.R.*, No. 5 (May 1969), p. 3.
26. *Katolícke noviny*, 21 November 1971, p. 1.
27. See Erika Kadlecová, *Bozí a lidé* (Gods and People), (Prague: Nakladatelství politické literatury, 1966), especially pp. 423–79.
28. *Ibid.*, p. 433.
29. Reported in *Czechoslovak Press Survey*, No. 2308 (84), Radio Free Europe Research, 11 May 1970, pp. 1–19.

15 Towards Normalisation of Church–State Relations in Hungary

LESLIE LASZLO

The heroic but futile Hungarian revolution of 1956 was followed by severe repression and the reimposition of Communist Party domination in all spheres of public activity. The Churches,[1] which during the turbulent days of the uprising seized the opportunity to regain their freedom, were gradually brought back under control and made again to serve the purposes of the militantly atheistic regime's domestic and foreign policies. During the Revolution, the clerical collaborators and fellow-travellers, members of the Communist sponsored 'Peace Movement of the Clergy', who served as the chief tool of subversion within the Churches under the Rákosi regime,[2] had been removed from their key positions on order of Cardinal Mindszenty. The 'purge' in the Protestant Churches was accomplished by their respective synods. Soon both these groups returned to their abandoned posts.[3] The State Office for Church Affairs, established in 1951 with full powers over all church institutions and personnel, resumed its functions and declared that it 'would take under its protection those priests who have been relieved of their duties because of their progressive views'.[4] In March 1957 the Presidential Council issued a decree which in effect annulled all ecclesiastical appointments made since 1 October 1956 and made all future appointments subject to state approval.[5] In the following months scores of priests and ministers were arrested on charges of having participated in the 'counter-revolution' and many others were removed from their positions and replaced by collaborators, nicknamed 'peace priests'. When, in September 1957, Pope Pius XII issued a directive to the Hungarian Catholic clergy in which he explicitly forbade participation in political activity, the Government accused the Vatican of interference in the internal affairs of Hungary and insisted that three notorious 'peace priests' take their seats in parliament. When the Holy See placed the three under most severe interdict, the Government prevented the church authorities from enforcing the ban and rewarded the excommunicated priest-parliamentarians – who in defiance of Rome continued to say mass and dispense the sacraments – with lucrative appointments and high honours.[6]

Simultaneously with the reimposition of control over church administration and personnel, a vigorous indoctrination campaign was launched with the avowed aim to extirpate religion and inculcate atheism, especially in the youth. Registration for religious instruction, which in 1957 embraced 80 and 90 per cent of the pupils in all elementary and high schools,[7] was subsequently reduced through administrative trickery, coupled with intimidation of students and parents, to under 10 per cent.[8] While religious belief was ceaselessly assaulted and the Churches were persecuted, the leaders of all religious denominations were called upon to praise the Government and thank it for its generosity towards the Churches – exactly as they were wont to do under the Stalinist regime of Mátyás Rákosi before the 1956 revolution. The intimidated and by now thoroughly conditioned church leaders complied with abject servility. They gave public blessing to the forcible collectivisation of the countryside,[9] took active part in the so-called peace campaign, praising the great Soviet Union as the defender of peace while denouncing the U.S.A. as an aggressive imperialist power.[10] In short, by 1960 the pre-revolutionary *status quo* was fully restored, the Churches were reduced once again to impotence and subservience *vis-à-vis* the Government. The church policies of János Kádár seemed to follow the prescriptions of his predecessor and erstwhile mentor, Mátyás Rákosi, in whose prisons he suffered unspeakable degradation and tortures.[11]

THE VATICAN AGREEMENT OF 1964

The initial phase of Kádár's attempt to rebuild the shattered Communist power structure in Hungary was accompanied by a vicious campaign against the 'counter-revolutionaries' and 'revisionists', culminating in the judicial murder of Imre Nagy and his associates in June 1958. This was followed by a thorough purge of the Stalinist 'dogmatists', as the loyal followers of the former party boss Rákosi were now labelled. The task of crushing both leftist and rightist 'deviationists' thus accomplished, and his enemies out of the way, the workers' councils suppressed, the peasants safely locked into the kolkhozes, János Kádár, secure in Khrushchev's unequivocal support, quite unexpectedly embarked on a new policy of national reconciliation, best expressed in his famous slogan first enunciated in December 1961: 'Whoever is not against us is with us.' The 'new' Kádár, who now became benignly tolerant towards his subjects' ideologically not always correct preferences in tastes and mores, was pursuing moderate 'centrist' policies and visibly courted popular acceptance. The unprecedented freedom permitted artists and intellectuals, just as the daring economic innovations under the sign of 'goulash communism', were designed to make his regime palatable and help people to forget its terrible birth amid treachery and blood.[12]

As an integral part of his policy of achieving a true 'socialist national unity' Kádár made new peace overtures towards the Churches calling for improvement in Church–State relations and the solution of all outstanding questions 'in a mutually acceptable way, namely, with full respect for the laws and legal order of the State, but also taking into consideration the internal laws and order of the Church'.[13] A real departure from earlier practice became manifest when the Hungarian Government approached the Vatican offering to negotiate – it should be recalled that the previous 'agreement', still in force today, which legalised the total enslavement of the Church in return for promises of religious freedom and financial support was forced upon the bishops in 1950 without allowing them to consult the Pope and obtain his consent.[14]

In a sense this development was in line with the Kremlin's renewed emphasis on peaceful coexistence with the non-Communist world. Khrushchev, who on his home territory waged a relentless battle against religion, made repeated friendly gestures towards the Vatican. He permitted some Lithuanian prelates, together with a delegation from the Russian Orthodox Church, to attend the Vatican Council – the latter as observers. Then in February 1963 the ranking archbishop of the Ukrainian Uniate Church, Josyf

Slipyj of Lviv, was released from Soviet captivity and allowed to go to Rome where he was given a cardinal's hat. Pope John XXIII reciprocated these favours by receiving Khrushchev's son-in-law, Alexei Adzhubei, together with his wife, in private audience and by sending Franz Cardinal König, Archbishop of Vienna, on a goodwill tour in several of the Eastern European countries.

The ice was broken and for the first time since 1948 two Hungarian bishops, accompanied by five priests and two lay Catholics, were permitted to go to Rome to attend the first session of the Council which opened on 11 October 1962. Shortly thereafter representatives of the Vatican Secretariat of State travelled to Budapest on the invitation of the Hungarian Government.

It seems that the regime was prompted towards rapprochement with the Vatican by both domestic and foreign policy considerations. On the domestic scene Kádár must have realised that any genuine reconciliation with the Catholic clergy and faithful whose support he was now actively seeking,[15] would be impossible without papal approval. At the same time, parallel with his efforts of gaining popular endorsement for his policies at home, Kádár expended great effort to convince the international community of his regime's legitimacy.[16] Following the brutal suppression of the 1956 revolution the 'Hungarian question' was raised year after year in the United Nations, while the validity of the Hungarian U.N. delegation's credentials remained in dispute. Western and some Third World Governments ostentatiously shunned Hungary in their diplomatic dealings. At a time when in the neighbouring Communist states the U.S. diplomatic missions were raised to the ambassadorial level, the United States legation in Budapest was headed by a mere chargé d'affaires: a pointed reminder of Washington's displeasure with Kádár's Hungary. Under such circumstances to open up negotiations with the Church and win recognition from the Holy See must have seemed a good way for Kádár to show the world that the situation in Hungary had returned to normalcy and the regime was gaining international respectability.[17] In respect to relations with the United States, government spokesmen openly expressed hope that once the fate of József Cardinal Mindszenty was settled with the Vatican – meaning his removal from the United States' legation in Budapest – the greatest stumbling-block in the way to improvement of

Hungarian–U.S. relations would disappear.[18] Kádár apparently believed that the road to Washington would lead through Rome.

The negotiations thus begun with hopeful expectations ran almost immediately into a snag, due to Cardinal Mindszenty's categorical refusal to leave his sanctuary unless certain conditions were met by the Government. These included the restoration of full freedom to the Church and also a demand for his total rehabilitation, namely, that the Government should declare his innocence of the alleged crimes for which he was convicted to life imprisonment in 1949.[19] The regime, which for years used Mindszenty as its bogeyman, making him the real villain behind the 1956 'counter-revolution', accusing him of seeking to recover all the former wealth of the Church, including the great latifundia, in order to create the basis for a clerico-fascist dictatorship in Hungary, must have found it now well-nigh impossible to declare all the accusations against the Cardinal null and void and proclaim him innocent. The resulting deadlock was only broken when both sides agreed on side-stepping the issue by removing the so-called 'Mindszenty question' from the agenda, to be dealt with separately at a more appropriate time in the future. In the end, after one and a half years of negotiations, a partial agreement was signed in Budapest on 15 September 1964, by Monsignor Agostino Casaroli, Under-Secretary of the Sacred Congregation of Special Ecclesiastical Affairs, and by József Prantner, Chairman of the State Office for Church Affairs in Hungary.

Actually there were two documents signed on this occasion: an act (referred to by the Vatican as '*atto*') containing those points on which agreement had been reached, and a protocol ('*protocollo*') which listed those outstanding issues to which no solution was found.[20] The agreement ('*atto*') dealt with three subjects: (a) it listed the names of the new bishops who were to administer a number of vacant dioceses; (b) it specified that the loyalty oath demanded by the Government from the bishops and the clergy would be valid and binding only in as much as the constitution and the laws were not contrary to Christian faith and morals; (c) it settled the status of the Papal Hungarian Ecclesiastical Institute located on the second floor of the Hungarian Academy in Rome. For sixteen years the Institute was occupied by Hungarian émigré priests, to the great annoyance of the Communists living on the lower and upper floors of the Academy. Already in 1952 the

Hungarian Government had decreed the suppression of the Institute and ever since had tried to evict the 'squatters' from the second floor who in turn invoked papal protection and had behind them the goodwill of the Italian authorities. The Institute was now returned to the jurisdiction of the Hungarian Bench of Bishops, the émigrés had to vacate the premises on order from the Pope, while the Government pledged to maintain the Institute and to permit at least one priest from each Hungarian diocese to study there.[21]

The text of the protocol was not disclosed, the official communique stating only that both sides expressed in it their respective views on all issues which were raised during the negotiations but on which no agreement could be reached. Presumably this document was to serve as a basis for further negotiations. Anyone familiar with the well-publicised grievances of the Catholic Church in Hungary would be able to guess the content of the protocol. In fact, the leaders of the Catholic clergy engaged in pastoral work among Hungarians residing in Western Europe issued an official statement with the list of the outstanding issues which had to be settled before a genuinely good relationship could develop between Church and State in Hungary.[22] The essential points of the list are the following:

(a) The fate of Cardinal Mindszenty.

(b) Freedom of communication between the bishops and the Holy See. At the time of the signing of the partial agreement only 9 bishops out of the 19 invited were permitted to attend the third session of Vatican II.

(c) The fate of the bishops exiled from their dioceses. In spite of the general amnesty granted on 4 April 1963, and even after the Vatican agreement, the bishops of Vác and Veszprém (besides, of course, the archbishop of Esztergom, Cardinal Mindszenty) were not permitted to return to their sees.

(d) Recognition of the Pope's right to appoint bishops. The Government continued in its refusal to accept the appointment of Mgr Gellért Bellon who was named bishop by Pope Pius XII in 1959, and prevented his consecration.

(e) The freedom of bishops to administer their dioceses without interference from the State Office for Church Affairs which has its officials in every episcopal chancery whose function is to control the bishop's activities.

(f) The fate of the 'Peace Movement of the Clergy'. The Vatican considers this government-sponsored collaborationist movement as the most dangerous challenge to church unity and discipline, contrary to Canon Law, and wishes to bring back the defiant priests under obedience to their bishops.

(g) The freedom of religious instruction and the free exercise of religion. This is the greatest grievance of the Church. In spite of the freedoms guaranteed in the constitution of 1949 and subsequent legislation, religious instruction has been practically eliminated from city schools and severely restricted in the villages. Religious instruction outside the schools, even in the church or in the parish hall, is considered conspiracy against the State and the priest, or whoever is in charge, is thrown into jail. People who participate in religious services are discriminated against, e.g. denied admission to the universities, while large categories of employees, notably certain classes of civil servants and practically all educators, are expressly forbidden to attend church.

(h) The status of the religious orders and the fate of their members. Over 10,000 monks and nuns were evicted from their monasteries, convents, schools and hospitals in 1950. In the agreement concluded between the Government and the bishops later that year eight schools (out of some 3,000) were restored to the Catholic Church and three male and one female religious order were permitted to reoccupy two houses each and to provide the faculty for two schools each. The membership of these four orders is severely restricted and each one is permitted to admit only two candidates per year. The rest of the surviving religious orders, comprising several thousand priests, teachers, nurses, etc., are working in government-controlled co-operatives, producing gloves and various other textile articles for scandalously low wages.

(i) Finally, there was no agreement in regard to the Church's insistence on its right to have freedom to establish and maintain schools, hospitals and other charitable institutions; visit the sick in the hospitals, prisoners in jails; and to organise religious associations; to create a free Catholic press.

In view of the many unfulfilled expectations, the agreement signed was perceived by the Church as containing very meagre results indeed. The chief Vatican negotiator, Mgr Agostino Casaroli, admitted as much in his description of the negotiations in the 19 September 1964 issue of the *Osservatore Romano*. According to him, it would be misleading to claim that a *modus vivendi* between the Vatican and the Hungarian State had been achieved. The partial agreement falls even short of being an accord (*accordo*), and could only be called an 'agreement' on the practical solution of a few selected concrete problems, without clearing up the differences between the two parties regarding the legal principles involved. For example, agreement was reached on five individuals to be named bishops without the Holy See accepting, or the Hungarian Government abandoning its Decree No. 22/1957 which made all episcopal appointments subject to the approval of the Presidential Council of the Hungarian People's Republic.

On the other hand, one should not forget that these were the first bishops consecrated in Hungary since 1951, a sorely needed reinforcement of the legitimate hierarchy of the Church which had been depleted by death, illness, senility and forced absence of bishops from their dioceses to such an extent that before the agreement there was barely one or two normally functioning bishops left in the entire country.[23] Furthermore, it remains a fact that with all its limitations the partial agreement of 1964 was the first such document negotiated and publicly signed by a Communist Government and the Papacy, although one should mention that the Vatican was simultaneously conducting talks also with Belgrade and Prague. On the occasion of the signing ceremony Mgr Casaroli spoke with guarded optimism of the expectations which the Holy See attached to the document.

> The Holy See wishes to see in this agreement not the goal achieved but the starting point to further negotiations. That does not mean that it does not appreciate the results obtained. However, the continuation of the work that has been started depends on whether the Government of the Hungarian

People's Republic and the Holy See keep their assumed obligations. There is no lack of goodwill on the part of the Holy See. The sole concern of the Holy See is directed towards securing the rights and freedom of the Church, as well as the interests and spiritual welfare of the Catholics in Hungary; and it does this in the conviction that in this way it will contribute in all spheres of life to the development of the country.[24]

On the Government side, the Chairman of the State Office for Church Affairs, József Prantner, seemed more pleased and, perhaps, more sanguine in his appraisal of the regime's prestige gains due to the agreement:

> This agreement furthers the continuing improvement of relations between the State and the Roman Catholic Church. ... We note with satisfaction that in regard to some questions a more realistic appreciation of the development of the Hungarian People's Republic prevailed also in the Vatican and, due to the growing prestige of the socialist states it (the Vatican) showed willingness to regulate relations. ... In continuing this realistic policy it will be possible to settle also other questions in the relationship between State and Church which still await solutions.[25]

CONFUSION ON THE IDEOLOGICAL FRONT

The Kádár regime went out of its way in publicising the newly-found good *entente* with the Vatican. Commentators praised the significance of the event and pictures showed the papal emissary surrounded by happily smiling Government officials. While the Communists thus created the impression that the rapprochement with the Church corresponded to their most sincere wishes and expressed gratification over the successful signing of the agreement, that same policy unexpectedly landed them in a quandary as to the proper ideological 'line' that could be understood and followed by the rank and file of the Party. Apparently there was some confusion among the Party cadres, quite a number of whom, seeing the Government's friendly gestures towards the Vatican and the Churches,[26] accepted the loud pronouncements about freedom of religion at face value and concluded that religion had been 'rehabilitated'; everybody was now free to go to church and to enrol his child for religious instruction at school.[27] An editorial entitled 'The Ideological Offensive of Marxism' in the monthly *Társadalmi Szemle* (Social Review) took up the cudgel against this erroneous view, reminding the readers of the party's continued commitment to the eradication of religion and to education along strictly atheistic lines. In the words of the editorial:

> Recently there has been confusion in some of the party organisations regarding this question. This happened because in some places – where they can conceive the fight against religion only in a simplistic fashion – they misunderstand the normalisation of relations between the State and the Churches, certain changes in the Vatican's stand, the recently concluded agreement between our State and the Vatican. . . . This is why the conference on ideology deemed it necessary to recall to attention: religion remains a retrograde world-view also in our days, and the ideological fight against religion continues to be the daily task in our ideological work.[28]

Also the correct meaning of the constitutionally guaranteed freedom of conscience had to be explained, lest the citizens, and even Party members, would think that it applied equally to believers and non-believers. Reproaching Party members who shy away from exercising their freedom of conscience to voice their atheistic conviction in the combat against religion, a Party ideologue characterised the situation

> as if in some Party organisations confusion reigned in regard to the anti-religion enlightenment activities. It seems that they do not see clearly the tasks of atheistic educational work and its principal methods. Their clear perception should not be obscured by the newest normalisation of Church–State relations. Although the leaders of the Church today do not oppose our State any longer, our constructive work, or the principal questions regarding the defence of peace, in our homeland this does not mean that in numerous areas of life the ideological struggle has ceased . . . the task of our age is to do our work in such a way that people who are still believers should be liberated from the opium of religion.[29]

The journal of the Hungarian atheists *Világosság* (Light), commenting on the partial agreement, warned that

> from the conclusion of the agreement, of course, it does not follow that we would approve if one should confuse the good relations between the believing and non-believing builders of socialism with the peaceful coexistence of religion and Marxism, with the dissolution of their ideological antagonism. On the contrary: exactly in order that the Catholic masses could participate with growing activity in the constructive work which aims also at assuring their welfare, it is necessary to debate their views; to help their further development in the direction of socialism. To help them also to combat the religious limitations of their ideas.[30]

That the confusion was widespread is evident from the spate of articles, especially in the provincial press, dealing with the problem of religion and atheism. One writer complained that 'in recent times we can meet with increasing frequency views which, misinterpreting our present social development, maintain that religion and Marxism had been reconciled and united into a common unified ideology'.[31] Another provincial paper reported that when at a Party meeting a Communist father was questioned about how he was able to reconcile his Marxist ideology with having his child baptised, his reply was: 'After all, the Churches too are participating in the much hailed broad co-operation in our political life, and so I thought that nowadays adherence to religious beliefs would not play a part in judging Party members, as it used to in older times.'[32] The Party leadership was clearly alarmed by such 'incorrect' conclusions drawn from its coexistence policy *vis-à-vis* the Churches. There was complaint that

> in several Party organisations they don't see clearly the tasks and methods in the struggle against the religious world-view. From the normalisation of Church–State relations, the negotiations with the Vatican, the partial agreement, the priestly peace movement, the growth in the number of loyal priests, the flexibility of the Churches and their striving for modernisation, as well as from a number of other facts, some even among the Communists deduced the wrong conclusions . . .[33]

The need for authoritative Party directives became pressing. The correct interpretation was spelled out in the official 'Guidelines for Ideological Work' which were adopted at the meeting of the Central Committee Plenum held on 11–13 March 1965. The relevant passage reads:

> In recent times we noted that in many places they do not see clearly the tasks and correct methods of spreading our scientific world-view at the time when in our homeland it came to further normalisation of relations between the State and the Churches. In our homeland the State is ready to continue to co-operate with the Churches in numerous areas of social life. In the framework of socialist national co-operation the Communists and non-party materialists work together with the believers. In our state and social organisations and institutions we co-operate also with the clergy. However, we continue to criticise the political stand and activity of ecclesiastics when these mirror strivings contrary to our policies which are the expression of the interests of the entire population.[34]

In plain language: co-operation is welcome, but the Communists reserve for themselves the right to 'criticise the Churches'. On the other hand, there is no mention of the right of the Churches to criticise, or oppose, Communist policies.

Actually, the regime's response to the challenge of ideological erosion was twofold: on the one hand, a stepped up ideological campaign, including greater stress on atheistic materialism in all school curricula[35] and, on the other hand, a return to terroristic methods against churchmen and believers who were bold enough to test the sincerity of the Government's policy of religious toleration. Since the signing of the partial agreement scores of priests had been arrested in almost regular intervals and charged with conspiracy.[36] Their trials were invariably held *in camera,* but enough had transpired to show that their true 'crime' consisted of spreading religious views, distributing devotional literature, and having given religious instruction for the young 'illegally', although this was often done at the explicit request and always with the consent of the parents. The house searches, arrests and various other harassments of priests, seminarians, former monks and nuns are apparently designed to intimidate, to render harmless those who otherwise could become the most likely *avant-garde* of the Church Militant, who would zealously proselytise for God and combat atheism. It is significant that, unlike the show trials under Rákosi, these more recent acts of terror receive but scant publicity. Kádár does not want to create martyrs. The man on the street knows only that the Churches support the Government and in turn receive money for their sustenance. All he sees is open collaboration, while the moral courage of the persecuted remains hidden behind the veil of silence.[37]

THE SITUATION SINCE THE AGREEMENT

While the regime boasts of greatly improved relations, the Church remains muzzled. To be sure the bishops and the 'peace priests' issue plenty of statements echoing the regime's propaganda lines on U.S. imperialism, Vietnam and the Soviet Bloc's peaceful intentions. The Foreign Affairs Committee of the Hungarian Bench of Bishops dominated by the 'peace priests' conducts propaganda tours abroad, disguised as 'pilgrimages', and also invites distinguished foreigners to Hungary who are given red-carpet treatment together with the rosiest description of the state of religion and the well-being of the Churches.[38] In glaring contrast to these political activities, the Church keeps silent on the gravest moral issues of the times. Hungary leads the world in the number of suicides, and abortions have reached truly catastrophic proportions.[39] Since the early sixties Hungary has had the lowest birthrate in the world and year after year there are more abortions registered than live births. A number of concerned doctors, sociologists, demographers and economists have mastered enough courage to speak up against this 'national suicide' resulting from policies permitting, and even encouraging, frequent abortions.[40] Only the Church seems to be unconcerned. It is inconceivable that the Hungarian bishops could ignore the problem and default in their sacred duty to give moral guidance to their flock – the Polish, Yugoslav and East German episcopate had taken a public stand against similar legislation in their respective countries – unless one assumes that they are under the heaviest pressure not to criticise Government policy, even if only implicitly, in their pastoral letters.[41]

Amid the continuing discrimination against religion it is difficult to see how the Communists could talk about their good relations with the Churches and expect better understanding with the Vatican. It was relatively easy for them, having all the means of coercion at their disposal, to force the Hungarian Churches to toe the line. It is, however, hard to imagine that they would be so naïve as to believe that they could fool the Vatican with their Orwellian 'newspeak', calling slavery freedom. True, the general relaxation and liberalisation in recent years also benefited the Churches in that travel and exchange of ideas with the outside world became easier. One could also mention that on some special occasions, such as the celebrations of the 400th anniversary of Calvinism in Hungary which was held in Debrecen in 1967, or the festivities staged by the Catholic Church in Székesfehérvár and Budapest in 1970[42] to commemorate the one thousandth anniversary of both the birth of St Stephen, first king of Hungary, and the introduction of Christianity by his father, Prince Geyza, the regime gave a helping hand to the organisers, especially in accommodating the invited foreign guests, while high-ranking government representatives took part in the activities, even attending the solemn church services.

More significantly, official contacts with the Vatican had been maintained, even if these served – with one notable exception – only to bargain from time to time over episcopal appointments. The exception was, of course, the departure of Cardinal Mindszenty from his self-imposed exile in the Budapest U.S Embassy. For years the regime made it clear that it would let him go abroad and even facilitated visits to him by Cardinal König of Vienna and various other representatives of the Vatican in the hope that they would persuade him to leave. Finally, Mindszenty acceded to the Pope's pleas and on 28 September 1971 departed for Rome – later to settle in Vienna – ostensibly to receive proper medical treatment for an unspecified illness. He was not 'rehabilitated', but the Hungarian Government granted him a special amnesty, for which he did not ask. According to the Vatican his release and the amnesty was an unsolicited favour from the Hungarian Government for which no *quid pro quo* concession was asked by Budapest. However, a few days later Jean Cardinal Villot, Papal Secretary of State, notified Archbishop József Ijjas of Kalocsa, the present Chairman of the Hungarian Bench of Bishops, that the Holy See transferred the right to absolve the excommunicated 'peace priests', until then specifically reserved to the Pope, to the

Hungarian bishops.[43] Should this gesture of the Vatican imply that the 'extraordinary situation of the Church in Hungary', which was the stated reason behind the papal reservation, had now ended (in other words that the Vatican considers the present *status quo* in Hungary as normal), this would mean a signal victory for the Kádár regime, well worth the hollow amnesty for the exiled Cardinal.

On the other hand, the experiences of the Holy See during the eight years since the 1964 partial agreement demonstrate that the regime consistently evades all the important issues laid down in the protocol and, instead, engages the Vatican in interminable haggling over the filling of episcopal vacancies. While this is an admittedly important matter, the long procrastination in each case and the tactics of always leaving some vacancies open for yet another round of negotiations,[44] prompted a close observer to speculate that the regime in reality uses the issue of episcopal appointments to divert attention from the most important questions, namely, freedom of religious instruction, the bishops' freedom to administer their dioceses, the issue of the 'peace priests', and the issue of the religious orders, while giving the impression of busily and amicably – and interminably – negotiating with the Holy See in good faith.[45]

This might be so, but then the question remains, why does the Government negotiate about the church appointments with the Vatican? It could ignore the Pope and prevent his appointees from taking office, as was done between 1951 and 1964. And, furthermore, why would the Communists want to establish fully-fledged diplomatic relations with the Holy See?[46] Surely the quest for legitimacy and respectability, so potent in the early years of the regime, does not play a role any more. The United Nations dropped the 'Hungarian Question' long ago from its agenda,[47] while the United States not only resumed normal diplomatic relations with Hungary, but at the same time in 1967 it also elevated the Budapest legation to the rank of an embassy. All around the world Kádár's Hungary is regarded today as a respected member of the international community. Could it be that for Kádár Vatican recognition would mean the ultimate in prestige and respectability? Or, perhaps, Kádár's and his party *élite*'s yearning for popularity at home, their desire for genuine acceptance and love by the whole Hungarian people, would provide the clue as to the real motive behind the puzzle.

Kádár has to be credited with the truly astonishing feat of having transformed his image in a short decade from that of a vile traitor to a genuinely popular leader of the nation who has made Hungary easily the most liveable country within the Soviet orbit. For this he earned the gratitude even of the non-Communist majority of his people. Still, he must be aware that as long as a substantial segment of the populace remains attached to religion, they cannot support whole-heartedly a regime which denounces and ridicules their most sacred beliefs and persecutes their Churches. Thus the most likely explanation for Kádár's conciliatory attitude towards the believers and their Churches can be found in his apparently sincere desire to gain broad popular support for his regime and its policies. One could add, perhaps, a psychologically understandable personal motive too, namely, his penchant to bask in the love and affection of the masses, from whom not so long ago he received nothing but scorn and spite.

But if this is so, why the hesitancy to go all the way and allow genuine religious freedom? Why not create the conditions, as in Yugoslavia,[48] which would induce the Vatican to extend willingly its recognition to the Communist regime of Hungary? There is no clear-cut answer to these questions, however, the reasons for the hesitancy could be reduced to three main factors, namely, insecurity, distrust and fear.

The feeling of insecurity must be a basic ingredient in a system which dares not to test its support at free elections, or even by means of opinion polls, and as a last resort it does not hesitate to enforce compliance by 'administrative means', i.e. police methods of intimidation and force. The Party proclaims the superiority of its Marxist–Leninist ideology and the political and socio-economic system which it has introduced in the name of that ideology, but it is unwilling to allow competition from opposite views for fear that the people might not be as firmly convinced of the sole righteousness of Communism as they are expected to be, and might still be liable to being seduced by exponents of erroneous ideas. Thus in the case of religion, while the Communists believe it to be an outdated, rapidly vanishing phenomenon, and openly congratulate themselves on the fact that among the youth religion has declined to such an extent that it hardly constitutes a real challenge to the atheistic–materialistic world-view any more,[49] at the same time they must have lingering doubts about the reliability of their own statistics since these reflect data collected in an unfree society where the young had learned at a very tender age how to dissimulate, how to show attitudes pleasing to the authorities and advantageous for themselves. In the same vein, when Communists point to the fact that there is little demand for religious instruction, they must know that this is due in great part to the harassment and pressure to which they subjected parents and children.[50] What if in an atmosphere of true freedom the experience of the 1956 revolution recurred when, after years of suppression, pratically all schoolchildren again attended classes in religion? Perhaps this would not happen now. In the opinion of impartial observers, under the impact of steady Communist propaganda and pressure the Churches have lost their hold on the people and amidst the greater economic opportunities and better entertainment and leisure the importance of religion has receded in the minds and lives of many, perhaps the majority, of Hungarians.[51] This is likely the case today, but what if the religious orders were permitted again to operate freely? What if the Churches could again start proselytising through the media of the written word, radio, television? What if they organised spiritual retreats, engaged in education, led youth groups, etc.? Would there not be a danger that the trend towards secularisation, materialism and atheism could be reversed and thus many years of Communist efforts frustrated?

For the Communists, however, the stakes are even higher than merely the revival of religious belief, no matter how unpalatable that alone would already be. Above all, Communists nurse a deeply felt distrust towards the Churches on political grounds. Steeped in dogmatic Marxism, they regard religion as an adjunct of capitalistic society and the Churches as instruments of the exploiting classes. They cannot forget, or forgive, that in the past the Churches served as important props for the authoritarian pre-war regime, while after 1945 they put up the longest and most obstinate resistance to the Communist take-over. In Communist minds the Churches were harbingers of political reaction, advocates of clerico–fascist ideologies and, of course, they were always virulently anti-Communist. Any assurances to the contrary, all talk about Christianity and the Churches not being bound to any particular socio-economic order, or political system, any profession of a sincere desire to live and serve the people loyally in a socialist state, would be up against a profound mistrust and the charge of opportunism. It will be a long uphill road for those who believe in Christian–Marxist co-operation to convince each other of their sincerity. Just as many, if not most, Christians do not trust Communist intentions, it is equally hard for a Communist to believe that the Churches are ready to accept the socialist order of things without mental reservations and that they would be willing once and for all to abandon dreams of restoring the old order and would withhold their support from those who might plot for such an end.[52] When, rocked by the spiritual waves stirred up by the Second Vatican Council, many Catholics have lost their firm footing and find themselves in a state of bewilderment and uncertainty, wouldn't it be too much to expect that the Communists should instantly accept the new image of the Church and should hasten to make their peace with it? Isn't it rather more in line with human nature that old images and prejudices persist, though we know that these serve more our emotional needs than reality? Moreover, one should not forget that distrust of the Catholic Church as the enemy of freedom and true democracy, and as the supporter of authoritarianism and fascism, is widespread also in the West. This image did not disappear with Vatican II. In view of all this it would be surely unrealistic to expect a sudden change of mind and attitudes from the Hungarian Communists. Kádár might be a supreme pragmatist, even a clever opportunist, but he is not a Constantine the Great who would issue a new Decree of Milan.

Finally, there is fear, fear of the leap into the unknown. We know from the testimony of a number of ex-Communists what a traumatic experience it was for them when they began to doubt the tenets of the tightly organised and well-defined belief system of Marxism–Leninism. Dialectical materialism is not only a basic ingredient of Marxist philosophy and thus part of the binding faith for a Communist, but every Party member was also taught that it was his duty to spread scientific atheism in the interest of progress, and to combat religion, the harmful 'opiate' for the masses. Tolerance towards religion, the granting of freedom to the Churches to engage in their mission, i.e. in preserving and even spreading religion, must seem to a Communist as a betrayal of his own upbringing and beliefs, giving comfort to the enemy, the first step on the slippery slope of 'revisionism'.

And there is another fear. Suppose Kádár and his similarly pragmatic associates were willing to give a new interpretation to the Marxist–Leninist injunctions against religion. Would this kind of tampering with the Faith be left unchallenged by Big Brother from across the North-East border? The memory of 1956 and the example of what happened to Czechoslovakia in 1968 is still fresh in the minds of all Hungarian would-be revisionists and reformists.

And so the Hungarian leadership remains impaled on the horns of the dilemma: it wants to be accepted and loved by all people, including the believers; it wants to normalise its relations with the Churches; it wants to gain international respectability and establish full diplomatic relations with the Vatican. At the same time, however, it feels compelled to combat religion; it does not dare to remove the shackles from the Churches; and it continues to play a waiting game with the Vatican. In the autumn of 1964, following the signing of the partial agreement, Kádár spoke optimistically about the possibility of a real understanding between the Catholic Church and the governments of the socialist countries. In his view the agreement between Hungary and the Vatican was proof of this possibility, even if it was only a beginning.[53] Since that initial step eight years ago the problems in Church–State relations remain frozen in virtual immobilism. Kádár still has the option to be once again boldly innovative, to find the way to normalise Church–State relations in Hungary on a mutually acceptable basis and show an example to the other countries in the Soviet Bloc. What he will do with this option only time would tell.[54]

NOTES

1. In 1947, the last time the census contained information about religion, 70 per cent of the population was Catholic, 22 per cent Calvinist, 6 per cent Lutheran, and just over one per cent Jewish. The remaining one per cent consisted of Eastern Orthodox, Unitarians, Baptists, Methodists and a small number of non-believers. The present-day population of Hungary is ten million.
2. Andras Muranyi (pseud.), 'Church, "Peace Priests" and State', *East Europe*, VIII (June 1959), pp. 12–17.

3. 'The Cross and the Party', Part I, *East Europe*, VI (December 1957), pp. 7–11.
4. *Esti Hirlap*, 24 February 1957.
5. Decree No. 22/1957, published in *Magyar Közlöny*, 24 March 1957. Two years later new enacting clauses were added (*ibid.*, 6 April 1959) which made church appointments a routine function of the State Office for Church Affairs. Cf. 'A Pápa aggodalma a magyar egyházért' (The Pope's Anxiety for the Hungarian Church) in *Katolikus Szemle*, XI, No. 2 (1959), pp. 81–5.
6. József Kala, 'A magyar egyház kálváriája' (The Calvary of the Hungarian Church), *Katolikus Szemle*, IX, No. 3 (1957), pp. 142–3. Further developments in the affair of the excommunicated 'peace priests' was reported by Lajos Szentpéteri in his column entitled 'Hirek a magyar egyház életéböl' (News from the Life of the Hungarian Church) in *Kotolikus Szemle* (Catholic Review) the emigré quarterly journal published in Rome, Vol. X (1958), No. 2, pp. 88–9; No. 3, pp. 135–6; No. 4, pp. 185–6.
7. See the article by J. Kala, cited above, *Katolikus Szemle*, IX, No. 3 (1957), p. 142; also Ádám Wirth, 'A kommunisták és a vallás' (Communists and Religion), *Társadalmi Szemle*, XIV (November 1959), p. 26. According to Wirth, the high percentage was due to the 'spiritual terror' to which the priests and ministers subjected the pupils and their parents.
8. *Katolikus Szemle*, XVIII, No. 4 (1966), pp. 367–9; XIX, No. 3 (1967), pp. 270–71.
9. *Népszabadság*, 25 September 1958; *Hungarian Review*, December 1958; see also the pastoral letters of the Catholic Bench of Bishops and the circular letters from the Calvinist and Lutheran Churches praising collectivisation, reported in *Magyar Nemzet*, 4 January 1960; also *Református Egyház*, 15 February 1960.
10. Samples of such foreign propaganda pronouncements are given by A. Muranyi in his article cited above (n. 2), 12–13. See also the 'Peace Resolution' adopted by the Catholic bishops' *Opus Pacis* on 22 January 1959, *Magyar Nemzet*, 24 January 1959.
11. See my essay 'Az egyház és állam viszonyának alakulása a második világháború után' (The Development of Church–State Relations in Hungary since the Second World War) *Katolikus Szemle*, XVI, No. 1 (1964), pp. 17–29.
12. Vincent Savarius, 'János Kádár: Man and Politician', *East Europe*, XV (October 1966), pp. 16–21; Sándor Kiss, 'The Kádár Imprint on the Hungarian Party', *East Europe*, XVIII (March 1969), pp. 2–9.
13. The passage is from his opening address to the newly elected parliament in the autumn of 1962, quoted by Károly Fábián in 'Szavak és tények Kádár egyházpolitikájában' (Words and Deeds in Kádár's Policy towards the Churches'), *Katolikus Szemle*, XV, No. 2 (1963), p. 146.
14. Leslie Laszlo, 'The Agreement between the Government of the Hungarian People's Republic and the Roman Catholic Bench of Bishops' (unpublished M.A. thesis, Columbia University, 1958). The agreement with the Catholic Church was preceded by similar documents signed with the three historic Protestant Churches of Hungary, namely, the Calvinist, Lutheran and Unitarian, whose resistance was broken two years earlier, in 1948. English translation of the texts is provided by Vladimir Gsovski, ed., *Church and State Behind the Iron Curtain* (New York: Frederick A. Praeger, 1955), pp. 134–41.
15. *Új Ember*, 22 October 1961.
16. Imre Kovács, 'Hungary: The Quest for Respectability', *East Europe*, XIV (December 1965), pp. 2–8.
17. *Új Ember*, 7 October 1962.
18. See the statement by Deputy Premier Gyula Kállai reported in *Népszabadság*, 12 December 1961.

19. Károly Fábián, 'Tárgyalások az egyház és állam között' (Negotiations between the Church and the State), *Katolikus Szemle*, XVI, No. 2 (1964), pp. 150–51; see also *Frankfurter Allgemeine Zeitung*, 11 March 1966.

20. A detailed analysis of the nature of the documents was provided by Mgr Casaroli himself in *Osservatore Romano*, 19 September 1964.

21. Péter Magyar, 'A pápai magyar egyházi intézet' (The Papal Hungarian Ecclesiastical Institute) *Katolikus Szemle*, XVI ,No. 4 (1964), pp. 325–7.

22. *Katolikus Szemle*, XVI, No. 3 (1964), pp. 235–9.

23. *Katolikus Szemle*, XI, No. 2 (1959), p. 149.

24. *Osservatore Romano*, 19 September 1964.

25. *Népszabadság*, 16 September 1964.

26. Simultaneously with the Vatican agreement negotiations were conducted also with the Protestant Churches aimed at improving relations between them and the Government.

27. Péter Magyar, 'Egy évvel a megállapodás után' (One Year after the Agreement), *Katolikus Szemle*, XVII (1965), pp. 370–77.

28. *Társadalmi Szemle*, XIX (November 1964), pp. 14–15.

29. *Délmagyarország*, 4 October 1964.

30. *Világosság*, VI (October 1964), pp. 577–8.

31. *Veszprém Megyei Napló*, 14 March 1965.

32. *Csongrád Megyei Hírlap*, 1 May 1965.

33. *Vas Népe*, 4 July 1965.

34. *Trásadalmi Szemle*, XX (April 1965), pp. 22–3.

35. This aim was served also by the new course entitled 'Basic Principles of Our Ideology' which was introduced as compulsory subject in all schools in September 1967.

36. János Kisbíró, 'A megegyezés után' (After the Agreement), *Katolikus Szemle*, XVII, No. 1 (1965), pp. 81–3; *idem*, 'Letartóztatott papok Magyarországon' (Arrested Priests in Hungary), *ibid.*, XVII, No. 3 (1965), pp. 285–7. Further arrests were reported in *Katolikus Szemle*, XVII, No. 4 (1965), pp. 375–7; XVIII, No. 3 (1966), pp. 276–8; XVIII, No. 4 (1966), pp. 369–70; XIX, No. 1 (1967), pp. 81–3; XIX, No. 3 (1967), p. 272; XX, No. 1 (1968), pp. 81–2; XXII, No. 4 (1970), pp. 351–2; XXIII, No. 1 (1971), pp. 64–5; XXIV, No. 2 (1972), pp. 166–7.

37. 'Hungary Revisited', *East Europe*, XV (October 1966), p. 6.

38. *Katolikus Szemle*, XVIII, No. 4 (1966), pp. 370–71; XIX, No. 2 (1967), pp. 164–6; XIX, No. 4 (1967), pp. 361–4; XXIII, No. 4 (1971), pp. 365–6.

39. Károly Nagy, 'The Impact of Communism in Hungary', *East Europe*, XVIII (March 1969), p. 16.

40. Extensive documentation on the widespread criticism of the regime's abortion policy is provided in the following studies: Zoltán Kovács, 'Népesedési földcsuszamlás Magyarországon' (Demographic Landslide in Hungary), *Katolikus Szemle*, XV, No. 4 (1963), pp. 244–58; *idem*, 'A hazai népszaporodás kérdése' (The Question of Population Growth in our Homeland), *ibid.*, XVI, No. 1 (1964), pp. 86–8; Károly Hokky, 'Adatok a hazai néppusztításról' (Data on the Population Destruction in our Homeland), *ibid.*, XV, No. 3 (1963), pp. 229–31; K. Z., 'Újabb demográfiai hullámvölgy Magyarországon' (A New Demographic Wave-Trough in Hungary), *ibid.*, XXIV, No. 2 (1972), pp. 169–72.

41. *Katolikus Szemle*, XXIV, No. 1 (1972), pp. 76–7.

42. Originally the Church planned the St Stephen Jubilee for 1972–73. Under government pressure the date was advanced to 1970 in order to coincide with the 25th anniversary of Hungary's liberation by the Red Army and also with

the centenary of Lenin's birth. See *Katolikus Szemle*, XXI, No. 4 (1969), pp. 364–6.

43. *Magyar Kurir*, 13 October 1971.

44. Even after the most recent batch of episcopal nominations – the third such agreement since 1964 – still only four of the eleven dioceses are governed by full-fledged diocesan bishops. Károly Fábián, 'Magyar egyházpolitikai események' (Events in Hungarian Ecclesiastical Politics), *Katolikus Szemle*, XXIV, No. 1 (1972), p. 80.

45. *Ibid.*

46. This was the reported mission of József Prantner and Imre Miklós, the Chairman and Vice-Chairman, respectively, of the State Office for Church Affairs, who during their prolonged stay in Rome in the Fall of 1970 paid several visits to the Secretariat of State in the Vatican. *Katolikus Szemle*, XXII, No. 4 (1970), pp. 352–4.

47. The U.N. quarantine of Hungary ended on 20 December 1962, when the General Assembly resolved that 'the position of the United Nations representative on Hungary need no longer be continued'.

48. Four years after a preliminary accord signed on 25 June 1966, and a genuine improvement in regard to freedom of religion, Yugoslavia and the Vatican resumed full diplomatic relations on 15 August 1970.

49. According to a poll taken among working and student youth between sixteen and twenty-five years of age, only 32 per cent said that they believed in God, one per cent was unsure, and 66 per cent described themselves as materialists. (*Kortárs*, November 1968). Using the sparse data derived from the few and extremely limited sociological research projects undertaken in Hungary to test the ideological beliefs of the youth, Jenö Bangó arrived to the conclusion that (a) the number of youth with firm religious belief was found to be in each case above 15 per cent; (b) the number of convinced Marxists is between 25–30 per cent; (c) the rest, that is the majority, has no firm conviction: they are, in the terminology used by the Marxist researchers, 'still wavering'. ('Vallásszociológia Magyarországon' [Sociology of Religion in Hungary], *Katolikus Szemle*, XXII, No. 2 [1970], pp. 143–55.)

50. This was admitted by the journal of the militant atheists when it confessed that 'the contraction of religious instruction in the schools was not a natural, but an irrealistically forced, speeded up, process'. *Világosság*, VII, No. 2 (1965), p. 4.

51. See Nagy, *loc. cit.*, pp. 11–17.

52. See the warning against reactionary attempts on the part of the Catholic hierarchy in József Lukács, 'A marxista valláskritika mai problémái' (Contemporary Problems in the Marxist Criticism of Religion), *Társadalmi Szemle*, XX (January 1965), pp. 29–30.

53. See the interview published in the West German *Welt am Sonntag* on 27 September 1964.

54. Since this article was written Pope Paul VI has relieved the 82-year-old exiled József Cardinal Mindszenty of his title as archbishop of Esztergom, Primate of Hungary. On the same date, 5 February 1974, the appointment of two bishops and two apostolic administrators to vacant dioceses was announced by agreement between the Holy See and the Hungarian government. This is another example of how the Kádár regime uses its stranglehold over episcopal appointments to wring concessions from the Vatican. Moreover, since seven of Hungary's eleven dioceses remain without full-fledged bishops, the regime retains a strong hand for future bargaining.

16 The Romanian Orthodox Church and the State

Keith Hitchins

Developments in Romania in the years immediately following the end of the Second World War brought profound changes in the relationship between Church and State. Along with the rest of Romanian society, the Othodox Church found itself in the midst of a far-reaching social revolution and was forced to adapt itself to new theories and methods of government. The church hierarchy understood clearly what was expected of it by both Church and State, and, drawing upon the experiences of the past when the Church had faced similar crises in its relations with the State, it decided to yield on secondary, mundane issues in order the better to protect the Church's essential, spiritual mission.

Before the war harmony had generally prevailed between the Church and the monarchy. The Church enjoyed certain privileges as a State Church, and its presence was strongly felt in most spheres of public life. Although no clerical party as such existed, the political influence the Church could bring to bear was at times considerable, and its clergy occupied a position of leadership in local affairs that a tradition of centuries had consecrated. In spite of its involvement in civic affairs, the Church avoided controversy over secular domestic and foreign issues and tended, instead, to follow the lead of the State. It also acquiesced in the rather loose supervision that the State exercised over its legislation and personnel. There were of course, differences, but they were never tests of strength between two diametrically opposed bodies or ideologies. The State was officially a Christian kingdom and it accepted the teachings of the Church about man and the final judgement and recognised the Church's right to carry out its spiritual responsibilities unhindered.

The coming to power of the Romanian Communist Party in 1947 drastically altered the relations between Church and State. The crisis which now confronted the Church was not simply a formal contest between Church and State over precedence or some privilege; religion itself was in jeopardy. Both the Party's long-range aspirations and its immediate objectives were openly hostile to the Orthodox tradition. Guided by a materialist ideology, it taught that religion was retrograde and was rooted in the exploitation of the working masses, and it confidently predicted that 'mysticism' would gradually disappear, as the transition from Capitalism to ideal Communism gained momentum. In the meantime, the Party admonished its members not to take a passive attitude towards religion, but to recognise it as a serious obstacle to the attainment of Communism and to 'unmask' its true character by promoting a 'scientific' understanding of natural and social phenomena.

The immediate goal of the Party was the political and economic transformation of Romania into a socialist state, and its instrument was the people's democracy, which replaced the monarchy on 30 December 1947. Following the example of the Soviet Union, whose dominance of Romanian affairs was largely unchallenged until the early 1960s, it rapidly nationalised industry and business and began the collectivisation of agriculture. Through the new state apparatus the Party also assured itself of a monopoly of political power and brought under its direct control every element of social life; no institution or organisation, public or private, was henceforth able to function without its approval. The Church was no exception, as it, too, was obliged to accept a subordinate role in the new totalitarian system.

Confronted by a hostile secular authority and deprived of its traditional sources of financial and political support, the Church seemed powerless to defend itself. However, it had retained its greatest resource (fifteen million faithful) who were unswayed by atheist propaganda and attempts to denigrate the Church's role in the historical development of the Romanian nation. The great mass of Romanians venerated the Church as both a spiritual and a national institution which seemed to them to embody the very essence of their distinctive national character. The clergy had done much to strengthen these sentiments by preserving the national culture in the 17th and 18th centuries and by taking a leading part in the movements for independence and unity in the 19th century. These bonds between the Church and the people, at once spiritual and social, again proved durable despite constant pressure from outside.

Under these circumstances the People's Republic chose to recognise the Church as a social institution, which could, if properly managed, become a useful instrument in promoting its own policies. The State decided to treat the Church like the school or the labour union, all of which were enlisted in the struggle to build Socialism. The regime continued to condemn religion and 'otherworldliness' as being out of step with the times, but its militant atheism was never as strong as in the Soviet Union. In general, it allowed the clergy to exercise their strictly spiritual functions unhindered within the limits set by law. The authorities were none the less deeply concerned about the activities of the clergy wherever they might be in a position to influence large numbers of people, and it arrogated to itself the power to determine the nature and extent of those activities. The State demanded of the Church a total commitment to further its domestic policies (industrialisation, collectivisation, unquestioning obedience to its laws) and its foreign policy, whatever it might be at a given moment – attachment to the Soviet Union or 'independence'.

The legislation enacted in the early years of the People's Republic prescribed the legal limits of the Church's religious and social activities. The constitution of 1948, subsequently amended in 1952, dealt with general principles. It guaranteed freedom of conscience to all citizens and acknowledged the right of all religious bodies to organise and administer themselves in accordance with their own doctrines and traditions, subject, of course, to the provisions of state law. It abolished the special prerogatives of the Orthodox Church, which the constitutions of 1923 and 1938 had conferred upon it, and declared all religious denominations equal before the law. Detailed regulations governing church activities were contained in a special law passed by the Grand National Assembly on 4 August 1948. It provided for extensive state control of the Church – confirmation in office of its leading personnel, supervision of its landed and movable property, approval of pastoral letters and other significant public communications, regulation of the training of candidates for the priesthood, supervision of its relations with Churches abroad (other foreign contacts were forbidden), and the convocation of the Holy Synod, the National Church Congress and other church bodies and full representation of the State in their deliberations.[1] Liaison between the State and Church was to be maintained by the Ministry of Cults (reorganised in 1957 as the Department of Cults attached to the Council of Ministers), which saw to it that state policy was carried out and had the power to pass judgement on all matters affecting the Church before submitting them to higher state bodies for formal action.[2]

This law also required the Church to submit to the Ministry of Cults a new statute bringing its government and institutions into conformity with the constitution and laws of the republic. A committee of eminent scholars under the personal direction of the Patriarch prepared a draft in several months of intensive work. They took as their model the so-called Organic Statute, which had been drawn up in the 1860s in large part by the great Romanian Orthodox Metropolitan and canonist of Transylvania, Andreiu Şaguna. It had embodied the principle of church government by a hierarchy and a synod with lay representation on all church bodies except those dealing with purely doctrinal matters and the discipline of the clergy. This new constitution differed from both the Organic Statute and church legislation after the First World War in one significant respect. It invested the Patriarch with extensive powers over church government and allowed him to intervene in the internal affairs of dioceses with or without the approval of the bishops.[3] Such sweeping authority was contrary to earlier practice, which had permitted the bishops wide discretionary powers and had made the welfare of their dioceses dependent upon their own abilities and ideas. This provision was characteristic of the statute as a whole. It created a highly centralised and uniform system of church government, which was undoubtedly intended to satisfy the demand of the State for order and efficiency so that the Church might then better serve as an instrument of its policies. Although the representative forms of earlier legislation were preserved and the full participation of clergy and laity in church business encouraged, unanimity of opinion and the avoidance of public controversy were the rule. As was true of corresponding state bodies, debates and final action were expected to conform to decisions already made by higher, executive authority. The Ministry of Cults and the National Assembly approved the new statute which became law on 23 February 1949.

The relationship between Church and State which this legislation created may, to a certain extent, be characterised as a separation. The term is accurate if it refers to the virtual elimination of any church initiative in public affairs. Party and government leaders have reduced to nil the Church's role in the formulation of public policies and programmes. They have repeatedly declared that the 'era of Byzantinism' is over; a phrase intended to convey the notion that the State no longer has anything in common with the Church and that each goes about its particular tasks without interference from the other.[4] In keeping with this doctrine of 'non-interference', the State drastically reduced the Church's capacity for independent social action. It closed church-operated elementary and secondary schools and charitable institutions, abolished religious instruction in state schools and substituted courses in historical materialism, and generally discouraged religious influences upon the young and public manifestations of religious faith. As a result, worship and the study of religion were restricted to the home or to buildings and institutions specifically intended for these purposes.

The church hierarchy acquiesced in this separation and attempted to reconcile its transcendental mission and its supernatural universality, on the one hand, with its responsibilities for the material welfare of the faithful and its obligations as citizens and patriots to serve the best interests of the fatherland, on the other.[5] Theologians have interpreted these functions as complementary, but have at the same time drawn a fine distinction between the Church's dual roles as spiritual body and social institution. They point out that as an organisation of Christians it pursues a mystical goal (eternal salvation through faith in the teachings of Jesus Christ) which transcends time and place. Thus, political forms cannot and should not affect this otherworldly mission. They also recognise that, as a social institution, the Church does enter into close relations with the State and necessarily assumes commensurate secular responsibilities. As a 'social reality' it lies within the State, which is greater and more comprehensive than the Church, since it includes the faithful of many religions and non-believers as well as believers. According to this line of reasoning, the Church is subordinate to the State and depends completely upon it; it does not engage in controversy with the State, nor does it have an opinion about the State; and it accepts the State as it is and follows the instructions that emanate from it. The State, in turn, may choose to recognise the Church as a public institution, as has happened in the Socialist Republic, but it relinquishes none of its power to decide how the Church may perform its social functions. In its capacity as a social institution the Church develops in accordance with changing historical conditions. Its goal is necessarily adaptation rather than independence or dominance.[6] A separation of Church and State thus exists in the delimitation of different spheres of activity: the province of the State is the material world, the Church's, the realm of the supernatural.

This separation is not nearly so clear-cut in practice as it is in theory. To be sure, the State has recognised the existence of the Church and has allowed it to propagate its teachings; houses of worship are open and services are regularly held and well attended; theological institutes and seminaries train several hundred priests each year; church government functions in accordance with its own statute; and theologians are free to pursue their research and to present their findings in any of numerous reviews published by the Church. However, it is apparent that the State has tolerated the Church and has permitted such latitude largely because it has lived up to expectations and has proved its usefulness. Owing to its very utility, the State has made the Church fully subordinate to its interests and ultimately determines the value and range of all church legislation and the nature and extent of its activities in ecclesiastical as well as social affairs.

An example of how forcefully the State can intervene in the internal affairs of the Church is provided by the monastery crisis of the late 1950s. Shortly after his accession in June 1948, Patriarch Justinian had instituted a sweeping reform of monastic life.[7] His goal was to revive the regimen of prayer, study and work and to restore the spirit of service to others. The new ordinances which he promulgated in 1950 soon began to yield the desired results, as the monasteries became important spiritual and intellectual centres. This renaissance attracted the close scrutiny of the Government. It decided that the monasteries had become centres of reaction and opposition, and in 1958 it began a campaign against them which led to the closing of monastic schools, a reduction in the number of monks and nuns and a severe limitation on the number of novices. In 1959 the authorities obliged the Holy Synod to approve a new and very summary ordinance governing monastic affairs.[8] This episode reveals both the power of the State and its limitations, and illustrates the resilience and perhaps even the bargaining power of the Church. The monasteries were not suppressed, and after the period of open conflict ended with a general improvement in Church–State relations in 1961 they slowly began to recover.

Rather than a separation, what has emerged between Church and State is a kind of coexistence, a *modus vivendi* which has enabled each side to pursue its special aims with the support, albeit at times half-hearted, of the other. As a result, the state has had the benefit of the Church's influence and prestige among its faithful in consolidating its political power and developing the national economy, and the Church has been able to carry on its spiritual mission, at least within the confines of its own buildings, and to develop a cultural existence of its own with the material support of a regime which officially disavows religion.

On the Church's side the success of this often precarious balance was assured by the determination of Patriarch Justinian and most of his clergy to defend the Church by working within a legal framework which they had not power to change. The personality and ideas of the Patriarch himself decisively influenced the direction the Church was to take for more than a quarter of a century. Born of peasant parents in Oltenia in 1901, Ioan Marina was ordained a priest in 1924. He served his apprenticeship in village parishes and, moved by the poverty of the peasantry, he advocated greater church involvement in social questions and became active in the co-operative movement. In 1930 he published a brochure entitled *Cooperație și Creștinism,* in which he argued that Holy Scripture and the writings of the Church Fathers justified the clergy's efforts to improve the material as well as the spiritual well-being of the faithful. From this time on he became increasingly vocal in his criticism of existing economic and social conditions, deploring what seemed to him to be the steady concentration of wealth in fewer and fewer hands and the growing impoverishment of large sections of the peasantry and working class.[9]

In 1945 he was appointed episcopal vicar at Iasi, in Moldavia, where he directed the clergy's important contribution to the recovery of that province from the effects of the war. Now a monk and known by his monastic name, Justinian, after the 6th-century Byzantine Emperor, he was elected Metropolitan of Moldavia on 28 December 1947. Two days later, the Romanian People's Republic was proclaimed, which he hailed as the 'enthronement of social justice'. He used the occasion of his installation as the third Patriarch of the Romanian Orthodox Church in June 1948 to urge his clergy and faithful to combine the Christian virtues of peace and love with labour and self-sacrifice on behalf of the people and he promised to devote all his efforts to the creation of harmony between Church and State for the mutual benefit of Orthodoxy and the fatherland.[10]

Church policy has conformed to these dictates ever since and has, as a consequence, placed heavy burdens upon the clergy. The priest must reconcile his own inclinations for the religious life with the constant necessity to demonstrate his exemplary citizenship through public acts of support for government policies.[11] His superiors, on the one hand, recommend the need for constant prayer and meditation and warn that a priest cannot be true to his calling unless he is attracted to the inner, spiritual life, but, on the other hand, they stress 'theology for the sake of life'[12] rather than 'theology for the sake of theology', and continually admonish him to direct his faith and study to the solution of contemporary problems.[13] The dilemma which thus confronts the priest is profound: he has somehow to reconcile his religious convictions with the obligation to contribute to the building of Communism; but, even more, he must carry out his civic responsibilities without daring to organise his parishioners and thereby place himself and the Church in competition with organisations of the State. In short, he must provide leadership by example, but he must not lead.

The State itself recognised the seriousness of the problem and, suspicious of the 'bourgeois mentality' of the majority of the clergy, prescribed a programme of 'social reorientation' for all priests. The first courses opened in the summer of 1949 and have been held regularly ever since. Their main purpose is avowedly indoctrination: to provide the priest with a new social theory and interpretation to enable him to harmonise his religious training and career goals with the social and economic plans of the State, and to show him how he must contribute to their fulfilment. As a supplement to these courses, 'conferences of sacerdotal orientation' have been held periodically in each protopopiate under the direct supervision of the metropolitan or bishop.[14] It is unlikely that these courses have won any converts to materialism, but they have undoubtedly impressed the clergy with the importance that the State attaches to their role in society, and have deepened their awareness of their own responsibility for the survival of the Church and the welfare of the masses.

Both the church hierarchy and the parish clergy have accepted the terms of their *modus vivendi* with the State, and, overtly at least, they regard the question of Church–State relations as settled. They raise no public objections to the regime's domestic policies, and their official pronouncements voice full support for them. For example, at a reception on 29 February 1968 hosted by the First Secretary of the Romanian Communist Party and President of the State Council, Nicolae Ceauşescu, for the leaders of the various Churches in Romania, Patriarch Justinian pledged the full devotion of his clergy and faithful to the State's endeavours to raise the living standards of the people, explaining that their sense of patriotism as citizens was reinforced by religious convictions which obliged them to serve the State, the people and its leaders.[15] The Church has also continually professed its satisfaction with the freedom it enjoys to propagate the faith. Even in the 1950s when state pressure upon the Church was at its most unrelenting,[16] it tried, and largely succeeded, in persuading its faithful and clergy that such freedom must not be jeopardised by 'thoughtless' acts of opposition.[17] In so doing, it has been at considerable pains to reconcile Christian doctrine, and its own role, with the policies of the regime: it preaches the coexistence of believers and non-believers, interprets Communist social and economic theories as essentially Christian, discovers the roots of Communism in the primitive Christian Church, and seeks traces of communistic thought in patristic literature.[18] The Patriarch considers the social activism of the Church perfectly in keeping with its traditional historical role of sharing the hardships and aspirations of the Romanian people, and has on numerous occasions declared collaboration between Church and State not only possible but desirable, even though the State is guided by a materialist philosophy.[19]

The Church has also consistently supported the State's foreign policy. It takes no independent initiative in international affairs, and its public pronouncements conform strictly to the Party's own position at any given time. For example, in the late 1940s and 1950s, the period of greatest Soviet influence in Romania, it was obliged to join in the general chorus of praise for Stalin and the Soviet version of democracy and to express gratitude to the Soviet Union for ensuring liberty of conscience and freedom of religion throughout Eastern Europe.[20] During this period, as part of Romania's reorientation from West to East, the Romanian Orthodox Church re-established relations with the Russian Orthodox Church. In its relations with the Western Churches, and even with the Ecumenical Patriarch, it followed the lead of the Russian Church, which, of course, in turn followed the lead of the Soviet Government.[21] For a time in 1947 and 1948 it appeared that an 'Orthodox Front' under Russian leadership might be formed to unite all the Orthodox Churches against the West, but after the Orthodox church conference in Moscow in July 1948, for unknown reasons, the plan was shelved.[22] Instead, the Orthodox Churches of Eastern Europe were enrolled in the 'defence of peace', a movement organised by the Communist-dominated World Peace Council. As portrayed in the theological reviews of the period, they alone wanted peace, while the World Council of Churches and, especially, the Roman Catholic Church were condemned as tools of Anglo-American imperialism.[23]

In the 1960s as the Romanian Communist Party sought increased economic and cultural ties with the West, and succeeded in reducing Soviet influence and gaining greater flexibility in its international relations, the Romanian Orthodox Church was able to extend its own direct contacts beyond the boundaries of Eastern-bloc Orthodoxy. The year 1961 marked the beginning of its broad participation in common Orthodox affairs and its formal entrance into the ecumenical movement. In September of that year it took part in the first Inter-Orthodox Conference at Rhodes, and in November it joined the World Council of Churches at its Third Assembly in New Delhi. Since then it has become more deeply involved in international Christian affairs than ever before.

The renewal of a dialogue with the Roman Catholic Church took longer to achieve. The reasons were partly historical and theological and partly political. To the disputes over doctrine which went back to the Middle Ages, the sometimes extravagant claims of the Pope to supremacy, and the aggressive proselytism practised by the Roman Catholic Church, were added the hostile confrontations of the post-Second World War period. The general assault on the Roman Catholic Church undertaken by all the Communist states of Eastern Europe made progress towards a rapprochement in the 1960s extremely slow. The official attitude of the Romanian Church towards the Second Vatican Council, for example, was one of suspicion and hostility, from the first announcement of its convocation by Pope John in 1959 until 1967, when the rapprochement between the two Churches was already under way.[24] As late as May 1966 Justinian declared that the Roman Catholic Church did not yet fully comprehend the meaning of Christian co-operation and brotherhood and was still animated by a spirit of centralism and dominance.[25]

The visit of the Ecumenical Patriarch Athenagoras to Bucharest in October 1967, seems at last to have set in motion a serious dialogue between the Romanian and Roman Churches.[26] It was followed by exchanges of visits between leading Roman Catholic prelates and Justinian and members of his hierarchy, and a more reasoned tone in print concerning outstanding differences. During Justinian's two-week trip to Western Europe in October 1970, as the guest of the German Churches, he displayed a spirit of conciliation towards the Roman Catholic Church and an enthusiasm for ecumenism which surprised and delighted his hosts. Discerning a new spirit of 'openness' in Catholicism since Vatican II, he spoke more concretely than ever before about the possibility of a reunion of the Churches and lamented the mutual isolation and misunderstanding of the past.[27] It must be remembered, however, that the boldness with which he has approached ecumenical problems has been possible only because his actions correspond to the State's new internationalism and, hence, have its blessing.

The Church's enhanced international role is evidence of the fact that Justinian's policy of creating and maintaining a workable relationship between Church and State has succeeded, at least to the extent that the State now recognises the Church as a useful and even necessary social force. At the National Church Congress held in Bucharest in December 1967, the Government's representative, Dumitru Dogaru, Secretary General of the Department of Cults, praised the clergy for their comprehension of the bases and moral goals of Socialism and their support 'by word and deed' of the 'great manifestations of renewal of Romanian society'. He also congratulated them for showing that in a socialist society, led by Communists, Christian Churches could organise and carry out their religious mission unimpeded.[28] President Ceaușescu, in his unprecedented reception for religious leaders on 29 February 1968, also took note of the Orthodox Church's contributions to a more prosperous and powerful Romania.[29] More recently, on 8 April 1970, Secretary Dogaru at a meeting in Bucharest with the Roman Catholic Bishop of Ratisbonne explained that the leadership of the Romanian Communist Party recognised the necessity of offering the people the 'opportunity for a religious life' because the majority of the population were believers. He held out the prospect that this coexistence between materialism and Christianity would evolve into some kind of permanent relationship, as Socialism had begun to discover that it was essentially a type of humanism, and the more it departed from revolution, the more humanistic it became.[30]

Under these improved circumstances the Romanian Orthodox Church enjoys a far more favourable position than its sister Churches in the socialist-bloc countries. It is well organised and efficiently administered; its secular clergy numbers about 12,000, and although some small parishes remain vacant, recent increases in the number of theological students will presumably ease the situation. The calibre of its clergy is high, and the level of training provided candidates for the priesthood is excellent.[31] The Church possesses two theological institutes of university standing and six seminaries, more than any other Orthodox Church in the socialist bloc. It sends theological students to the West in increasing numbers every year (there were approximately thirty in 1971). These students are the equals of their Roman Catholic and Protestant counterparts in theological scholarship and sophistication. The Church regularly publishes no fewer than eight theological reviews of the highest quality, three at the Patriarchate in Bucharest and one in each of the five Metropolises. Besides learned articles on church history and doctrine, these contain significant articles for the priest as pastor, preacher and confessor. Undoubtedly the reviews serve the priest better than in the past. The publication of prayer and ritual books has increased in number and variety in the past decade and is done on the Patriarchate's own press in Bucharest or at its branches in the metropolitan sees.[32] The importance of the Church's role in civic affairs has steadily increased, in spite of the State's ideological opposition to religious influences.

It must also be evident that this relative prosperity has largely been at the pleasure of the State and that, as never before in its history, the Church is a part of the State and is deeply dependent for its continued existence upon changes in the State's domestic priorities and the vicissitudes of its international relations.

NOTES

1. D. C. Amzăr, 'Partei, Staat und Kirche im heutigen Rumänien', *Ostkirchliche Studien*, Vol. 14, No. 2–3 (1965), pp. 172–4.
2. The most recent information on the functioning of the Department of Cults is given in *Irénikon*, Vol. 44, No. 1 (1971), pp. 94–6.
3. Liviu Stan, 'The Statute of the Romanian Orthodox Church', *Studii Teologice* (*Theological Studies*), Vol. 1, No. 7–8 (1949), pp. 636–61; Gheorghe I. Soare, Ecclesiastical Legislation', *Biserica Ortodoxă Română* (*Romanian Orthodox Church*), Vol. 69, No. 3–6 (1951), pp. 173–204; Liviu Stan, 'The ecclesiastical legislation of His Beatitude Patriarch Justinian', *Biserica Ortodoxă Română* (*Romanian Orthodox Church*), Vol. 71, No. 5–6 (1953), pp. 503–16.
4. *Biserica Ortodoxă Română* (*Romanian Orthodox Church*), Vol. 67, No. 11–12 (1949), pp. 32–5.
5. P. Justinian, *Apostolat social*, Vol. 5 (Bucharest, 1955), p. 119; Vol. 7 (Bucharest 1961), pp. 54–7.
6. Liviu Stan, 'Relations between Church and State', *Ortodoxia* (*Orthodoxy*), Vol. 4, No. 3–4 (1952), pp. 353–461; 'Church and worship in international law', *Ortodoxia* (*Orthodoxy*), Vol. 7, No. 4 (1955), pp. 560–92.
7. D. I. Doens, 'La Réforme législative du Patriarche Justinien de Roumanie: sa Réforme et sa Règle monastiques', *Irénikon*, Vol. 27, No. 1 (1954), pp. 67–9, 73–7; 'Monastic life during the last ten years', *Biserica Ortodoxă Română* (*Romanian Orthodox Church*), Vol. 76, No. 5–6 (1958), pp. 509–23.
8. Flaviu Popan, 'Die Organisation der Rumänischen Orthodoxen Kirche', *Ostkirchliche Studien*, Vol. 10, No. 4 (1961), pp. 277–8; 'Statutes concerning the organisation of monastic life', *Biserica Ortodoxă Română* (*Romanian Orthodox Church*), Vol. 78, No. 1–2 (1960), pp. 171–83.
9. Doens, 'Réforme législative . . .' (see n. 7), pp. 51–2.
10. P. Justinian, *Apostolat social*, Vol. 4 (Bucharest, 1952), p. 25.
11. Flaviu Popan, 'Der Priester in der orthodoxen Kirche Rumäniens', *Stimmen der Zeit*, Vol. 167, No. 4 (1961), pp. 272–87.
12. Nicolae, Mitropolitul Banatului, 'Theology in the service of life', *Studii Teologice* (*Theological Studies*), Vol. 20, No. 5–6 (1968), pp. 327–42.
13. Orest Bucevschi, 'Jesus Christ in the confessional life', *Studii Teologice* (*Theological Studies*), Vol. 7, No. 7–8 (1955), pp. 511–19; P. Justinian, *Apostolat social*, Vol. 9 (Bucharest, 1968), p. 51; D. Belu, 'Concerns and studies in pastoral homiletics and catechitics', *Studii Teologice* (*Theological Studies*), Vol. 20, No. 5–6 (1968), pp. 454–69; Bartolomeu Popescu, 'The pastoral work

of the priest with reference to the concept of *oikonomia'*, *Biserica Ortodoxă Română (Romanian Orthodox Church)*, Vol. 87, No. 7–8 (1969), pp. 788–90.

14. Flaviu Popan, 'Die Rumänisch-orthodoxe Kirche in ihrer jüngsten Entwicklung (1944–1964)', *Kirche im Osten*, Vol. 9 (1966), pp. 72–4.

15. *Biserica Ortodoxă Română (Romanian Orthodox Church)*, Vol. 86, No. 1–2 (1968), p. 19.

16. P. Justinian, *Apostolat social*, Vol. 4 (Bucharest, 1952), pp. 50–54; *Ortodoxia (Orthodoxy)*, Vol. 5 (1953), pp. 160–61.

17. P. Justinian, *Apostolat social*, Vol. 4, p. 458.

18. Ioan G. Coman, 'Christian teaching about economic goods', *Studii Teologice (Theological Studies)*, Vol. 3, No. 3–4 (1951), pp. 223–40; Teodor M. Popescu, 'The Church in Contemporary Society', *Ortodoxia (Orthodoxy)*, Vol. 5 (1953), pp. 27–45; Dumitru Stăniloae, 'Christian teaching about work', *Studii Teologice (Theological Studies)*, Vol. 5, No. 1–2 (1953), pp. 24–37; Sorin Cosma, 'Communal work and Christian morality', *Studii Teologice (Theological Studies)*, Vol. 15, No. 3–4 (1963), pp. 173–89.

19. P. Justinian, *Apostolat social*, Vol. 1, 2nd ed. (Bucharest, 1949), pp. 197–8; Vol. 4, pp. 43–9, 435–9; Vol. 5 (Bucharest, 1955), pp. 169–73; Vol. 6 (Bucharest, 1958), pp. 156–7; Vol. 10 (Bucharest, 1971), pp. 44, 56–7, 226.

20. *Ortodoxia (Orthodoxy)*, Vol. 5 (1953), pp. 6–8.

21. I. Pulpea, 'The Orthodox Churches, with special reference to the Russian Orthodox Church', *Studii Teologice (Theological Studies)*, Vol. 1, No. 1–2 (1949), pp. 69–90.

22. Amzăr, 'Partei, Staat und Kirche', (see n. 1), pp. 168–9; P. Justinian, *Apostolat social*, Vol. 4, pp. 70–75.

23. Corneliu Sârbu, 'The missionary spirit of The Vatican and the papal conception of the unity of the Churches', *Ortodoxia (Orthodoxy)*, Vol. 3, No. 4 (1951), pp. 581–5; P. Justinian, *Apostolat social*, Vol. 4, pp. 308–11.

24. For a general survey see, Flaviu Popan, 'Das Zweite Vatikanische Konzil und die Rumänische Orthodoxe Kirche', *Ostkirchliche Studien*, Vol. 17, No. 2–3 (1968), pp. 113–33. For early reactions to Vatican II consult the following articles in *Ortodoxia (Orthodoxy)*: Vol. 11, No. 2 (1959), pp. 341–3; Vol. 12, No. 3 (1960), pp. 471–93; Vol. 14, No. 1–2 (1962), pp. 269–80; Vol. 16, No. 1 (1964), pp. 3–46; and those by Dumitru Stăniloae, Vol. 17, No. 2 (1965), pp. 267–82, and Vol. 18, No. 1 (1966), pp. 8–34.

25. *Biserica Ortodoxă Română (Romanian Orthodox Church)*, Vol. 84, No. 5–6 (1966), p. 486.

26. *Ibid.*, Vol. 85, No. 9–10 (1967), pp. 886–97.

27. D. Gelsi, 'Une rencontre d'Églises: La visite du Patriarche Justinien de Roumanie en Allemagne', *Irénikon*, Vol. 43, No. 4 (1970), p. 605.

28. *Biserica Ortodoxă Română (Romanian Orthodox Church)*, Vol. 85, No. 11–12 (1967), p. 1316.

29. *Ibid.*, Vol. 86, No. 1–2 (1968), pp. 24–6.

30. *Irénikon*, Vol. 43, No. 3 (1970), pp. 420–21.

31. A detailed account is given in Alf Johansen, *Theological Study in the Rumanian Orthodox Church under Communist Rule* (London, 1961).

32. For a review of publications since 1948 see Ene Braniște, 'Religious books printed between 1948 and 1968', *Studii Teologice (Theological Studies)*, Vol. 20, No. 5–6 (1968), pp. 471–82.

17 Church–State Relations in Bulgaria under Communism

MARIN PUNDEFF

The years since 1944, when Bulgaria became a part of the Soviet sphere of influence, show in retrospect three fairly distinct phases in Church–State relations. During the first phase, from September 1944 to the end of 1947, the Communists faced the paramount tasks of converting the Fatherland Front coalition government into a Communist regime and securing that regime through international recognition and conclusion of the peace treaty Bulgaria's status as a German ally in the war required. These necessities inhibited the Communists from taking drastic decisions affecting the Bulgarian Orthodox Church and the religious minorities until 1947 when the opposition within the Fatherland Front was overpowered, the peace treaty was signed, international recognition was secured, and a constitution patterned after the Stalin Constitution in the Soviet Union was enacted in December. The second phase, 1948 through 1952, was marked by a series of tough measures ranging from enactment of the Law on Religious Denominations to trials, executions and, in the case of the Turkish minority, mass deportations. These policies were designed to reduce the Churches to organisations totally unable to stand their ground against the totalitarian and atheist state of the Communists. In the third phase which began in 1953, and this coincided with the end of Stalin's rule and the relaxation of Stalinist methods, relations between the Bulgarian Orthodox religion, traditionally the Church of the vast majority of the Bulgarians, and the Communist regime have developed an equilibrium by the Church accepting a helpmate role in certain areas of domestic and foreign policy and the regime providing it with the subsidy it needs for survival. Relations with the religious minorities – Muslims, Catholics, Armenians, Protestants and Jews[1] – also show an equilibrium in this current phase, or at least absence of the repressive measures taken earlier against some of them. The details of each case, however, are varied and can become intelligible only if related within a general chronological framework.

In the complex circumstances of the first phase the policy of the Bulgarian Communists towards the Bulgarian Orthodox Church, the religious minorities and religion in general followed the policy which the Soviet regime had developed by 1944: separation of Church and State, but recognition of the special usefulness and role of the national Church; removal of religion from the education of the young and restriction of proselytising activities; control of the affairs of the religious minorities, especially those with ties to the capitalist world; and propagation of the atheist outlook. Closely attuned to thinking in Moscow, the Bulgarian Communists were also mindful of the projected post-war role for the Russian Patriarchate as leader of Orthodoxy and of its need for support from the Bulgarian Orthodox Church.

The position of the Communists thus dovetailed in a fashion with the view held by church leaders and their friends in the Fatherland Front that the advent of the coalition to power presented an opportunity to deal with the accumulated problems of the Church – above all the election of a primate (exarch or patriarch) and an end to the schism with the Ecumenical Patriarchate[2] – and to prepare it for a vigorous role in the life of the nation. The hierarchy, to be sure, was not of one mind as to what was to be done. While the upper clergy tended to be traditionalist and conservative, the lower clergy, long organised in a Priests' Union, contained proponents of various degrees of radicalism – from endorsement of the idea of separating the Church from the State (to which the Fatherland Front was committed) to 'democratisation' of what in their view was a 'Church of dictatorial bishops' – as well as priests linked to the Communists. In these circumstances the National Committee of the Fatherland Front took the initiative and set up a group of nine clergymen (all from the lower clergy) and thirteen laymen to produce guidelines and reforms in the Church. The group's recommendations were based on the principles of democratisation of the Church by means of participation of the lower clergy and the laity in its administration and participation of women in church elections and active participation of the Church in the social policies of the new regime. Suggestions included re-establishment of the medieval patriarchate, organisation of monasterial lands into collective farms, active participation of the priests in the collectivisation of agriculture, revision of the curricula of the theological schools to cultivate a scientific and social outlook, and elimination of the authoritarian viewpoint.[3]

The Synod, with the possible exception of the Metropolitan of Sofia, Stefan, who had the ambition to become head of the Church, was disinclined to move along such lines and in the matter of the election of a primate resolved to use the exarchal, rather than patriarchal, title in order not to antagonise the Ecumenical Patriarchate and jeopardise the likelihood of overcoming the schism. With the co-operation of the Government it convened a *subor* of ninety-six delegates which on 21 January 1945 elected Stefan as the leading candidate for the office.[4] Within a month, with the assistance of the newly-elected Russian Patriarch, Alexii, the Ecumenical Patriarchate was swayed to recognise Stefan and thus end the schism.[5] On his part Stefan made it a point to stress this assistance and began to build close ties with the Russian Orthodox Church which was to him a sort of model for relations with a Communist state and potential protector.

At the same time the coalition Government, undoubtedly pressed by the Communists, took the first steps to curtail the role of the Church established by the existing Turnovo Constitution of 1879 and move towards a separation of Church and State. By two decrees in January and May 1945, religion was made an elective rather than a required subject in the elementary schools of the Bulgarian majority and was abolished in the high schools – the history of the Church being absorbed into general Bulgarian history. The recommendations for new educational policy, furthermore, stated that 'religion [was] incompatible with science' and was 'the private affair of every citizen' and that as such had no place whatever in the schools.[6] Not having parochial schools of its own, the Church attempted to preserve, with sporadic success, its traditional place in the public schools, but the Communists responded with 'a directive to the teachers who were members of the Party and the local Party units in the schools to intensify anti-religious propaganda'. The new policy eventually prevailed.[7] In the schools for the 'recognised ethnic minorities', that is, the Turks, Jews and Armenians, a law transformed religious instruction into an elective subject taught at the schools by teachers rather than clergymen.[8]

The complete disestablishment of the Church, however, had to await the adoption of a new constitution. In May 1946 the commemoration of the millennium of the death of the national saint, Ivan of Rila, and the visit of Patriarch Alexii for the occasion provided the Communists with an opportunity to indicate their views. In Alexii's presence Georgii Dimitrov, who had returned after years in the Soviet Union to lead the Party and later in 1946 became Prime Minister, made a brief speech which has since become the classical position of the Party on the national Church.[9] The Church, Dimitrov said, had great historic merits in that it had preserved Bulgarian national consciousness during the centuries of Turkish rule. He was proud of it and proud of patriotic clergymen like Ivan of Rila, 'a truly people's saint'. However, the Church had also had in its ranks 'traitors, scoundrels, and Judases from the point of view of the national interests of the Bulgarian people'. The present Synod included some old men of 'ossified brains and extremely conservative views'. These old men needed to learn from the experience of the Russian Church after the Revolution: at first it had failed to understand the spirit of the new times and had brought upon itself misfortunes, including persecution of clergymen for being tools of the counter-revolution. The Bulgarian Church could have a role to play if it became 'a truly people's, republican and progressive church'. Above all, Dimitrov said, the exarch and the clergy must stop singing prayers for the reigning dynasty and glorifying 'that which the people reject'.

The immediate problem, as Dimitrov indicated, was the abolition of the monarchy and establishment of a republic, which was accomplished later in September by plebiscite. This cleared the way for the enactment of the so-called Dimitrov constitution, planned by the Communists and published in draft form in October. Alarmed by its provisions, the Synod issued a long and closely-reasoned statement which seemed to bear the imprint of the thinking and personality of Stefan.[10] The statement objected to all segments 'which radically change in a legal as well as moral sense the agelong relationship between the Bulgarian state and the Bulgarian Orthodox Church' (such as the provisions that 'the church is separated from the state', that 'all education is secular', and that 'only the civil marriage has legal effect') and called for constitutional recognition of the fact, acknowledged by Dimitrov, that over the centuries the Church had played a central and vital role in the life of the nation. To preserve this beneficial role the Synod asked for continued union of Church and State, especially since there was no history of antagonism between the two or favouritism at the expense of the other religions in the country. The Bulgarian Church did not have 'the ultraclerical spirit of the Roman Catholic Church' which might endanger, as in France or Mexico, the democratic republican government and the liberal national development. Nor did the Bulgarian nation have the background of religious heterogeneity and violent religious struggles, as did the Swiss Confederation, Holland and the United States, which might compel the State to divorce itself from any leading Church and take a neutral stand towards all. The negative views towards religion held by some persons and the idea that through separation the Church was to be crippled and destroyed could not be shared by any 'true Bulgarian statesman'. In any case, even in countries where there is hostility to religion and Christianity, 'the Church has emerged invulnerable'. If, however, the separation were enacted, provision should be made to preserve the loyal and benevolent relations between the State and the Church on the basis of recognition of the Church as a corporation of the same type as agencies of the State, as in Belgium, Holland and France; of the Church's rights of internal self-organisation, self-government, ritual, teaching of the faith and charity, as in Yugoslavia, the Soviet Union and France; and of assurance of state subsidies 'as needed', as in Belgium, Holland and Yugoslavia. The principle that religion was to be offered in the schools only as an elective subject was acceptable, but the stipulation concerning 'secular education' contained a threat that an anti-clerical and anti-religious outlook would be fostered. For this reason the Synod required a clause that the State would be 'neutral in regard to the philosophical outlook'.

The strongly-worded statement, with its allusions that Dimitrov was not a true Bulgarian statesman if he held the views of a true Communist and that even in the Soviet Union the Church had survived its ordeals, indicated that the Church was determined to fight for its rights and that the backbone of this determination was Exarch Stefan. To the Communists he became not only a symbol of what they hated[11] but an individual in a key position who threatened to block their way and had to be removed. They had old as well as new reasons to get him out of the way. In the inter-war period he had taken stands against them. In 1925, when elements from the Party blew up his cathedral in Sofia in an attempt to kill the king and members of the Government, he published a pamphlet denouncing the outrage.[12] One of the men closest to him was Georgii Shavelsky, the last chaplain of the Russian imperial army and navy and a refugee in Bulgaria.[13] In the early part of 1947 he published with Shavelsky a book, *Sotsialniiat vupros v svetlinata na Evangelieto,* which openly criticised the main tenets of the Communist outlook and equated Communism with Fascism and Nazism as varieties of materialism seeking to destroy Christianity.

The efforts of Stefan and the Synod to sway the Communists from the objectives they pursued were no more successful than those of the opposition that left the Fatherland Front, and in December 1947 the Dimitrov constitution became law.[14] In regard to religion, it stipulated (Articles 76, 78 and 79) that only civil marriage had legal effect; freedom of conscience and of religion as well as freedom to perform religious rites were guaranteed; the Church was separated from the State; a special law was to regulate the legal status, financial support and right of internal self-organisation and self-government of the various religious communities; the misuse of the Church and religion for political purposes and the formation of political organisations on a religious basis were prohibited; education was 'secular with a democratic and progressive spirit'; and the national minorities had the right to be taught in their language and develop their national culture, with the study of the Bulgarian language being compulsory. Thus, while it provided for freedom of conscience and religion, 'the people's democratic state' was 'strongly interested in the enlightenment of the popular masses and the eradication of the religious prejudices' and proposed to achieve that through anti-religious education and atheist propaganda.[15]

Once the constitution was enacted, Stefan took the position that it contained some 'constructive stipulations' and that the

Church, being separated from the State and no longer constrained by a special status and considerations of state policy, was able to begin a vigorous programme of evangelical, educational and charitable activities and deepen its roots among the people. The parish clergy were accordingly instructed to increase Sunday-school activities and more effectively involve the lay Orthodox Christian Brotherhoods existing around many of the churches in evangelical, educational and charitable work. The clergy were furthermore put on notice that separation from the State also signified that the servants of the Church should stay out of government-sponsored political organisations and out of politics in general.[16]

In the second phase (1948–52), following the adoption of the constitution the Communists proceeded with a variety of measures, timed and conducted in a manner indicating a concerted campaign, to turn the Church into a pliable tool for their own purposes, repress the Protestants and the Catholics as 'problem' denominations tied to mother Churches abroad, and thin out the Jews and the Turks as ethnic and religious minorities having too strong an identity from their religion and nationalism. In regard to the Church, the Communists made an issue of the activities of Bishop Andrei, then the acting head of the Bulgarian Orthodox communities in North America, which they said were aimed against the new regime in Bulgaria.[17] The charges were levelled by Dimitrov himself who asked that Andrei be dismissed. Stefan and the Synod held, however, that the dismissal might provoke a schism and dissension among the Bulgarians overseas and even their secession from the Church in Bulgaria. They requested that a member of the Synod be allowed by the Government to investigate the matter on the spot. In a meeting on 8 April Stefan told the Synod that, despite his numerous requests, Dimitrov had refused to see him and that in these circumstances it was necessary for the Church to demonstrate its goodwill for an understanding with the Government 'and more particularly with the Prime Minister' by relieving Andrei of his duties.[18]

Yielding to Dimitrov on the issue of Andrei did not, of course, end the crisis since the main target was Stefan himself. Keeping up the pressure, the Director of Religious Denominations in the Ministry of Foreign Affairs, Dimitur Iliev, addressed a long communication to the Synod demanding that all church leaders stop criticising the Government, support its measures, acknowledge and preach that the State stood above the Church, counteract any propaganda against the Party and the Soviet Union from the pulpit and in the religious press, display the portraits of the Communist leaders and preach love for them, prevent the polarisation of opposition sentiments and activities around the churches, acknowledge and support the Government organisations for children, youth and women, and stop barring the lower clergy from joining the Fatherland Front and involving themselves in politics on the side of the Government and the Party.[19] The struggle that ensued has remained shrouded in secrecy, but in July 1948 the organ of the Church explained that according to 'assurances received from most authoritative persons', Iliev's communication did not express the views of the Bulgarian Government on relations between the Church and the State and on the mission of the Bulgarian Orthodox Church; that it was to be regarded as 'unsent, unreceived, and invalid'; and that the Synod's policy asking the priests to stay out of politics and political organisations in order to devote themselves fully to their direct and proper concerns was in accordance not only with the tradition of the Church since the country's liberation in 1878, but with *the view and practice of the Russian Orthodox Church*, which have been taken into account in organising our own church life.'[20]

In his further efforts to relieve the crisis Stefan had several discussions with Dimitrov's closest associates, Traicho Kostov (Deputy Prime Minister) and Vasil Kolarov (also Deputy Prime Minister and Minister of Foreign Affairs and as such in charge of religious denominations), leading to a special meeting of the Synod on 4 September 'for urgent consideration of certain important questions which needed immediate attention'. An explanatory 'Communication from the Holy Synod', which was published a month later and provides the only known details of the climax of the crisis,[21] indicates that the situation was tense – the Synod's members were summoned by telegram to meet on a Saturday and had to continue the discussions the following Monday – and that at the meeting on 6 September, described as 'stormy', Stefan, having already told an unnamed government representative that he would resign, submitted his resignation. Published to allay 'false and harmful rumours', the communication attributed Stefan's resignation to an 'imprudent' attitude towards his office 'in a tense and strenous time when the Holy Church is moving, not without pains, into new conditions of existence resulting from its separation from the State'. It also castigated him for 'autocratic' and 'arbitrary' rule and mentioned his ambition to become patriarch.

In a third meeting on 8 September the Synod accepted Stefan's resignation, relieved him also of the office of Metropolitan of Sofia, and chose its oldest member, Metropolitan Mikhail of Dorostol and Cherven, as acting chairman and acting head of the Sofia eparchy, without reference to the exarchal office. (Mikhail was replaced in these functions later in December by Metropolitan Paisii of Vratsa who was succeeded in January 1951 by Kiril of Plovdiv.) With Stefan removed, the Synod quickly turned to appeasing the Communist leaders and complying with their wishes. The following day, which was the anniversary of the establishment of the Fatherland Front Government in 1944, it 'hastened' to express to Dimitrov and Kolarov 'most cordial and sincere' greetings and fulsomely praised their 'statesmanlike wisdom'.[22] On 13 September Mikhail, Paisii and Kliment of Stara Zagora paid a visit to Iliev and achieved 'complete understanding', while Iliev assured representatives of the Priests' Union in a separate meeting that Dimitrov and Kolarov harboured 'goodwill towards the Church and the priesthood' and stressed 'heavily' that the State would continue to provide financial support.[23] This was followed by a letter from the Synod to all parish churches indicating that the priests were henceforth allowed to take an active part in the Fatherland Front units, that the Church would refrain from 'any religious propaganda among the youth', that the constitutional provisions must be obeyed, that due respect was to be shown to the political leaders and the authorities, and that in the future only the religious and ethical truths of the Church were to be expounded from the pulpit.[24]

Among the minor denominations, the Jewish community underwent the most radical change in this phase. Having survived the war without falling victim to the Nazi extermination programme, the Bulgarian Jews emerged from internment in the provinces and from the economic disabilities a larger community than they had been before the war: from the total of 48,398 in 1934 and the 47,154 'racial' Jews counted in 1943, the revived Jewish Central Consistory in 1945 found 49,172 Jews, more than half of them in Sofia.[25] Their first impulse was to resume the religious and cultural autonomy which they traditionally enjoyed (and which was again guaranteed by the armistice agreement and the subsequent peace treaty)[26] and to reopen the Jewish schools. The Communists attempted to exert control through a Central Jewish Committee under the Fatherland Front's Commission for National Minorities, but tension developed between their aims and those of the Zionists and the religious leaders who dominated the community. At first Zionist views were allowed to be heard, but, suspect because of their ties in the English-speaking countries, the Zionists were gradually silenced and, to reduce them as an internal problem, a mass exodus to Israel was allowed in 1948–49. With only about 6,000 Jews remaining in Bulgaria, the Jewish schools were then declared closed for 'lack of pupils'.

The Bulgarian Protestants and Catholics had also experienced disabilities during the war and expected to resume their relations with mother Churches in the West and rebuild their religious, educational and cultural life. The Protestants had been particularly restricted because of their ties with the United States and England: the Bulgarian Y.M.C.A. and Y.W.C.A. had been banned and the schools, maintained and largely staffed by Americans, had been closed.[27] After 1944, however, the Y.M.C.A. and Y.W.C.A. were not allowed to be revived nor the schools reopened – a decision which led representatives of the Protestants to address pleas to the United States and England at the peace conference in Paris to write guarantees of religious and cultural freedom into the Bulgarian peace treaty. The Communists, it appears in retrospect, had plans to ban all 'foreign schools' once the treaty was signed, including those of the Catholics maintained by religious orders and sources from abroad and largely staffed by French priests and nuns.[28] A decree in August 1948 closed these schools, dealing a severe blow to the educational and religious life of the Bulgarian Catholics.

The general plans of the Communists were indicated by the law on religious denominations stipulated by the constitution and enacted on 1 March 1949, and by a statement made by Kolarov at its adoption. Speaking in tough and uncompromising terms, Kolarov dwelled at length on 'what will not be tolerated': no church or clergyman would be allowed to preach against the new regime or conduct open or covert activities to restore the old; no church or clergyman would be allowed to preach against the economic plans or be an agent of the imperialists and conspire with the remnants of Capitalism against Socialism; the Government would not tolerate any use of religious meetings, the church building, the pulpit, the sermon, or prayer and confession for the purpose of subverting directly or indirectly the people's unity and the regime's stability; it would not permit the youth to be split on religious grounds and would 'never tolerate the meddling of any religious organisation in the area of public education'. Kolarov singled out the Bulgarian Catholic and Protestant clergy as being agents of foreign centres and involved in traitorous activities that had to be stopped. The Vatican, he said in specific terms, had shown interest in maintaining an outpost in Bulgaria, but since no concordat and diplomatic relations existed with it, the Government had decided to end the activities and presence of Vatican representatives in the country.[29]

The law itself set forth a system of strict and thoroughgoing controls over religious communities.[30] It made special mention of the Bulgarian Orthodox Church as 'the traditional religion of the Bulgarian people', which 'may become the people's democratic church in form, substance and spirit', but it gave the Church no special legal status. Its thirty-two articles[31] stipulated that a denomination could exist and enjoy legal rights only if recognised by the State. Recognition took the form of approval of the denomination's statute by the Council of Ministers or an official delegated by it. Each denomination was to submit a statute for approval within three months. Denominations having canonical relations with Churches abroad were required to submit the names of their clergymen for approval by the Director of Religious Denominations (the post presently occupied by Mikhail Kiuchukov with the title of Chairman of the Committee on the Problems of the Bulgarian Orthodox Church and the Religious Cults in the Ministry of Foreign Affairs) before they could hold office. Although these denominations were permitted to receive financial aid and gifts from abroad, the Director was to be notified of all such transactions. Only Bulgarian nationals could be clergymen or hold office in any denomination. The Director was empowered to suspend or remove any clergyman or church official for violation of the laws, public order and good morals or for acts 'in conflict with the democratic institutions of the State'. The denominations could collect revenues and make expenditures according to their own budgets, but the budgets were to be submitted to the Director, with all their financial activities subject to government control; 'if needed' the Government might provide financial subsidies. Establishment of secondary and higher theological schools for the training of clergy was permitted, but the organisation and curriculum of these schools were subject to state regulation and special permission was required for any student to be sent to study in religious institutions abroad. The denominations were to submit to the Director in advance all messages, circular letters and materials of public importance issued by them, and the Director could stop their distribution if he found them 'contrary to the laws'. Each denomination was also to submit the names of the officers of its central and local bodies as well as complete rosters of its clergy, and, if the Director raised no objections, they could exercise their duties. The denominations were specifically prohibited from working among the youth and from establishing or maintaining charitable institutions. Relations with Churches and individuals abroad were to be maintained only if authorised by the Director. Foreign Churches were prohibited from establishing or maintaining missions, orders and the like in the country; all existing subdivisions of foreign Churches were to be closed within one month and their property taken over by the State.

Kolarov's statement and the 1949 law on religious denominations foreshadowed the drastic measures designed to repress Protestants and Catholics and isolate them from contacts abroad. While the law was being passed, fifteen leading pastors from the Supreme Council of the United Evangelical Churches in Bulgaria, secretly arrested in 1948 with other pastors, were put on trial and charged with espionage on behalf of the United States and England, high treason, foreign exchange speculation, and efforts to 'restore the bourgeois capitalist regime'.[32] Their leader, Vasil Ziapkov, was also charged with betraying secrets of the Bulgarian peace delegation in Paris to American and British delegates. The trial ended on 5 March with Ziapkov and three others sentenced to life imprisonment and the rest to various prison terms.[33] The question of what was happening to religious freedom in Bulgaria (as well as Hungary and Romania) was taken by the United States and England to the United Nations General Assembly, which expressed deep concern and established an *ad hoc* Political Committee on Observance of Human Rights in the three countries however, when the International Court of Justice found, in two advisory opinions of 30 March and 18 July 1950 that they could as bound by the peace treaties. The case reached a dead end, block the creation of joint commissions stipulated by the treaties to settle such disputes.[34]

The arrests of Catholic clergy and laymen began in 1950, leading to executions without trial, one open trial, and apparently several secret ones. The open trial involved Mgr Evgenii Bosilkov, bishop of the diocese of Nikopol, two editors of the suspended Catholic weekly *Istina,* and some thirty other priests, nuns and laymen. The charges included spying for the Vatican, concealing arms and carrying on propaganda against Communism. The trial ended on 3 October 1952 with death sentences for Bosilkov and three others and various terms of imprisonment for the rest.[35] On 15 December Pope Pius XII issued an encyclical protesting, without results, the 'wave of terror' against the Bulgarian Catholic leaders. As in the case of the Protestants, the terror against Catholics brought their life as a religious community to a virtual standstill.

The turn to drastic measures also involved the Turkish minority. Settled in compact masses and traditionally isolated from the life of the Bulgarian majority, the Turks had a strong sense of religious and ethnic identity which stood in the way of the various cultural and economic changes the Communists were bent on achieving. The method of dealing with the problem which they adopted in August 1950 was to thin out the Turkish areas and rid themselves of the most religious and nationalistic Turks by resettling, within three months, 250,000 of them, or more than one-third of the minority, in Turkey. In the ensuing period to November 1951, when Turkey closed the border to further movement, some 155,000 Turks were resettled in dire conditions, with a minimum of personal belongings in their hands.[36]

The Bulgarian Orthodox Church, on the other hand, moved slowly but steadily towards a *modus vivendi* determined not only by Dimitrov's formula repeated in the law of 1949 and the pattern established by the Russian Orthodox Church in the Soviet Union, but also by Communist plans to restore the patriarchal office in order to make it a national institution on equal footing with the Balkan Orthodox patriarchates and give the Russian Patriarch an even stronger voice of support. In accordance with the law of 1949, the Church submitted for approval a statute which, however, did not become effective until 31 December 1950.[37] The selection of Metropolitan Kiril of Plovdiv three days later to be acting head of the Church indicated that the agreements reached on the *modus vivendi* included his installation as Patriarch.[38]

Kiril's elevation to the patriarchal office on 10 May 1953 coincided with the end of the Stalin era and may be taken as the beginning of the third and current phase in Church–State relations. The ceremony was carried out by a *subor* of clergy and laity addressed by Kiuchukov who emphasised that 'the new relations' between Church and State had produced good results in the internal life of the Church: the Church was 'freed from the heavy burden of functions not befitting it' and was able to 'direct its resources exclusively into the field of religious questions where its real calling is'. The Church, he said, was giving 'uncoerced' support to the new order and was an active participant in the peace movement in the country and abroad. It was true to its traditions of 'strict and unconditional' defence of national and religious independence and patriotism and was 'in unison' with the people's aspirations.[39] In his own detailed report on the state of the Church, Kiril devoted only a page to 'relations with the State', pointing out that they were governed by the Lord's principle 'Render to Caesar the things that are Caesar's and to God the things that are God's', that is rendering to God faith and conscience and to the State 'complete loyalty' and civil obligations. The Church had given evidence on many occasions since 1944 of this loyalty and of its goodwill to co-operate, according to its abilities in terms of principles and actual resources, in the peace movement and other policies of the Government and thus carry out its 'patriotic duty'.[40]

These statements became the public guidelines for the stance of the Church under Kiril in the years ahead. In particular Kiril cultivated the theme of 'patriotic service' as the common ground where the Church and the Communists have joined forces, since the early 1960s, in promoting patriotism and pride in the nation's history, heroes and achievements. It has provided the Church with excellent opportunities to be seen in a favourable light since many of these heroes and achievements were associated with it. In this atmosphere the Church elevated among its saints Father Paisii, the author of the passionately patriotic *Istoriya Slavyanobolgarskaya* of 1762, and Bishop Sofronii of Vratsa, an ardent follower of

Paisii and author of the first book in modern Bulgarian. The Party press frequently publishes pictures of monasteries as 'citadels of the Bulgarian spirit' and historians give an almost traditional recognition of the role of the Church in the nation's history. The present Prime Minister and Party leader, Todor Zhivkov, endorsed the theme in an interview with Austrian journalists, pointing out that 'in contrast to the situation in other countries, our Church has always been patriotic' and that it had established 'a very meritorious record in the struggle against the foreign Turkish rule'.[41] Kiril himself, asked in an interview about dialogue between believers and Communists, explained:

> Our dialogue is carried on every day through work and love of country. Every day we work together for the good of our country. To many persons abroad who have asked me, either provocatively or out of curiosity, whether there is sincere closeness and co-operation between believers and non-believers in Bulgaria, I have replied in conformity with the reality: 'In a family there can be both believing and non-believing members, but they love each other because they are bound together by blood. Our national family is like that. In it there are both non-believers and believers, but all work together for the well-being of our country. This is called creative dialogue which rather significantly differs from the verbal one.'[42]

Despite the recognition of its patriotism, the Church has not fared well. Far from entering into a verbal dialogue with it on philosophical or ethical questions, the Communists have put great effort into fighting the religious outlook by atheistic propaganda as well as by the creation of secular rituals of marriage, registration and naming of infants, funerals and other family occasions, including new holidays and festivities to supplant the religious ones. For example, the Party document 'On Measures to Intensify and Improve the Atheistic Propaganda' described the tenets of the Church as a 'reactionary ideology' opposed to Communism, 'the ruling ideology in our society', and noted that, after being closely tied to the capitalist class, the Church had turned to 'realistic ways' to achieve 'closeness and co-operation with the people's democratic state' in a number of areas of domestic and foreign policy. This shift in the Church's position and the reliance of party workers on 'the old atheist traditions in our country and the religious indifference of the greater part of the population' had led to an 'underestimation of the ideological struggle' against religion. Following the denunciation of Stalinism and during the Hungarian revolution 'clergymen of a reactionary bent became brazen and openly called for disobedience of the laws and the provisions of the constitution'. What was needed, the document concluded, was expansion and intensification of anti-religious propaganda and development of meaningful 'socialist' rituals and holidays.[43]

The result of the efforts of the Communists, who have the resources of the State at their disposal, has been a steady loss of ground by the Church, although the exact loss is difficult to determine. According to a comprehensive survey involving 42,664 persons born before 1944 and conducted by the Institute of Philosophy of the Bulgarian Academy of Sciences in 1962, only 32·76 per cent of the Orthodox Bulgarians questioned were found to be religious, while among the ethnic minorities the corresponding figures were 67·02 per cent of the Turks, 38·58 per cent of the Armenians, and 29·17 per cent of the Jews. The trends the survey presumably revealed are that the Orthodox believers are decreasing both in absolute numbers and as a percentage of the population; the Muslims and the Catholics are increasing in percentage of the number of believers; and the Protestants are increasing both in absolute numbers and as a percentage of the believers in the country.[44] Perhaps a more reliable index of the loss is the drop in the number of parish priests from 2,486 in 1938 to 1,785 in 1966 for the twelve eparchies constituting the Church. A parish, according to the statute of the Church, must have at least 300 wedlocks in rural areas and 400 in urban ones.

In its reduced role the Church has been allowed to have a publishing office (established in 1936 and now averaging less than ten books a year), a bookshop, a seminary at the Cherepish Monastery, and a theological academy (formerly the Faculty of Theology of the University of Sofia, separated from it in 1950). It issues the periodicals *Tsûrkoven Vestnik* (Church Herald) (thirty-two issues per year, 4,500 copies), *Dukhovna Kultura* (Spiritual Culture) (monthly, 2,000 copies), and *Godishnik na Dukhovnata Akademiya Sv. Kliment Okhridski* (Yearbook of St Clement of Ohrid Theological Academy) (annual, 600 copies).

Patriarch Kiril himself sought to emphasise by example an area of activity where leaders of the Church could make enduring contributions and command attention and respect even from the ideological enemies of the Church. He involved himself heavily in historical studies, producing in the years after 1953 eight major works on the history of the Church in the 19th century and other subjects. His singular contribution elicited recognition by the Bulgarian Academy of Sciences which made him an academician in 1970. At the time of his death in March 1971 he was in the middle of publishing his muti-volume history of the exarchate in Turkey before the Balkan wars.[45]

Kiril's death came shortly before the Communists enacted a new constitution, in preparation since 1968, to fit the new stage of 'building the advanced socialist society' in Bulgaria.[46] Its Articles 38 and 53 continue the essential regime established by the 1947 constitution: only civil marriage has legal effect; freedom of conscience and of religion as well as freedom to perform religious rites are guaranteed; the Church is separated from the State; the legal status, financial support and right of internal organisation and self-government of the various religious communities are regulated by legislation; and the misuse of the Church and religion for political purposes and the formation of political organisations on a religious basis are prohibited. There are, however, also significant innovations and changes of emphasis: parents must give their children a 'Communist upbringing'; the upbringing of youth 'in a Communist spirit is the duty of the entire society'; citizens of non-Bulgarian origin have the right to study their language 'in addition to the compulsory study of Bulgarian', but the provision concerning their right to develop their national culture has been dropped. The rights of citizens include conducting 'anti-religious propaganda'; and lastly, religion cannot be invoked for refusing to fulfil obligations imposed by the constitution and the laws.

Within the prescribed period of four months from Kiril's death, a *subor* met on 4 July 1971 and elected the Metropolitan of Lovech, Maksim, to the combined offices of Patriarch and Metropolitan of Sofia.[47] Clearly a church leader of lesser stature than Kiril, in his public statements following his election Maksim has stressed that the Church, guided by the 'great example' of Kiril, will continue on the course charted by him. On his part Zhivkov stated on receiving Maksim after the election that the State not only 'values highly the patriotic services of the Church in the past, but greets with appreciation all real contributions of the Church to the progress of our socialist fatherland, the patriotic unity of the people, Bulgarian–Soviet friendship and the defence of peace in the entire world.'[48] Predictably, Maksim has backed the Government's position on the American mining of North Vietnam's harbours by sending telegrams to the United Nations and expressing the solidarity of the Church with the Communist cause in Indochina.[49]

The second-largest religious community, the Muslim, has also suffered loss of ground in the past two decades. It has been the object of intense efforts by the Party and the State to overpower the tenacious adherence to Islam, 'fanaticism' and 'Turkish bourgeois nationalism' and to mould a 'unified' socialist nation.[50] The Turkish minority schools were mereged in 1958 with the schools of the Bulgarian majority and the development of a separate Turkish national culture is no longer allowed by the constitution. The precipitous drop in the number of priests (*hodzas*) from 2,393 in 1956 to 462 in 1965 for the Turks and from 322 in 1956 to 95 in 1965 for the Pomaks indicates a drastic reduction of organised religious life.[51] The community is headed by a Chief Mufti and a regional Mufti for the Pomak area and has a theological seminary for the training of Muslim clergy. The other two ethnic and religious minorities, the Armenians and the Jews, are too small to be of much consequence: the believing Armenians have ten priests (under the jurisdiction of a bishop for Romania and Bulgaria residing in Bucharest and member of the hierarchy of the Armenian Gregorian Church in Soviet Armenia), while the believing Jews have seven rabbis. Nevertheless, since the Israeli–Arab war of 1967 there have been manifestations of Zionist sentiments among the Bulgarian Jews which the Party press has sought to combat with frequent articles about Zionism being a reactionary ideology and Israel being an outpost of American 'imperialism' in the Middle East.[52] The remaining two religious minorities, the Catholics and the Protestants, continue to be viewed by the Communists not only as irreconcilable ideological antagonists, but as outposts of hostile foreign centres interested in subverting the Communist regime. The policy of keeping them isolated from the mother Churches in the West is still in effect, although the Stalinist methods of repression are no longer applied and leading clergymen are occasionally permitted to travel abroad. This was notably the case during the Second Vatican Council when the Apostolic Vicar heading the Bulgarian Catholics of Latin rite and the Apostolic Exarch heading the Bulgarian Uniates were allowed to attend it. The Catholics have altogether about sixty priests, the Protestants about 170 pastors and preachers. Neither religious community has been able to train clergy or publish for its needs.

NOTES

1. There are no reliable current statistics on the religious denominations. The last pre-war census in 1934 listed 5,128,890 Orthodox Bulgarians (in a total population of 6,077,939), 821,298 Muslims (Turks, Gypsies, Muslimised Bulgarians or Pomaks, and Tatars), 45,704 Catholics, 23,476 Armenians, 8,371 Protestants and 48,398 Jews. In an estimated total population of 8·6 million in 1971, some 2 million were by definition atheists as members of the Bulgarian Communist Party (699,476) and the Bulgarian Komsomol. The official publication of the Bulgarian Orthodox Church *NR Bulgariya i religioznite izpovedaniya v neya* (The P.R. of Bulgaria and Its Religious Denominations) (Sofia: Sinodalno izdatelstvo, 1966) gives no figures for the Orthodox Bulgarians (beyond stating that they are 'the prevalent denomination') or the atheists and lists (in approximate figures) 656,000 Muslims (Turks, Pomaks and Gypsies), 60,000 Catholics (of them 10,000 Uniates), 22,000 Armenians, 16,100 Protestants (consisting of 6,000 Pentecostalists, 5,000 Congregationalists, 3,000 Adventists, 1,300 Methodists, and 800 Baptists), and 6,000 Jews. On the Muslims, more reliable seem to be the figures indicated in *Isliamut v Bulgariya; sushtnost, modernizatsiya i preodoliavane* (Islam in Bulgaria: Essence, Modernization and Overcoming), by Nikolai Mizov, a specialist on Islam and atheism working in the Institute of Philosophy of the Bulgarian Academy of Sciences (Sofia: Izdatelstvo na Bulgarskata komunisticheska partiya, 1965). According to him, there are 650,000 Turks, 200,000 Gypsies, 140,000 Pomaks and 6,000 Tartars.

2. The Church had not had a primate (exarch) since 1915 when the last exarch died, and was governed by the Holy Synod made up of the metropolitans of the eparchies within Bulgaria. The Exarchate was created in 1870 as a result of the demands of the Bulgarians in the Ottoman Empire and was subordinated in matters of doctrine to the Patriarchate of Constantinople. In 1872, in retaliation for their national separatism, the Patriarchate declared the Bulgarian 'exarchists' schismatic and thus outside the pale of Orthodoxy. In the Middle Ages, before the Ottoman conquest, the Church was headed by a patriarch. For literature on the history of the Church, see M. Pundeff. 'Hundert Jahre bulgarisches Exarchat, 1870–1970,' *Österreichische Osthefte*, November 1970, pp. 352–8.

3. Text in *Slavianska Misŭl* (bimonthly published by the Metropolitanate of Sofia), No. 1 (1945), pp. 153–4.

4. D. Lazov, *Ekzarkh Stefan I; zhivot, apostolstvo i tvorchestvo* (Ekzarkh Stefan: Life, Apostolate, and Works) (Sofia, 1947), pp. 257–9. Stefan (1878–1957) was then acting chairman of the Synod. By virtue of the offices he held, his excellent training, impressive personality and great influence in Bulgaria and abroad, he was the natural choice. The son of a village priest, he was educated in Russia (Kiev Theological Academy) and Switzerland (univer-

sities of Geneva and Fribourg where he earned a doctorate of philosophy in 1919) and, after serving as secretary of the Exarchate in Constantinople and of the Synod in Sofia, became Metropolitan of Sofia in 1922. His education in Kiev had made him a devoted friend of Russia and Russian Orthodoxy, while his stay in Switzerland had introduced him to Western theological circles where his connections were wide. He also had the reputation of having stood up to the late King Boris on various occasions, including the threat to deport the Bulgarian Jews in 1943, and enjoyed the support of some Fatherland Front leaders.

5. The *tomos* of 22 February 1945 removing the schism and various related documents are in *Tsŭrkoven Vestnik* (organ of the Church), 19 May 1945.

6. Quoted *ibid.*, 16 June 1945.

7. P. Avramov, *BKP i formirane na sotsialisticheskata inteligentsiya* (The B.C.P. and the Formation of Socialist Intelligentsia) (Sofia: B.K.P., 1966). pp. 110–16.

8. *Dŭrzhaven Vestnik* (official law gazette), 12 October 1946.

9. Text in Dimitrov's *Sŭchineniya* (Works), Vol. 12 (Sofia: B.K.P., 1954), pp. 186–90.

10. Text in *Tsŭrkoven Vestnik*, 14 December 1946.

11. For example, the Soviet commanding general in Bulgaria and chairman of the Allied Control Commission until the conclusion of the peace treaty, S. S. Biryuzov, regarded Stefan as an 'extremely subtle and perfidious intriguer' and an 'accomplished cynic' ('for him there was nothing sacred') not above vice. See Biryuzov's memoirs *Sovetskii soldat na Balkanakh* (Moscow, 1963), pp. 282–7.

12. *L'attentat à la cathédrale de Ste. Nédélia, impressions et souvenirs de Stéphane, archevêque de Sofia, et de l'archimandrite Sophronii* (Sofia, 1925).

13. Shavelsky also taught at the Faculty of Theology of the University of Sofia from 1924 to 1939 and while in Bulgaria published a number of works, some of which were critical of the treatment of religion in the Soviet Union. See *Almanakh na Sofiiskiya universitet Sv. Kliment Okhridski; zhivotopisni i knigopisni svedeniya za prepodavatelite* (Almanac of the Sofia University of St Clement of Ohrid: Biographical and Bibliographical Data of the Faculty Members) (Sofia, 1940), pp. 673–4. Biryuzov refers to him as 'notorious for his hatred of everything Soviet'.

14. The draft proposed by the Agrarians in the opposition was quite favourable to the Church. On the circumstances of the adoption of the Communist constitution, see B. Spasov and A. Angelov, *Dŭrzhavno pravo na Narodna Republika Bŭlgariya* (Constitutional Law of the People's Republic of Bulgaria) 2nd ed. (Sofia: Nauka i Izkustvo, 1968), pp. 51–8.

15. *Ibid.*, pp. 496–9.

16. *Tsŭrkoven Vestnik*, 15 May 1948.

17. Andrei held the office after it was established (under the jurisdiction of the Metropolitan of Sofia) in 1937 to minister to the needs of Orthodox Bulgarians in the United States and Canada. He had become increasingly apprehensive about the future of the 'captive Church' and Church-State relations in Bulgaria and on 26 June 1947 he convoked a *subor* in Buffalo, New York, which elected him bishop of an expanded eparchy of North and South America and Australia. The eparchy was also incorporated under the laws of the state of New York so as to organise a self-contained religious life of the Orthodox Bulgarians overseas.

18. For these and other details of the affairs, see *Tsŭrkoven Vestnik*, 15 May 1948. The Synod relieved Andrei of his duties but he continued to exercise them and

on 4 July 1963, after a trip by Metropolitan Pimen of Nevrokop, the Synod reinstated him as 'canonical Metropolitan' of the eparchy; cf. *ibid.*, 6 July 1963. In 1971 he visited Sofia and, according to reports, delivered for keeping in the Bulgarian Academy of Sciences 'originals of valuable documents on Bulgarian history'.

19. Text in *Naroden Pastir* (People's Pastor – organ of the Priests' Union), 1 June 1948. The communication was also addressed to the eparchies and their sub-divisions, the dean of the Faculty of Theology, the heads of the theological seminaries in Sofia and Plovdiv, the head of the theological institute in Cherepish, the unions of priests, Orthodox Christian brotherhoods and church employees, the publications *Tsŭrkoven Vestnik*, *Naroden Pastir*, *Tsŭrkoven Sluzhitel*, and *Pravoslaven Pastir*, and the rector of the University of Sofia. It was obviously intended to have the widest possible notice.

20. *Tsŭrkoven Vestnik*, 19 July 1948. Italics in the text.

21. Text *ibid.*, 7 October 1948.

22. *Ibid.*, 21 September 1948.

23. *Ibid.* Iliev's statement suggests that financial pressure was also used, or at least that discontinuance of the annual state subsidy was rumoured. The subsidy was indeed discontinued in 1950, when the Church was put on a self-support-ing basis, but its main source of revenue, the sale of candles, proved in-adequate (it went down from 150–180 tons annually before the war to 55 tons in 1953) and the state subsidy was restored in undisclosed annual amounts.

24. *Ibid.*, 23 October 1948.

25. For details on the pre-war status of the Bulgarian Jews, their treatment during World War II, and post-war developments, see Peter Meyer and others, *The Jews in the Soviet Satellites* (Syracuse University Press, 1953), pp. 557–629. The fact that no Bulgarian Jews were delivered to the Nazis for extermination during the war has produced a number of publications, most of them by Bulgarian Jews; for a sample, see Kh. D. Oliver, *We were saved; how the Jews in Bulgaria were kept from the death camps* (Sofia: Foreign Languages Press, 1967).

26. The armistice agreement of 28 October 1944 provided for termination of all disabilities imposed during the war because of their ethnic origin or religion. The peace treaty signed on 10 February 1947 provided (Article 2) that 'Bul-garia shall take all measures necessary to secure to all persons under Bulgarian jurisdiction, without distinction as to race, sex, language or religion, the enjoyment of human rights and of the fundamental freedoms, including freedom of expression, of press and publication, of religious worship, or political opinion and of public meeting.'

27. The early history of the Bulgarian Protestants is detailed by William W. Hall, *Puritans in the Balkans: The American Board Mission in Bulgaria, 1878–1918* (Sofia, 1938). The most important of the Protestant schools was the American College in Sofia. On its history and role, see the account by its president, Floyd H. Black, *The American College of Sofia* (Boston, 1958).

28. On the Catholic schools, see K. Drenikoff, *L'Église Catholique en Bulgarie* (Madrid, 1968). The highest among them was the St Augustin College for men in Plovdiv.

29. *Rabotnichesko Delo* (organ of the party), 24 February 1949. The Vatican had since 1925 a Visitator (Mgr Angelo Roncalli, the future Pope John XXIII) who was raised to Apostolic Delegate without diplomatic status in 1935. Roncalli was succeeded in 1935 by Mgr Giuseppe Mazzoli upon whose death in December 1945 the post was assigned to Mgr Francesco Galloni, a long-time resident of Bulgaria.

30. *Dŭrzhaven Vestnik*, 1 March 1949; the law is translated n *The Church and State*

under Communism, Vol. II (Washington: Government Printing Office, 1965), pp. 23–6.

31. Articles 26–28 dealing with crimes involving religion were superseded by the Criminal Code (Articles 288 and 303–306) of 13 February 1951, which in turn were superseded by the new Criminal Code of 2 April 1968. Articles 164–166 provide for imprisonment for up to three years 'or correctional labour' in cases of advocacy of hatred on a religious basis; for imprisonment for up to one year in cases of hindering, by force or threat, citizens in freely confessing their religion or performing their religious rites and services unless they violate the laws, public order and rules of socialist life, as well as in cases of compelling a person to participate in religious rites and services; and for imprisonment for up to three years, if not subject to a heavier penalty, in cases of forming a political organisation on a religious basis or using the church and religion for propaganda against the Government and its measures.

32. The Government's version of the case is in *The Trial of Fifteen Protestant Pastors-Spies* (Sofia, 1949) and *Subversive Activities of the Evangelical Pastors in Bulgaria: Documents* (Sofia, 1949). See also Robert Tobias, *Communist-Christian Encounter in East Europe* (Indianapolis, 1956).

33. For an account by one of the fifteen pastors, see Haralan Popoff, *I was a Communist Prisoner* (Grand Rapids, Mich., 1966).

34. Department of State *Bulletin*, 23 October 1950, pp. 666–70.

35. A 'Bill of Indictment' was published in *Rabotnichesko Delo*, 21 September 1952. See also A. Galter, *Le Communisme et l'Église Catholique* (Paris, 1956) and Drenikoff, *L'Église Catholique en Bulgarie*.

36. H. L. Kostanick, *Turkish Resettlement of Bulgarian Turks, 1950–1953* (University of California Press, 1957).

37. Published as supplement to *Tsŭrkoven Vestnik*, 1951; amended *ibid.*, 9 June 1953.

38. Kiril (1901–71) was eminently qualified for the post. After study at the Sofia seminary and the theological faculty of the University of Belgrade, he took monastic vows in 1923 and was sent for advanced work in theology at Chernovtsy, where he earned the doctorate in 1927. His studies also took him to German and Austrian universities and – well educated – he rose quickly to general secretary of the Synod in 1935 and Metropolitan of Plovdiv in 1938. In addition to writing on theological subjects, he was a very active student of church history, having contributed well-researched biographies of three predecessors in the Plovdiv see. For his biobibliography, see *Godishnik na Dukhovnata Akademiya 'Sv. Kliment Okhridski'*, Vol. XIII (Sofia, 1964), pp. 345–432, and M. Pundeff, 'Patriarch Kiril of Bulgaria, 1901–1971,' *Slavic Review*, June 1971, pp. 471–2.

39. *Deianiya na tretiya tsurkovno-naroden subor, Sofiia, 8–10 mai 1953 g.* (Proceedings of the Third Ecclesiastical-Popular Council) (Sofia: Sinodalno knigoizdatelstvo, 1953), pp. 47–50.

40. *Ibid.*, pp. 98–9.

41. As quoted in *Tsŭrkoven Vestnik*, 21 September 1968.

42. *Slaviani* (monthly of the Slavic Committee in Bulgaria), March 1969, pp. 18–19.

43. Text of the document in *Bulgarskata Komunisticheska Partiya v rezoliutsii resheniya na kongresite, na plenumi i na Politbyuro na TsK na BKP, 1956–1962*, (Bulgarian Communist Party in Resolutions and Decisions of Congresses, Plenary Sessions and Politbureau of the C.C. of the B.C.P., 1956–62) Vol. V (Sofia: B.K.P., 1965), pp. 166–72.

44. The results of the survey are reported and analysed in *Protsesŭt na preodoliavaneto na religiyata v Bŭlgariya; sotsiologichesko izsledvane* (Process of the

Overcoming of Religion in Bulgaria: Sociological Investigation), (Sofia: Bulgarska Akademiya na Naukite, 1968). See also *Rabotnichesko Delo*, 18 April 1968.

45. For the titles of Kiril's works, see the references in n. 38 above. Two other works appeared posthumously in 1971: *Bŭlgarskoto naselenie v Makedoniya v borbata za sŭzdavadene na ekzarkhiyata* (Bulgarian Population in Macedonian the Struggle for the Establishment of the Exarchate) and *100 godini ot uchrediavaneto na Bŭlgarskata ekzarkhiya* (100 years since the Establishment of the Bulgarian Exarchate), a collaborative volume edited by Kiril.

46. Text in *Dŭrzhaven Vestnik*, 18 May 1971.

47. Maksim, born in 1914, received his secondary and higher theological education in Sofia and became a monk in 1941. In the post-war years he was head of the *podvorie*, the liaison rectory maintained by the Bulgarian Orthodox Church in Moscow, and general secretary of the Synod. He was made bishop in 1956 and Metropolitan of Lovech in 1960.

48. *Rabotnichesko Delo*, 8 August 1971.

49. *Ibid.*, 15 May 1972.

50. *Spravochnik na aktivista* (Activist's Manual) (Sofia: B.K.P., 1966), pp. 478–80. See also Wayne S. Vucinich, 'Islam in the Balkans,' *Religion in the Middle East: Three Religions in Concord and Conflict*, ed. by A. J. Arberry (Cambridge University Press, 1969), Vol. 2, pp. 236–52.

51. Mizov, *Isliamŭt v Bŭlgariya*, pp. 194–5.

52. See, for example, *Rabotnichesko Delo*, 8, 9 and 18 January 1972.

18 The Position and Activities of the Religious Communities in Yugoslavia

with Special Attention to
The Serbian Orthodox Church

There are over thirty active religious communities in Yugoslavia today. The largest is the Serbian Orthodox Church, followed in order by the Catholic Church, the Islam community and the Macedonian Orthodox Church which separated from the Serbian Orthodox Church in 1967.

This paper deals with the legal and the actual social position and activities of the religious communities in general, and specifically with the Serbian Orthodox Church in Yugoslavia in the post-war period. However, we must, first of all, observe that the relative scarcity of data on the Serbian Orthodox Church and other Churches in the post-war period makes it more difficult to carry out a sociologicial analysis of this problem.

THE POSITION AND ACTIVITY OF THE RELIGIOUS COMMUNITIES PRIOR TO AND DURING WORLD WAR II

In the period prior to the outbreak of the Second World War, the constitutions of 1921 and 1931 guaranteed, in principle, freedom of conscience and religious belief to all citizens. The notions of religious freedom and freedom of conscience naturally also imply the freedom to have atheistic convictions. The pre-war constitutions, however, severely restricted freedom of conscience both in law and in fact, by requiring the performance of religious rites '. . . on State holidays and celebrations and, in so far as the law stipulates, for persons under parental control, guardianship or military authority'.[1] These restrictions on freedom of conscience can be explained by the system of relations between the religious communities and the State. Under this relationship there was neither a State Church nor separation between State and Church, but rather a compromise solution which made religious communities *public institutions with a special status and privileges within the State.*

The restrictions on freedom of religion and conscience were a result, in part, of a distinction adopted in the Yugoslav law, between 'accepted' and 'recognised' religious communities. Under the heading of 'accepted' religious communities came those which had already been legally recognised before the adoption of the 1921 constitution; 'recognised' ones were those that were legally recognised at a later date. This solution was, both in law and in fact, discriminatory, and it frequently brought about the persecution of smaller religious communities, as most of them had not been 'recognised'.

It was forbidden to use the Church as a means of achieving various political ends. This constitutional provision, however, was violated openly and constantly, especially by the representatives of the Catholic Church. Thus the so-called Kancel clause, according to which 'recognised' Churches were to be apolitical institutions did not serve its purpose.

The unity of religion and nationality was one of the general rules of the social life of the time, since Yugoslavia then was a multi-national community, with relations among the nations not being based on the principle of equality and freedom of assertion for all nations. In such a situation, conflicts between individual Churches were inevitable. On the one hand, a cause and effect relationship was constituted among national, religious and political elements and, on the other, comparatively unrelated to this, a class differentiation was taking place which was later to become an essential basis for new social changes which were fully reflected in the creation of post-war Yugoslavia.

It is significant to note that the religious communities executed certain functions which were state functions by nature: keeping records of births and deaths; certain responsibility in contracting marriages and handling marital differences; and functions in the fields of education and culture.

On the whole, it can be said that the Church in pre-war Yugo-slavia constituted a specific part of and was complementary to the State. Since the State itself was marked by numerous contra-dictions, above all of a social, political and national nature, religion was necessarily in a similar position – conflicting, undemo-cratic and, to a large extent, fraught with religious intolerance and hatred.[2]

The Serbian Orthodox Church enjoyed a considerably more favourable position than other Churches. This can be readily explained by the fact that the Serbian leading circles had, for the most part, a decisive say in conducting state affairs. It should also be stressed that during World War II the Serbian Orthodox Church in Yugoslavia supported, as a rule, the popular struggle against foreign occupation. In the course of this struggle, the Patriarch of the Serbian Orthodox Church was deported to a German concentration camp and over 370 Orthodox priests (16 per cent) were murdered by the occupation forces and their col-laborators within the country. This helps to explain the active participation of a part of the Orthodox priests in the National Liberation Movement and its armed struggle.[3]

The number of Orthodox priests who collaborated with the occupational forces was comparatively small, a fact which was of rather great importance in the Church's later normalising rela-tions with the new State. This identity of the interests of the Serbian Orthodox Church with the liberation struggle explains the estab-lishment of the comparatively harmonious relations with the new State.

The activity of the Orthodox clergy during the war can be seen from several of their proclamations. Thus the well-known epistle issued by the Church after the meeting in Srpske Jasenice in 1942 condemns the crimes of the occupiers and their internal collaborators, and invites the peoples in the occupied territory to join the Army of Liberation. This proclamation also invited the Catholic and Muslim clergy to enlist their followers in the struggle against the occupiers. A proclamation issued in 1943 by the Ser-bian Orthodox clergy in the territory of Dalmatia is similar in content.[4] In supporting the people's interests a number of Ortho-dox clergymen, on that occasion too, reiterated the traditional stand of the Serbian Orthodox Church to share the destiny of the people not only in the religious domain but also in other important aspects of life.

Part of the clergy of other religious communities also collaborated with the Army of Liberation. They too, as was the case with the Orthodox clergy, were most often of lower rank, while the higher-ranking clerics were, as a rule, less ready for such co-operation. A prevailing part of the higher Catholic clergy, headed by the then Archbishop Stepinac, openly supported the occupiers and their internal collaborators.

THE POSITION AND ACTIVITIES OF THE RELIGIOUS COMMUNITIES IN THE POST-WAR PERIOD

An early indication of the lines along which the problem of the legal and social status of the Orthodox Church and other Churches was to be settled could be found in the attitude of the National Liberation Movement and in certain legal norms that were instituted by this movement, while the war was still in progress.

Taking into account class, political, national, religious and other contradictions which existed in Yugoslavia prior to the Second World War, the leaders of the National Liberation Movement endeavoured to create conditions in which social life would not be subordinated to the Church nor to any similar socio-philosophical orientation, but would be dependent on social and economic norms. The leaders of the movement further considered that Marxist teaching represented the most scientific world outlook, and they therefore endeavoured to shape social relations accordingly. In order to establish a socialist community based on a federal principle, and to ensure the full and equal rights of all nations and ethnic groups, the leaders of the movement stressed at the very beginning the need to separate Church and State. It was thought that such separation was the most conducive to freedom of religion and conscience and would protect the interests of both the people and the religious communities.

As early as 1942, according to the Foča Documents, which set forth the organisation and duties of the National Liberation Committee, all citizens were granted equal rights and obligations regardless of their political, religious, national or any other characteristics. At the first session of the Anti-Fascist Council of the National Liberation of Yugoslavia in 1942, and at the second session in 1943, the principles concerning the relations between

Church and State were broadened and elaborated, and further work was done on establishing administrative, legal and political institutions which would apply these principles. As early as 1944, all anti-fascist councils of the federal units formed *commissions for religious questions,* which were entrusted with the tasks of ensuring free expression of religious beliefs and of improving the relations both between religious communities and the State, and among religious communities.[5]

The constitution of the new Yugoslavia, which went into force in January 1946, set forth the following basic provisions concerning freedom of conscience, religious communities and the relations between Church and State (Article 25):

(a) citizens are guaranteed freedom of conscience and religious beliefs;

(b) the Church is separate from the State;

(c) Religious communities whose teachings are not in disagreement with the constitution are guaranteed full freedom in performing their religious functions and rites;

(d) the misuses of the Church and faith for political ends is forbidden as is the existence of political organisations on a religious basis;

(e) theological schools for the training of priests are granted freedom to work, provided they are subordinated to general state control;

(f) the State may aid religious communities financially.

Before the law, the rights and duties of all religious communities were rendered equal and, furthermore, new religious communities could be founded. This democratic principle was, above all, welcomed by the smaller religious communities which had not been 'recognised' in pre-war Yugoslavia. As far as the 'recognised' religious communities were concerned, this principle was considered to be significant in so far as it prevented the hegemony of a single faith which had existed sporadically before the war and had grave consequences on the course of the war itself.

Religion was legally made the private affair of all citizens, not to be interfered with by the State, any political authorities or by any other element external to the religious community itself. In a normative sense, man could freely decide whether or not he would have religious beliefs. Since post-war Yugoslavia was founded on Marxist teachings, it was only natural that the leading forces in society had no desire to organise social relations in such a way that the religiosity of the population would be encouraged. They were, however, at the same time conscious of the fact that the repression of religious beliefs would be in conflict with the humanistic emancipation of man, which was considered to be an essential criterion of social progress.

It should be noted that these constitutional principles occasionally offered the basis for the emergence of certain forms of state pressure over the leaders of some religious communities in the post-war period. This state attitude should be considered in the light of the circumstances existing at the time. Indeed the State was forced to use fairly strict measures, as many attempts were made by the leaders of certain religious communities (both larger and smaller) to act as organised political forces against the existing social system. As this system was struggling to establish itself, it could not run the risk of allowing greater tolerance and openr.1indedness as it is able to do today. During the so-called phase of administrative socialism in Yugoslavia, with its Stalinistic concepts in the organisation of social relations, there were no practical possibilities of achieving a higher degree of latitude or democracy. Tension was mainly reflected in the relations with the Catholic Church, particularly in the period after the end of the war, and later, in the period between 1952 and 1965, which ended with the signature of the Protocol with the Holy See in 1966. The major difficulties in relations with the Serbian Orthodox Church appeared in the year following the war, after which there was constant improvement in these relations, with only minor difficulties of short duration arising sporadically.

The expropriation of some church property was one of the major causes of tension in the relationship between the State and the religious communities. According to the 1945 Agrarian Reform and Colonisation Law, all large land-owners were expropriated. The more important and historically significant religious institutions were left with up to 30 acres of arable land and up to 30 acres of woodland. This government measure was often interpreted (especially outside the country) as proof of religious persecution. It is beyond any doubt that this expropriation seriously affected the economic interests of the religious communities. Nevertheless it was simply a general social measure aimed at establishing more equitable economic relations in society in general, and it is understandable that religious communities could not be exempted. The nationalisation of buildings and rented housing space (the law of 1958) did not extend to the buildings used by religious communities for the performance of their religious rites and other related activities.

The above-mentioned constitutional principles were further developed in the Law on Religious Communities of 1953 which helped to dispel misunderstanding and opposition by slightly liberalising and more precisely defining the legal status of religious organisations.

In the 1963 constitution, this tendency towards liberalisation became still more apparent. Apart from the provision according to which 'the abuse of religion and religious activities is unconstitutional if used for political ends', there is no other basis for repressive measures, or state control. The provision of the 1946 constitution concerning the control over religious schools was deleted. A new paragraph was formulated, stating that 'religious communities may have the right of ownership of real estate within the limits set by federal law'. The tendency towards liberalisation could be observed in 1965 when the Law on Religious Communities was made consistent with the new constitution. As there were actually many cases of arbitrary interpretation of what constituted the violation of religious freedom, an attempt was made to define precisely the basic aspects and elements of such a violation. In this sense, protection under the constitution became far greater.

Problems regarding the existence of religious communities were also settled by means of other laws which cannot be examined here in greater detail. The 1951 regulations on the social insurance of priests was, for example, of great importance. It was later modified, showing the greater understanding of the Government for the problems of the religious communities and their professional staff. Publishing by religious communities was regulated by the general law on publishing activities of 1949; this law did not discriminate against the religious communities, and it can be said that this question was settled in accordance with the constitutional principles concerning religious communities. The Yugoslav legislation on religion thus constantly evolved towards liberalisation and reflected a greater understanding of the State for the problems of religious communities. After the rather negative experiences and difficulties following the Second World War, the Yugoslav political leaders have in the past ten to fifteen years firmly held the opinion that full and unrestricted religious freedom constitutes a vital condition for preventing the politicisation of the religious communities. As this view has been borne out by experience, it is certain that the authorities will make every attempt to see that this freedom is realised in the fullest sense of the word; all the more so since they are convinced that integral atheism, as an expression of man's spiritual and social freedom, can only be achieved by a complete recognition of the right of religious belief.

The main purpose of the 1971 amendments to the constitution was to consolidate self-management and to provide for a greater assertion of ethnic groups. Consequently we can expect that in the near future certain republics will further develop the legal status of the religious communities. We can expect, with reason, that the process of liberalisation will, in this manner, be continued still further, and that the specific features of certain religious communities within the constituent republics will be given a more humane and precise treatment by means of new and specific legal acts. However, these prospects also carry the possibility of revived politicisation of certain religious communities, provoked by the very assertion of the ethnic groups and nationalities in some of the constituent republics. If this should occur, conflicts on an institutional basis are certain to take place between religious communities and the State.

PRESENT ANTAGONISMS AND DIFFICULTIES IN THE
RELATIONSHIP BETWEEN THE SERBIAN ORTHODOX
CHURCH AND THE STATE

Although, in general, the activity of the Serbian Orthodox Church has developed within the framework of the constitutional principles and legal norms, recent differences between this Church and the State have threatened the harmony which has generally prevailed in their relations. The source of contradictions and difficulties appears to be the Serbian Orthodox Church's concept of itself, its tasks and its role. Envisioning religion as the highest norm of life, and the initial source and shelter of all essential forms of human activities, the Church is attempting to become the supreme arbiter in defining the essence and the ways of fulfilling human existence.

The most frequent and most serious difficulties emerge in connection with the Church's treatment of the question of multinational relations – a problem which has always been complex and politically very delicate in Yugoslavia. Though the Serbian Orthodox Church has supported the principle of brotherhood and unity for all Yugoslav peoples and nationalities, its concept of the historical and even the present role of the Serbian nation differs from the official position on this matter. The point of departure for this Church is that religion is the essence of nationality and that the Serbian nation and the Serbian Orthodox Church are inseparable. The Church's cult of the Serbian past has made the latter appear to be greater and more glorious than it actually was. In a complex multi-national situation this glorification necessarily must have negative implications, above all in relation to the present position and development of other nations. By such an approach the Serbian Orthodox Church is attempting to affirm itself because, in the past conditions of temporary and partial domination by the Serbian nation, its role was also dominant both in relation to other religious communities and in relation to other social institutions.

The Serbian Orthodox Church does not treat the national problem as a separate political problem but as a form and element of religion. Nevertheless this Church has attempted to act as a national, and not only as a confessional institution. The Church's traditional stand on the national problem has recently acquired a new significance, with greater shift in the Yugoslav policy towards the affirmation of the component nations and their statehood. The Catholic Church, a traditional rival of the Serbian Orthodox Church, has also persistently endeavoured to affirm itself as the national Church of Croatia, which could not but encourage the Serbian Orthodox Church to act as a national institution. In this context there has been an increasing tendency within the Serbian Orthodox Church to revive the tragic memories of World War II when, in the Independent State of Croatia, the Ustashas, with the collaboration of the higher Catholic clergy, attempted the genocide of the Serbs. On the other hand, within the Catholic

Church, there has been a tendency to excuse this behaviour during the war.

Differences between the hierarchy of the Serbian Orthodox Church and the State became particularly strong in 1967 in connection with the separation of the Macedonian Orthodox Church from the Serbian Orthodox Church. In this case the Government took steps to prevent the dispute from negatively affecting multi-national relations. Given the very real existence of certain antagonisms and difficulties between particular nations in Yugoslavia, the thesis of 'endangered Serbian individuality', which has increasingly acquired currency among the higher Serbian clergy, is treated by the Yugoslav political leadership as an expression of political rather than religious conviction.

In recent times religious communities, particularly the Catholic Church and the Serbian Orthodox Church, have become increasingly vehement in their requests to use radio and television to inform their congregations and popularise religious convictions so it is possible that in the future disputes will emerge on this question as well.

The position of the Serbian Orthodox Church on the multinational relations represents the views mainly of the higher Orthodox clergy. It is manifested particularly in the quarterly of the Serbian Patriarchate, *Pravoslavlje*, especially since 1969. This tendency is less noticeable in the newspaper *Vesnik* published by the Association of the Clergy of Yugoslavia. The different approach of these two newspapers indicates serious differences between the higher and the lower strata of the clergy – differences which are not restricted to the national problem. The Association of the Clergy is more closely identified with political life and is rather critical of the higher clergy of the Serbian Orthodox Church. It advocates the democratisation of the Church and is more ready to co-operate with other forces of society and to develop both religious and social life in a generally accepted direction as regulated by the constitution.[6]

Another source of difficulty, closely connected with the multinational question, has been the attitude of the Serbian Orthodox Church to other, especially small, religious communities. Under the slogan 'against false teachers of faith' representatives of the Serbian Orthodox Church sometimes carry the polemics against their religious opponents to the extremes of intolerance and even fastidiousness, as was the case with polemics carried by *Pravoslavlje* in 1971 against Adventists and Jehovah's Witnesses. Recalling past manifestations of religious intolerance, individual government representatives sometimes condemn even those dialogues between religious communities which do not exceed the bounds of orderly debate.

In recent times questions of the upbringing of children and youth have increasingly attracted the attention of the State, socio-political organisations and religious communities. The activities of religious communities in this sphere exceeds the narrow frame-work of religious education and encompasses the entire moral, cultural and social development of the young. The Serbian Ortho-dox Church has fallen behind the Catholic Church in terms of the intensity and quality of activities in this field. It is characteristic, however, that the Orthodox Church has recently made consider-able efforts to become a significant influential factor on the general development of the young. The State and the Communist Party in particular are endeavouring to thwart the Church in this respect primarily by strengthening their own influence, rarely applying pressure against churches in the educational field. Should religious communities expand these activities, however, pressure may be applied more frequently.

It is characteristic that the Serbian Orthodox Church (as well as other religious communities) seeks to exert influence predomi-nantly in the domains where the educational activity of various state institutions is weakest. One such domain is the leisure activity of the young. It is interesting that this Church, which is generally deemed to be too preoccupied with the past, demonstrates a de-veloped sense for innovations – both in the content of leisure activity and in the method of its organisation. The Orthodox Church has, however, remained strictly traditional in its treat-ment of changing sexual mores among the youth. The so-called sexual revolution is most often qualified as the 'epidemic of de-bauchery'. The classical patriarchal marriage is viewed as the only acceptable form of sex relations and the only alternative to this tendency. Sex education is accepted only as a necessity, and only in so far as it contributes to the cult of virtue, particularly to the cult of maidenhood. In taking such a position, the Serbian Orthodox Church has not encountered resistance from the authorities but it has often aroused opposition from the liberally oriented circles of intellectuals.

In Yugoslavia there have long been efforts to make self-management the basic principle of social relations and the most essential characteristic of the socio-political system. The Serbian Orthodox Church has not long supported this orientation. In recent times the Orthodox publications have asserted that 'personality is a Christian discovery' and that self-management, in so far as it contributes to the development of personality and individuality, follows the same line as Christianity. This analysis rejected the official thesis that the development of self-management will bring about a gradual decline in religiosity. Although this dialogue is still within the framework of normal theoretical differences, it at the same time represents a latent contradiction.

Generally speaking, the causes of the tensions between the Serbian Orthodox Church and the State are not confined to the scope of the Church's activity alone. The behaviour of state institutions and political organisations has not always corresponded to the legal norms governing relations between Church and State. This behaviour most often takes the form of primitive atheistic articles in some newspapers or of arbitrary acts of individual local officials. It is characteristic that the religious press, as a rule, strongly and uncompromisingly reacts to such cases.

ECONOMIC POSITION OF RELIGIOUS COMMUNITIES AND SOME OF THEIR ACTIVITIES

According to official statistics for 1969, religious communities operate over 14,000 churches, monasteries, mosques and other church buildings. The Catholic Church owns 6,936 of them, the Serbian and Macedonian Orthodox Churches 4,154, and the Islamic community 2,180, while other religious communities have a total of 778 houses of worship. These figures do not include the large number of smaller chapels.

Approximately 2,800 church buildings have the status of cultural and historical monuments and are, as such, mainly preserved by the State, although they are owned by religious communities. The Catholic Church owns 1,900 such monuments, the Serbian and Macedonian Orthodox Churches 480, and the Islamic community 400

About 3,000 buildings (residences of bishops, school buildings, vacation centres, etc.), as well as some 2,000 parishes and other centres are in possession of religious communities. They also own several very valuable libraries and museums.

The main sources of income for religious communities are religious services and agricultural estates, proceeds from other church activities, contributions from inside and outside the country, and substantial revenues provided by the State.

Social insurance for priests is not compulsory, but depends on whether the supreme organ of the religious community or the association of priests signs a contract with the social security agencies. So far sixteen religious communities, including the Serbian and Macedonian Orthodox Churches, and priest associations have concluded such contracts. The cost and the kind of social insurance offered to religious communities do not differ from those extended to the rest of the Yugoslav population. The State makes a small contribution to the social insurance of the priests, and the remaining part is paid by the parishes or by the priests themselves.

The theological schools in Yugoslavia may be attended only by persons who have completed compulsory primary education. Persons attending such schools enjoy the same privileges as are guaranteed to persons attending other schools. There are some 50 advanced theological institutions, secondary and lower schools for the training of priests. The Catholic Church has the greatest number of such institutions: 19 secondary schools with 2,109 pupils, and 11 advanced schools (including two theological faculties with 1,256 students. In addition, 70 Catholic theology students study abroad. The Serbian Orthodox Church has only one theological faculty in Belgrade with a total of 120 students and five secondary schools which are attended by 647 pupils. The Macedonian Orthodox Church has one secondary school with 92 pupils. Several other religious communities also have secondary schools.

Religious communities engage in vast publishing activities, the scope of which increases every year. Thus the total annual printing of religious publications (reviews, magazines, books) amounted to over 5 million copies in 1963, over 7 million in 1964 and over 13·5 million in 1965, of which 11 million were published by the Catholic Church.[7]

DISTRIBUTION OF RELIGIOUS BELIEFS

There are no reliable data on the number of faithful and the intensity of religious beliefs among the Yugoslav population. It is also difficult to assess the scope of activities of certain religious communities. Some research findings suggest that there has not been any recent increase in the number of faithful in Yugoslavia, but an increase of the number of those who freely express their religious beliefs. Even though the State has always respected religious freedom, the atheistic social climate was considered by some faithful to be an obstacle to the public expression of their religiosity. With a more democratic social atmosphere, the tendency to conceal one's religious conviction has been disappearing. At the same time there has been less and less of a dogmatic interpretation of socialist ideology in Yugoslav life.

Recently, atheistic propaganda in Yugoslavia has been less intensive and has differed from that in the immediate post-war period. Marxist axiology has increasingly developed in an attempt to replace simplified atheistic propaganda. Frequent dialogues between Marxists and theologians (in joint publications, in public lectures, at faculty gatherings, etc.) represent some of the expressions of this new orientation.

Interesting data on the distribution of religious beliefs resulted from sociological research projects carried out over the past few years. The Institute of Social Sciences in Belgrade investigated the religiosity of students in 1960, 1965 and 1968. The 1960 survey examined the largest sample (4,000 respondents) selected from across Yugoslavia. Of the students who participated in this anonymous survey 19·7 per cent declared themselves to be religious. If this is considered in the light of the areas of influence of different religious communities, certain differences may be observed. The greatest number of those who declared themselves to be religious came from the area of influence of the Catholic Church, followed by those from the Muslim area and, lastly, those from the historically Orthodox area.

In terms of ethnic distribution, 33 per cent of the Croatian students declared themselves to be religious; 23 per cent of the Slovenian students (who are traditionally as Catholic as the Croats), and the same percentage of students of Muslim origin (23 per cent). Among those who are traditionally Orthodox, the highest percentage of students who declared themselves to be religious were Macedonians (19 per cent), then Serbians (16 per cent), and least of all Montenegrins (8 per cent).

The percentage of believers among female students proved to be higher (26 per cent) than the percentage among males (17 per cent).

In the first year of studies, religiosity was found to be 27 per cent and in the last year 19 per cent. While the social background showed little correlation with religiosity, it is interesting to observe that the greatest number of those holding atheistic beliefs came from the villages.

On this occasion, students gave their estimate of the religiosity of their parents. According to their statements, 58 per cent of the parents were religious, 30 per cent were atheists and 11 per cent oscillated between religiosity and atheism.[8]

Later investigations provided similar results, although in some cases noticeable changes were observed.

A research project carried out by this writer at the end of 1968 and the beginning of 1969 attempted, among other things to provide more precise data about differences in the expansion of religious beliefs in the Orthodox and Catholic environments. The respondents (545) were pupils in the final grades of secondary schools (gymnasia) in three smaller towns that were similar in all more important characteristics except in regard to religious orientation. Cacak was chosen as the typical Orthodox town in the territory of Serbia, Varazdin as a typical Catholic town in the territory of Croatia, and Bihac as a typical mixed town in the territory of Bosnia and Herzegovina. Using several methodological procedures we found that the percentage of religious pupils in the Orthodox environment was 15 per cent, while it was 40 per cent in the Catholic environment. Twenty-seven per cent of the respondents' fathers in the Orthodox environment were religious, while in the Catholic environment the percentage was 48 per cent; 43 per cent of the mothers in the Orthodox environment were religious, while in the Catholic environment 63 per cent belong to this category.

The Public Opinion Research Association in Japan carried out research on various aspects of the social consciousness of youth in 64 towns in 56 countries in the middle of 1970. Yugoslavia and Poland were the only socialist countries included in this research.

The respondents were secondary-school boys and girls, aged 16 to 22. Among other things data on religiosity were also collected. In Belgrade, where the Serbian Orthodox Church's influence is dominant, 63 per cent of the respondents declared themselves to be atheists, 23 per cent as religious and 14 per cent did not believe but habitually maintained religious rituals.

In 38 countries – out of a total of 53 – the majority of respondents declared belief in God. In four countries the majority chose the alternative 'pray to God out of habit' while in 11 countries the majority declared they were non-religious. The religious believers were dominant in Panama – 94 per cent, Egypt – 93 per cent, Indonesia – 91 per cent, Venezuela – 90 per cent, Spain – 88 per cent, Argentina – 87 per cent, Peru – 84 per cent, Chile – 84 per cent, Paraguay – 82 per cent, Italy – 90 per cent, etc. The atheistic orientation prevailed in the following 11 countries: the highest percentage was in Sweden – 72 per cent, then in Yugoslavia – 63 per cent, the Netherlands – 54 per cent, West Germany – 54 per cent, Finland – 52 per cent, France – 51 per cent, Japan – 49 per cent, Denmark – 49 per cent, Poland – 49 per cent, Austria – 46 per cent, and Hong Kong – 44 per cent.[9]

A statement issued by the Patriarch of the Serbian Orthodox Church in 1970 also speaks about the state of religious consciousness of the population living in the territory under the influence of this Church:

> By our statistics only an insignificant part of the Serbian Orthodox population accept priests to their homes, read religious publications and actively participate in the church's life. Where are the others? The others are fast asleep. . . .
>
> The question must be asked: Who are our people afraid of, when all that we demand of them is permitted by our positive state laws? So, these are hard times for our people when they themselves become indifferent towards all that is sacred duty and obligation to cherish and protect.[10]

NOTES

1. *Ustav Kraljevine Jugoslavie* (Constitution of the Kingdom of Yugoslavia), (Belgrade, 1931), Art. 11.
2. Stefanovic Jovan, *Odnos crkvizmedu i države* (Relationship between the Church and the State) (Zagreb, 1953), p. 101, 128.

3. *Spomenica pravoslavnog sveštenstva 1941–1945* (Anthology of Works on the Activity of the Orthodox Clergy, 1941–1945) (Belgrade, 1970), p. 9.
4. *Ibid.*, pp. 174, 180.
5. *Vjerske zajednice u Jugoslaviji* (Religious Communities in Yugoslavia) (Zagreb, 1970), p. 57.
6. *Politika*, 26 January 1971. A 1971 letter addressed by the Association to President Tito, stated: 'The Clerical Association, which beside its professional church nature has also a pronounced social character with a progressive orientation in its activities has grown to its proper expression and full affirmation precisely in Socialist Yugoslavia under your leadership. In this connection we are glad to emphasise that your exceptional attention and understanding of the cause of the Association of the Orthodox Clergy has provided a great impetus for its positive development.'
7. Statistical data are from the book *Vjerske zajednice u Jugoslaviji*, pp. 7–44.
8. M. Janićijević, M. Broćić, M. Glušćević, and J. Stanković, *Jugoslovenski studenti i socijalizam* (Yugoslav Students and Socialism) (Belgrade, 1966), pp. 253–72.
9. *How Young World. A Survey of Students in 63 Cities, 56 Countries* (Tokyo, 1970), pp. 12–15.
10. *Pravoslavlje*, No. 78 (1970).

19 Religion and Social Change in Yugoslavia

BOGDAN DENITCH

HISTORY

Before a sociologist or political scientist can begin to assess the relationship of religion to social change in Yugoslavia, he must turn to the social historian. In any complex polity the historical dimension is ignored only at the researcher's peril: this is particularly the case in the Balkans. The development of modern nationalism and state-building from the 19th century on has been greatly influenced by a variety of romantic historiography which, though often poor in scholarship, has served an essential function in helping to develop the national identity of peoples who had been submerged for almost five centuries by the two great empires in the Balkans.

The two empires, Austria and Turkey (and, to a lesser extent, the Republic of Venice), had distinctive religious policies which have affected the development of the religious communities and institutions in the Balkans.[1] To the beginning of the 19th century, membership in a religious community was the accepted definition of nationality throughout the Turkish empire, in so far as nationality was accepted at all. In the Austrian lands national identity was complicated in that the state religion, Roman Catholicism, was also often the religion of the subject peoples. However, when this was not the case, as with the Serbian Orthodox frontiersmen and the Romanian Uniate peasantry, religion, or rather religious institutions, formed the framework within which their modern nationalism developed.

Yugoslavia had the dubious fortune to be composed of lands with widely different political cultures, institutions and religions. Religious diversity was perceived as an obstacle to building a

modern nation throughout the 19th century, even by the non-
clerical intelligentsia influenced by the ideas of the French Revolution. This attitude was sharply stated by Spyridon Trikoupis,
a Greek historian in the 19th century: 'Blessed is the nation that
professes one and the same faith. We (Greeks) possess this blessing
– thanks be to God – and cursed by the nation is he who will
conspire against the unity of the faith of the Greeks, through
alien teachings, no matter what the pretext, or whatever the
means.'[2]

Early wars of national liberation in the Balkans started under
quasi-religious auspices, and the political slogans of the early
Serbian and Greek revolutionists did not distinguish between a
battle *for the faith* and a battle *for freedom and independence*.
This was because under the Turks the religious communities had
maintained a degree of communal self-government under their
own hierarchy, which in the case of the Orthodox was subservient
to the Ecumenical Patriarch in Constantinople. The Patriarchate
in effect provided a skeleton civil service for the subject Christian
populations within the Turkish Empire. Thus the struggle for
church autonomy among the Orthodox preceded in many cases
the struggle for political independence. The Patriarchate was perceived, rightly or wrongly, as one of the arms of Turkish
authority. By the mid-19th century the ecumenical patriarchate
in Constantinople was increasingly identified with the rival claims
of Greek nationalism, particularly in Macedonia and Bulgaria.
In Bulgaria, for example, we have an almost laboratory-pure case
of the birth of modern nationalism occurring within the framework
of a newly-autonomous Bulgarian Church (founded in 1872).
In the case of Serbian nationalism, an independent Serbian Patriarch existed from the mid-16th century to 1766, when it was
abolished in good part because of its continual involvement with
the various revolts against the Turks. In these early revolts, which
preceded the Serbian Revolution of 1804, the Orthodox Church
of Serbia provided much of the leadership and acted as the spokesman of the rebels, particularly in their dealings with the Austrian
Empire. An autonomous Church of Serbia was re-established in
1832, as soon as an autonomous principality was firmly organised.

These struggles for national independence under Turkish rule
set in motion one of the first of the major social changes in that
area, the effects of which are still present. The Church led a series

of mass migrations, culminating with the migrations of 1690 and 1739 to the Austrian lands. There it was given exceptional privileges within a basically unified territory, most of which was organised as the Military Frontier.[3] The Military Frontier was characterised by an absence of feudal relationships and the subordination of the social organisation to the needs of the military organization. The Church, therefore, for over a century represented the only legitimate civil leadership for the Serbs living within the Frontier – where most Serbian subjects of Austria lived, in any case. By the 19th century a small secular intelligentsia developed among the Serbs in Austria which played a major role in the reorganisation of the new Serbian state after autonomy was gained from the Turks (1815–30).

Further, the mass migrations of the Orthodox also changed the ethnic map of the Balkans by encouraging massive settlement in lands which previously had been Catholic. The long-drawn-out hostility between the Orthodox and Catholic Churches in those areas had obvious consequences in pre-war and wartime Yugoslavia. This hostility was based at least in part on repeated attempts by the Catholic hierarchy to force the Orthodox to become Uniates once Austrian rule was extended to these areas. Within the territory still controlled by the Ottomans, Catholic–Orthodox rivalry was often sharpened by the fact that the Orthodox Church, particularly during the existence of the Independent Serbian Patriarchate of Peč, attempted to exert its authority over, and even sometimes collect Church taxes from, the Catholic population in Bosnia–Herzegovina. The Turks, quite naturally, favoured a Church whose seat was under their control to one which not only accepted the authority and leadership of Rome, but also identified with the political claims of the rival and Catholic Empire, thus acting more or less consistently as one of the foci of opposition.

While the Orthodox Church in the Yugoslav lands was identified with newly awakened Serbian nationalism, the role of the other major faiths was more ambiguous. The Muslims were part of the ruling faith of a multi-religious empire. They therefore resolutely opposed the various struggles for national liberation, since religious indentification rather than language or ethnicity remained primary for Bosnian Muslim Slavs until very recently. The Bosnian Muslims, in many cases descendants of the Slavic feudal nobility, were thought of as Turks by their co-nationals of Orthodox and Catholic faith. More to the point, they participated as part of the ruling stratum in the Empire. It was not until the mid-19th century that Bosnian Muslims found themselves developing a national opposition to the Ottomans. This was, however, in good part because they were more traditionalist Muslims and consequently resisted the spasmodic efforts to modernise the Ottoman Empire through the introduction of Western-type administrative and military reforms by the Turkish Government.

In the case of the Catholics, their Church acted as one of the major factors which kept the multi-national Austrian Empire together. This was the case even after the religious reforms of the early 19th century. Although Catholicism was identified with Hapsburg Loyalism, by the mid-19th century, some Croat church leaders, particularly Bishop Strossmeyer, supported unity of the South Slavs. The Church, therefore, took a more complex stance towards the movements for the unification of the Yugoslav peoples. For the vast mass of Croatians, however, Catholicism remained practically synonymous with nationality. This was particularly the case since only the most minimal linguistic differences exist between the Serbs and the Croats. In the case of the Slovenian lands, the problem of religion as a surrogate for national identity hardly arose, since Slovenia was almost homogeneously Catholic, and the early Slovenian political rebirth in the 19th century was identified with a church-dominated Christian Social Party. Religious differences in practice played a major role primarily in those areas which were religiously mixed.

The inter-war period was characterised by a failure of the Yugoslav political *élites* to solve the national question. While the Royal Yugoslav Government practised religious tolerance during its entire existence from 1918 to 1941, the rival Churches continued to act as spokesmen for different nationalist claims. The Serbian Church was, of course, by and large loyalist, identifying itself with the dynasty and the new Yugoslav state. It entered into conflict with the Government only when the Belgrade Government signed a Concordat with the Vatican in 1936 giving what the Orthodox hierarchy and Serbian nationalists believed were too many concessions to the Roman Catholic Church. The Catholic hierarchy in Croatia and Bosnia not only identified with

Croatian nationalism, but for a variety of reasons tended to support a pro-Axis policy. The Slovenian Catholic leaders supported the central Government. Thus, after the dismemberment of Yugoslavia, following the German attack of April 1941, the Churches found themselves in very different situations. The Orthodox Church, identified as it was with Serbian nationalism, found itself proscribed and subject to massacres and forcible conversions within the territory of the new Axis satellite Croatian state. The Catholic hierarchy of Croatia and Bosnia not only welcomed the occupiers, but in a number of cases, including that of Archbishop Šarić of Sarajevo, actively supported the Croatian Uštasi (Fascist) authorities and their pogroms against the Orthodox and the Jews, as well as against Communist and anti-Fascist Croats. The Muslim notables by and large supported the Germans and their Croatian allies in the early years of the occupation. The result was a fanning of the national and religious hatreds which manifested themselves in the mutual massacres of the Catholic, Orthodox and Muslim inhabitants of the mixed areas. These massacres, involving the complicity of at least sections of the Catholic, Muslim and Orthodox hierarchies, made the Civil War victory of the Communist-led Partisans, who were not identified with any specific religion or nationality, an indispensible precondition for the restoration of a unified Yugoslavia. The traditional *élites* having failed, the continued existence of Yugoslavia required a rigorous separation of the Church and the State, and an attempt to break down religious and national particularism.

Modern nationalism in Yugoslavia took two basic forms. Briefly, they could be labelled Jacobin and Legitimist. Jacobin nationalism, drawing its inspiration from the French Revolution, tended to be secular and to identify national claims with the territory inhabited by the given national population, ignoring and often opposing the traditional and historical or religious divisions. It was particularly characteristic of Serbian and Macedonian nationalism. Legitimist nationalism based its claims on historic and legal claims, that is, it identified the nation with historic territorial units and areas in which the given nation might well not have a numerical majority. A well-known example of this was that of Hungarian nationalism within the Austro-Hungarian Empire, where the Magyar spokesmen spoke in terms of the unity of the 'lands of the crown of St Stephen', lands which were in many cases inhabited by absolute majorities of Romanians, Slovaks and South Slavs. The 'nation' was identified with the *political nation* and the other groups were 'inhabitants', having rights only in so far as they accepted the basically Magyar character of the State. At least some major strands of Croatian nationalism were based on clericalism and legitimism and the heirs of conservative parties of the 'Croatian Rights' and the 'Pure Party of Rights' demanded the 'historic' frontiers of Croatia, naturally including areas like Bosnia–Herzegovina, where the Catholic Croat population numbered approximately 25 per cent of the total, and where the claims were based on pre-15th century frontiers.

It is this historic nationalism which has generally been absolutist and uncompromising, and has been and remains associated with the more conservative groups within the church hierarchy and among the clerical intellectuals.

SOCIAL CHANGE

The basic unresolved social problem in pre-war Yugoslavia was the agrarian question.[4] It was also among the peasants that the religious institutions maintained the firmest organisation. The three major religious groups, however, did not have a similar attitude towards land reform, urgently needed by the peasantry. The Orthodox Church, in general more subservient to the day-to-day policies of the Government and owning less land, did not work against the land reform. The Catholic hierarchy was both politically more independent and more conservative, viewing itself as a bulwark against social revolution. A major landowner, it was hostile to a break-up of major land estates. The Muslim institutions basically reflected the interests of the semi-feudal Muslim landlords and notables and bargained very skillfully to delay the application of land reform to Bosnia and Macedonia, the two areas with substantial Muslim populations. The three Churches not only had divergent attitudes towards land reform, but also had entirely different linkages to the faithful. The Orthodox believers were the least organised and showed the lowest participation in church institutions. The Catholic Church, although threatened by anti-clerical currents which had begun developing among the more advanced intelligentsia in Zagreb, nevertheless maintained and still maintains the strongest hold over its believers – which is the major reason why the Catholic

Church was and remains a political force. Studies show that the Catholic Church is today probably the only serious church organisation in Yugoslavia.[5]

The role of the Churches during the war permitted the Party to move large sections of the peasantry from their traditional attitudes and made it possible to accelerate the process of urbanisation and modernisation. This role was, of course, primarily negative. The Churches had discredited themselves, even among many of the traditionally faithful, by either overt or covert collaboration with the occupier and proved incapable of forming an opposition to the policies of the Yugoslav Communists in the immediate post-war years.

For at least a decade after the end of World War II the Party and Government showed considerable direct, active hostility towards organised religion. This anti-clericalism aroused less resistance than might have been expected because the Churches had discredited themselves during the war. A part of the Muslim religious establishment was compromised by its collaboration with the new Fascist state of Croatia and by its acceptance of the Mufti of Jerusalem as a leader who helped to recruit an entire S.S. division of Muslim Slavs. All the figures in the Catholic hierarchy of Croatia and Bosnia, including Archbishop Šarić of Sarajevo and Archbishop Stepinac, collaborated with the new satellite Croat state and the Axis occupiers. The record of the lower hierarchy was not much better, and in parts of Bosnia and Herzegovina Franciscans were even involved directly in massacres of the Orthodox peasantry. To be sure, a few Catholic priests aided the Partisans, but this was clearly against the orders of their superiors, except in the case of Slovenia. The Orthodox hierarchy was less involved in collaboration. The Serbian Orthodox Patriarch Gavrilo had been imprisoned during the war, which of course helped him to retain his position after the war. However, although some priests supported the Partisans – one even became a member of the General Staff – they were suspected, with good reason, of monarchist and nationalist sentiments, and thus of backing the forces of Mihailovic in the civil war against the Partisans.

The repressive policies towards organised religion in the early post-war years failed to provoke substantial resistance, since many non-Communists felt that the Churches had clearly discredited themselves during the war and had had a substantial share of responsibility for the virulent nationalism and chauvinism which had led to fratricidal massacres. It is difficult to overestimate the revulsion which these massacres and civil war had aroused, even among the believers, and particularly among the young. The Churches found themselves in a situation where they had lost a good deal of their legitimacy, and where the old utilisation of religion as a surrogate for national identity began to break down. This was marked in the early post-war years in the situation of the Catholic Church in Croatia. Its titular leader, Archbishop Stepinac of Zagreb, had been tried as a collaborator and was effectively removed from any participation in church affairs by being exiled to his native village after being released from prison. Other church figures had found themselves exiled or compromised to such an extent that the Church in the early period had to cultivate a very low profile. In contrast to the situation in Poland, where the Party had to deal with a church organisation which had maintained its continuity and legitimacy as a national institution and which had actively participated in the Resistance, the Catholic Church in Yugoslavia had to compromise to continue to exist. Despite the current policy of the Yugoslav Government of religious toleration, land reform had expropriated the church holdings, and the influence of the Church among the young, educated and modern has been declining sharply until very recently.

This paper deals only with the three major religious groups in Yugoslavia: the Serbian and Macedonian Orthodox, Roman Catholic and Muslim. There are, to be sure, over thirty registered religious communities; however, the other ones are small, localised and without particular importance. The fate of existing religious communities has been drastically affected by the war and its consequences. The Jewish community was almost exterminated by the Germans and their allies and was subsequently further reduced by emigration. The Protestant community had been based in large part on the German minority in Vojvodina, which was, by and large, deported after the war. The more recent Yugoslav censuses do not break down the population by religious affiliation. However, a comparison of the pre-war and post-war breakdowns can, however, be adequately seen from the following table:[6]

TABLE 1

	Year: 1931		1953	
Total population:	13,933	100%	16,937	100%
(*in thousands*)				
Orthodox	6,785	48·7	7,011	41·4
Catholic	5,218	37·4	5,383	31·8
Protestant	231	1·7	148	0·9
Muslim	1,561	11·2	2,083	12·3
Other Christian	68	0·5	71	0·4
Jewish	68	0·5	—	—
Others and undeclared	2	—	156	0·9
Atheists	—	—	2,085	12·3

From Table 1 it can be seen that the major changes which emerge are: the relative drop in membership of the Orthodox and Catholic Churches and the development of the atheist category to the third rank numerically. The Muslim community does not show a drop, primarily because the much higher birth rate is in the Muslim areas. At the same time one must be extremely careful not to identify those who declare themselves as being *members of a confession* with the religious. In all cases, but particularly with the Orthodox, this declaration is often to be taken as a declaration of nationality. As Table 3 shows, the majority of students who do declare themselves as belonging to a particular faith are not practising believers. This is less the case with the population as a whole, but is a qualification which should always be kept in mind.

A factor further affecting the Churches in Yugoslavia in the post-war period was the massive social shift caused by the urbanisation of the country. From a country with barely 20 per cent of the population in the cities, Yugoslavia moved to a ratio of 50 per cent rural, 50 per cent urban, between 1948 and 1960. This shift brought the peasantry into a whole network of relationships and institutions where the Church had little place. This process did not affect all areas equally. One has to turn to the political cultures of Yugoslavia to explain the differential impact of a unitary governmental policy over a range of religions and regions.[7] Today the level of religiosity is lowest in the cities. However, there are certain areas such as Montenegro which, although quite undeveloped and rural, show consistently lower participation and identification with religion, while Slovenia, the most advanced republic, shows the lowest percentage of atheists. The reason for this is to be sought not only in historical background, but also in the shifts of attitudes towards religion by the local political leadership, in what is an increasingly decentralised state. The political establishment in various republics of Yugoslavia often pursues different *de facto* policies towards Churches and believers.

In a recent study of Yugoslav public opinion, by the Centre for Public Opinion of Belgrade,[8] a question was included about the attitude of the public towards the growing activity of the Church in organising social activities for the young.* The results were, for the country as a whole, that 25 per cent approved, 48 per cent disapproved, and 26 per cent had no opinion. In terms of the republics, the rate of approval was highest in Slovenia (48 per cent), and lowest in Montenegro (16 per cent) and the autonomous province of Kosovo (11 per cent). Sixty-nine per cent of the Montenegrins disapproved, against only 26 per cent in Slovenia. Some other breakdowns, however, are probably more indicative of the present attitude towards religion. For example, if we break down the public by age, we will find the age cohort 18–25 was far less religious (21 per cent positive) than the age cohort of 65 and over (41 per cent).

Briefly stated, one can begin to see that the Church has been losing ground, at least among the young. This is confirmed by the most interesting breakdown of responses, by the educational level of the respondents.

TABLE 2

	Positive	Negative	Don't know
Illiterate	37%	24%	38%
4-years school	30	39	30
8-years school	26	53	20
Skilled workers school	16	66	17
Gymnasium	9	73	17
Faculty or higher school	6	83	10

* The exact wording of the question was: 'Do you consider it positive or negative that the Church has increased its activity among the young?'

As this table shows, the effect of education in anti-religious socialisation is considerable, and from that the prognosis for a growing
influence of the Church in Yugoslavia would be pessimistic. This
is particularly the case since, of course, there is a continual increase
in the number of people exposed to higher education, especially
the young. Since higher education is increasingly the major factor
in careers and social mobility, this also means that the influence
of religion will probably keep declining among the influential
and modern strata – which act as role-models for the young and
ambitious.

In the long run, social changes in Yugoslavia, creating as they
do a fundamentally modern and mobile society, will probably
begin to break down religious identification. My own studies of
the Yugoslav students, a group most sensitive to such changes,
indicates that religion today acts primarily as a national self-
description. Some minimal figures might be illustrative: the sample
was composed of 2,528 students at the Universities of Belgrade,
Zagreb and Sarajevo.[9] When asked about their religious identification, 1,017 stated that they did not believe in God. The other
figures, however, are more interesting:

TABLE 3
Religious Identification

	Practising (with rituals)			Not practising		
	Ego	Father	Mother	Ego	Father	Mother
Catholic	268	326	451	358	394	375
Orthodox	133	358	416	454	519	556
Muslim	18	73	125	95	106	78

(N = 2,528, with 1,017 listing no religion)

As this table shows, a larger proportion of even those students
who do identify as religious are not practising, and this also holds
for their fathers. In the case of their mothers, a considerably
higher proportion, except for the Orthodox, are practising.
Mothers, in general, and unsurprisingly, show a higher religiosity,
which is a reflection of the fact that they are less likely to be participating in the modern sector. The increasing normalisation of
social relations in Yugoslavia, characterised by the fact that the

State and Party no longer seek to mobilise broad layers of the population for various campaigns, has led, of course, to a privatisation and depoliticisation of large sectors of the population. This is more the case in the rural areas, creating a vacuum into which organised religion may move. This factor generally affects women more than men (for all the well-known reasons), the modern more than the backward areas, and areas with a tradition of high religiosity more than those exposed to secular influences from the cities.

The data from the student survey also show that Catholicism had maintained itself to a much higher extent than Orthodoxy. Our sample was broken down as follows: 1,268 students from Belgrade, 925 students from Zagreb, and 335 from Sarajevo. Thus, although there were considerably fewer Croats or Catholics in the sample, *more than twice as many still* practise their religion than the Orthodox. The greatest drop-off is among the Muslims. I would interpret this to be because Islam is not merely a religion but a way of life, the unity of which is more brittle, and, therefore, fragile when faced with a fundamentally lay modern society.

It is probably because of findings such as these that the Party intellectuals and other Marxists have increasingly turned to a reasonably objective and scholarly study of the role of the Church in Yugoslavia, perceiving it as no real political threat. There are a number of Yugoslav sociologists who have addressed themselves to the role of religion in Yugoslavia, and their studies are refreshingly free of any attempts at mere crude atheist propaganda.[10] An increasing sensitvity to the non-institutional appeals of religion is found among some of the younger scholars. Dr Djuro Susnjić, in a recent article on 'Science and Religion',[11] summarised some of his views as follows:

If religion is a consequence of ignorance, how is it then that the advances in human knowledge have not eliminated religion as a misconception? If religion is an expression of misery and a revolt against it, how is it then that we have not encountered the disappearance of religion in countries with high standards of living? If religion is the opium of the masses, how is it then that people in spite of so many other more effective and concrete opiums have chosen precisely religion, the least concrete opium? If religion is really an illusion, is it possible then to have a reality which does not need any illusion? Is it not better to start with a simple assumption that man cannot live without illusions, that otherwise his life would be meaningless? What kind of a reality would this be without illusions? If religion does not satisfy the essential needs of individuals, groups and the society, how can we explain its survival throughout the history of mankind? Can the stubborn endurance of religion be explained exclusively by the forces of tradition and inertia?

He concludes that these, of course, are the serious questions to In his last paragraph of conclusions, he adds a most interesting statement:
which any study of religion by a Marxist should address itself.

> The function of religion is not to describe empirical facts but rather to give meaning to these facts and to guide man in his actions. In human life, science carries out the former and religion the latter. *Therefore, science cannot eliminate religion just as the abolition of private ownership cannot eliminate human egoism.* The power of science in the criticism of religion is very restricted.   (My italics).

This is a far cry from the crude atheism which characterised early Yugoslav Communist works on religion. Today a section of the Yugoslav intelligentsia, firmly identifying itself with Marxism, believes that in terms of ideals and values, it has to turn from the relatively arid official pronouncements to many questions traditionally dealt with by religion.

The Yugoslav critical Marxists identify themselves as Marxist Humanists. This is no accident. Marxism has ceased to be for them primarily a political action programme, and they have begun to search for an ethic and a view of life within the framework of Marxism. It is Marxism, not as an expression of the political platform of the ruling party, but rather Marxism as a representation of a modern secular philosophy and view of man's place in the universe, that attracts the younger intellectuals of Yugoslavia. Thus, perhaps ironically, some of the most articulate opponents of specific measures and policies of the Government are Marxist, and in general the political and philosophical debates taking place in Yugoslavia are between various strands of Marxism.

In pointing to the factors in the social transformation of Yugoslavia which militate against an expansion of religion in its organ-

ised form, one must be careful not to overlook two counter-tenden-
cies. The first is found in the enormous flexibility of modern Catholicism and particularly its radical wing. Radical Catholicism has
been the subject of a number of articles in Yugoslav journals, and
the work of the revolutionary priests in Latin America and worker
priests in France has created a model of Catholicism which may
well prove attractive to the young and even to the young intellectuals.[12] The other factor is a resurgence of traditionalist nationalism
among some Croatian intellectuals, particularly literary intellectuals. The nationalism of this group expresses itself not only in
linguistic polemics, but also in an attempt to identify with the
historic roots of Croatian identity, which is interpreted as fundamentally Catholic.

In the spring 1971 elections for a student pro-Rector at the
University of Zagreb, the victor was a Catholic traditionalist
nationalist, much to the distress of the establishment and non-
establishment Marxists. This may well be a reflection of the fact
that religious groups can act as a focus for generalised discontent
which is not otherwise expressed. It must be added that such
successes represent a peril for the Church. The Roman Catholic
Church has worked out a *modus vivendi* with the Yugoslav
authorities, and although there are polemics occasionally directed
at the church press, it would be foolhardy for the Church as an
institution with a stake in the social order to identify itself with
an opposition, particularly with separatism. Despite this cautious
attitude towards nationalist opposition which I believe to be prevalent within the hierarchy, the more recent development of
Croatian separatist-nationalism certainly found an echo among
the lower clergy and the clerically-oriented traditionalist intellectuals. We can, therefore, expect continued debate within the
Church about the attitude to be taken towards the Yugoslav social
system and even the desirability of the continuation of a unified
Yugoslavia. Here, perhaps, is one of the points of contact between
some of the nationalist elements in Croatia and the political
emigration. Given the fact that Yugoslavia has permitted a freedom of travel far more like that of Western European countries
than of its Eastern European neighbours for years, and the further
fact that close to a million Yugoslav workers, mostly Croat from
traditionally religious areas, work in Western Europe, an obvious
field for the activity of the clerical right-wing exists. By and large,

both the Croat and some Serbian Churches outside of Yugoslavia are controlled by émigrés violently hostile to the present social order.

In recent years the Catholic Church has expanded its activity in Croatia and Slovenia, especially in publications of journals and a fortnightly, the *Glas Koncila* (Voice of the Council) which is distributed through the parish churches. According to Professor Bošnjak, the yearly circulation of church publications in Yugoslavia was 8,200,000 in 1968,[13] an enormous quantity, given the literacy rates and general low readership of the press in that country.

The activity of the Orthodox and Muslim groups does not begin to compare with that of the Catholics. To be sure, in recent years there has been a minor revival of Serbian traditionalist nationalism, which has often in part existed in a symbolic relationship with Orthodoxy. Since the Serbian Church has been identified intimately with the Serbian medieval state and national struggles for independence, a revival of traditionalist national motifs almost inevitably involves a renewed interest in some aspects of church history and in the restoration and maintenance of religious monuments which are also regarded as national shrines. Traditional Serbian nationalism has had a minor revival since 1969, in the reaction of the Serbian Orthodox Church figures to other nationalisms in Yugoslavia. For example, the establishment of a separate Macedonian Orthodox Church was one of the few cases where the Orthodox hierarchy had resisted an official policy of the Government. Uneasiness about the fate of the Serbian Orthodox population in Croatia during the period of fairly extensive nationaalist (often Catholic-oriented) propaganda in that republic has also been voiced, as well as a resentment about the growing de-Serbianisation of the Province of Kosovo. Kosovo now has a clear Albanian majority, but has been historically considered the 'cradle' of the Serbian nation, and contains most of the major medieval churches and monasteries of the Serbian Orthodox Church.

It must be added, however, that a number of Catholic church leaders, including the Archbishop of Split, have taken a very positive attitude towards the two major contributions of Yugoslav Socialism: decentralisation and workers' self-management. Both of these are often defended in church publications as aspects of a humane and just social order conceived of as closer to the present teachings of the Roman Catholic Church than the practices of either the capitalist or Communist world. Yugoslav Marxist spokesmen recognise this support, and in turn make a distinction between the various currents within the Church.

SUMMARY AND CONCLUSIONS

In Yugoslavia the major denominations have, for historical reasons, often served as a surrogate for national identity. Thus, even today, after major social transformations, the large majority of the populations identifies with particular religious groups. This is specifically recognised in the census of 1971, where the category *Muslim – as an ethnic group* exists for the Muslim Slavs of Bosnia-Herzegovina.

The period immediately after the war witnessed a weakening of the Churches – in part because of repressive policies of the new Communist authorities, in part because they had been compromised by tacit or active collaboration with the war-time occupation authorities. This coincided with the period of a major shift of the peasantry into industry and the cities, further weakening the hold of religion on the day-to-day lives of the previously faithful.

Indications from the available research are that atheism is a phenomenon most often found in the modern sector, that is in the cities and among the social groups which have most directly benefited from the social changes resulting from the revolution. *Religion and tolerance towards religion are inversely related to education.*

The present policy of the Yugoslav Government is one of continued separation of the Church and the State, combined with religious toleration. While all religious groups have continued to exist, the Roman Catholic Church, being by far the best organised and most flexible, has displayed the greatest activity and has retained the greatest hold on the believers. It is not, however, a Yugoslav national Church, but is identified with only two of the Yugoslav nations (Slovenes and Croats) and one major minority (Hungarians).

In so far as a dialogue can be said to exist between the Marxists and the religious groups, it is directed primarily at the Catholic Church. The present coexistence of the Catholic religious institutions and press with the authorities may be threatened by a separatist and nationalist laity which attempts to use the Church as a framework within which to operate. Continued tension between the Catholic Church and the League of Communists can be expected because of conflicting claims in the area of education, social and family policy. This tension is mitigated, however, by the plurality of approaches which is now present in *both* organisations. The secularisation of the political system removes the external pressure on the faithful; on the other hand, the development of a progressive current within the Church make co-operation more likely.

The increasing flexibility of the Yugoslav Marxists, as well as their growing heterogeneity, will probably lead to the development of a form of Marxist Humanism which will address itself to questions similar to those traditionally in the domain of religion. It is probably in this form that Marxism will offer genuine competition to the appeal of organised religion. This appeal, however, since it requires considerable education and sophistication, will be directed primarily at the young and educated – two groups not particularly subject to appeals of organised religion at this time.

The continued social changes in Yugoslavia – the ever-increasing proportion of persons with secondary and higher education, effect of urban existence, devolution of provincialism and the slow decline of the peasantry through the expansion of the industrial working class – indicate a continued decline of religion as a focus for social life and national identity. This decline, however, will probably at some point reach relative stability. At that time, when religion is truly a citizen's private affair, one can postulate several forms and levels of religious life. The traditional forms will continue, primarily among the old, rural and passive sectors. In the modern sector the Catholic Church will probably remain the only genuine competitor to a form of Marxist Humanism, while both will compete with indifference.

A few tentative generalisations can be made about the situation of religion, particularly organised religion, in Eastern Europe, and more specifically in Yugoslavia. Much of the the post-World War II Western scholarship in this area has tended to be unduly influenced by pro-Church or at least pro-religious scholars, or in any case by émigré scholars who were in many cases traditionalist and church-oriented. Thus the general image developed was that of religious persecution, where the Church appears as the major contender of the secularised Communist *élites* and presumably as a major force for the democratisation of those societies. The major conflicts between the State and Church today appear to be based less on the religious than on the *secular* claims of the Church. The religious organisations are the *only* organisations outside of the formal political system permitted to exist. In so far as they are subject to governmental and Party pressure, they are far less subject to that pressure than any other group making a claim to independence and separate loyalty would be. No other group which does not support the legitimacy and desirability of the existing social order, irrespective of its political pedigree, has been permitted an independent organised existence. Certainly no group with supra-national organisational ties has been allowed to exist. The Church gets into conflicts with the State not over its profession of religion but primarily in those 'grey' areas of conflicting Church–State claims: institutional loyalty, education, social policy, abortion, family, and the like, where it also gets into conflicts with *non-Communist* secular states. The demands the Catholic Church makes in the field of education in Poland and Croatia, for example, are rejected by the courts in the United States. The demands of the Church that Catholic doctors be permitted to refuse abortions to patients and still continue to use hospital facilities would pose a problem in any secular state.

Many scholars writing about the Church in Eastern Europe in the recent past took for granted a violent bias against those political orders. More recently, a broader, more scholarly approach towards the study of religion *as a social phenomenon* has been characteristic in both Communist and non-Communist countries. Of course, the changing situation of the Church in Yugoslavia *is* related to the growing liberalisation of that country, but this can be taken on two levels: on the one hand, any greater pluralism of institutions presumably will widen the possibility of democratic dialogue; on the other hand, the attitude of the Church towards increased democratisation has been, to put it mildly, ambivalent. Thus, for example, we have a case where, in Slovenia in 1969, the local Archbishop used the courts of the Communist state to ban a book of poetry on the grounds that the poet attacked God and religion and thus violated the constitutional provision against 'spreading national and religious hatreds'. In this particuar case, since the local court *upheld the Church,* it was only after considerable agitation by Communist and non-party writers and intellectuals in the name of freedom of speech that the Supreme Court decided that the more recent extension of freedom of speech also applies to atheists. It is also the case that two of the more articulate groups calling for more rigid censorship of books, films and journals on grounds of morality in Yugoslavia have been the Catholic and Orthodox Churches. It would appear that some church leaders even today have no objections to censorship when it is on their behalf. On the contrary, they actively seek it, even in a Communist secular state.

A continued *modus vivendi* between the religious organisations and the State of Yugoslavia is not only possible but probable. The long-range prospects will probably lead to a type of realignment of intellectual forces which will affect both the Party and the Church. In effect, increasingly a dialogue will develop with the radical Catholics and Marxist Humanists, on one side; and the keepers of social stability, the governmental and Party hierarchies *and* the formal church institutions, on the other.

Yugoslavia is a particularly suitable arena to study the adaptability of religious organisations in modernising societies. The diversity of religions and levels of economic development, all subject to a uniform influence of a secular polity, create an almost ideal laboratory situation for the study of *comparative* adaptability of religions to social change.

NOTES

1. Most useful for the non-specialist as general references are: Charles and Barbara Jelavich (eds.), *The Balkans in Transition*, (Berkeley: U. Cal. Press, 1963); Traian Stoianovich, *A Study in Balkan Civilization* (New York: A. Knopf, 1967); and the first part of Jozo Tomasevich's *Peasant, Politics and Economic Change in Yugoslavia* (Stanford Univ. Press, 1955). See also Bogdan Denitch, 'Political Cultures and Social Mobility in Yugoslavia,' (available from the B.A.S.R., Columbia U.) *Proceedings. 7th World Congress of the ISA*, (Varna, Bulgaria, 1970).
2. Cited from George Arnakis, 'The Role of Religion in the Development of Balkan Nationalism', in *The Balkans in Transition*, p. 115.
3. For a description of the Military Frontier, see Gunther E. Rothenberg, *The Austrian Military Frontier in Croatia, 1522–1747* (Urbana, Ill.: University of Illinois Press, 1960) (Illinois Studies in the Social Sciences: Vol. 48).
4. By far the best discussion of the agrarian crisis in inter-war Yugoslavia is found in Tomasevich, *op. cit.*
5. This is the general consensus of the Yugoslav scholars working in the field. See particularly Branko Bošnjak, ed., *Religija i Društvo* (Religion and Society) (Zagreb, 1969).
6. Cited from Fred Neal and V. Hoffman, *Yugoslavia and the New Communism* (New York: Twentieth Century Fund, 1962), p. 33.

7. See my 'Political Cultures . . .', *loc. cit.*, for a more detailed discussion.
8. The study in question is Ljiljana Bacević, *Javno Mnenje o Jugoslovenskoj Omladini* (Public Opinion on Yugoslav Youth) (IND Centar za Javno Mnenje, 1967).
9. The study was conducted by the author in 1966 in co-operation with the Institute of Social Sciences in Belgrade as a part of the comparative studies of students directed by Seymour Martin Lipset. Code book and data available from B.A.S.R., Columbia U.
10. See the already cited *Religija i Društvo*; also Branko Bošnjak and Stefica Bahtijarević, *Socialističko Društvo, Crkva i Religija* (Socialist Society, Church and Religion) (Zagreb: Institute for Social Research, 1969), Esad Ćimić, *Socialističko Društvo i Religija* (Socialist Society and Religion) (Sarajevo, 1966). The Zagreb institute has a special department for the study of religion.
11. Djuro Susnjić, 'Nauka i Religija', (Science and Religion) in *Sociologiski Pregled*, Vol. IV, No. 1 (1970), pp. 21–34. I am citing his summary. Susnjić is a young Marxist scholar associated with the group around the review *Praxis*.
12. For example, see Boris Vusković, 'Kršćanska raskrsca', in *Pogledi*, Vol. II, No. 3 (1970), and especially Nikola Visković, 'Svećenik Revolucionar', (Priest Revolutionary) in *Pogledi*, Vol. II, No. 2 (1970), which is a favourable review of the book by the left-wing Catholic priest, Camilo Torres.
13. Cited from *Religija i Društvo*, p. 30.

20 Albania – Towards an Atheist Society

PETER PRIFTI

In September 1967 the Albanian literary monthly *Nëndori* announced that all religious edifices in Albania, including 2,169 churches, mosques, monasteries and other religious institutions had been closed, and that Albania had thus become 'the first atheist state in the world'.[1] A fatal blow had been dealt to religion in a corner of Europe, midway between Rome and Athens, the centres of world Catholicism and Eastern rites of Orthodoxy, respectively, yet it hardly attracted the attention of the world press. The event, however, did not come as a surprise to those familiar with domestic affairs in Albania, and was in a way foreshadowed by an incident at the United Nations two years earlier. When Pope Paul VI delivered his historic address to the U.N. General Assembly in New York, on 5 October 1965, the Albanian delegation, alone of all delegations to the U.N. boycotted the address. The action of the Albanians was a dramatic revelation of the hostile attitude of Albania's Communist leaders towards the Vatican, and of their mood and thinking about religion in general. It was an illustration, moreover, of the fact that the religious establishment in socialist Albania was weak, and its future uncertain.

Speaking at the 6th Congress of the Albanian Party of Labour in November of 1971, Enver Hoxha, the Party's First Secretary, described the abolition of the religious establishment as 'a decisive victory' which prepares the ground for the 'complete emancipation [of the people] from religious beliefs'.[2] What were the forces and contradictions within Albanian society that led to so radical a development in the life of the Albanian people?

Albania is a nation of slightly more than two million people, and the only country in Europe with a majority Muslim population. According to the last religious census available, taken in 1937, roughly 70 per cent of the population was Muslim, 20 per cent Orthodox, and 10 per cent Catholic. The Muslim percentage includes also the Bektashi sect, which at that time was estimated at 200,000 or 20 per cent of the pre-war population of Albania.[3] Following Albania's independence in 1912, the three religious groups, while not entirely independent of the State, enjoyed a large measure of autonomy. The situation changed drastically after the Communists seized power in November 1944.

Indeed, the conflict between Church and State in socialist Albania began during the Partisan struggle for power in World War II. Albanian Communists charge that in the course of the civil war, 'traitorous clergymen' called on the faithful to oppose the Partisans, who were leading the struggle for national liberation against the Italian and German occupiers.[4] Following the war, 'reactionary' clergymen engaged in counter-revolutionary activity against the Party and the 'people's power', by distributing anti-government tracts, forming opposition groups such as 'Albanian Unity' and 'Catholic Action', sheltering criminals in churches and mosques, opposing the agrarian reform, and seeking to incite the people with slogans such as, 'We must not trust those who do not believe in god'.[5] In fact, the agrarian reform law of 29 August 1945 deprived the religious institutions of nearly all their property, and met with resistance on the part of 'the clerical caste' which, like all propertied classes, 'had no intention of renouncing its privileges without a struggle'.[6]

The tensions between the Albanian leadership and the Church,[7] which came to the surface during the war, were aggravated in the post-war period. The Communists now began to characterise dissenting clergymen as class enemies, and to view the religious establishment as an antagonistic contradiction within Albanian society. Accordingly they took steps to combat and neutralise, at least, the threat which religion and religious bodies presented to their power and authority, as well as to their programme for building a socialist society. Their larger design, in strict accord with their Marxist–Leninist outlook, was to eliminate religion as a feature of Albanian life. But since 'the conditions were not ripe' for such a move, the Party resorted to interim methods in dealing with the Church – methods intended to render the Church impotent as an institutional force, but viable enough to use it, whenever possible, for furthering Communist ends.

The Church and State confrontation during 1945–50 was sharp and often violent. Albanian sources claim that the policy of the Party towards religion at this time had a twofold aim: (1) to separate the Church completely from the State; and (2) to end the Church–school relationship; that is, to separate education from religion. The intention was to make religion a purely 'private affair', in contrast to its role in former times, when the Church served as an 'official instrument of politics' in the hands of the ruling classes. This policy was subsequently described as 'an important political step towards totally divorcing men from the spiritual shackles . . . of religion'.[8]

Such was the theory and the justification put forth by the Party, as it moved to apply pressure on the religious establishment in order to make it conform to its demands. In the course of about five years, from 1945 to 1950, the Government proceeded to limit severely the Church's autonomy and freedom of action. Its sources of revenue were curtailed. Religious instruction was forbidden, and the education of youth became the responsibility of the State alone; that is, all education was secularised. All religious publications and communications such as sermons, pastoral letters and memoranda had to be approved by the Government before being made public. The State exercised control over the election and appointment of personnel to all religious posts. Religious communities were enjoined from maintaining and operating hospitals and other charitable institutions. Lastly, the land reform of 1945 deprived the Church of considerable property, including monasteries, libraries and seminaries.[9] The implementation of these measures curbed the influence of religion, and in turn provoked much resistance on the part of the church leadership. The Party responded by indicting, arresting, trying and sentencing recalcitrant clergymen.

In the case of the Orthodox Church, this confrontation resulted in the virtual elimination of the church leadership. Among those purged were Bishop Agathangjel of Berat, Bishop Irenei, deputy Metropolitan of Korçë and Gjirokastër, and Archbishop Kristofor Kisi, Primate of the Albanian Orthodox Church. Kisi was deposed on 28 August 1949 for the crime of 'plotting to detach the Church from the Eastern Orthodox faith and surrender it to the

Vatican'.[10] All three reportedly were interned. Subsequently Kisi was succeeded by Archbishop Paisi (Pashko) Vodica, who had given strong support to the Communists during the war.

Similar purges occurred in the Muslim community, many of whose clergymen were charged with aiding the Fascist and Nazi cause. The list of those who were executed or imprisoned included Mustafa effendi Varoshi, Mufti of Durrës, Hafëz Ibrahim Dibra, former Grand Mufti of Albania, Baba Zylfo, Sheh Xhemal Pazari of Tiranë, Bexhet Shpati, Hafëz Tahir Kolgjini and Qerim Shehu.[11] Two prominent figures of the Bektashi sect, Baba Fajo of Martanesh and Baba Fejzo, both of whom supported the Communists, reportedly died violently in March 1947, under circumstances that are not entirely clear.

Communist pressure was particularly strong against the Catholic hierarchy. Tirana justified this stance on the ground that the Catholic clergy were the most organised and most active' religious body in the country, and moreover was allied, through its link with the Vatican, with the 'imperialist and aggressive West'. Almost from the time they seized power, the Communists began to attack the Catholic clergy as willing servants of foreign interests and powers. They complained that certain high members of the Catholic hierarchy in Shkodër – a city in northern Albania, and main centre of Catholic power in the country – considered themselves 'citizens of the Vatican' rather than Albania, and operated as a 'fifth column of Italian Fascism' prior to Mussolini's invasion of Albania in April 1939. Father Gjergj Fishta (1871–1940), a Franciscan monk who is widely recognised as Albania's national poet,[12] came under attack for allegedly proposing that Albania become an Italian mandate.[13] Party spokesmen claim that Catholic clergymen helped organise terrorist bands against the people's power, and that on 9 September 1946 several such bands converged from different directions for a concerted attack on Shkodër, but were beaten back by the people's forces.[14] The incident led to the arrest, trial and execution of a number of prominent Catholic clergymen. Among those who reportedly perished were Mgr Vincenc Prennushi, Archbishop and Metropolitan of Durrës, Mgr Gjergj Volaj, Bishop of Sappa, Mgr Gasper Thaçi, Archbishop of Shkodër, Father Bernardin Palaj and Father Ndre Zadeja. Some of the victims had attained distinction in Albanian letters and academic circles as poets, novelists and scholars.[15] One of these was Father Anton Harapi, who became a special target for Communist attacks. Harapi was condemned as 'an agent of the Vatican', and a Nazi collaborator, owing to his membership in the High Regency, the ruling body which the Germans set up in Albania during the war.[16]

The Party's drive against the clergy resulted in the virtual decimation of the Catholic, Muslim and Orthodox leadership. According to a report of the Free Albania Committee in New York, by 1968 some 200 clergymen had been executed or sent to labour camps in Albania. It was a grim and major Church and State confrontation, in which the State apparently gained decisive supremacy. The Communists seemed now to be in a position to deal a crushing blow to the religious establishment, yet for tactical reasons they did not press their advantage. For the moment they were content with the gains they had achieved, and these were considerable. They had eliminated the dissident and recalcitrant clergy and greatly weakened the capacity of the Church to function effectively. Moreover, by portraying opposing ecclesiastics as reactionaries, subversives and anti-nationalists, it is possible that they inspired doubts in the public mind concerning the role and position of the Church in Albanian society.

In brief, by the late 1940s the Albanian Communists had succeeded in bringing the Church almost entirely under their control. Aware of its strength, Tirana now set out to reorganise the religious establishment, and to channel the expression of religious life in such a manner as to make it consistent with, rather than opposed to, the Party's domestic and foreign policies. On 26 November 1949, the Government issued a decree entitled, 'On Religious Communities', which made it mandatory for all religious bodies to profess loyalty to the Party and the People's Republic of Albania. On 4 May 1950 new statutes were approved for governing the Muslim community and the Orthodox Church, based on Article 18, Chapter III, of the Albanian constitution, which says: 'Freedom of conscience and religion is guaranteed to all citizens'.[17] Similarly, on 30 July 1951 the Government approved new statutes for the Catholic Church, on the basis of decisions taken by a 'general assembly' of Catholic ecclesiastics in Shkodër the previous month. In the meantime the Party 'approved' the appointment, as heads of the various church bodies, of clergymen who were co-operative or sympathetic to the Communists. In theory the new Government statutes were sufficiently liberal and flexible to accommodate the church-going public. In practice, the Church as an institution had been 'nationalised'.

MISSIONARIES OF MATERIALISM

Throughout this period, and in the years that followed, the Albanian leadership carried out a vigorous propaganda campaign against religion and in favour of atheism. As early as April 1947 the Party recommended the introduction of 'anti-religious propaganda' in the schools and other sectors of society.[18] In April 1955 a meeting of the Party plenum on the question of 'ideological work' stressed the need to 'strengthen the materialist and scientific world outlook among the workers', and to combat religious beliefs and backward customs which were hindering 'the spread of . . . socialist culture among the masses'.[19] The ideological drive to denigrate religious belief and promote atheism was based on the principle – as Hoxha put it – that 'the religious world outlook and the communist world outlook are irreconcilable, [in as much as] they express and uphold interests of antagonistic classes',[20] that is the capitalist class and the working class, respectively. Hoxha was further quoted as saying that the religious ideology, being idealistic and mystical, distorts one's thinking and leads to the commission of serious political errors. Party ideologists and propagandists drew on the writings of Lenin and other Communist classics to propagate the view that belief in God is 'enslaving', and that all contemporary religions are organs of bourgeois reaction, which deceive, stupefy and exploit the masses.

Albanian Communists took note of the fact that religion was not an isolated phenomenon in the people's lives, but that it had penetrated deeply into their lives and was intertwined with their customs, moral values, education, work ethic, family and social relations. Consequently the offensive against religion had to be a prolonged and many-sided one if it was to be effective. In mounting their offensive the advocates of atheism relied not only on Communist doctrine, but on such disciplines as history, science, cultural anthropology, biology, medicine and philosophy. In their zeal and industry, if not in originality, they proved themselves worthy heirs of Holbach, De la Mettrie, Cabanis and other renowned figures of the French Enlightenment, as they set about to dethrone God and replace him by the triumvirate of materialism, science and reason.

The arguments marshalled by the Party in its campaign against religion went beyond straightforward repetition of Marxist rhetoric. Presumably they were intended, for the most part, for a fairly sophisticated audience, and above all, perhaps, for the cadres on whom the Party leadership relied heavily for the success of its drive against the Church.

Albanian missionaries of materialism argued that scientific Marxist materialism and religious idealism are diametrically opposed to each other.[21] The former, they said, explains the world, life on earth and society on the basis of empirical evidence and the causal principle of natural law, while the latter relies on fanciful and infantile notions contained in revelation – notions which have been thoroughly discredited by science. It is no accident, they contended, that organised Christianity has traditionally opposed science and vilified or persecuted great men like Galileo, Giordano Bruno, Darwin and others, for 'every new discovery, every new success of science is a blow to the teachings of the Bible, which to this day . . . remains the basis of [Christian] theology'.[22] Darwin's theory of evolution dealt religion a particularly heavy blow, for it proved the oneness and continuity of life forms, and that man is not a passive and obedient creature of 'God', a mere plaything in 'his' hands, but an active agent, a creator who is able to alter his environment and, indeed, create new breeds of plants and animals.[23]

As for reports of 'miraculous' cures and other 'miraculous' events which religion attributes to saints, shrines and prayer and uses to build up its credit with the public, Albanian Marxists answered that all such 'miracles' can be explained scientifically, except in cases of hoax which crafty priests perpetrate on innocent and superstitious people.[24] Moreover, prayer is in itself a vain attempt to defy nature. In the words of one Albanian writer: 'At the foundation of every prayer stands the belief that god can change the course of nature [i.e. contravene natural law] and grant what is asked of him',[25] which is absurd. To believe in prayer is to believe in word magic. In this connection an Arab who toured Albania in 1968 reports that his Albanian guide said to him: 'Why do you insist on seeing the mosque [in Tirana]? . . .

The Six-Day War did not teach you anything. The Arabs lost precious time praying to Allah.'[26]

In their spirited drive to demolish the philosophical, moral and psychological foundations of religion, Albanian atheists wrestled with the question of the origin of religion and religious belief, and claimed that the entire history of the development of human society demonstrates that man himself created religion and the idea of God according to his image and fancy. This came about not because man has a 'religious instinct', but because our primitive ancestors, being weak and ignorant, trembled before the powerful forces of nature, and sought to placate them by means of ritual and sacrifice.[27] In fact, fear, ignorance and class oppression created the first gods. Science and history prove that all religions 'emerged under definite historical conditions, have changed in accordance with changing economic, social and political [conditions],' and will disappear from the earth when new conditions make the institution of religion an unbearable anachronism.[28]

The disciples of Marxist atheism in Albania also polemicised against religion over the doctrine of 'original sin', which views men as 'inherently corrupt and evil', and which is utilised by the clergy to justify the misery and oppression of the working people, with the explanation that they are being 'punished by "god" for their sinful nature'. In opposition to this view, they argued that man is not predestined from birth to become either good or evil. He is born morally neutral, and what he becomes in life depends on the conditions under which he grows up. In brief, human nature is not unchangeable; man can change his nature and become a better being by changing the circumstances of his life.[29] Nor is religion essential to morality. According to Albanian materialists, those who ground morality in religion, or more precisely in doing the 'will of God', are but apologists for the ruling classes, 'for the "will" of God is none other than the will of the class which holds power over the workers'.[30] Moral conduct among men antedates religion by many millennia, and shall exist long after religion makes its exit from the human scene.

Such was the theoretical attack on religion by Albanian advocates of atheism. But they also utilised a more practical approach to this question, as will be seen below.

RELIGION AND THE ALBANIAN REALITY

Focusing on the concrete experience of the Albanian nation, Albanian Communists found additional arguments to use against religion and the religious establishment. They contended that the history and culture of the Albanian people and their struggle for national independence show that religion has not been a strong force in their lives. According to Zihni Sako, Albania's leading spokesman on cultural history and folklore, the culture of the Albanian people is 'in its core atheist' and pagan. To this day one hears people in Albania swear 'by this earth', or by the sun, or the bread they eat. 'Our people,' Hoxha has remarked, 'have never been . . . [much] attached to religion.'[31] This view is widely shared by Albanians, and is supported by the research of Professor Stavro Skendi, a leading Albanian scholar in America, who notes that the Albanians, owing to historical conditions, have never been a religious people.[32] Indicative of this light-hearted approach to religion is the fact that the priest in the Albanian village was often the butt of jokes and anecdotes. Indeed the favourite comic character in Albanian folklore is none other than Nastradin Hoxha, a bungling, often roguish and rather irreverant Muslim priest.

Tirana maintains that religion is alien to the Albanian people, since all three faiths in contemporary Albanian society were brought into the country by alien powers. In Hoxha's view:

> All the religious sects existing in our country were brought into Albania by foreign invaders, and served them and the ruling classes of the country. Under the cloak of religion, god and the prophets, there operated the brutal law of the invaders and their domestic lackeys. The history of our people demonstrates clearly how much suffering, distress, bloodshed and oppression have been visited upon our people by religion; how [religion] engendered discord and fratricide in order to oppress us more cruelly, enslave us more easily, and suck our blood. . . .[33]

The above citation shows the emotional intensity and bitterness of the Albanian leadership towards the Church. It is an attitude, moreover, which to a large degree was shaped by the religious experience of the Albanian people over many decades, especially during the movement for national independence. Prior to Albania's independence from the Turks in 1912, religious services were conducted in three different languages: Arabic for Muslim Albanians, Greek for the Orthodox and Latin for the Catholics. Furthermore, since the Turks identified nationality with religion, Muslim Albanians came to be called 'Turks', the Orthodox were called 'Greeks', while the Catholics were regarded as 'Latins'. Religion thus became a source of discord and division within Albanian society and a great obstacle to national unity and the struggle for independence. This condition led leaders of the Albanian national movement to downgrade religion in order to upgrade nationalism, and to rally the people under the slogan: 'The religion of the Albanian people is Albania'.[34]

Here we have one of the basic contradictions between religion and the Albanian reality, between the Church and the State, which made possible the abolition of religion in Albania. In the words of Hoxha, the road to Albania's independence was 'watered with the blood of the martyrs of Albania's Rennaissance, such as Papa Kristo Negovani [1875–1905] and Petro Nini Luarasi [1865–1911]. . . .'[35] Both men were victims of Greek fanaticism, incited by their devotion to the teaching of the forbidden Albanian language and their efforts to introduce Albanian into the liturgy of the Orthodox Church.

Albanian nationalism thus provided Tirana with a powerful base from which to mount an attack on the various religious bodies in the country. As Albanian Marxist–Leninists saw it, the Church had lost its *raison d'être*. It had no valid philosophical or rational basis. It had lost all credit with Albanian nationalism – although they granted that there had been a few patriotic clergymen, like Papa Kristo Negovani, and Fan S. Noli (1882–1965), founder of the Albanian Orthodox Church in America. Lastly, they were convinced that the Church had become a serious obstacle to the social, economic and political development of the country.

Albanian materialists argued that the Church had a medieval outlook on life, and expounded a pernicious social philosophy, including fatalism, inequality between men and women and submission and passivity in the face of evil and injustice. In grappling with the pronounced backwardness of Albanian society, the Albanian leadership inevitably linked the Church with the backward customs and traditions which cluttered and plagued Albanian social life. The relentless struggle against the heavy legacy of backwardness thus became a struggle against the Church as well. Indeed the Church was seen not only as an accomplice, so to speak, of a pervasive social evil, but as the ideological basis for the evil.

A major aspect of this evil was the inferior and restricted position of woman in Albanian society, for which religion was severely blamed. Speaking at the 4th Congress of the Union of Albanian Women in October 1955, Enver Hoxha said: 'Aside from the despotism of the male, religion intervened at every moment to keep woman in the miserable state of slavery . . . by means of its savage tenets, which crushed her spiritually, kept her in the most profound darkness, terrified her by putting in her the imaginary fear of the lord, of sinning, etc.'[36] Albanian atheists pointed out, for example, that the Koran calls woman 'a submissive creature who lacks the perfection of man',[37] and grants the husband the right to beat his wife, divorce her at will and even kill her.[38]

The economy, too, became an issue in the relations between Church and State. From Tirana's viewpoint, the religious establishment was an obstacle to the full utilisation of the labour potential in the country and the rapid development of the economy. Party propagandists complained that 'religious festivals and holidays did great harm to the economy, since on such days believers would not go to work'.[39] They further attacked the clergy for perpetuating harmful superstitions among the people, claimed that many religious practices such as the kissing of ikons and circumcision of Muslim boys were unhygienic and potentially deadly, and derided ecclesiastics as parasites who lived by fraud and guile.[40]

In addition to the internal pressures, which brought the Church and State in Albania into a fateful confrontation, there were external pressures as well, which heightened the confrontation and influenced its final outcome. The Albanian leadership saw the Church not only as an internal handicap but as an ideological 'fifth column' of the imperialists, the revisionists and the Vatican. From Tirana's standpoint, Washington, the Kremlin and the Vatican comprised a Holy Trinity, bent on suppressing national liberation movements and carrying out counter-revolution against Marxist–Leninist countries like China and Albania. Party polemicists denounced Pope Paul's visit to the U.N. in 1965 as a manoeuvre to help Washington achieve its imperialist objectives in Vietnam. Worse still, they charged that during the Italian occupation of Albania the Vatican sought to turn Orthodox Albanians into Uniates – that is to have them recognise the Pope as their spiritual leader – and even 'set up a special office, under Cardinal Tisserant, to deal with [this] question.'[41]

Turning to Moscow's policy on the Vatican, the defenders of the Communist faith in Tirana were bitterly critical of Gromyko's audience with Pope Paul VI in 1966,[42] and other subsequent contacts between Soviet leaders and the Pope. They reminded the Kremlin of the many sins committed by the Vatican against Communism, including attempts by the Catholic Church to mobilise 'crusades' against the U.S.S.R., following the October Revolution, and the part played by Cardinal Mindszenty in 'organising' the Hungarian counter-revolution. Tirana further charged that the 'traitorous Soviet revisionists' were fostering the revival of religion in 'the first socialist state', in order to 'numb the revolutionary will of the Soviet people',[43] and attacked the Soviet religious monthly *Nauka i religiya* as an organ for the propagation of religious ideology. Analysing the Vatican's relations with Moscow and Washington, Albanian Stalinists concluded that the cross of religion and the sword of the military remain as ever natural allies, the 'arms of tyrants and reaction'.

1967 – THE 'DETHRONEMENT' OF GOD

The struggle of the Party to eliminate the Church as a refuge for 'remnants of the past', and as a competitor for the 'hearts and minds of the people', intensified in the years immediately following the war, and reached breaking point by the mid-1960s. Early in 1966 the Albanian Party of Labour began its 'ideological and cultural revolution', with the avowed goal of preventing the restoration of Capitalism and bourgeois ideology in Albania. Stated more positively, a major goal of the revolution was to rid Albania of backward customs and 'futile beliefs'. In February 1967, at the height of the ideological and cultural revolution, students at the Naim Frashëri High School in Durrës, Albania's major seaport, 'initiated' a movement to close down the churches and mosques in the country. The movement spread, and by May 1967 all places of public worship – described by Hoxha as 'centres of obscurantism and mysticism' – had been eliminated. God had finally been 'dethroned' in socialist Albania. Tirana's theoreticians now asserted that the 'last and most parasitical form of exploitation' of the masses had been swept away,[44] and that the Albanian people were freed not only from economic and social exploitation, but from spiritual enslavement as well.

During this period and throughout 1967 numerous mass meetings were held in towns and villages, at which the Church was 'hailed before the popular courts of reason' and condemned for its sins. At these meetings old men and women, students, workers, farmers and party cadres denounced the Churches as 'spider's webs'; renounced all belief in God and saints; reviled the clergy as parasites, exploiters and frauds; and pledged never again to engage in religious worship or observe religious holidays. Some vowed to give up religious expressions in social greetings and toasts, and to refrain from naming their children after saints, as was the custom.[45] In certain cases children denounced their clergymen fathers as fakers. 'Thunder sheets' (*fletë-rrufe*) appeared in the streets attacking parents who had given religious names to their children.[46] At the same time the Party presses turned out a spate of pamphlets and books satirising religion and 'exposing' the Church and the clergy. One such publication, a book of poems about clergymen entitled *Religion Stripped Naked*, contains the following lines:

> Forever the people swept away
> These pillars of fanaticism
> And rid themselves of clericalism
> Which for many centuries past
> Through deception, artful craft
> Using Christ and Mohamet
> Holy men, saint and prophet –
> Made of life a sorry mess.[47]

The Party put the official seal, as it were, on the death of the Church on 13 November 1967 when the People's Assembly of Albania approved a decree annulling the religious statutes of November 1949, May 1950 and July 1951, which affirmed the right of believers to worship freely within the framework of the Muslim, Orthodox and Catholic Churches. The obituary notice appeared in *Gazeta Zyrtare* (The Official Gazette) on 22 November 1967.

Albania – Towards an Atheist Society

401

Addressing the 6th Congress of the Albanian Party of Labour in November 1971, the Party's First Secretary explained that there was no alternative to the abolition of religion in Albania. 'As a Marxist–Leninist Party,' he said, '[the A.P.L.] is clearly aware that . . . the socialist revolution cannot but cut off and uproot, when all objective and subjective conditions are ripe, all the strands that link the masses with the old world and hinder them from marching forward.'[48]

Following the dissolution of the Church, the Party advised that new festivals must replace the old religious ceremonies and holidays in order to prevent the creation of a void in the people's lives. Accordingly a new calendar of secular festivals began to emerge, including national holidays such as Albanian Independence Day (28 November), and Liberation Anniversary (29 November); days for honouring the workers, such as Builders' Day, Miners' Day, Printers' Day; agricultural festivals in connection with the harvesting of grapes, olives, etc.; and celebrations in honour of local martyrs or heroes of labour, as well as events of historical significance to a particular community or region. Albanian sources complained, however, that many people – especially the old, but sometimes even Communist youth – continued to believe in God and to practise religion, either privately or in some indirect way as, for example, observing one's name-day on one's birthday. Religious influence was particularly strong in the countryside. A publication of the Union of Working Youth observed that 'religious beliefs are the most durable of all remnants of capitalism'[49] – an open admission that popular resistance to institutionalised atheism in Albania was strong.

It is now five years since Albania procaimed itself 'the first atheist state in the world'. After a twenty-year 'struggle for survival', the Church in Albania succumbed to the State – a victim of the 'cultural revolution'. More precisely, however, the Church fell victim to a combination of forces and contradictions within Albanian society, chief among which was the Party's inveterate animosity towards religion and its relentless drive for hegemony over every phase of Albanian life, including the material and the spiritual. As long as God and the Church lived in Albania, there existed also an alternative centre for the people's loyalty, affection and support, and the Party had no intention of tolerating such competition.

In this attack the Stalinist leaders in Tirana were apparently helped by a number of circumstances, more or less peculiar to Albania, including the historical friction between religion and Albanian nationalism, a largely uneducated clergy, the identification of religion with the backwardness of the country, and the fact that Albanians have never been a deeply religious people.

It is ironic that the downfall of the Church in Albania should have occurred at a time when religion was experiencing a revival of sorts in other countries in Eastern Europe and the Soviet Union. The Albanian experiment ran counter to the seeming religious revival in Eastern Europe. One might therefore ask: Was the 'dethronement' of God in Albania the result of a strange but temporary aberration of the human mind and spirit? Or is it perhaps a 'sign of things to come', an experiment in social extremism which presages the eventual disappearance of organised religion as we know it today?

The answer would seem to depend primarily on the evolution of political and economic life within Albania, and the Party's ability to guide or control such evolution. More exactly, it depends on whether the Party can truly substitute itself for the Church, whether the Marxist faith can replace traditional theology, and whether secular holidays and festivals can effectively displace religious ritual and myth. It depends on whether the Albanian leadership succeeds in its struggle to eliminate the pervasive backwardness of Albanian society, and raise the economic level of the country to such a degree that the people will identify their own welfare – and the good of the country – with that of the Party. The answer depends also on the fortunes of religion in Eastern Europe and in the world in general.

The determination of the Albanian leaders to change almost completely the face of Albanian society is a remarkable example of the faith of a revolutionary *élite*, with regard to remaking society in accordance with a preconceived model – in this case the Marxist–Leninist model of society, as envisioned by Tirana. The abolition of religion in Albania was a part, it seems, of what Kenneth Jowitt has called the first task of 'nation building' – the elimination of structures, values and behaviour patterns which, in the eyes of the revolutionary *élite*, make up or could become alternative centres of political power.[50]

In the case of Albania, it is an open question whether radical social experiments, such as the abolition of religion, will succeed. For their part, the disciples of 'scientific atheism' in Tirana remain confident that the day will surely come when *Requiem Aeternam* shall be sung to religion, along with the Vatican, revisionism and imperialism.

NOTES

1. *East Europe*, Vol. 16, No. 11 (November 1967), p. 35.
2. *Z̆ëri i Popullit* (The Voice of the People), 2 November 1971.
3. Stavro Skendi (ed.), *Albania* (New York: Praeger, 1956), pp. 287–91.
4. Hulusi Hako, *Akuzojmë fenë* (We Accuse Religion) (Tirana, 1968), p. 80.
5. *Të shkulim nga rrënjët besimet fetare* (Let us abolish Religious Beliefs Root and Branch), published by the Central Committee of the Union of Working Youth of Albania (Tirana, 1967), p. 61, hereafter, *Të shkulim . . .*; Hako, *op. cit.*, pp. 81–2.
6. Hako, *op. cit.*, p. 71.
7. For simplicity, the term 'Church', unless otherwise specified, is used in this study in a broad sense, so as to include both the Christian and the Muslim religious establishments.
8. Hako, *op. cit.*, p. 121.
9. *ACEN News* (New York), No. 128 (March–April 1967), p. 18.
10. Skendi, *op. cit.*, p. 297.
11. Hako, *op. cit.*, p. 75; *ACEN News, loc. cit.*, pp. 19–20.
12. Fishta's *Lahuta e Malcis* (The Lute of the Mountains) is generally regarded as the greatest Albanian epic poem.
13. Hako, *op. cit.*, p. 52.
14. *Ibid.*, p. 82.
15. *ACEN News, loc. cit.*, p. 19.
16. Hako, *op. cit.*, pp. 53, 79.
17. *Shqiptari i Lirë* (New York), XII, 1–2 (January–February 1968), p. 1.
18. *PPSH Dokumenta Kryesore, I* (Main Documents of the A[lbanian] P[arty] of L[abour], Vol. I) (Tirana, 1960), p. 329.
19. *Ibid.*, p. 357.
20. *Report on the Role and Tasks of the Democratic Front for the Complete Triumph of Socialism in Albania* (Tirana, 1967), p. 64. Hereafter, Hoxha, *Report on Democratic Front . . .*
21. Zihni Sako, *Populli dhe feja* (The People and Religion) (Tirana, 1967), p. 32.
22. Fehmi Xhuglini, *Mjëkesia dhe feja* (Medicine and Religion) (Tirana, 1967), p. 3; *Të shkulim . . ., loc. cit.*, p. 17.
23. See G. Konomi, *Darvinzmi dhe feja* (Darwinism and Religion) (Tirana, 1967).
24. See Mina Qirici, '*Çudirat*' *e fesë* (The 'Miracles' of Religion) (Tirana, 1967).
25. Sotir Melka, *Dëmet e riteve dhe festave fetare* (The Harm of Religious Rites and Festivals) (Tirana, 1967), p. 15.
26. Ahmed il Drrha, 'Mission to Albania,' *Nea Politeia* (Athens), 1–5 December 1968.
27. See G. Konomi, *Mbi origjinën e fesë* (On the Origin of Religion) (Tirana, 1967); Sako, *op. cit.*, pp. 3–7.
28. *Të shkulim . . ., loc. cit.*, p. 8.
29. *Rruga e Partisë* (The Party Road), XVII, 2 (February 1970), pp. 104–5.
30. Hako, *op. cit.*, p. 85.

31. Hoxha, *Report on Democratic Front* . . ., p. 65.
32. Skendi, 'Skenderbeg and Albanian National Consciousness,' *Südost–Forschungen*. XXVII (R. Oldenbourg/Munich, 1968), pp. 83–8.
33. Hoxha, *Report on Democratic Front* . . ., p. 65. Hoxha's remark about 'foreign invaders' refers to the Romans who introduced Christianity into Albania in the first centuries of the Christian era, and to the Ottoman Turks who introduced Islam following their invasion of Albania in the 14th century.
34. *PPSH mbi fenë dhe edukimin ateist-shkencor të punonjësve* (The A.P.L. on Religion and the Atheist-Scientific Education of the Workers) (Tirana, 1967), p. 5.
35. *Ibid.*, p. 5.
36. Hoxha, *Mbi problemin e gruas* (On the Problem of Woman) (Tirana, 1967), p. 71.
37. Mina Qirici, *Thelbi reaksionar i Muslimanizmit* (The Reactionary Core of Islamism) (Tirana, 1967), p. 651.
38. Hako, *op. cit.*, p. 98.
39. C. Konomi, *Mbi festat dhe të kremtet fetare* (On Religious Festivals and Holidays) (Tirana, 1967), p. 9.
40. See especially, Petro Marko, *Urata, dhia dhe perëndia* (The Priest, the Goat and God) (Tirana, 1967) – a book which portrays the clergy as deceivers, gluttons, degenerates and agents of Albania's enemies.
41. Hako, *op. cit.*, p. 76.
42. *Zëri i Popullit*, 28 April 1966.
43. Enver Muça, 'Religion in the Service of the Ruling Bourgeois-Revisionist Dictatorship', *Bashkimi* (Unity), 19 November 1969. For a particularly violent attack on the Kremlin's relations with the Vatican, see Hako, 'The Vatican and Modern Revisionism,' *Rruga e Partisë*, XI, 6 (June 1964), pp. 61–75.
44. Hako, *op. cit.*, p. 73.
45. The testimonials and pledges made at these meetings were published in several volumes, including: *Lufta kundër zakoneve prapanike dhe besimeve fetare–shprehje e luftës së klasave* (The Struggle against Backward Customs and Religious Beliefs is an Expression of the Class Struggle) (Tirana, 1967); and *Nuk ka liri të vërtetë shoqërore pa emancipimin e plotë të gruas* (There can be no True Social Freedom without the Full Emancipation of Woman) (Tirana, 1967).
46. *Rruga e Partisè*, XVII, 6 (June 1970), p. 44.
47. Bik Pepa, *Feja Lakuriq* (Religion Stripped Naked) (Tirana, 1967), p4.
48. *Zëri i Popullit*, 2 November 1971.
49. *Të shkulim* . . ., *loc. cit.*, p. 31.
50. Kenneth Jowitt, *Revolutionary Breakthroughs and National Development: The Case of Romania, 1944–1965*, Berkeley and Los Angeles: (University of California Press, 1971), p. 7.

Index